AT HOME WITH THE EMP

This pioneering volume addresses the question of how Britain's empire was lived through everyday practices – in church and chapel, by readers at home, as embodied in sexualities or forms of citizenship, as narrated in histories – from the eighteenth century to the present. Leading historians explore the imperial experience and legacy for those located, physically or imaginatively, 'at home', from the impact of empire on constructions of womanhood, masculinity and class to its influence in shaping literature, sexuality, visual culture, consumption and history writing. They assess how people thought imperially, not in the sense of political affiliations for or against empire, but simply assuming it was there, part of the given world that had made them who they were. They also show how empire became a contentious focus of attention at certain moments and in particular ways. This will be essential reading for scholars and students of modern Britain and its empire.

CATHERINE HALL is Professor of Modern British Social and Cultural History at University College London. Her previous publications include, with Keith McClelland and Jane Rendall, *Defining the Victorian Nation: Class, Race, Gender and the British Reform Act of 1867* (2000) and *Civilising Subjects: Metropole and Colony in the English Imagination, 1830–1867* (2002).

SONYA O. ROSE is Emerita Professor of History, Sociology and Women's Studies at the University of Michigan, Ann Arbor. Her recent publications include *Which People's War? National Identity and Citizenship in Wartime Britain, 1939–1945* (2003), and, as a co-editor with Kathleen Canning, *Gender, Citizenships and Subjectivities* (2004).

AT HOME WITH THE EMPIRE

Metropolitan Culture and the Imperial World

EDITED BY

CATHERINE HALL AND SONYA O. ROSE

CAMBRIDGE
UNIVERSITY PRESS

CAMBRIDGE UNIVERSITY PRESS
Cambridge, New York, Melbourne, Madrid, Cape Town, Singapore, São Paulo, Delhi

Cambridge University Press
The Edinburgh Building, Cambridge CB2 8RU, UK

Published in the United States of America by Cambridge University Press, New York

www.cambridge.org
Information on this title: www.cambridge.org/9780521670029

First published 2006
Reprinted 2008

Printed in the United Kingdom at the University Press, Cambridge

A catalogue record for this publication is available from the British Library.

Library of Congress Cataloging-in-Publication Data

At home with the empire : metropolitan culture and the imperial world / [edited by]
Catherine Hall and Sonya Rose.
p. cm.
Includes bibliographical references and index.

1. Imperialism – Social aspects – Great Britain. 2. Great Britain – Civilization – 19th century.
3. Great Britain – Civilization – 20th century. 4. Great Britain – Social life and customs – 19th
century. 5. Great Britain – Social life and customs – 20th century. I. Hall, Catherine. II. Rose,
Sonya O. III. Title
DA16.A78 2006
909′.0971241–dc22
2006025229

ISBN 978–0–521–85406–1 hardback
ISBN 978–0–521–67002–9 paperback

Contents

Notes on contributors

ANTOINETTE BURTON is Professor of History and Bastian Professor of Global and Transnational Studies at the University of Illinois at Urbana-Champaign. The author of several books on gender and empire, she is most recently the editor of *Archive Stories: Facts, Fictions and the Writing of History* (2005). She is currently working on a study of the Cold War cosmopolitan writer Santha Rama Rau.

JAMES EPSTEIN is Professor in the Department of History, Vanderbilt University. He is the author most recently of *In Practice: Studies in the Language and Culture of Popular Politics in Modern Britain*. He is presently working on a study of Britain and Trinidad in the age of revolution.

JOANNA DE GROOT teaches at the University of York. Her main interests are the intersections of gender, race and empire in cultural politics and political cultures since 1700, and histories of the Middle East (especially Iran) and India in the era of modernity and imperialism. Recent work includes 'Oriental Feminotopias? Montagu's and Montesquieu's Seraglios Revisited', *Gender and History* (2006) and *Religion, Resistance, and Revolution in Iran c. 1870–1980* (2006).

CATHERINE HALL is Professor of Modern British Social and Cultural History at University College London. She has published widely on race, gender and empire in the nineteenth century and her most recent book is *Civilising Subjects: Metropole and Colony in the English Imagination, 1830–1867*. She is currently working on Macaulay and the writing of history.

CORA KAPLAN is Visiting Professor in the School of English and Drama, Queen Mary, University of London. Her most recent book is *Victoriana: Histories, Fictions, Criticism* (2007) and she has published widely on race and gender in the nineteenth century.

CHRISTINE KINEALY is a Professor in the University of Central Lancashire and teaches modern Irish history. She has published extensively on the impact of the Great Irish Famine in Ireland, including *This Great Calamity: The Irish Famine 1845–52* and *The Irish Famine: Impact, Ideology and Rebellion*. She is currently researching the impact of the 1848 nationalist uprising in Ireland.

PHILIPPA LEVINE is author, most recently, of *Prostitution, Race, and Politics: Policing Venereal Disease in the British Empire*, and editor of *Gender and Empire*, Oxford History of the British Empire Companion Series. She teaches history at the University of Southern California.

KEITH McCLELLAND is a former editor of *Gender and History* and author with Catherine Hall and Jane Rendall of *Defining the Victorian Nation*. He is currently working on British socialism and empire since the late nineteenth century.

CLARE MIDGLEY is Research Professor in history at Sheffield Hallam University and is the author of *Women Against Slavery* and editor of *Gender and Imperialism*. Her work focuses on exploring the intersections between British women's history and the history of British imperialism, and she is currently completing a new monograph entitled 'Feminism, Philanthropy and Empire'.

JANE RENDALL is an Honorary Fellow in the History Department at the University of York. Her publications include *The Origins of Modern Feminism*, with Catherine Hall and Keith McClelland *Defining the Victorian Nation* and, most recently, edited with Mark Hallett, *Eighteenth-Century York: Culture, Space and Society*. She has published many articles on women's and gender history and is currently working on a study of the gendered legacies of the Enlightenment in Scotland.

SONYA ROSE is the author of *Limited Livelihoods: Gender and Class in Nineteenth-Century England* and *Which People's War? National Identity and Citizenship in Wartime Britain, 1939–1945*. Most recently she has been interested in questions of citizenship, masculinity and empire, especially during and in the aftermath of war in twentieth-century Britain.

LAURA TABILI is Associate Professor of Modern European History at the University of Arizona, and author of *'We Ask for British Justice': Workers and Racial Difference in Late Imperial Britain*, as well as articles on migration, interracial marriage and the racialisation of masculinity. Her book in progress enquires into the cultural impact of long-distance migration on the Tyne port of South Shields between 1841 and 1939.

SUSAN THORNE teaches modern British history and the history of European colonialism in the Department of History at Duke University in Durham, North Carolina. She is the author of *Congregational Missions and the Making of an Imperial Culture in Nineteenth-Century England.* Her current research explores the social and ethnic boundaries of competing conceptions of the family as reflected in the social history and cultural construction of homeless children in Britain and the Empire during the eighteenth and nineteenth centuries.

CHAPTER ONE

Introduction: being at home with the Empire

Catherine Hall and Sonya Rose

What was the impact of the British Empire on the metropole between the late eighteenth century and the present?[1] This is the question addressed in a variety of ways and across different timescales in this volume. Such a question has a history that perhaps needs remembering: for it is both a repetition and a reconfiguration of a long preoccupation with the inter-connections between the metropolitan and the imperial. Was it possible to be 'at home' with an empire and with the effects of imperial power or was there something dangerous and damaging about such an entangle-ment? Did empires enrich but also corrupt? Were the expenses they brought worth the burdens and responsibilities? These questions were the subject of debate at least from the mid-eighteenth century and have been formulated and answered variously according both to the historical moment and the political predilections of those involved.

The connections between British state formation and empire building stretch back a long way, certainly into the pre-modern period.[2] It was the shift from an empire of commerce and the seas to an empire of conquest, however, that brought the political and economic effects of empire home in new ways. While the American War of Independence raised one set of issues about native sons making claims for autonomy, conquests in Asia raised others about the costs of territorial expansion, economic, political and moral.[3] From the 1770s questions about the effects of empire on the metropole were never entirely off the political agenda, whether in terms of the worries about the impact of forms of Oriental despotism or the practice of slavery abroad on the liberties of Englishmen at home, debates as to the status of British subjects and British law across the empire, or

---

[1] Thanks to the contributors to this book for comments on this piece and to Bill Schwarz.

[2] For a discussion of some of the relevant material see David Armitage, 'Greater Britain: A Useful Category of Historical Analysis?' *American Historical Review*, 104 (2) (1999), 427–55. See also his *The Ideological Origins of the British Empire* (Cambridge, 2000).

[3] See, for example, Eliga Gould, *The Persistence of Empire: British Political Culture in the Age of the American Revolution* (Chapel Hill, 2000); P. J. Marshall, 'Empire and Authority in the Later Eighteenth Century', *Journal of Imperial and Commonwealth History*, 15 (2) (1987), 105–22.

hopes for a 'Greater Britain' that could spread across the world.[4] During the period that we cover in this book there were moments of profound controversy about the empire – about what form it should take, and what should be its purpose. How Britain's imperial stance was envisaged was always contested and changed over time. But there were few if any voices arguing the Empire should be disbanded, and that Great Britain should no longer remain an imperial nation. Important issues were seen as at stake in the metropolitan/colonial relation and both supporters and critics of empire recognised that Britain's imperial power could have consequences for her native population, never mind the effects on populations farther afield.

The chapters in this book are not solely concerned, however, with the political or ideological debates over empire, critical as these were. Rather, we argue that empire was, in important ways, taken-for-granted as a natural aspect of Britain's place in the world and its history. No one doubted that Great Britain was an imperial nation state, part of an empire. J. R. Seeley famously argued that the British 'seemed to have conquered and peopled half the world in a fit of absence of mind'.[5] In commenting on this Roger Louis notes that 'he was drawing attention to the unconscious acceptance by the English public of the burdens of Empire, particularly in India'.[6] It is this 'unconscious acceptance', whether of the burdens or benefits of empire, that we are in part exploring in this volume. The Empire's influence on the metropole was undoubtedly uneven. There were times when it was simply there, not a subject of popular critical consciousness. At other times it was highly visible, and there was widespread awareness of matters imperial on the part of the public as well as those who were charged with governing it. The majority of Britons most of the time were probably neither 'gung-ho' nor avid anti-imperialists, yet their everyday lives were infused with an imperial presence. Furthermore, important political and cultural processes and institutions were shaped by and within the context of empire. Our question, therefore, is not whether empire had an impact at home, fatal

---

[4] See, for example, on Hastings, Nicholas Dirks, *The Scandal of Empire* (Cambridge, MA, 2006); on slavery, David Brion Davis, *The Problem of Slavery in the Age of Revolution, 1770–1823* (Ithaca, 1975); on Morant Bay, Bernard Semmel, *The Governor Eyre Controversy* (London, 1962); on the tradition of radical critics of imperialism, Miles Taylor, 'Imperium et Libertas? Rethinking the Radical Critique of Imperialism during the Nineteenth Century', *Journal of Imperial and Commonwealth History*, 19 (1) (1991), 1–23.

[5] J. R. Seeley, *The Expansion of England: Two Courses of Lectures* (London, 1883), 10.

[6] Wm. Roger Louis, 'Introduction', in Robin W. Winks (ed.), *The Oxford History of the British Empire*, vol. V: *Historiography* (Oxford, 1999), 9.

or not.[7] Rather, we ask how was empire lived across everyday practices – in church and chapel, by readers at home, as embodied in sexualities or forms of citizenship, as narrated in histories? To what extent did people think imperially, not in the sense of political affiliations for or against empire, but simply assuming it was there, part of the given world that had made them who they were?

This question is possible precisely because we are no longer 'at home' with an empire. It is both the same and different from the questions which preoccupied both supporters and critics of empire prior to decolonisation. It is a reconfiguration – a new way of seeing associated with a different historical moment. Empire was always there between the eighteenth century and the 1940s, albeit in different forms with varied imperatives according to the particular conjuncture, different questions provoking debate about the metropolitan/colonial relation. But the questions were all thought within an imperial paradigm. After decolonisation that frame had gone and the end of empire has brought with it new concerns and pre-occupations. In the 1940s and 1950s the Empire was decomposing, despite attempts by Churchill and others to hold on. Capturing public imagination at the time were the sectarian and inter-tribal conflicts taking place as independence was granted to former dependencies. Decolonisation was figured by the government and in much of the press as relatively conflict-free. Unlike the French who were fighting an all-out war to keep Algeria French, the British public generally understood that Britain was making a graceful exit, defending the Commonwealth and keeping the interests of colonised peoples at the forefront of their policies. Yet we now know and to a certain extent it was known then but not always consciously registered, that the leave-taking from Malaya and Kenya was anything but peaceful. In the case of Kenya, as has recently been demonstrated, the Mau Mau rebellion was portrayed in the press as an outbreak of utter savagery on the part of the Kikuyu in the name of nationalism gone wild. It was repressed with horrific brutality by the Colonial administration with the full knowledge and complicity of the British government.[8] Those suspected of active participation with Mau Mau were tried and hanged at the very same time that Parliament was debating the abolition of capital punishment by hanging in the metropole.[9] Many thousands more, including women and

---

[7] The reference is to P. J. Marshall, 'No Fatal Impact? The Elusive History of Imperial Britain', *Times Literary Supplement*, 12 March 1993, 8–10.

[8] Caroline Elkins, *Britain's Gulag: The Brutal End of Empire in Kenya* (London, 2005).

[9] David Anderson, *Histories of the Hanged: The Dirty War in Kenya and the End of Empire* (New York, 2005), 7.

children, were herded into detention camps where they suffered starvation, disease and death. Caroline Elkins has illuminated this terrible story, indicating that the facts about these camps were debated in parliament and received some coverage in the press. Yet, there was no public outcry. The reason for this, she argues, was that Mau Mau had been portrayed in the press and by the government as African savagery at its most primitive and violent.[10] Some Afro-Caribbean migrants, arriving in England during this period, discovered that they were perceived through a Kenyan lens: 'Are you a Mau Mau lady?' Beryl Gilroy was asked.[11]

The Empire had gone and was best forgotten. The West Indians and South Asians who were arriving were thought of as postwar migrants rather than imperial subjects with a long history connecting them to Britain. In the aftermath of the Second World War it was the great struggle between the United States and the Soviet Union that dominated global politics. Britain, no longer an imperial power, was drawn into the Cold War, a loyal supporter and friend of the USA, part of the West now united against communism. Modernisation would solve the problems of underdevelopment now that colonies were a thing of the past. It was not until the 1980s that questions about 'after empire' became high on the political agenda. This was associated with both the emergence of new forms of globalisation and, by the late 1970s and early 1980s, with the now substantial second-generation communities of black Britons in the inner cities making claims for equality and recognition. At the same time acknowledgement of the failure of new nations established after decolonisation brought with it a critique both of the limits of nationalism, and the recognition that while the political forms of empire had been dismantled, neo-colonialism and colonial ways of thinking were alive and well. This was the reconfiguration that made possible the emergence of a postcolonial critique from the 1980s – lifting the veil of amnesia about empires and making it imperative to recognise the persistence of their legacies. As Derek Gregory has put it, postcolonialism's critique disrupted the 'unilinear and progressive trajectory of episodic histories that dispatch the past to the archive rather than the repertoire'.[12] The collapse of the Soviet bloc and the end of the Cold War meant that the United States now emerged as *the* superpower and questions of empire began to arise anew, alongside reconfigured languages of civilisation and barbarism. The

---

[10] Elkins, *Britain's Gulag*, 307–9.

[11] Beryl Gilroy, *Black Teacher* (London, 1976), 121, cited in Wendy Webster, *Englishness and Empire, 1939–1965* (Oxford, 2005), 123.

[12] Derek Gregory, *The Colonial Present* (Oxford, 2004), 265.

dam that had earlier been erected against the memory of the British Empire broke down and in recent years books, television and radio programmes have poured out exploring that legacy in innumerable different ways. In this moment after one kind of empire (the British), and contemplating another (that of the United States), it has become not only possible but necessary to rethink the imperial relation in the light of the present, no longer inside but outside an imperial although postcolonial paradigm.

We are all too well aware of the dangers of focusing yet again on the British, to the neglect of the lives of colonial peoples across the Empire. Yet our object here is the metropole and the ways in which it was constituted in part by the Empire. Thus our focus in this book is on the period when the Empire existed and was a presence in metropolitan life: not on the equally important topic of the effects of empire after decolonisation. It is British history which is our object of study. Imperial historians have always thought in a variety of ways about the metropole, the seat of government and power, but British historians, those concerned with the national and the domestic, have seriously neglected the place of empire on that history. British history, we are convinced, has to be transnational, recognising the ways in which our history has been one of connections across the globe, albeit in the context of unequal relations of power. Historians of Britain need to open up national history and imperial history, challenging that binary and critically scrutinising the ways in which it has functioned as a way of normalising power relations and erasing our dependence on and exploitation of others. In exploring the ways in which the British were 'at home' with their empire, we aim to destabilise those relations and explore the dangerous parameters of white British culture.

A NOTE ON TERMINOLOGY

It is important that we define the terms that we are using here. This is no easy task for as any number of scholars have suggested, the central terms of 'empire' and 'imperialism', 'colony' and 'colonialism', 'race and racism' are slippery, contested, and their historical referents have changed over time. This is not the place to review and assess all of the different uses of these terms on offer. Instead, we will draw upon the work of other scholars in clarifying what we mean when we use these terms.

Empire is a large, diverse, geographically dispersed and expansionist political entity. A central feature of this unit is that it 'reproduces differentiation and inequality among people it incorporates'.[13] Thus, at its heart, empire is about power, and is 'usually created by conquest, and divided between a dominant centre and subordinate, sometimes far distant peripheries'.[14] In challenging the traditional focus on the centre/ periphery relation scholars have recently emphasised the importance of connections across empires, the webs and networks operated between colonies, and the significance of centres of power outside the metropole, such as Calcutta or Melbourne. Thus, 'webs of trade, knowledge, migration, military power and political intervention that allowed certain communities to assert their influence ... over other groups' are constitutive of empires.[15] Empires also may be considered as 'networks' through which, in different sites within them, 'colonial discourses were made and remade rather than simply transferred or imposed'.[16]

Imperialism, then, is the process of empire building. It is a project that originates in the metropolis and leads to domination and control over the peoples and lands of the periphery.[17] Ania Loomba helpfully suggests that colonialism is 'what happens in the colonies as a consequence of imperial domination'. Thus, she suggests that 'the imperial country is the "metropole" from which power flows, and the colony ... is the place which it penetrates and controls'.[18] One might add that the penetration often has been extremely uneven and that resistance on the part of the colonised has been central to that unevenness. As Guha has aptly put it, '(I)nsurgency was ... the necessary antithesis of colonialism.'[19]

As Robinson and Gallagher argued long ago, imperialism can function without formal colonies, but the possession of colonies is essential to what is termed colonialism.[20] Colonies, themselves, differ enormously even within a particular empire such as the British Empire. The process of colonisation involves the takeover of a particular territory, appropriation of its resources and, in the case of the British Empire, the migration of people from the metropole outward to administer or to inhabit the

---

[13] Frederick Cooper, *Colonialism in Question: Theory, Knowledge, History* (Berkeley, 2005), 26.

[14] Stephen Howe, *Empire: A Very Short Introduction* (Oxford, 2002), 30.

[15] Tony Ballantyne, *Orientalism and Race: Aryanism in the British Empire* (Basingstoke, 2002); see also Tony Ballantyne and Antoinette Burton, 'Introduction', in Ballantyne and Burton (eds.), *Bodies, Empires and World History* (Durham, NC, 2005), 3.

[16] Alan Lester, *Imperial Networks: Creating Identities in Nineteenth-century South Africa and Britain* (London, 2001), 4.

[17] Ania Loomba, *Colonialism/Postcolonialism*, 2nd edn (London, 2005), 12.   [18] *Ibid.*

[19] Ranajit Guha, *Elementary Aspects of Peasant Insurgency in Colonial India* (Delhi, 1983), 2.

[20] Ronald Robinson and John Gallagher, 'The Imperialism of Free Trade', *Economic History Review*, 2nd ser., 6 (1) (1953), 1–15.

colony as settlers. Regardless, colonisation involves various forms of dispossession of those who lived on the lands prior to their being colonised.[21] As Loomba has put it, colonisation meant '*un-forming* or *re-forming* the communities that existed there already', often violently, and that would be the case whether or not people from the metropole went there to form their own permanent communities. Furthermore, colonial empires such as the British Empire were not omnipotent. They had to administer and assert control under constraints 'intrinsic to the vastness and diversity of imperial spaces' that inevitably aroused discontent among those who were subordinated in the process. At the same time imperial authority attempted to insist upon the idea that the Empire was a 'legitimate polity in which all members had a stake'.[22] One mode of exerting imperial power depended upon negotiating with existing colonial wielders of power, whether Indian *rajahs*, African 'chiefs', or mercantile or cultural elites, thus aligning the Empire with pre-existing social and cultural hierarchies. But this strategy coexisted both with attempts to offer all subjects of empire a form of belonging and with the persistent deployment of racial distinctions as a way of underscoring their superiority.[23]

Although as James Donald and Ali Rattansi argue, people continue even today to act as if race was a fixed, objective category, most scholars recognise that not only is race not an essential, 'natural' category, but that the meanings and valence of race have changed historically.[24] Both during the heyday of the British Empire and its aftermath, race, in its many guises, 'naturalises difference' and reinscribes the always unstable distinction between coloniser and colonised. As a number of scholars have demonstrated, ideas about colonial difference became increasingly influential as they 'intersected with, and helped to reformulate, British domestic discourses of class, ethnic and gender difference'.[25] Furthermore, the process by which the meanings of race became the focus and

---

[21] Howe, *Empire*, 31. [22] Cooper, *Colonialism*, 28. [23] *Ibid.*
[24] James Donald and Ali Rattansi (eds.), *'Race', Culture and Difference* (London, 1992), 1–4.
[25] Alan Lester, 'Constructing Colonial Discourse', in Alison Blunt and Cheryl McEwan (eds.), *Postcolonial Geographies* (London, 2002), 38. See also Ann L. Stoler, *Race and the Education of Desire: Foucault's History of Sexuality and the Colonial Order of Things* (Durham, NC, 1995), 104; Leonore Davidoff, 'Class and Gender in Victorian England', in Judith L. Newton, Mary P. Ryan and Judith R. Walkowitz (eds.), *Sex and Class in Women's History* (London, 1983), 17–71; Joanna de Groot, '"Sex" and "Race": The Construction of Language and Image in the Nineteenth Century', in Catherine Hall (ed.), *Cultures of Empire: Colonizers in Britain and the Empire in the Nineteenth and Twentieth Centuries* (Manchester, 2000), 37–60.

product of scientific inquiry was intimately bound up with empire.[26] And although there was contestation about the fixity of racial distinctions over the course of the period covered by this book, the grounding of difference in 'scientific' authority and the creation of 'the natural' was a political process involving both colony and metropole.[27] Historically, racism and the 'scientific' authority behind the notion of immutable, biologically based difference were co-constitutive. The idea of race, like that of essential differences between women and men, was to become so wide-spread as to be part of the 'taken-for-granted' world in which the people of the metropole lived their lives. As G. R. Searle has put it, 'the super-iority of "whites" over "blacks" was widely treated as self-evident'.[28] This, however, does not mean that everyone was a racist just as everyone was not an imperialist. In Britain open conflict between people of different 'racial' or 'ethnic' origins was anything but constant, and, as Laura Tabili's essay in this volume suggests, racial violence and antagonism may well have been the product of particular moments of economic and imperial crises. She argues that outside of these particular conjunctures people of different ethnicities could and did live relatively harmoniously. Yet when conflict did erupt Britons adopted and adapted 'commonsen-sical' or 'taken-for-granted' views of 'natural' difference that had been and continued to be present in metropolitan culture.

HISTORIOGRAPHY

The end of the European empires, the construction of new nation states and the major changes that took place in the world in the 1970s and 1980s resulted in shifts in patterns of historical writing, both in Britain and elsewhere. Here we are concerned with those effects in the writing of British history. Once Britain was no longer the centre of an empire and a great power, long-established assumptions about the writing of national history began to dissolve. A binary divide between nation and empire had been central to the nationalist historiography that emerged in mid-nineteenth-century Britain and survived for much of the twentieth. It was challenged by Seeley in the 1880s when he made the case for England's past, present and future being intimately associated with that of its

---

[26] Catherine Hall, 'Introduction: Thinking the Postcolonial, Thinking the Empire', in Hall (ed.), *Cultures*, 19.

[27] Nancy Stepan, *The Idea of Race in Science: Great Britain, 1800–1960* (London, 1982); also see her 'Race, Gender, Science and Citizenship', in Hall (ed.), *Cultures*, 61–86.

[28] G. R. Searle, *A New England? Peace and War, 1886–1918* (Oxford, 2004), 32.

empire.[29] His intervention, however, far from producing a more connected history, was significant in the development of imperial history as a separate subject. 'The disjuncture between national and extra-national histories has been particularly abrupt within the history of Britain', as David Armitage has argued.[30] English exceptionalism has indeed been difficult to dismantle built as it was on wilful amnesia, as Catherine Hall suggests in her essay on Macaulay in this volume. In the last twenty-plus years, however, efforts to reconnect the histories of Britain and empire and to challenge both the myopia of nationalist histories, and those forms of imperial history that do not engage with the metropole, have come from a variety of different sources and perspectives. Some are critical of the whole project of empire, others more revisionist in their focus, while some defend the imperial legacy.[31] The various contributors to the debate over national history and its relation to the imperial have engaged with the different literatures to different degrees. What is clear is that this is a most productive area of historical research and one with which many of the protagonists feel passionately, albeit with very different investments and positions.

The 1960s and 70s saw a flowering of social history in Britain, but that work was for the most part resolutely domestic in its focus. By the 1980s increasingly sharp debates over questions of race and difference, riots in Britain's inner cities, and the Falklands War put issues of empire firmly back on the historical agenda. Racism, as Salman Rushdie argued at the time, was exposing Britain's postcolonial crisis.[32] In this context some British historians who had been focused on the nation began to think more about empires. Work by anthropologists, themselves engaged in critical reflection on their discipline and its origins in colonial knowledge, provided important insights. Their refusal of the established lines of division between history and anthropology, one dealing with 'modern' peoples, the other with 'primitive' peoples, understood as without a history, destabilised conventional understandings. In 1982 Sidney Mintz and Eric Wolf, both influenced by Marxism, published classic texts which

---

[29] Seeley, *The Expansion of England.*

[30] Armitage, 'A Greater Britain', 428; Peter Mandler, *History and National Life* (London, 2002).

[31] Obviously there have been crucial international influences – especially postcolonial theory and Subaltern Studies. But here we are confining our attention to the efforts by historians to reconnect the domestic and the imperial. We are also not discussing all the ideas that have come from historical geographers, those working in literary and visual culture etc., as this would have been a major essay in its own right.

[32] Salman Rushdie, 'The New Empire within Britain', in *Imaginary Homelands: Essays and Criticism 1981–1991* (London, 1991).

insisted on the importance of grasping the connections between peoples in different parts of the globe, the power relations between them, and the circuits of production, distribution and consumption within which they lived.[33] Mintz traced the history of sugar, from luxury to everyday commodity, in the process exploring the plantation as one of the formative sites of modern capitalist production. Sugar, he argued, was one of the first commodities to define modern English identities.[34] Wolf argued that it was no longer enough to write the history of the dominant or the subjugated. The world of humankind was a totality: it was the specialised social sciences which had insisted on separating out the parts. He aimed to 'delineate the general processes at work in mercantile and capitalist development, while at the same time following their effects on the micro-populations studied by the ethnohistorians and anthropologists'. In his account, 'both the people who claim history as their own and the people to whom history has been denied emerge as participants in the same historical trajectory'.[35]

Another anthropologist, Bernard Cohn, again someone who was preoccupied with the relationship between history and anthropology, has been a key figure in reshaping imperial history, bringing it into the same field as the history of early modern and modern South Asia.[36] One of his central preoccupations has been with the development of classificatory systems and the ways in which India was utilised as a laboratory for new technologies of rule. Long before the publication of Said's *Orientalism*, as Dipesh Chakrabarty has noted, Cohn 'was teaching his students in Chicago some of the fundamentals of the relation between knowledge and power' that shaped colonialism in South Asia and beyond.[37] His work, along with that of Thomas Metcalf, who has emphasised the play of similarity and difference as central to British conceptions of India, has significantly shifted understandings of the Raj.[38] Since the East India Company was London based, its shareholders, proprietors and Directors

---

[33] Mintz and Wolf were both drawing on the radical-Marxist critique of empire, which also informed work going on in Britain. See, for example, Michael Barratt Brown, *After Imperialism* (London, 1963); V. G. Kiernan, *The Lords of Human Kind: European Attitudes to the Outside World in the Imperial Age* (London, 1969).

[34] Sidney Mintz, *Sweetness and Power: The Place of Sugar in Modern History* (New York, 1985). David Scott, 'Modernity that Predated the Modern: Sidney Mintz's Caribbean', *History Workshop Journal*, 58 (2004), 191–210.

[35] Eric R. Wolf, *Europe and the People Without History* (London, 1982), 23.

[36] Bernard S. Cohn, *An Anthropologist Among the Historians and Other Essays* (Oxford, 1990); *Colonialism and its Forms of Knowledge: The British in India* (Princeton, 1996).

[37] Dipesh Chakrabarty, 'Foreword', in *The Bernard Cohn Omnibus* (Oxford, 2004), x–xi.

[38] Thomas R. Metcalf, *Ideologies of the Raj* (Cambridge, 1994).

interested in enjoying an income at home, the history of the Company has required a direct engagement with domestic issues. This work has informed a new generation of British historians trying to understand the connected histories of Britain and its empire. Some, while challenging the metropolitan/colonial divide, have remained inside an imperial paradigm, assuming that empire is 'a legitimate political and economic form'.[39] P. J. Marshall, one of the most influential of British scholars of India, has insisted on seeing the connections between Britain and India while placing both in a larger imperial frame.[40] At the same time he has downplayed the centrality of colonial ideology to the emergence and expansion of a territorial empire, in part because of his interest in private trade and in the significance of Bengali merchant groups and cultural brokers.[41] Following this trajectory Philip Lawson, for example, both in his history of the East India Company and his later work, brought together India and Britain. He argued that the Company was inextricably bound up with the development of a fiscal-military state in the eighteenth century and that 'the most striking and rewarding aspect of studying the East India Company's experience is that it confounds nationalist histories of one sort or another'.[42]

From a different but connected perspective, one that has insisted on connection and collaboration, C. A. Bayly's *Imperial Meridian* marked the beginning of an attempt to map the complicated history of the British Empire from the late eighteenth century, considering the domestic in relation to the imperial.[43] His starting point was the transformations of the Islamic empires of Eurasia and the decline of Mughal, Safavid and Ottoman authority. It was this that paved the way for the expansion of British power, and an aggressive imperial strategy driven by the army, the military-fiscal state and the evangelical revival of the late eighteenth century. New forms of absolutism and a revivified ruling class were critical to this 'Second Empire'. More recently, Bayly's *The Birth of the Modern World* has again insisted on the interconnected and global

---

[39] Dirks, *Scandal*, 329.
[40] P. J. Marshall, *The New Cambridge History of India*, vol. II, part 2: *Bengal: The British Bridgehead, Eastern India, 1740–1828* (Cambridge, 1987); *Trade and Conquest: Studies in the Rise of British Dominance in India* (Aldershot, 1993).
[41] Thanks to Tony Ballantyne for advice on Marshall and Bayly.
[42] Philip Lawson, *The East India Company: A History* (London, 1993), 164; *A Taste for Empire and Glory: Studies in British Overseas Expansion, 1660–1800* (Aldershot, 1997).
[43] C. A. Bayly, *Imperial Meridian* (London, 1989); 'The British and Indigenous Peoples, 1760–1860: Power, Perception and Identity', in Martin Daunton and Rick Halpern (eds.), *Empire and Others: British Encounters with Indigenous Peoples, 1600–1850* (London, 1999), 19–41; *The Birth of the Modern World, 1780–1914* (Oxford, 2004).

processes associated with the West's rise to power in the nineteenth century, even though he minimises the significance of key axes of division such as race, class and gender to this process. A. G. Hopkins has also argued for a reconnection of the imperial and the domestic, again from the perspective of an interest in globalisation, and an insistence that globalisation has a complicated history that includes the epoch of the European empires.[44] Another historian of empire, Stephen Howe, was one of the first to raise the issues of decolonisation in relation to metropole and colony in his work on anti-colonialism and the British left. More recently, he has emerged as a strong critic of postcolonial work and a sceptic on questions of the impact of the Empire on metropolitan life.[45]

The Manchester University Press 'Studies in Imperialism Series' has marked a sustained effort to turn away from the institutional and high political traditions of imperial history writing to a greater focus on the social and the cultural, both in their 'domestic' and imperial contexts. Edited by John MacKenzie and inaugurated in 1985 with his *Propaganda and Empire*, it has transformed our knowledge of many aspects of the Empire at home. Of the sixty volumes now published, at least half deal with aspects of Britain's imperial culture – from his own classic edited volume *Imperialism and Popular Culture*, to work on children's and juvenile literature, the army, music, representations of the Arctic, considerations of the end of empire, and the place of West Indian intellectuals in Britain.[46] This constitutes a body of work that has significantly shifted the parameters of knowledge about the interplay between the domestic and the imperial. In an evaluation of the debates over empire and metropolitan culture written for the *Oxford History of the British Empire* (a series that had almost nothing to say on the subject), MacKenzie discussed the arguments of those sceptics who see 'no impact' and concluded that 'Empire

[44] A. G. Hopkins, 'Back to the Future: From National History to Imperial History', *Past and Present*, 164 (1999), 198–243; (ed.) *Globalization in World History* (London, 2002).

[45] Stephen Howe, *Anticolonialism in British Politics: The Left and the End of Empire, 1918–1964* (Oxford, 1993); *Ireland and Empire: Colonial Legacies in Irish History and Culture* (Oxford, 2000); 'Internal Decolonisation? British Politics since Thatcher as Postcolonial Trauma', *Twentieth Century British History*, 14 (2003), 286–304.

[46] These include John M. MacKenzie, *Propaganda and Empire* (1984); John M. MacKenzie (ed.), *Imperialism and Popular Culture* (1986); Jeffrey Richards (ed.), *Imperialism and Juvenile Literature* (1989); Kathryn Castle, *Britannia's Children: Reading Colonialism Through Children's Books* (1996); Rob David, *The Arctic in the British Imagination, 1818–1914* (2000); Jeffrey Richards, *Imperialism and Music: Britain 1876–1953* (2001); Stuart Ward (ed.), *British Culture and the End of Empire* (2001); Bill Schwarz (ed.), *West Indian Intellectuals in Britain* (2003); Heather Streets, *Martial Races and Masculinity in the British Army, 1857–1914* (2004).

constituted a vital aspect of national identity and race-consciousness, even if complicated by regional, rural, urban, and class contexts'.[47] Other historians of Britain have also been part of the turn to integrating the domestic with the imperial. Miles Taylor's body of work on nineteenth-century imperial ideas and their connections with other traditions of political thought, alongside his investigation of the impact of empire on 1848, stands out here.[48]

Meanwhile, historians of Scotland, Ireland and Wales have been concerned to explore the relation between empire and the making of the United Kingdom. John MacKenzie raised these questions for Scotland, at a time when issues of Scottish national identity (and therefore separate and specific contributions to empire) had come to the fore in the context of devolution. Both Tom Devine and Michael Fry have adopted a somewhat celebratory note, and both suggest that access to empire was a very significant reason for Scotland to stay in the Union. The Scots, Devine argues, were particularly important in the Caribbean and he concludes that 'the new Scotland which was emerging in the later eighteenth century was grounded on the imperial project. The Scots were not only full partners in this grand design but were at the very cutting edge of British global expansion.'[49] The complex position of Ireland, both part of the UK and colonial, has been a subject of much debate among historians. Christine Kinealy argues in this volume that Ireland continued to be treated as a colony by successive British administrations after the Act of Union, despite its constitutional position within the United Kingdom. 'Ireland's rulers in the nineteenth century,' as David Fitzpatrick concludes, 'whether grim or benevolent, tended to regard the Irish as a separate and subject native population rather than an integral element of a united people.'[50] Furthermore, as many have noted, Ireland provided an important model for imperial government, as the debates over landownership and taxation in Ireland and India demonstrate. But as Keith Jeffery has suggested for Ireland, and Aled Jones and Bill Jones for

---

[47] John M. MacKenzie, 'Empire and Metropolitan Cultures', in Wm. Roger Louis (ed.), *The Oxford History of the British Empire*, 5 vols. (Oxford, 1998–9), vol. III: *The Nineteenth Century*, ed. Andrew Porter (1999), 292.

[48] See, for example, Miles Taylor, 'Imperium et Libertas?'; 'John Bull and the Iconography of Public Opinion in England c1712–1929', *Past and Present*, 134 (1992), 93–128; 'The 1848 Revolutions and the British Empire', *Past and Present*, 166 (2000), 146–80.

[49] John M. MacKenzie, 'Essay and Reflection: On Scotland and the Empire', *International History Review*, 15 (1993), 714–39; T. M. Devine, *Scotland's Empire, 1600–1815* (London, 2003), 360; Michael Fry, *The Scottish Empire* (Edinburgh, 2001).

[50] David Fitzpatrick, 'Ireland and the Empire', in Porter (ed.), *The Nineteenth Century*, 495–521.

Wales, the Irish and the Welsh were often content to be British in pursuit of imperial lives across the Empire.[51]

Linda Colley has been in the forefront of arguing for a global context for British history. Her classic work on the centrality of France and of Protestantism to Britons' notions of a distinctive national identity was followed up with an important essay that linked Britishness to questions of empire. More recently her focus has been on captivity as a lens through which to consider what she defines as the fragility of empire and the vulnerability of 'the small island' at the heart of the imperial web.[52] David Cannadine has also ventured into the debates over reconnecting the metropolitan and the colonial. His *Ornamentalism*, conceived as a popular intervention in the current debates over empire, sees imperialism as a safety-valve for Britain's aristocracy.[53] Questions of race, he argues, have been given far too much emphasis to the exclusion of the class dynamics of empire, a position which has earned the book much deserved criticism. As many commentators have noted, Cannadine's focus on the role of the elite in empire building has masked issues of power, violence and exploitation.[54] Even more controversially, Niall Ferguson's recent work provides an apology for empire, with an ideologically driven account that refuses the complexities of imperial histories.[55]

Feminist historians of Britain, alongside those working in the fields of literary and visual representation, have also been in the forefront of exploring the imperial legacy. This scholarship is often more interested in interdisciplinary approaches than other historians would countenance. In the past fifteen years a large body of research, much of it influenced by postcolonial as well as feminist theory, has challenged the domestic/ imperial divide from an explicitly theoretical and anti-colonial position and has established the salience of empire from the beginnings of modernity. Fanon has been a critical influence here, with his insistence on the

---

[51] Keith Jeffery (ed.), '*An Irish Empire? Aspects of Ireland and the British Empire* (Manchester, 1996); Aled Jones and Bill Jones, 'The Welsh World and the British Empire, c. 1851–1939', in Carl Bridge and Kent Fedorowich (eds.), *The British World: Diaspora, Culture and Identity* (London, 2003), 57–81.

[52] Linda Colley, *Britons: Forging the Nation, 1707–1837* (London, 1992); 'Britishness: An Argument', *Journal of British Studies*, 31 (4) (1992), 309–29; *Captives: Britain, Empire and the World, 1600–1850* (London, 2002). For a thought-provoking critical review of *Captives* see Miles Ogborn, 'Gotcha!', *History Workshop Journal*, 56 (2003), 231–8.

[53] David Cannadine, *Ornamentalism: How the British Saw Their Empire* (London, 2001).

[54] For a number of incisive critical evaluations see the special issue of *Journal of Colonialism and Colonial History*, 3 (1) (2002), 'From Orientalism to Ornamentalism: Empire and Difference in History'.

[55] Niall Ferguson, *Empire: The Rise and Demise of the British World Order and the Lessons for Global Power* (New York, 2002).

racialised systems of imperial rule and his recognition of the ways in which 'Europe' was created by colonialism.[56] Thanks to this recent scholarship we now know a great deal about the ways in which representations of the imperial world and its peoples circulated in the metropole, about the place of written and visual texts in producing and disseminating racial thinking, about the significance of museums and exhibitions in representing peoples of the empire to the metropolitan public, and about the place of empire in the construction of English/ British identity. We also know some of the ways in which the management of colonial sexuality was central to British rule at the intersection of national and imperial interests, about how debates over key political questions, such as suffrage, intersected with empire, about the impact of the two world wars on understandings of nation, race and colonialism, about debates over the category of British subject and the issue of nationality, and about the presence of colonised subjects in the metropole.[57] Work on the legacy of empire in the period after decolonisation has also been critical to challenging the idea that since the Empire was disbanded without significant debate at home, this provides evidence for the notion that the British were not really affected by it. Bill Schwarz's work on the memories of empire alongside Wendy Webster's analyses of popular culture have effectively disrupted any claim that the end of empire was unremarked in metropolitan culture and politics.[58]

An initiative from a group of historians working on the dominions has resulted in an effort to place the 'British World' back at the centre of concerns. This was the world first described by Dilke in his *Greater*

---

[56] Franz Fanon, *The Wretched of the Earth* (London, 1967).

[57] Because of space we can cite only a small portion of this literature, see, e.g. Antoinette Burton, *At the Heart of the Empire: Indians and the Colonial Encounter in Late-Victorian Britain* (Berkeley, 1998); Sonya O. Rose, *Which People's War? National Identity and Citizenship in World War II Britain* (Oxford, 2003); esp. chs. 3 and 7; Philippa Levine, *Prostitution, Race, and Politics: Policing Venereal Disease in the British Empire* (London, 2003); Kathleen Wilson, *The Island Race: Englishness, Empire and Gender in the Eighteenth Century* (London, 2003); Catherine Hall, Keith McClelland and Jane Rendall, *Defining the Victorian Nation: Class, Race, Gender and the British Reform Act of 1867* (Cambridge, 2000); Ian Christopher Fletcher, Laura E. Nym Mayhall and Philippa Levine (eds.), *Women's Suffrage in the British Empire: Citizenship, Nation and Race* (London, 2000); Laura Tabili, *'We Ask for British Justice': Workers and Racial Difference in Late Imperial Britain* (Ithaca, 1994); Susan Thorne, *Congregational Missions and the Making of an Imperial Culture in Nineteenth-Century England* (Stanford, 1999); Deborah Cherry, *Beyond the Frame: Feminism and Visual Culture, Britain 1850–1900* (London, 2000); Annie E. Coombes, *Reinventing Africa: Museums, Material Culture and Popular Imagination in Late Victorian and Edwardian England* (London, 1994).

[58] Bill Schwarz, *Memories of Empire* (Oxford, forthcoming); Webster, *Englishness and Empire*; *Imagining Home: Gender, 'Race' and National Identity, 1945–64* (London, 1998); Ward (ed.), *British Culture and the End of Empire*.

Britain and taken up by Seeley in his *Expansion of England* – the world created by British migration and settlement.[59] In 1974 Pocock, thinking from a New Zealand perspective, raised questions about the possibilities of a new form of British, not English, history. He was troubled by the new enthusiasm for Europe and the forgetting of empire and Commonwealth. British history, he argued, needed to be reinvested with meaning; a remapping of historical consciousness was required which would result in more plural and multicultural accounts. The new history should be one of contact and penetration, encompassing the three kingdoms, and the settlements in east and west. It needed to be 'post Commonwealth, extra European and highly internationalist'.[60] One effect of this can be seen in the turn to 'four nations' histories. Another long-term effect of this may have borne fruit in the sequence of 'British World' conferences and publications. Some of the energy for these has come from those working in the white colonies of settlement and struggling with the silence on empire in societies where the effort to create a national history has resulted in a repudiation of the significance of the imperial past.[61]

Most recently Bernard Porter has raised the issue of 'how much' the Empire mattered. The British generally, argues this king of the sceptics, were not much interested in or affected by empire. A particular kind of imperialism – blatant, 'dominating imperialism' – did not saturate British society and the 'everyday life' of Britain that included consuming the products of empire was not an effect or manifestation of 'dominating imperialism'.[62] It was sugar, for example, that rotted the teeth of the people, not the Empire. Nor did other forms of Britain's involvement in the wider world, such as travel, necessarily have imperial undertones. Porter is concerned with how much, or how significantly (in comparison to other factors such as class) empire (specifically 'dominating imperialism') affected the British people and how imperialist it made them. He is also concerned with whether empire or imperialism can be seen as the

[59] Charles Wentworth Dilke, *Greater Britain: A Record of Travel in English-Speaking Countries During 1866–7* (London, 1869); Seeley, *The Expansion of England.*

[60] J. G. A. Pocock, 'British History: A Plea for a New Subject', *New Zealand Historical Journal,* 8 (1974), repr. in *The Journal of Modern History,* 47 (4) (1975), 601–21; 'The Limits and Divisions of British History: In Search of the Unknown Subject', *American Historical Review,* 87 (2) (1982), 311–14.

[61] Roundtable on 'Was there a British World?', Institute of Commonwealth Studies, 6 December 2005. Bridge and Fedorowich (eds.), *The British World*; Philip Buckner and Doug Francis (eds.), *Rediscovering the British World* (Calgary, 2005); Kate Darian-Smith, Patricia Grimshaw and Stuart Macintyre (eds.), *Britishness Abroad: Transnational Movements and Imperial Cultures* (Melbourne, forthcoming).

[62] Bernard Porter, *The Absent-Minded Imperialists* (Oxford, 2004), 313.

origin of particular aspects of British life, including the development of racism. Andrew Thompson's recent assessment of the impact of imperialism on Britain is closer to the position that we take in this book.[63] Like MacKenzie he argues that there was no single or monolithic imperial culture in Britain. While the effects of empire may at times have been 'relatively discrete', he suggests, 'in certain areas of British public life they were so closely entwined with other influences and impulses as to become thoroughly internalised'.[64]

From a very different perspective historians of Britain's population of colour have worked to recover 'hidden histories' and dismantle the metropolitan/colonial binary by documenting the presence of black and South Asian peoples in Britain over a long period and exploring the complex diasporan histories of different colonised peoples. Since the 1980s there have been sustained efforts to open up these histories, demonstrating the diverse ways in which subjects of empire have challenged racial hierarchies and claimed a place as citizens both in the metropole and on multiple imperial sites.[65] This work has helped to undo the erasures that have been part of the practice of historical writing in Britain, for, as Trouillot argues, 'the production of traces is always also the creation of silences' and history is always 'the fruit of power'.[66]

Many of the historians working in these varied initiatives share the impulse to reconnect the histories of Britain and empire. Yet the developments in this field have been hotly contested and a site for 'history wars' over interpretation. In part this has to do with politics and the new salience of debates over race and empires. It also has to do with the demarcations of the discipline and the anxieties evoked by new developments that threaten long-established boundaries. While imperial historians are concerned by the claims of some historians of Britain to move on to their terrain, plenty of British historians are alarmed by the decline of national history and the increased demand, particularly in the United States, for transnational skills. At the same time the interdisciplinary nature of the new scholarship, fed as it is by literary, visual, anthropological and geographical concerns, has

[63] Andrew Thompson, *The Empire Strikes Back? The Impact of Imperialism on Britain from the Mid-Nineteenth Century* (Harlow, 2005).

[64] *Ibid.*, 5, 6.

[65] Classic texts include, Peter Fryer, *Staying Power: The History of Black People in Britain* (London, 1984); Rozina Visram, *Asians in Britain: 400 Years of History* (London, 2002); for a recent example see Jan Marsh (ed.), *Black Victorians: Black People in British Art 1800–1900* (Manchester and Birmingham, 2005).

[66] Michel-Rolphe Trouillot, *Silencing the Past: Power and the Production of History* (Boston, 1995), 29, xix.

raised other issues. Interdisciplinarity, as we have learned, means more work, the hard discipline of engaging with different bodies of scholarship.

THIS BOOK'S PERSPECTIVE

The authors writing in this volume have come to questions of metropole and colony variously influenced by feminism, Marxism and post-colonialism. The inspiration to engage with imperial history came from feminist politics and the politics of race both in the UK and the USA from the 1980s. Questions of class had been made more complex by gender. The category of gender was disrupted in its turn as issues of race and ethnicity became increasingly pressing in British society. Once the empire had 'come home', the geographical gap between metropole and colony destabilised by the arrival of large numbers of Afro-Caribbean and South Asian men and women, questions about the legacy of imperial power in the heartlands of London, Birmingham or Glasgow became more pressing. What was the place of race in British society and culture? What was the relation between feminism and imperialism? Were constructions of masculinity in Britain and in other parts of the Empire connected and if so, how? These were some of the first questions to occupy feminist historians who began to explore the relation between an imperial past and a postcolonial present.[67]

Transnational feminism, with its focus on the construction of racialised and gendered subjects, was critical to this work, but so was Fanon, as we suggested earlier, Said (for his insistence that the colonial was at the heart of European culture), Foucault (for new understandings of the nature of power and the technologies of governmentality) and many others.[68] At the centre of the common project of colonial critique was a focus on the politics of difference – how difference, meaning inequality (as it did in colonial societies), was produced and reproduced, maintained and contested. What was the imperial 'rule of difference' at any given historical

---

[67] Antoinette Burton, *Burdens of History: British Feminists, Indian Women and Imperial Culture, 1865–1915* (Chapel Hill, 1994); Mrinalini Sinha, *Colonial Masculinity: The 'Manly Englishman' and the 'Effeminate Bengali' in the Late Nineteenth Century* (Manchester, 1995); Catherine Hall, *White, Male and Middle Class: Explorations in Feminism and History* (Cambridge, 1992); Vron Ware, *Beyond the Pale: White Women, Racism and History* (London, 1992); Clare Midgley, *Women Against Slavery: The British Campaigns, 1780–1870* (London, 1992).

[68] M. Jacqui Alexander and Chandra Talpede Mohanty (eds.), *Feminist Genealogies, Colonial Legacies, Democratic Futures* (New York, 1997); for two accounts of some of the influences at work see Hall (ed.), *Cultures of Empire*, esp. 12–16; Catherine Hall, *Civilising Subjects* (Cambridge, 2002), 8–20.

moment? And while empires certainly did not create difference they thrived on the politics of differences – not just those associated with race and ethnicity but also those of gender and of class, of sexuality and religion.[69]

Grammars of difference and hierarchies of inequality existed of course long before the late eighteenth century. Property ownership, gender and forms of religious belonging marked subjects centuries before the languages of class or of separate spheres were codified. Cultural essentialism in early modern England, Ania Loomba argues, did the ideological work that race later did. Associations between Islam and blackness were already established in medieval and early modern writing and outsiders were never safely outside, as the figures of Othello and Shylock so evocatively demonstrate.[70] By the eighteenth century colonial encounters had produced forms of racial thinking as a body of scholarship has now shown – and Englishmen and women understood themselves in relation to multiple others of the nation, empire and beyond.[71]

But a new historical conjuncture at the end of the eighteenth century and beginning of the nineteenth century brought with it reworked conceptions of race, nation and empire – the starting point for our volume. Revolutionary thinking and religious revival, the defeat of Napoleon's empire, the end of one British Empire and the expansion of another, engendered new forms of colonial rule.[72] Systems of classification became more central, partly associated with new technologies of measurement such as the census. As Nancy Stepan argued long ago, once slavery was abolished in the British Empire in 1834 new ways had to be found of explaining inequalities between peoples – the language of race was a key instrument in this process.[73] Increased classification may also be associated, as Frederick Cooper has suggested, with the shift from ascribed status associated with land to a new polity associated with rights, though such an argument might work better for France than for England.[74] After 1815 British colonial officials and their collaborators explicitly constituted

---

[69] For Partha Chatterjee's notion of 'the rule of colonial difference' see *The Nation and its Fragments: Colonial and Post-Colonial Histories* (Princeton, 1993), 10.

[70] Ania Loomba, *Shakespeare, Race and Colonialism* (Oxford, 2002).

[71] E.g. Kathleen Wilson, 'Citizenship, Empire and Modernity in the English Provinces, c. 1720–90', *Eighteenth Century Studies*, 29 (1) (1995), 69–96; *The Island Race*; Kathleen Wilson (ed.), *A New Imperial History: Culture, Identity and Modernity in Britain and the Empire 1660–1840* (Cambridge, 2004); Felicity Nussbaum, *Torrid Zones: Maternity, Sexuality and Empire in Eighteenth Century English Narratives* (Baltimore, 1995); Roxanne Wheeler, *The Complexion of Race: Categories of Difference in Eighteenth-Century British Culture* (Philadelphia, 2000); Colley, *Captives*.

[72] Bayly, *Imperial Meridian.*   [73] Stepan, *The Idea of Race in Science.*

[74] Cooper, *Colonialism in Question*, 28.

populations into ethnically specific, gendered subjects, marked peoples as different and ruled them according to those differences. They utilised categories and classifications that legitimated inequalities of power. The marking of difference across the Empire was never only about race, and never only the binary of coloniser/colonised. Rather there were multiple axes of power. But race was critical to imperial power because empires were constituted of diverse peoples, living in varied sites, some of whom ruled others. 'Race is a foundational colonial sorting technique', as Ann Stoler argues, and 'like all classificatory techniques, it is based on establishing categories and scales of comparison'.[75] These could work on the register either of biology or of culture. Such differences never could be fixed for they were neither natural nor self-evident. And the British Empire with its complex mapping of difference across European, South Asian, African, Caribbean, Antipodean and North American territories never produced a set of stable dichotomies of coloniser and colonised, citizens and subjects: rather these were always matters of contestation. Since empires depended on some notion of common belonging, there was a constant process of drawing and redrawing lines of inclusion and exclusion. The British Empire was held together in part by the promise of inclusion, all British subjects were the same, while at the very same time being fractured by many exclusions. These included the practices of citizenship and sexuality as the chapters by Philippa Levine and Keith McClelland and Sonya Rose show in this volume.

The classification of subjects across the Empire was also a process of positioning in a social space demarcated by notions of the metropolitan and the colonial – here/there, then/now, home/away. Dissolving these idealised dualities and insisting on considering metropole and colony within the same analytic frame has been a concern for many historians in the past decades as we have seen. The chapters in this book dissolve the metropole/colony binary, a fiction that was at the very heart of the taken-for-granted view of Britain as an imperial power by showing how, in different ways that varied over time, the British metropole was an *imperial* 'home'. As Alan Lester has argued, 'colony and metropole, periphery and centre, were and are, co-constituted'.[76] We maintain that while 'home' – metropolitan Britain – was a part of the Empire, it was imagined by those within the metropole as a place set apart from it in spite of Britain's role

---

[75] Ann L. Stoler, 'Haunted by Empire: Domains of the Intimate and the Practices of Comparison', in Stoler (ed.), *Haunted by Empire* (Durham, NC, forthcoming).
[76] Lester, 'Constructing Colonial Discourse', 29.

within it. This imagined sense of impervious boundaries allowed for and was promulgated by a historical sensibility portraying Britain as an 'island nation' mostly untroubled by its imperial project.

Historical specificity is also critical to our project in this book. The detail of how relations shifted in time and place, the varied chronologies – of political ideologies, of racial thought, of traditions of resistance and contestation, of patterns of production and consumption, of religious belief, of class and gender relations and family forms, of popular culture – all of these and many other variables need to be explored if we are to properly comprehend the place of empire in metropolitan life. The essays in this book focus on the nineteenth century, in part because this has been the period which has been most researched to date. Those that do consider the twentieth century rarely go beyond the 1930s, and only Philippa Levine and Cora Kaplan make connections with the postcolonial period. Fortunately work is now in progress on the twentieth century and in the next few years our grasp of the impact of empire both in the interwar period and in the second half of the century, when the Empire came home, is bound to increase.

As was so clear at that moment of 'coming home', empire linked the lives of people in the metropole to global circuits of production, distribution and exchange, to the exploitation and oppression of millions of other imperial subjects. National and local histories were imbricated in a world system fashioned by imperialism and colonialism. We need, as Mrinalini Sinha argues, 'a mode of analysis that is simultaneously global in its reach and conjunctural in its focus'.[77] At the same time, prior to decolonisation, 'being imperial' was simply a part of a whole culture, to be investigated not as separate from but as integral to peoples' lives. Britain's imperial project affected the everyday in ways that shaped what was 'taken-for-granted' and thus was not *necessarily* a matter of conscious awareness or deliberation. With the exception of those in some official or quasi-official roles, for most people, empire was just there – out there. It was ordinary.[78] We do not argue that empire was the sole influence on the constitution of 'Britishness', which was always an unstable form of national belonging or identity. Influences from the Continent and after the late eighteenth century from the United States, Russia, Turkey and Japan were felt at home in Great Britain. It is important, however, to

---

[77] Mrinalini Sinha, 'Mapping the Imperial Social Formation: A Modest Proposal for Feminist History', *Signs*, 25 (4) (2000), 1077–82.

[78] Gail Lewis, 'Racialising Culture is Ordinary', in Elizabeth B. Silva and Tony Bennett (eds.), *Contemporary Culture and Everyday Life* (Durham, 2004), 111–29.

keep in mind that during the period that we cover in this book, European empires were critical in a world-historical perspective and on occasion had a direct impact on the British metropole as Laura Tabili's essay in this volume emphasises.

Even when Britishness, itself, was rejected by people within Great Britain as a national identity, that very rejection could well indicate the insidious presence of imperial Britain in the lives of its inhabitants. For example, when Raymond Williams was asked if he recalled from his childhood if the Welsh thought of themselves as British, he replied, 'No, the term was not used much, except by the people one distrusted. "British" was hardly ever used without "Empire" following and for that nobody had any use at all, including the small farmer.'[79] While this might appear to indicate that empire had no influence in early twentieth-century Wales, Williams' statement suggests that it helped to shore up a Welsh national identity in contrast to a British/English one.

EMPIRE AND THE EVERYDAY

Empire was omnipresent in the everyday lives of 'ordinary people' – it was there as part of the mundane – of 'a familiar and pragmatic world which under normal circumstances, is taken for granted, neither questioned nor especially valued', to quote Patrick Wright.[80] Britain's imperial role and its presence within the metropole shaped peoples' identities as Britons and informed their practical, daily activities.[81] It was a part of what Michael Billig has termed, 'banal nationalism'.[82] Billig suggests that people are reminded in many little ways 'of their national place in a world of nations. However, this reminding is so familiar, so continual, that it is not consciously registered as reminding. The metonymic image of banal nationalism is not a flag which is being consciously waved with fervent passion; it is the flag hanging unnoticed on the public building.'[83] Racial thought was

---

[79] Raymond Williams, *Politics and Letters* (London, 1979), 26. For a discussion of Williams' statement in connection with an idealised English/British 'home', see Simon Gikandi, *Maps of Englishness* (New York, 1996), 28–9.

[80] Patrick Wright, *On Living in an Old Country* (London, 1985), 6. We thank Geoff Eley for reminding us of Wright's discussion of the nation and everyday life.

[81] These ideas draw upon those of Pierre Bourdieu – and, to use his language, we are arguing that Britain's status as an imperial nation and the presence of the Empire within the metropole shaped what Bourdieu has called the *habitus* or set of more or less durable predispositions that lead individuals to act in particular ways. See Pierre Bourdieu, *Logic of Practice*, trans. Richard Nice (Cambridge, 1990); for a helpful introduction to Bourdieu's ideas see John B. Thompson's 'Introduction' to Pierre Bourdieu, *Language and Symbolic Power*, ed. Thompson (Cambridge, 1991).

[82] Michael Billig, *Banal Nationalism* (London, 1995).   [83] *Ibid.*, 8.

also part of the everyday, intimately linked with though not contained by the imperial. The colour of skin, the shape of bones, the texture of hair as well as less visible markers of distinction – the supposed size of brain, capacity for reason, or form of sexuality – these were some of the ways that modern metropolitans differentiated between themselves and others. 'Race yet lives', as Thomas Holt puts it, 'because it is part and parcel of the means of living.'[84] The story of how race was naturalised, made part of the ordinary, is both linked to and overflows from that of the Empire. But as a number of the chapters in this volume suggest, there are particular historical moments when those everyday, taken-for-granted ideas become questioned or consciously underlined. These include times of imperial crises such as the Indian Mutiny, the Morant Bay uprising and the Amritsar massacre, periods when fears became rampant that 'hordes' of 'aliens' were threatening the national fabric, moments of widespread political debate over fraught imperial issues such as Home Rule for Ireland or in wartime when the imperial nation and the Empire were threatened or were perceived to be under threat. As Paula Krebs noted, for example, the contradictions of imperialism were exposed to public view during the Boer War 'through the publicity awarded by newspapers to the concentration camps' that housed Boer women and children.[85] As a consequence, ideas such 'as the right of the British to control Africa seem to have moved from the sphere of ideological hegemony into the openly negotiable realm of public opinion'.[86] The extraordinary is present within the everyday, but it is only at particular moments – instances of disruption or some intense experience – that it provokes conscious awareness and the possibility of critique.[87] Thus the everydayness of empire held within itself a potential for visibility and contestation that its ordinariness disguised.[88]

It is this 'everydayness' or 'taken-for-grantedness' of empire in the British metropole that we are underlining by giving this volume the title, *At Home with the Empire*. Being *at home* has a number of different resonances. The word 'home' means a 'domestic' space that refers to both the 'private' domain of family whose members are related to one another

---

[84] Thomas C. Holt, 'Race, Race-making and the Writing of History', *American Historical Review*, 100 (1) (1995), 1–20.

[85] Paula Krebs, *Gender, Race and the Writing of Empire: Public Discourse and the Boer War* (Cambridge, 1999), 35.

[86] *Ibid.*

[87] Ben Highmore, *Everyday Life and Cultural Theory: An Introduction* (London, 2002), 115. Highmore is drawing here on the ideas of Henri Lefevbre.

[88] Elizabeth B. Silva and Tony Bennett, 'Everyday Life in Contemporary Culture', in Silva and Bennett (eds.), *Contemporary Culture and Everyday Life*, 5.

by virtue of kinship and the imperial metropole.[89] The term 'domestic' also has a number of different resonances. According to the Oxford English Dictionary, from 1545 it pertained to one's own country or nation; internal, inland home; from 1611 its meaning included belonging to the home, house or household; household, home, family; and from 1660 it also came to mean indigenous, home-grown and home-made. In a very provocative discussion, Amy Kaplan writes, ' "Domestic" and "foreign" are ... not neutral legal and spatial descriptions, but heavily weighted metaphors imbued with racialized and gendered associations of home and family, outsider and insider, subjects and citizens.'[90] She suggests that 'domestic has a double meaning that links the space of the familial household to that of the nation, by imagining both in opposition to everything outside the geographic and conceptual borders of home'.[91] The metaphorical connections between domestic, home and nation on the one hand, and their opposition to the Empire on the other, were especially evocative during the nineteenth and early twentieth centuries as the Empire expanded and the ideology of domesticity in middle-class England held sway. Towards the end of the nineteenth century as the ideology of domesticity was threatened by the growth of feminism and as the imperial nation was perceived to be in danger of degeneration on the one hand, and competition from other imperial nation states on the other, and later by nationalist movements in the colonies, the emotional power of the connection between home, the domestic and the imperial metropole, if anything, was strengthened. These were places of safety and security, of family and emotional bonds.

It signifies the comfort of being taken into the bosom of one's family as well as being utterly at ease with a subject or issue and being on familiar ground. As Guha has suggested, it is a world of 'known limits', and as such it is a space of 'absolute familiarity' outside of which is its opposite – the 'unimaginable and uncomfortable'.[92] The outside, in other words, is imagined as the world of difference. Home is built upon a 'pattern of select inclusions and exclusions'.[93] This is a utopian vision as difference is also uncomfortably present within the familiar, familial home divided as it is by gender and age differences – differences that unsettle an imagined

---

[89] For a helpful discussion of this point see Alison Blunt and Robyn Dowling, *Home* (London, 2005), esp. ch. 4.

[90] Amy Kaplan, *The Anarchy of Empire in the Making of U.S. Culture* (Cambridge, MA, 2002), 3.

[91] *Ibid.*, 25.

[92] Ranajit Guha, 'Not at Home in Empire', *Critical Inquiry*, 23 (3) (1997), 483.

[93] Rosemary Marangoly George, *The Politics of Home: Postcolonial Relocations and Twentieth-century Fiction* (Cambridge, MA, 2002), 3.

sense of absolute unity signified by the word 'home'. Just as the nine-teenth-century distinction between the domestic or private sphere and the public sphere was an imagined one, so too is the boundary between 'home' and its 'outside' illusory. Indeed, the association between 'home' and comfort and ease or security and protection may be understood within the realm of fantasy. As such, it is always unstable and a space that must be defended. As Morley and Robins have put it, 'home'

is about sustaining cultural boundaries and boundedness. To belong in this way is to protect exclusive, and therefore, excluding identities against those who are seen as aliens and foreigners. The 'Other' is always and continuously a threat to the security and integrity of those who share a common home.[94]

Furthermore, to be 'at home' with the Empire is to imagine the imperial world under control by the metropole and a state of affairs that one can and does 'live with'. But that sense of being in control is persistently haunted by the consequences of the violence upon which that control is based.

Ironically, being 'at home' with the Empire, being comfortable with the idea of being imperial, being accustomed to its sometimes shadowy presence fostered and was dependent upon a geographical imagination that bifurcated the political and economic space of empire into a bounded 'home' which was physically and culturally separated from the colonised 'other'.[95] As Rosemary Marangoly George has put it, 'ulti-mately ... distance in itself becomes difference'. As a home place, a place that was thoroughly familiar, it was imagined to be essentially impervious to the Empire of which it was a part. Home kept the 'other' peoples of the Empire at a distance, 'their' strange climates, fruits and vegetables and peoples of colour were living in places that were incommensurable. As for the temperate zones, there it was easier to imagine a home from home – but always marked by difference, for Australia had its sugar plantations and rainforests as well as its sheep, its Aboriginal peoples as well as its hardy settlers. And yet, the notion of 'home' was informed by tropes of material comfort associated with food, cleanliness, etc., themselves dependent upon imperial products.

The history of home was to be comprehended as one that was internally driven by special virtues that inhered in a homogeneous people

---

[94] David Morley and Kevin Robins, *Spaces of Identity, Global Media, Electronic Landscapes and Cultural Boundaries* (London, 1995), 89.

[95] Edward W. Said, *Orientalism* (London, 1978), 55. For further discussion see Gregory, *The Colonial Present*, 17.

as Catherine Hall's essay on Macaulay suggests. The imagined boundedness of the metropolitan 'home' was based on a common-sense geographical history of an island nation mostly untroubled by its imperial
project. This imagined geography of separation was a crucial logic of
difference that enabled the Empire to persist and then to dissolve, doing
so in ways that inexorably shaped metropolitan life.

Henri Lefebvre has helpfully theorised the difference between the sub-
jective and objective aspects of space. Subjectively social space is the
environment of the group and of the individual within the group. It
appears as 'the horizon at the centre of which they place themselves and in
which they live. Objectively ... social space is made up of a relatively dense
fabric of networks and channels. This fabric is an integral part of the
everyday.'[96] As Doreen Massey has argued, notions of a geographical place
'called home' often were popularly associated with a sense of belonging that
depended on notions 'of recourse to a past, of a seamless coherence of
character, of an apparently comforting bounded enclosure'.[97] Such views,
she suggests, occur especially with nationalism, and, we would argue, are
central to an imperial nationalism that must maintain an imaginary
impervious boundary that distinguishes and distances metropole from
colony; home from empire. 'Such understandings of the identity of places',
Massey writes, 'require them to be enclosures, to have boundaries and –
therefore or most importantly – to establish their identity through negative
counterposition with the Other beyond the boundaries.'[98] Along with
Massey we are arguing that what distinguishes Britain as a place, as a 'home
place', 'does not derive from some internalised history. It derives, in large
part, precisely from the specificity of its interaction with the "outside" ...
[I]n part it is the presence of the outside within which helps to construct
the specificity of the local place.'[99]

At the same time as Great Britain has been imagined to be a geographically bounded home comprised of a homogeneous people, the
Empire was frequently and quite insistently understood to be 'a family
affair'.[100] The metaphor of the imperial family was a useful one in a
number of different ways. It could be used to suggest, as in the frequently
deployed term 'kith and kin', that the settler colonies, the Dominions,

---

[96] Henri Lefebvre, *Critique of Everyday Life*, 2 vols. (London, 1991–2002), vol. II: *Foundations for a
Sociology of the Everyday*, trans. John Moore (2002), 231.
[97] Doreen Massey, *Space, Place and Gender* (Cambridge, 1994), 168.   [98] *Ibid.*, 169.
[99] *Ibid.*, 169–70.   [100] See, for example, Percy Hurd, *The Empire: A Family Affair* (London, 1924).

were *naturally* related to one another and to the 'mother country'. In his book published in 1924, Percy Hurd, a former Tory MP wrote:

Great Britain is the Family Hearth, the Homeland. Close round it stand the Dominions, the Five Free Nations of the Empire – Canada, Australia, New Zealand, South Africa, Newfoundland ... the Five ... owe allegiance to the same Sovereign; have common traditions with the people of Great Britain, a common Citizenship and common interests. All rests upon free consent and good will.[101]

So for these areas of the Empire, the family metaphor hinted at 'blood ties' and an allegiance based upon 'free consent and good will'. Hurd went on to say, 'A Dominion is a daughter in her mother's house and mistress in her own.' However, 'Crown Colonies are still under parental care.'[102] And as benevolent parents, it was Great Britain's responsibility to train the people of these colonies 'to become self-dependent "when the time was right"'. As Elizabeth Buettner has put it, '[l]ove, trust, worship, reverence, gratitude: all were recurring terms for depicting coloniser/colonised interactions as at once harmonious and hierarchical'.[103] Thus familial language marked 'both kinship and a gap between individuals and groups with vastly unequal access to power'.[104] The trope of the family naturalises social hierarchies and helped to foster the domestication of Britain's imperial relations on the home front. In other words, the homely terms of family helped to make empire ordinary and a part of everyday life.

Gender difference was complexly involved in the construction of the familial trope of empire. Great Britain was portrayed as the 'mother country', and yet, as an imperial nation raising up its offspring to some future independence, the family metaphor speaks of a patriarchal paternalism. Symbolically, empire building and maintenance was a masculine task whereas the home-place was feminised. British women's roles in the colonies were envisioned as making new homes away from home. The 'mother country' was 'home' to her children who would be educated and helped towards self-dependence 'when the time was right' by imperial men in the colonies. Such metaphors used in various metropolitan discursive arenas also helped to naturalise and to make ordinary Britain's imperial relations.

Gender was relevant in other ways to making metropolitans at home with their empire. The chapters by Philippa Levine and Jane Rendall are

---

[101] *Ibid.*, 3.   [102] *Ibid.*, 5.
[103] Elizabeth Buettner, *Empire Families: Britons and Late Imperial India* (Oxford, 2004), 262.
[104] Hall, *Civilising Subjects*, 19.

concerned with women and sexuality. Philippa Levine examines how and why empire was a crucial source of anxiety about and a site for the construction of female sexuality. Jane Rendall explores the place of empire in women's writings and how perceptions of gender relations in the Empire served as a 'rule of difference' distinguishing metropole from colony.[105]

There were numerous other avenues through which empire became commonplace. As we have already suggested, John MacKenzie and his colleagues have demonstrated the infusion of matters imperial into the cultural life of the metropole. Other scholars have stressed the role of schooling, especially in the late nineteenth and twentieth centuries. Importantly, from the 1880s as Stephen Heathorn has shown recently, young children first learned to read in primary school classrooms from readers featuring stories of imperial adventure, 'racial others' and images of their national home.[106] He argues that these texts were 'used to promote literacy among children still in the early stages of their formal schooling'.[107] Heathorn proposes that the 'boundaries of student subjectivity were circumscribed by the vocabulary and syntax of identity presented to them in the process of becoming reading literate ... Learning to read the alphabet and learning to read the nation, therefore, went hand-in-glove.'[108] Importantly, he maintains that imperialist ideas were 'an integral part of an evolving hegemonic nationalist ideology that

---

[105] The issue of masculinity is a theme in the chapter, below, by Keith McClelland and Sonya Rose, and in James Epstein's discussion, below, of the significance of imperialism to upper-class life. As there is a rich literature that explores how imperialism shaped masculinity at home and conceptions of masculine 'others' in the colonies we do not include a chapter specifically on men and masculinity. Because of space we can cite only a small portion of this literature, see, e.g. Sinha, *Colonial Masculinity*; John Tosh, *A Man's Place: Masculinity and the Middle-Class Home in Victorian England* (New Haven, 1999), esp. ch. 8; Graham Dawson, *Soldier Heroes: British Adventure, Empire and the Imagining of Masculinities* (London, 1994); Hall, *Civilising Subjects*; A. James Hammerton, 'Gender and Migration', in Philippa Levine (ed.), *Gender and Empire* (Oxford, 2004), 156–80; Richards (ed.), *Imperialism and Juvenile Literature*, esp. chapters by Richards and John Springhall; Robert H. MacDonald, 'Reproducing the Middle-Class Boy: From Purity to Patriotism in the Boys' Magazines, 1892–1914', *Journal of Contemporary History*, 24 (1989), 519–39; Kelly Boyd, *Manliness and the Boys' Story Paper in Britain: A Cultural History, 1855–1940* (Basingstoke, 2003), esp. 123–52; John Springhall, *Youth, Empire and Society, 1883–1940* (London, 1977); J. A. Mangan (ed.), *'Benefits Bestowed'? Education and British Imperialism* (Manchester, 1988) and *Making Imperial Mentalities: Socialisation and British Imperialism* (Manchester, 1990); Joseph Bristow, *Empire Boys: Adventures in a Man's World* (London, 1991); John M. MacKenzie (ed.), *Popular Imperialism and the Military* (Manchester, 1992).
[106] Stephen Heathorn, *For Home, Country, and Race: Constructing Gender, Class, and Englishness in the Elementary School, 1880–1914* (Toronto, 2000). On schooling see also, Valerie E. Chancellor, *History for their Masters: Opinion in the English History Textbook, 1900–1914* (Bath, 1970); J. A. Mangan, *Athleticism in the Victorian and Edwardian Public School* (Cambridge, 1981); J. A. Mangan, *The Games Ethic and Imperialism: Aspects of the Diffusion of an Ideal* (Harmondsworth, 1986); Alan Penn, *Targeting Schools: Drill, Militarism and Imperialism* (London, 1999).
[107] Heathorn, *Home, Country, and Race*, 19.   [108] *Ibid.*, 20.

was ... a fundamental feature of the curriculum. Imperial-nationalism was a major constituent, in other words, of the parameters of the contemporary cultural hegemony.'[109] Along with Heathorn we argue that the culture of everyday life was infused with imperial nationalism structured around logics of difference that operated in '*both* a conscious *and* unconscious manner'.[110] As Bob Crampsey reflected on books, films and texts to which he was exposed in his years growing up in Glasgow in the 1930s, '(t)he Asian seamen we met on the Glasgow streets, shuffling through the winter weather in freezing, bewildered, miserable groups, were simply "the coolies". There was nothing whatever consciously demeaning or pejorative in our use of this word for them, we just knew no other.'[111]

Religion, consumption and literature were other routes through which empire became commonplace. Given the significance of religion to Victorian society, as Susan Thorne discusses in her essay in this volume, missionary activity brought the Empire home so that parishioners, even those who were not devout evangelicals, might become a part of the missionary endeavour through their routine religious lives. As Thorne puts it, 'the foreign missionary movement constituted an institutional channel through which representations of colonised people and sometimes colonised people themselves were displayed to British audiences on a scale unrivalled by any other source emanating from the colonies'. Furthermore, people consumed the products of empire as well as the advertisements that portrayed the spaces and places over which the British flag was flown. As they shared in the fruits of empire, the exotic was domesticated and made ordinary as Joanna de Groot suggests in her essay. Imaginative literature, as Cora Kaplan argues, provided a space in which wishes relating to empire and its discontents could be expressed as heightened and highly condensed stories and figures, soldering together disparate elements in the national imaginary. Readers absorbed and identified with the charged poetics of empire so that the social fantasies embedded in fiction and poetry became woven into their own subjectivities and so into their everyday lives.

Thus far we have highlighted the 'ordinariness' of empire – how the imperial nation became lived and part of what was simply 'taken-for-granted' at home in Great Britain. Antoinette Burton's essay in this volume, in contrast, shows how and in what sense empire was anything but background or ordinary. Instead, she focuses on nineteenth-century

---

[109] *Ibid.*, 211. [110] *Ibid.*, 212. Emphasis in original.
[111] Bob Crampsey, *The Empire Exhibition of 1938: The Last Durbar* (Edinburgh, 1988), 18, 20.

imperial politics where empire was visibly in the foreground. Her essay highlights the yet untold or little examined political events and processes that a new focus on how empire affected metropolitan life reveals. Among other issues she takes note of the imperviousness of histories of left-liberal politics to matters imperial, and discusses the benefits of extending what has become a transnational study of social reform and welfare state development to include the colonies. Empire was not ordinary either to women who participated in both pro-imperialist and anti-imperialist movements, and through their activities brought imperial matters into the heart of the metropole as Clare Midgley discusses in her essay. Midgley suggests how an examination of women's imperial activism adds significant insight into the ways that gender shaped ideologies of class, and argues that many upper- and middle-class women were fully aware of how the domestic and imperial were intertwined. James Epstein's essay takes a less often travelled historical route to explore how empire unevenly inflected British class relations, meanings and identities. As other historians have suggested, imperial influence was arguably most visible and significant in fashioning elite power, but Epstein also reviews the complex ways that the anti-slavery movement affected class politics. He also suggests that perceptions of empire and class identities were mutually constitutive, although not in uniform ways, for working-class soldiers who served in the imperial army. Finally he explores how attitudes towards the poor were shaped by imperial concerns and suggests the possibility that the racial language of 'Anglo-Saxonism' may have penetrated metropolitan thinking in ways that cut across the class divide. Importantly, we argue, the 'taken-for-grantedness' of empire enables the mobilisation of imperial concerns in metropolitan debates about such 'domestic' issues as women's suffrage, as Keith McClelland and Sonya Rose explore in their essay.

CONCLUSION

The chapters in this book, then, explore the different ways that Britain's status as an imperial power became a part of the lived lives of Britons. And they trace some of the contributions of that imperial hegemony to significant historical processes. The importance of the Empire for the British 'at home' did not depend on whether or not Britons were consciously 'imperialist' or if they applauded or denounced imperialism. Empire mattered to British metropolitan life and history in both very ordinary and supremely significant ways: it was simply part of life. This was always recognised, as we argue in this volume, and contemporary critics of empire, while frequently making powerful critiques of the operation of imperial power, rarely challenged empire itself. In returning to the question of the place of empire in the nineteenth and twentieth centuries, in this period after the end of the British Empire but when neo-colonialism and new forms of imperial power are all too evident in the world, we hope to direct attention to the damaging effects and the treacherous silences that follow from being 'at home' with empire.

CHAPTER TWO

At home with history: Macaulay and the History of England

Catherine Hall

How has the relation between nation and empire been imagined by British historians? What part has history played in the construction of a binary divide between 'here' and 'there', 'home' and 'away'? In what ways has the discipline of history constituted metropole and colony as intimately linked, or distinct and unconnected? These are the questions raised in this chapter, which takes Thomas Babington Macaulay's *History of England* as an exemplary case study to explore the split that was created between domestic history (which became defined as national history) and the history of empire. Macaulay, I suggest, wrote a history of the nation (England) that banished the Empire to the margins. Yet empire was critical to Macaulay's own life experience and its presence essential to his narrative of the English as an imperial race. For how could a race be imperial without an empire? History was immensely popular in the mid-nineteenth century, a time of self-conscious nation formation and of nationalist enthusiasm, and historians played a vital part in defining this nation. Macaulay's narrative of England was designed to give his readers a confidence in themselves and their future, for he told 'how our country ... rose ... from a state of ignominious vassalage ... to the place of umpire among European powers'.[1] His 'island story' profoundly influenced English common sense and historiography. It was paradigmatic in sharply distinguishing between the nation – a place that could be at home with its history, and the Empire – a place for the peoples without history. One site for the construction of a 'we' and a 'them', those who were included in the modern world and those who were consigned to the 'waiting room of history', was history itself.[2]

The first two volumes of Macaulay's *History of England* were published at the end of 1848, in the immediate aftermath of the sequence of

---

[1] T. B. Macaulay, *The History of England from the Accession of James II* (1848–61) (London, 1906), 3 vols., I, 9. All subsequent references are to this edition.
[2] Dipesh Chakrabarty, *Provincializing Europe: Postcolonial Thought and Historical Difference* (Princeton, 2000), 8.

European revolutions, and the fears generated by the mobilisation of Chartists in Britain. They were an immediate and spectacular success: 3,000 copies were sold in the first ten days, the next 3,000 almost immediately, 13,000 copies in less than four months. There had been nothing like it since the publication of Scott's *Waverley*. Macaulay was more than delighted. 'I have aimed high', he wrote in his Journal on 4 December, 'I have tried to do something that may be remembered; I have had the year 2000, and even the year 3000, often in my mind; I have sacrificed nothing to temporary fashions of thought and style.'[3] This was a triumph indeed and it confirmed Macaulay's view of the influence he could have as a historian. 'Napoleon', he had told his father Zachary Macaulay many years before, had done no more than 'force the often reluctant service of a few thousand hands for ten or twelve years'. Yet Homer had 'through six and twenty centuries ... influenced the feelings, interested the sympathies, governed and fixed the standard of taste of vast and enlightened empires'.[4] The chances of immortality were much greater as a literary man than as a politician. Macaulay aimed high – and had reached the stars, an extraordinary feat for a historian.

So what story did Macaulay tell in his *History*? It was the story of the creation of a great nation and an imperial race. And it was a story of progress that enabled his readers to feel 'at home' with their society, for dangers had been kept at bay and their place secured in the world. It was a story full of drama and excitement, and it told of threats contained and improvements effected, celebrating the present through an evocation of the past. For Macaulay, the contemplation of the past was interesting and delightful 'not because it furnished a contrast to the present, but because it had led to the present'.[5] He himself was at the heart of his narrative: 'I purpose to write the history of England' he opened in epic fashion. He would recount the errors of the Stuarts, trace the causes of the revolution, relate the new settlement of 1688 with its 'auspicious union of order and freedom'. He would tell how 'our country' emerged from 'ignominious vassalage' to become the greatest maritime, commercial and imperial power ever to be seen. He would tell of national crimes and disasters, yet, he maintained, 'the general effect of this chequered narrative will be to excite thankfulness in all religious minds, and hope in the breasts of all

---

[3] G. O. Trevelyan, *The Life and Letters of Lord Macaulay* (London, 1881), 517.

[4] *The Letters of Thomas Babington Macaulay*, ed. Thomas Pinney, 6 vols. (Cambridge, 1974–81), I (1807–18), 163.

[5] Macaulay, 'History', in *The Collected Works of Lord Macaulay*, ed. Lady Trevelyan, 8 vols. (London, 1866), VI, 141. The point was made in relation to Livy.

patriots ... the history of our country is eminently the history of physical, of moral, and of intellectual improvement'.[6]

His *History* was really a history of Britain, since Scotland and Ireland were
included. Wales got little more than a brief mention. It was the history of
the first fully modern nation, the one that others would follow. England
was a providentially favoured country, by circumstances, by the spirit of its
peoples and institutions, and by its history. Drawing on a tradition of
eighteenth-century writing, Macaulay assumed that England in its constitutional essentials 'was qualified to be the tutor of a more distracted
world'.[7] At the heart of the narrative was the revolution of 1688 – a revolution which was essential in order to affirm and secure already existing
liberties. England had become a nation in the thirteenth century and its
monarchy emerged as the best of the continental European monarchies. By
the seventeenth century, however, its constitution needed confirmation
and preservative innovation. 1688 was a liberating moment – James II was a
tyrant and was dethroned because of a growing spirit of liberty, independence and confidence. 'The people' – meaning the elite – effected this.
And 1688 marked the way forward to the future – with its limited monarchy, established rights of property and permanent army and navy. William
of Orange brought a new stability to England, despite his engagement with
continental wars. His reign brought with it a new order and balance, marked
by the harmony between crown and parliament, the development of parties
and ministerial government, new ways of organising government finance
through the creation of the Bank of England, and an energetic free press.

At the same time the *History* told the story of an imperial race. In the
thirteenth century the old enmities of race were completely effaced.
Hostile elements melted down into 'one homogeneous mass' and an
'amalgamation' of races took place.[8] The distinctions between Saxon,
Norman and aboriginal Briton disappeared and the great English people
was formed. National character emerged, the peculiarities of the English –
they were islanders with a free constitution, of English stock with English
feelings, English institutions, stout English hearts. They valued the common law, limitations on absolutism, the freedom of the press, the freedom
of speech, the making of an English Protestant empire. The conquest
of Ireland and the union with Scotland – all of this was the history of
England. The great antagonists at the centre of the story were James II and

---

[6] Macaulay, *History*, I, 9–10.
[7] J. W. Burrow, *A Liberal Descent: Victorian Historians and the English Past* (Cambridge, 1981), 35.
[8] Macaulay, *History*, I, 20, 21.

Macaulay's hero, William of Orange. It was William who triumphed over both France, with its absolutist king Louis XIV, and the insidious Spanish, thus marking the borders between Protestant and Catholic nations. And the Empire – the savage Indians of the New World, the enslaved Africans of the Caribbean, the fabled Moguls of India – these peoples marked the outer peripheries, the ghostly presences of the *History*, making possible the delineation of the peculiarities of the English.

Macaulay's tale was lucid. His readers were encouraged to dispel doubt and anxiety. There was no need to puzzle over unresolved mysteries or dwell with complexities. Their historian could assure them that England was simply the best place to be. If empire was a place experienced as uncanny, as Ranajit Guha has argued, riven with uncertainty and diffi-culty for the coloniser, the nation as Macaulay constructed it was a homely place, a place where English people could belong.[9] Macaulay evoked a long-established linkage between home and nation. The double meaning of domestic – associated both with household and nation – had been in use since the sixteenth century. While his narrative had little to say about homes in the sense of households, it relied on well-established ideas of separate spheres, of the family as the bedrock of society, of men engaged in war and politics and women bearing children and managing homes. Such households provided the stable base that allowed nations to be domestic, to be like home. England was all the more homely because of the dangers expelled – whether Irish 'hordes', Chartist 'mobs', con-tinental Catholics, or colonised peoples. The homeliness was predicated on the unhomely nature of the outside and the work of the *History* was to keep those outsides at bay and secure the safety of the island home.

Macaulay's narrative offered a simple morality of good and evil, peace of mind for the present and boundless hope for the future. His history encouraged people to feel comfortable with their place in the world. Readers could identify with the England that was pictured: an ordered society with regulated forms of government, a settled population, culti-vated fields, towns, streets, churches, mills, schools and houses. While the Empire expanded territorially and wars were fought in faraway South Asia and New Zealand, while every other part of Europe had been the 'theatre of bloody and devastating wars' and 'while revolutions have taken place all around us', this nation had enjoyed peace and liberty.[10] England was a

[9] Ranajit Guha, 'Not at Home in Empire', *Critical Inquiry*, 23 (3) (1997), 482–93.
[10] Macaulay, *History*, I, 218. On the link between domesticity and imperial expansion see Amy Kaplan, *The Anarchy of Empire in the Making of U.S. Culture* (Cambridge, MA, 2002).

place to want to be, unlike those places where savagery still potentially
ruled (the Empire) or which had not yet achieved equivalent stability and
prosperity (the Continent). Yet the safety was a fragile one, as the events
of 1848 made all too apparent, and the dangers that threatened could only
be kept at bay by constant vigilance. Macaulay's idealised picture of an
England that was coherent and safe depended on a series of exclusions,
excisions and silences. Macaulay's 'emplotment', to use Hayden White's
terminology, worked as much on the basis of what he left out as what he
put in.[11]

While many aspects of 'the Empire at home' have been examined in
the past decade, as evidenced in this volume, so far little work has been
done to rethink the significance of history writing in nineteenth- and
twentieth-century Britain from a postcolonial perspective.[12] From the
establishment of history as an academic discipline in Britain it was
assumed that history was British domestic history. Imperial history
emerged as a sub-discipline in the late nineteenth century, understood as
separate from domestic history. The large body of work on British historiography in both its amateur and its professional guises does little to
address this division or to explore the ways in which historians have
shaped ideas of the relation between nation and empire. A re-reading of
history might reveal some of the same patterns that the re-reading of the
literary or the visual canon has revealed. Are the canonic histories of
England 'raced', to use Toni Morrison's term?[13] What part did history
writing play in the construction of British imperial identities? As Kathleen
Wilson has noted, 'Britons' own self-conceptualisation as "modern"
hinged on the emergent historical consciousness ... that was produced
by contact and exchange with and narratives about a widening world and
Britain's place in it.'[14] History, in other words, as Nicholas Dirks has put
it, 'is itself a sign of the modern'.[15] Britons' special status in the world was
articulated in part through possession of their history, a narrative that
took them from the barbarism of their ancestors to the civilisation of the
present. The peoples without history had not yet achieved modernity.
Perhaps, therefore, it is time to address history writing and ask what kind

[11] Hayden White, 'The Historical Text as Literary Artifact', *Clio*, 3 (3) (1974), 277–303.
[12] Jane Rendall's work, including her essay in this volume, has demonstrated the significance of
Scottish Enlightenment thinkers to the shaping of particular notions of 'civilisation' for women
historians.
[13] Toni Morrison, *Playing in the Dark: Whiteness and the Literary Imagination* (London, 1993).
[14] Kathleen Wilson, 'Introduction: Histories, Empires, Modernities', in *A New Imperial History:
Culture, Identity and Modernity in Britain and the Empire 1660–1840* (Cambridge, 2004), 7.
[15] Nicholas Dirks, 'History as a Sign of the Modern', *Public Culture*, 2 (1990), 25–32.

of home was being imagined in histories of the nation and how those outside national boundaries and those in the Empire were constructed? Macaulay seems a good place to start since his *History of England* was a resounding success from the moment of its publication. While scorned by later generations of professional academics for being too popular and literary, he has nevertheless featured continuously on university history syllabuses and in the national imagination.[16] The central concern of the Whig historians, of whom Macaulay is seen as a prime example, was with the constitution and its place at the centre of a progressive national history.[17] 'Empire [was] not salient in Whig history.'[18] But new ways of thinking about questions of race, nation and people may provide a lens through which to read the 'island story' with its constitutional spine and story of progress rather differently. Once the 'unsettling of national histories'[19] is a central way of organising historical work, the iconic texts that have provided the bedrock of those national histories may begin to look rather different.

Macaulay started work on his *History* in 1839 aged thirty-nine. He had recently returned from three and a half years in India, as the very powerful lay Member of the Governor-General's Council. He already had an established literary and political reputation. The chapters that he had been publishing since the mid-1820s in the *Edinburgh Review* had secured a place for him as a successful writer. While in the House of Commons between 1830 and 1832 he had established a position as a leading orator, the most eloquent exponent of the Whig case for parliamentary reform. As a reward for his parliamentary services he was made a Commissioner of the Board of Control for India, and following his sterling work on drafting and articulating the case for the new Charter Act for India in 1833 he received the appointment in India. India was banishment for him, a place of exile from home and the England to which he was deeply attached. It was a place of alarming racial difference and he refused to engage with its culture. Furthermore, his time in India was shadowed by

---

[16] A recent series of TV programmes on 'Historical Genius' introduced by Simon Schama featured three: Gibbon, Macaulay and Carlyle. Macaulay's *History* is still in print as a Penguin Classic.

[17] There are debates as to what extent Macaulay was a Whig. See Joseph Hamburger, *Macaulay and the Whig Tradition* (Chicago, 1976); William Thomas, *The Quarrel of Macaulay and Croker: Politics and History in the Age of Reform* (Oxford, 2000).

[18] Burrow, *Liberal Descent*, 233. However, it should be noted that there was a tradition of Whig historiography about empire that included Coupland, Hancock and Mansergh. Wm. Roger Louis, 'Introduction', in Robin W. Winks (ed.), *The Oxford History of the British Empire*, vol. V: *Historiography* (Oxford, 1999), 7.

[19] Durba Ghosh, 'Decoding the Nameless: Gender, Subjectivity and Historical Methodologies in Reading the Archives of Colonial India', in Wilson (ed.), *New Imperial History*, 297–316.

the traumatic emotional loss of his two beloved younger sisters, Margaret and Hannah, who he had hoped would be his intimate companions for life. Both chose to marry, a loss which was then compounded by the untimely death of Margaret from scarlet fever. Experiencing a deep loneliness and finding that his chief consolation lay in books, he began to think that a literary career would be more satisfying than a political one. Having saved much of his substantial salary in Calcutta he was able on his return to England in 1838 to live a life of independence: this facilitated his decision to write the *History*.[20]

'I have at last begun my historical labours', he wrote to his friend Napier, the editor of the *Edinburgh Review*, in 1841, 'English history from 1688 to the French Revolution is even to educated people almost a *terra incognita*. The materials for an amusing narrative are immense. I shall not be satisfied unless I produce something which shall for a few days supersede the last fashionable novel on the tables of young ladies.'[21] Initially his plan was to cover the period from 1688 to 1832: 'between the Revolution which brought the Crown into harmony with the Parliament, and the Revolution which brought the Parliament into harmony with the nation'.[22] Six volumes later (and the last was published posthumously in 1859) he had covered the period from 1685 to 1702. It soon became apparent to him that he had embarked on a life's work and he hoped that over twelve to fifteen years he might be able to 'produce something which I may not be afraid to exhibit side by side with the performances of the old masters'.[23]

Macaulay had been thinking about history writing since the 1820s. 'A perfect historian', he wrote in 1828, 'must possess an imagination sufficiently powerful to make his narrative affecting and picturesque' and history should be 'a compound of poetry and philosophy'. It had become too anatomical and driven by theory rather than facts. There were 'good historical romances' and 'good historical essays' but the two genres had become separated. Historians should reconnect imagination and reason, 'make the past present ... bring the distant near'. 'These parts of the duty which properly belong to the historian have been appropriated by the historical novelist', he argued. Yet history was not fiction, for the historian aimed also to tell the truth, to make judgements, 'to trace the connexions of causes and effects', and draw 'general lessons of moral and

---

[20] For biographical material on Macaulay see Trevelyan, *Life and Letters*; John Clive, *Thomas Babington Macaulay: The Shaping of the Historian* (London, 1973).
[21] Pinney (ed.), *Letters*, IV, 15.   [22] Trevelyan, *Life and Letters*, 347.
[23] Pinney (ed.), *Letters*, IV, 41.

political wisdom'.[24] Historians needed to learn from Scott and capture once again the art of narration. But evidence must be sifted, generalising done with care, theories always tested against facts rather than the other way around. It was experience, not theory, that provided the key to understanding the world. What could be seen, heard and felt, verified by common sense. There was no mystery that could not be unravelled. Historians needed to look beyond 'the surface of affairs' and think of what was going on underneath, the 'noiseless revolutions' that transformed a social world. 'The perfect historian', he concluded,

is he in whose work the character and spirit of an age is exhibited in miniature. He relates no fact, he attributes no expression to his character, which is not authenticated by sufficient testimony. But, by judicious selection, rejection and arrangement, he gives to truth those attractions which have been usurped by fiction ... He shows us the court, the camp, and the senate. But he shows us also the nation.[25]

He was very critical of most contemporary historians and his chosen points of reference were always the writers of Greece and Rome. By the 1840s his especial love was Thucydides, a master of the history of men, of war and of politics.[26] While the 'conjectural' and 'philosophical' Enlightenment historians were concerned to deal with an ambitious set of questions about the social, the economic, the political and the cultural, Macaulay's scope was much narrower. Despite his stated commitment to writing the history of the whole nation, his major focus was political – a repudiation, P. R. Ghosh argues, of the Enlightenment legacy in favour of 'a thoroughgoing Thucyididean classicism'.[27] In his essays written during the 1830s and early 40s Macaulay tested out and developed many of his ideas about the writing of history. Most of these essays were focused around great men, either literary or historical, for the man, he believed, could give access to an historical moment. From his childhood he had been fascinated by Caesar, Napoleon, Wellington, 'the rapacious Clive, the imperious Hastings, the lavish Wellesley'. Reflections on the delights of nature were not for him: 'Men and manners, the camp, the court, the

---

[24] Macaulay, 'History', 122–3; 'Hallam's Constitutional History', in *Literary and Historical Essays Contributed to the Edinburgh Review* (Oxford, 1913), 1.

[25] Macaulay, 'History', 157.

[26] On the differences between Herodotus and Thucydides see Ann Curthoys and John Docker, *Is History Fiction?* (Sydney, 2005), chs. 1 and 2.

[27] P. R. Ghosh, 'Macaulay and the Heritage of the Enlightenment', *English Historical Review*, 112 (446) (April 1997), 358–95. Ghosh argues that the form of the *History* severely constrained Macaulay.

city, and the senate,' he declared aged fifteen, 'are the subjects which
interest and enchant my vulgar taste.'[28] Issues of war and politics were the
things worth writing about – and it was men who engaged in them. But
while the classical historical vision was that of a universal human nature,
Macaulay was emphatically an Englishman, writing a national history for
the English people.[29] His father, who was descended from two generations of Presbyterian ministers, had left Scotland for Jamaica at sixteen
and after a stint in Sierra Leone had lived the rest of his life in England.[30]
Macaulay, born in Leicestershire on Saint Crispin's Day, was thoroughly
assimilated into English culture – the very model he was to recommend
to others.

Macaulay's historical writing was richly imaginative and had many of the
qualities of fiction, that most favoured genre for the Victorians.[31] It took
character as central to meaning, it painted vivid scenes and told stories,
it moved from one plot to another, it told great set-piece dramas – from
Monmouth's rebellion and the Bloody Assizes to the siege of Londonderry
and the massacre of Glencoe. It had strong elements of melodrama with a
constant play of good and evil and the promise that justice would triumph.
At the same time the detail piled upon detail, the careful description of
places and people, the use of footnotes to indicate sources all contributed to
the air of historical authenticity and verified the truth of the tales being
told. And history, after all, was 'stranger than fiction'.[32] But history was also
intimately linked to politics and morality. It was history that demonstrated
the necessity of reform in time, that peculiarly English pattern that so
marked her difference from France. England's revolutions were calm and
managed interventions; France's bloody and violent. Macaulay would
guide his readers through the entangled thickets of his narrative – pointing
the morals, distinguishing between responsible and irresponsible actions,
drawing lessons for the present.

Macaulay's imagined nation was homogeneous and the successful
growth of nationhood was associated with reconciliation and amalgamation. As the nation grew, new groups were absorbed into it. This had a
political manifestation – as with Magna Carta, 1688 and 1832, all moments
when the nation was strengthened by the inclusion of new constituencies,

---

[28] Pinney (ed.), *Letters*, I, 71.
[29] On the shift from universal to national histories see A. Dwight Culler, *The Victorian Mirror of History* (New Haven, 1985), 1–19.
[30] Viscountess Knutsford, *Life and Letters of Zachary Macaulay* (London, 1900).
[31] George Levine, *The Boundaries of Fiction: Carlyle, Macaulay, Newman* (Princeton, 1968), 6.
[32] Macaulay *History*, I, 564.

whether the barons, the financial and commercial elite or middle-class men. Then there was the Union with Scotland (Ireland was a more difficult story). Other sectors of the society could not hope for political citizenship – women were excluded on account of their sex, 'the mob' because they were not ready to exercise political responsibility. Brought up in the Tory and evangelical heartlands of Clapham, Macaulay shared a fear of revolution in the French style, a fear confirmed by the weight of Burke's influence upon him and the tempestuous days of 1831/2 and 1848 when revolution seemed a real possibility. Both in his account of the seventeenth century and in his speeches on the Reform Act and on Chartism his fear of an undisciplined working class, of highwaymen, marauders, prostitutes and criminals, was tangible. These people were the enemy within, to be kept at bay.[33] Universal male suffrage was not a feasible project for the present or the immediate future.

It was men of property who constituted the rulers of the nation. Threaded through the volumes of the *History* are portraits of different kinds of men, their vices and virtues. His characterisations were vivid but static. There was no sense of an identity that developed or shifted over time. He greatly admired Addison's capacity to 'call human beings into existence and make them exhibit themselves' and he drew on the tradition of English character writing, seeing men in their essentials.[34] As Bagehot remarked, no one described so well the spectacle of a character, but there was 'no passionate self-questioning, no indomitable fears, no asking perplexities'.[35] William represented the ideal of independent masculinity, for an ordered public life rooted in the rational control of feelings (the special province of men) was critical to Macaulay's values. By the time he entered the narrative, a variety of characters had already crossed the stage: Charles I, constantly violating royal authority, and with 'criminal contempt of public feeling'; Strafford, who exercised 'military despotism' in Ireland; Cromwell, with his ruthless exercise of power, but whose iron rule made Ireland prosperous and who made England great again, 'the most formidable power in the world'.[36] Then came the Restoration and the reaction against the severity of the Puritans. Macaulay judged Charles II harshly – he was addicted to indulgence, lacking principles, frivolous

[33] James Vernon, 'Narrating the Constitution: The Discourse of 'the Real' and the Fantasies of Nineteenth Century Constitutional History', in his *Re-reading the Constitution: New Narratives in the Political History of England's Long Nineteenth Century* (Cambridge, 1996).

[34] Macaulay, *Essays*, 642–3; Jane Millgate, *Macaulay* (London, 1973).

[35] Walter Bagehot, 'Mr Macaulay', in *The Collected Works of Walter Bagehot*, ed. Norman St John-Stevas, 8 vols. (London, 1965), I, 411.

[36] Macaulay, *History*, I, 79, 74, 112.

and shallow: 'honour and shame were scarcely more to him than light and darkness to the blind'.[37] He had no serious ambitions, hated business and only wanted power in order to satisfy his material wants. His brother James, on the other hand, was diligent, methodical, narrow, obstinate and unforgiving: the opposite of his easy-going sibling, the stuff of whom tyrants were made.

James was proud, small-minded and obstinate. Given authority over Scotland James's administration was 'marked by odious laws, by barbarous punishments, and by judgements to the iniquity of which even that age furnished no parallel'.[38] Not only was he personally cruel, but he enjoyed the pain of others under torture. Once king he permitted the most tyrannical acts from his subordinates: most notably Judge Jeffreys and Tyrconnel. His 'acts of Turkish tyranny' eventually convinced the entire nation, in Macaulay's narrative, that 'the estate of a Protestant English freeholder under a Roman Catholic King must be as insecure as that of a Greek under Moslem dominion'.[39] He took advice from flatterers and inferiors, his understanding was 'dull and feeble', he could be 'the fiercest and most reckless of partisans', and possessed a 'sluggish and ignoble nature'.[40] He had no capacity to learn from experience, wanted to be feared and respected both at home and abroad, yet made himself a slave of France. He had no skills of statesmanship and drove away even his most ardent supporters by his actions. Faced with danger he was a coward, sinking to the dismal level of throwing the Great Seal into the Thames before escaping for France. His 'womanish tremors and childish fancies', his 'pusillanimous anxiety about his personal safety' and his abject superstitions prevented him from exercising even the limited intelligence he had.[41] He lacked the qualities of a manly Englishman: he was enslaved by his dependence and effeminate in his actions.

William on the other hand, was 'destined ... to save the United Provinces from slavery, to curb the power of France, and to establish the English constitution on a lasting foundation'.[42] Having lost both his mother and his father he could not enjoy a childhood and was never young, with a 'pensive, severe and solemn aspect'.[43] Endowed 'by nature' with the qualities of a great ruler, he was always reserved and stoical in public, seeming cold but with strong passions underneath. While a statesman first and foremost, he was capable of great courage in the face of adversity in battle. His frail body was ruled with an iron will; he found

---

[37] Ibid., I, 135.   [38] Ibid., I, 211.   [39] Ibid., I, 722.   [40] Ibid., II, 156; I, 611; II, 697.
[41] Ibid., II, 156, 697.   [42] Ibid., I, 171.   [43] Ibid., I, 630.

'even the most hardy field sports of England effeminate'; his was a strength of mind not body, his passions contained in the interests of his aim: that 'the great community of nations' should not be threatened with subjugation by France.[44] Hard working and single minded, he would never 'reign in our hearts', but Macaulay hailed him as 'the deliverer', stressed his grief at his wife's death rather than dwelling on his infidelities and passed over such aberrations as the massacre of Glencoe with mild criticism for his neglect of Scottish affairs.[45] William had rescued England from the tyranny of James and the danger of subjection to France: he had secured English freedom. While never becoming an Englishman he had made the new settlement of church, crown and parliament possible.

Macaulay had occasionally played with the idea that relations between the sexes were historically significant. In his 1838 essay on Sir William Temple he defended the use of Dorothy Osborne's letters to Temple during their seven-year courtship as an important source. To us, surely, he wrote, 'it is as useful to know how the young ladies of England employed themselves ... how far their minds were cultivated', as it was to know about continental war and peace. 'The mutual relations of the two sexes', he continued, 'seem to us to be at least as important as the mutual relations of any two governments in the world'. Love letters could throw much light on the relations between the sexes while 'it is perfectly possible, as all who have made any historical researches can attest, to read bale after bale of despatches and protocols, without catching one glimpse of light about the relations of governments'.[46] Unfortunately this insight had little impact on the history he wrote. Despite protestations about the significance of social history, the vast majority of his writing was concerned with the doings of public men. Challenged by a reader after the publication of the *History* that 'as the father of a family' he was unhappy about passages referring to immorality, Macaulay responded: 'I cannot admit that a book like mine is to be regarded as written for female boarding schools. I open a school for men: I teach the causes of national prosperity and decay.'[47]

But Macaulay's imagined readership was not only men – indeed, he regularly read draft chapters to his sister Hannah, who had provided an audience for him since her adolescence. Women were part of the imagined community of the reading nation, but as subjects not political citizens. Their role was to succour and support men, run households, care

[44] *Ibid.*, I, 635, 649.   [45] *Ibid.*, III, 113, 74.   [46] Macaulay, 'Sir William Temple', in *Essays*, 427.
[47] Pinney (ed.), *Letters*, V, 41–2.

for children. Accustomed from his earliest years to a father who was primarily preoccupied with the public world and a mother who loved home, this was the pattern he assumed. He had little time for women whom he saw as too strong-minded or for women intellectuals. He was critical when women historians tried to write about a world they could not properly know. It pained him, he told Napier on one occasion, to criticise a female author: 'it goes much against my feelings to censure any woman even with the greatest leniency'.[48] 'In a country which boasts of many female writers', however, 'inaccurate history' and 'unsound philosophy' should not pass uncensored, though criticisms should be made with extra courtesy. Not surprisingly in his view, a woman could not be expected to grasp classical scholarship in the way that men could: they were simply not trained for it.[49] Macaulay had learned from his years on the *Edinburgh Review* to demarcate the appropriate arenas for women's writing. The Edinburgh Reviewers, as Judith Newton argues, claimed a masculine authority based on new forms of knowledge and expertise. This required the drawing of boundaries with both women and other kinds of men.[50] The notion of a 'dispassionate and disembodied authority' meant that women could only have limited authority as interpreters of history or social relations. Harriet Martineau or Mrs Marcet could be praised by the Reviewers for preaching practical truths, but for Macaulay the only women's writing that he really cared for was the novel, more specifically the controlled worlds of Jane Austen and Maria Edgeworth.

In the six volumes of the *History* only a handful of women had cameo roles. Most prominent was Mary, the daughter of James II and wife of William of Orange. For Macaulay, she was the perfect wife, a young and blooming queen with a very proper sense of her husband's position and dignity. In the early days of their marriage, a union made for political reasons, Mary had to put up with William's adultery. She 'bore her injuries with a meekness and a patience' which gradually 'obtained William's esteem and gratitude'. It was she who was the heir to the English crown and she eventually realised that her husband could not stomach being treated only as her consort. She reassured him as to her subordination. While the laws of England might make her a Queen, the laws of God ordered her to obey her husband. 'I now promise you', Macaulay has her say, 'that you shall always bear rule: and, in return, I ask

[48] *Ibid.*, IV, 128.   [49] Macaulay, 'The Life and Writings of Addison', in *Essays*, 601, 606.
[50] Judith Newton, 'Sex and Political Economy in the *Edinburgh Review*', in *Starting Over: Feminism and the Politics of Cultural Critique* (Ann Arbor, 1994).

only this, that, as I shall enjoin the precept which enjoins wives to obey their husbands, you will observe that which enjoins husbands to love their wives.'[51] When in 1694 Mary learned that she had smallpox she heard of the danger with 'true greatness of soul' and sent away all those servants, even the most menial, who had not had it. When told that she was dying she 'submitted herself to the will of God . . . with that gentle womanly courage which so often puts our bravery to shame'.[52] In contrast, Madame de Maintenon, the French and Catholic wife of Louis XIV, exerted only a bad influence on her husband. A pious believer, she sympathised deeply with the Stuart cause and was a friend to the displaced Queen. 'An artful woman', she encouraged Louis after the death of James II to recognise the Pretender and thus ensure that war and conflict would continue.[53]

Other women were given bit parts as martyrs to the Protestant cause. Alice Lisle, for example, the widow of John who had sat in the Long Parliament, described as highly esteemed even by Tories, and related to respectable and noble families. It was widely known that she had wept at the execution of Charles I and regretted the violent acts her husband had been engaged in. When two rebels from the Monmouth rebellion sought refuge in her house, 'the same womanly kindness, which had led her to befriend the Royalists in their time of trouble, would not suffer her to refuse a meal to the wretched men who had intreated [sic] her to protect them'.[54] The prisoners were taken and the terrible Judge Jeffreys demanded her death by burning. A wise ruler, commented Macaulay, would have dealt with this crime generously. There was a tradition in England and 'to women especially has been granted, by a kind of tacit prescription, the right of indulging, in the midst of havoc and vengeance, that compassion which is the most endearing of all their charms'.[55]

Macaulay's nation, in other words, was imagined as hierarchically constituted – with propertied men exercising responsible government while women and the poor occupied their respective spheres. The 'ordinary men' whom he had once argued should be part of a proper history had only walk-on parts – as soldiers, ploughmen or shepherds. The 'miners of Northumbrian coalpits', or 'the artisans toiling at the looms of Norwich and the anvils of Birmingham' felt changes but did not understand them.[56] Only their betters could interpret the world to them. But the growth and expanding potential of Macaulay's nation was also associated with the amalgamation of races and peoples – the creation of a homogeneous

[51] Macaulay, *History*, I, 644.   [52] *Ibid.*, III, 320, 321.   [53] *Ibid.*, III, 732–3.
[54] *Ibid.*, I, 487.   [55] *Ibid.*, I, 487–8.   [56] *Ibid.*, III, 528.

Englishness. This had begun in the thirteenth century but had taken a major step forward with the successful assimilation of the Scots. The accession of James I to the English throne brought Scotland into 'the same empire with England'.[57] The population of Scotland, apart from the Celtic tribes in the Hebrides, Macaulay argued, was 'of the same blood with the population of England'. 'In perseverance, in self-command, in forethought, in all the virtues which conduce to success in life, the Scots have never been surpassed.'[58] For a century Scotland was treated in many respects as a subject province, and while the events of 1688 were interpreted as a pre-serving and conserving revolution for England, it was more destructive in the north, for the level of maladministration had been very high. After the Restoration it had become clear that 'there was only one way in which Scotland could obtain a share of the commercial prosperity which England at that time enjoyed. The Scotch must become one people with the English.' The merchants were keen to enjoy the benefits of larger con-nections, particularly with the West India trade; the politicians wanted the theatre of the court and Westminster, but the religious question was dif-ficult. 'The union accomplished in 1707', Macaulay argued, 'has indeed been a great blessing both to England and to Scotland', though 'in con-stituting one state, it left two Churches'. This he believed, however, had made possible the amalgamation of the nation and the 'marvellous improvements' which had changed the face of Scotland. If the Anglican Church had been imposed the story might have been the same as in Ireland. 'Plains now rich with harvests would have remained barren moors. Waterfalls which now turn the wheels of immense factories would have resounded in a wilderness. New Lanark would still have been a sheepwalk and Greenock a fishing hamlet.'[59]

The disenchantment with the Stuarts in 1689 ensured the proclamation of William and Mary. War, however, then broke out in the Highlands, a region unknown in the South, for there was at that time no interest in 'the Highland race'. It took Sir Walter Scott to effect that. The English in the seventeenth century, Macaulay instructed his readers, were 'abundantly inquisitive about the manners of rude nations separated from our island by great continents and oceans'. They were fascinated by 'the laws, the superstitions, the cabins, the repasts, the dresses, the marriages, the funerals of Laplanders and Hottentots, Mohawks and Malays ... the usages of the black men of Africa and of the red men of America'. 'The

---

[57] *Ibid.*, I, 57–8.   [58] He later associated the Celts with the Highlands. *Ibid.*, III, 56–7.
[59] *Ibid.*, II, 408–10.

only barbarian about whom there was no wish to have any information was the Highlander': yet these Highlanders had been as exotic as any Hottentot.[60] He utilised both the notion of societies progressing through distinct stages and the idea that societies coexisting in time could represent 'earlier' or 'later' stages respectively to paint a picture of the Highlanders as primitive people, living in archaic time, unwilling to adapt to the modern.[61] Since the Catholic Highlands supported the Stuarts, war broke out. The clan system, in Macaulay's account, was 'widely different from that which is established in peaceful and prosperous societies'. Its acceptance of robbery, its dislike of steady industry, its expectation that the weaker sex would do the heaviest manual labour, all provided markers of its barbarian characteristics. Plundering the land of others was more acceptable than farming and a mixture of Popery and paganism served as religion. Furniture, food and clothing were primitive, yet there was something 'in the character and manners of this rude people which might well excite admiration and a good hope'.[62] They had courage and an intense attachment to the patriarch and the tribe, heroic notions of hospitality, patrician virtues and vices, the arts of rhetoric and poetry. Their values were reminiscent of those heroic sixteenth-century Englishmen, Raleigh and Drake. Lochiel, one of the clan leaders, was painted as the Ulysses of the Highlands (a tribute indeed to link him to the Greeks). He was a generous master, a trusty ally, a terrible enemy, a great warrior and hunter. There was no reason to believe that the Celts suffered from 'a natural inferiority'. With efficient policing, the Protestant religion and the English language they could expect 'an immense accession of strength'.[63] Yet the clans were doomed to defeat in 1689 for they were beset with petty squabbles and could not form a nation. There was no cooperation, only 'a congress of petty kings'. Eventually the English government learned that 'the weapons by which the Celtic clans could be most easily subdued were the pickaxe and the spade'. 'The Anglosaxon [sic] and the Celt have been reconciled in Scotland,' enthused Macaulay, and 'in Scotland all the great actions of both races are thrown into a common stock, and are considered as making up the glory which belongs to the whole country'.[64]

But this was not the case in Ireland, reflected Macaulay, writing at the end of the 1840s, in the wake of the Famine. There 'the feud remains unhealed' and racial and religious divisions flourished.[65] This made the

---

[60] *Ibid.*, II, 444.   [61] Burrow, *Liberal Descent*, esp. 37.   [62] Macaulay, *History*, II, 445.
[63] *Ibid.*, II, 448–9.   [64] *Ibid.*, II, 483, 493.   [65] *Ibid.*, II, 494.

task of the historian 'peculiarly difficult and delicate'.[66] For Macaulay the history of the two countries was 'a history dark with crime and sorrow, yet full of interest and instruction'.[67] He applauded Cromwell's brutal attempt to make Ireland English – for this, he believed, was the only possible resolution of 'the Irish problem'. If civilisation had taken root then how different the history would have been. But Ireland was 'cursed by the domination of race over race and of religion over religion'. It 'remained indeed a member of the empire, but a withered and distorted member, adding no strength to the body politic, and reproachfully pointed at by all who feared or envied the greatness of England'.[68] In the Ireland of the seventeenth century there were two populations – the English settlers, knowledgeable, energetic and persevering, and the aboriginal peasantry, living in an almost savage state. 'They never worked till they felt the sting of hunger. They were content with accommodation inferior to that which, in happier countries, was provided for domestic cattle.' The Catholic was persecuted for being an Irishman: 'the same lines of demarcation which separated religions separated races, and he was of the conquered, the subjugated, the degraded race'.[69] These two populations were morally and politically sundered, living at widely different levels of civilisation. 'There could not be equality between men who lived in houses and men who lived in sties, between men who were fed on bread, and men who were fed on potatoes.'[70] Freemen and 'the aboriginal Irish' were different branches of 'the great human family'.[71] There was the dominion of wealth over poverty, knowledge over ignorance, and civilisation over barbarism.

James II attempted to reverse this inequality and make the Catholics dominant, with the aid of the tyrannical Tyrconnel. This mistake was compounded by his use of Irish troops in England when he grasped the danger to his crown. 'Of all foreigners', Macaulay claimed, as he depicted the difference between the English and the Irish in racial terms,

they were the most hated and despised ... they were our vanquished, enslaved and despoiled enemies ... The blood of the whole nation boiled at the thought ... To be conquered by Frenchmen or by Spaniards would have seemed comparatively a tolerable fate ... But to be subjugated by an inferior caste was a degradation beyond all other degradation. The English felt as the white inhabitants of Charleston and New Orleans would feel if those towns were occupied by negro garrisons.[72]

[66] *Ibid.*, I, 604.   [67] *Ibid.*, II, 312.   [68] *Ibid.*, I, 10.   [69] *Ibid.*, I, 605–6.   [70] *Ibid.*, I, 611.
[71] *Ibid.*, II, 33.   [72] *Ibid.*, II, 34.

Having fled from England, James, with his ally Louis, made Ireland the centre of his struggle to survive. The end was predictable. Protestants of Anglo-Saxon blood, English and Scots, united to defeat the Irish. In a dramatic reconstruction of the siege of Londonderry, Macaulay depicted 'the imperial race turned desperately to bay'.[73] Like Spartans the Protestants of Ulster had developed peculiar qualities that might have remained dormant in the mother country. They had kept in subjection 'a numerous and hostile population' and had cultivated 'the vices and virtues of masters, as opposed to the vices and virtues of slaves'. They had 'all of the noblest virtues of a sovereign caste', something of the tyrant as well as the hero.[74] The contest that ensued, the 'most memorable siege in British history', was 'between nations' and it was inevitable that victory would be 'with the nation that though inferior in numbers was superior in civilisation, in capacity for self-government, and in stubbornness of resolution'.[75] Once completely defeated in the battles that followed, the spirit of this 'unhappy nation' was cowed for generations. 'A rising of the Irishry against the English was no more to be apprehended than a rising of the women and children against the men.' Macaulay could only wish that one day all those who inhabited the British isles would be 'indissolubly blended into one people'.[76] His narrative was structured through the struggle to bring Scotland and Ireland safely into home ground. They should be part of the same body politic and his desire for homogenisation was powerful. While it was possible for the Scottish lowlands to be successfully assimilated, with their 'barren moors' turned into 'rich plains' and waterfalls trained to turn the wheels of 'immense factories', the landscapes of the Highlands and of Ireland remained resolutely unhomely: gloomy, swampy, boggy and undomesticated – places for rude and barbaric Celts. Here the languages of race, of religion and of civilisation were entangled, disrupting Macaulay's vision of one people on the grounds of both cultural and racial difference.

Being at home in the nation was supposed to mean being one people, naturally ordered by the hierarchies of gender and of property. If the peripheries were so difficult to deal with, what then of the Empire? Despite Macaulay's own years in India and his father's lifelong preoccupation with matters imperial, the Empire was banished to the margins of his volumes. This was a history of an imperial nation that made England its centre and placed the colonies on the very outer limits, his own experience of India as profoundly alienating ensuring the

[73] *Ibid.*, II, 338.   [74] *Ibid.*, II, 361–2.   [75] *Ibid.*, II, 395.   [76] *Ibid.*, II, 853–6.

impossibility of imagining it as belonging with the white nation. Colonies were there for metropolitan purposes: to make Englishmen rich. Despite the development of the Royal Africa Company under Charles II and James II, there was no discussion of the slave trade or plantation slavery, the subjects that had occupied most of Zachary Macaulay's waking hours. The Caribbean featured in one paragraph – on the terrible earthquake in Port Royal, Jamaica. 'The fairest and wealthiest city which the English had yet built in the New World, renowned for its quays, for its ware-houses, and for its stately streets, which were said to rival Cheapside, was turned into a mass of ruins,' wrote Macaulay. Here the focus was on the city, built by Englishmen and brought into the domestic by comparison with Cheapside. The markets where slaves were sold as commodities, the wharves where the slavers docked, the Africans who peopled the island – none of these were in his line of vision. It was the impact on home that preoccupied him, the effect of the disaster on 'the great mercantile houses of London and Bristol'.[77]

The East India Company figured in the same way: its history relevant to the growth and prosperity of the city and the nation. From its first introduction into the narrative, India was signalled to the reader as the land that was to be entirely subjected to the East India Company, which would 'one day rule all India from the ocean to the everlasting snow'.[78] Englishmen at the time of Queen Elizabeth, however, when the Company was first formed, had no thought of this future. They were enraptured by the tales of this fabled land with its bazaars, its silks and precious stones, its treasuries and palaces. There had been nothing to suggest that the great Mogul emperors would collapse in the face of modern commercial and mercantile power. Yet the Company laid the foundations for the sub-sequent conquest (a story that Macaulay had already told in his celebrated essays on Clive and Hastings).[79] In the *History* his emphasis was on the struggles in the metropole for control of the trade between powerful City merchants. Empire was only significant as it was enacted in London – in the over-mighty conduct of Sir Josiah Child, or the dreams of Montague, when Chancellor of the Exchequer, that India House and the Bank of England could together sustain the political mastery of the Whigs. While the ploughmen and artisans of England were at least summoned up to provide an occasional chorus, the ghostly presence of the natives of India

---

[77] *Ibid.*, III, 140.   [78] *Ibid.*, III, 17.
[79] Unfortunately there is no space to discuss these essays in this chapter. This essay is part of a larger work in progress.

was barely suggested: peopling the armies, building the palaces, tending the silkworms and looms, bearing the children who would labour.

It was the disastrous attempt to colonise Darien that provided Macaulay with an opportunity for a dramatic set piece, contrasting a failed Scottish enterprise with the greater success of their more careful neighbours. The story, he opined, was 'an exciting one' and had 'generally been told by writers whose judgements had been perverted by strong national partiality'.[80] He, of course, was above this. The ingenious speculator William Paterson, one of the brains behind the Bank of England, disappointed by his lack of recognition in England (probably, as Macaulay notes, in part because he was a Scot), returned to Scotland with a scheme for a new colony. Paterson was joined by Fletcher of Saltoun, a man whose 'heart was ulcerated by the poverty, the feebleness, the political insignificance of Scotland' and enraged by 'the indignities which she had suffered at the hand of her powerful and opulent neighbour'. Together they proposed a glorious future for Scotland, as the new Tyre, or Venice or Amsterdam. 'Was there any reason to believe that nature had bestowed on the Phoenician, or the Venetian, or on the Hollander, a larger measure of activity, of ingenuity, of forethought, of self command, than on the citizen of Edinburgh or Glasgow?' they asked.[81] The Scots had never been surpassed in commercial life – why should they not command an empire? Paterson proposed to colonise Darien, on the isthmus between North and South America. It would provide the key to a new trading universe, the link between east and west of which Columbus had dreamed. He had seen the place and it was a paradise. Scotland was seized as if by a mania, Paterson became an idol, appearing in public looking 'like Atlas conscious that a world was on his shoulders'.[82] All rushed to subscribe to the Company, formed in 1695 without thought for the Spanish (who had already claimed territorial rights). 'The Scotch are a people eminently intelligent, wary, resolute and self possessed,' wrote Macaulay, but they are also 'peculiarly liable to dangerous fits of passion and delusions of the imagination'. Indeed, 'the whole kingdom had gone mad'.[83] The English, anxious that their own trading companies might suffer, and that they might be drawn into a war not of their own making, were deeply hostile to the scheme. But this only increased the determination of the proud Scots.

A first fleet sailed in 1698, their stores full of periwigs, bales of Scottish wool that could never be worn in the tropics, and hundreds of English-language Bibles that neither the Spaniards nor the Indians would be able

---

[80] Macaulay, *History*, III, 670.   [81] *Ibid.*, III, 671.   [82] *Ibid.*, III, 672.   [83] *Ibid.*, III, 679.

to read. They anchored near Darien and took formal possession, naming the area Caledonia and laying the foundations of New Edinburgh. They attempted to negotiate with local potentates. Macaulay depicted the 'savage rulers' as enacting a pastiche of the power struggles of continental Europe: they were dressed, if at all, in strange combinations, they squabbled like children over their relative treatment at the hands of the Spanish, and played at being kings. 'One mighty monarch', Macaulay related, 'wore with pride a cap of white reeds, lined with red silk and adorned with an ostrich feather.' He received the strangers hospitably, 'in a palace built of canes and covered with palmetto royal, and regaled them with calabashes of a sort of ale brewed from Indian corn and potatoes'.[84] But the colony was doomed. The Scots had to do for themselves 'what English, French, Dutch, and Spanish colonists employed Negroes or Indians to do for them'.[85] They toiled in the pestilential swamps and mangroves, dying like flies. Those who survived soon determined to leave, and lost many more of their fellows to the sharks of the Atlantic. Meanwhile a second fleet had embarked only to discover a wilderness – the castle of New Edinburgh in ruins, the huts burned, the Amsterdam that was to be overgrown with jungle. Many of the adventurers who had left home with dreams of wealth, were glad to escape to Jamaica and hire themselves out to the planters there, relieved to find a colony established on a proper system of order. The Scottish effort to colonise outside of the protection of her mighty neighbour was over. Scotland could not go it alone. Her fate was tied to that of the real imperial race – the English.

Macaulay, as Gladstone put it, 'established a monarchy over his readers'.[86] He told them a story they were thrilled to hear – of their romantic and exciting past; of mistakes made, lessons learned and justice done; of civilisation gradually dawning at home and savagery and barbarism abounding abroad; of a prosperous present and future. At the centre of the story was the imperial race, drawing into their web all those who were close enough to adapt and become part of that future. The price was to become fully English. This was a narrative with which his public could be comfortably at home. Oppression and exploitation had been banished, fault-lines papered over, the nation made whole through its history.

[84] *Ibid.*, III, 687.   [85] *Ibid.*, III, 690.   [86] Quoted in Joseph Hamburger, *Macaulay*, 163.

CHAPTER THREE

A homogeneous society? Britain's internal 'others', 1800–present

Laura Tabili

Popular belief and oral tradition treat British cultural and racial diversity as unprecedented and disturbing, blaming recent migrants for disrupting a previously homogeneous, thus harmonious society. Yet the history of prior migration from elsewhere in the British Empire and outside it shows Britain was never a monolithic, closed society, detached from global flows of population or cultural influence. While other chapters of this volume treat class, gender and other power relations, this essay argues that British and European empire building, among other structural shifts and historical contingencies, rendered different 'internal others' visible and apparently problematical at various times over the past two centuries.

Grandchild of migrants, common to my generation, I grew up hearing their stories: a child orphaned in a war zone, a dispossessed farmer, a draft-dodger, childbirth at sea, the random but systemic cruelties of a strange land. Drawn to study British race and migration by its distorted echoes of the familiar, I remain uneasy with scholarship that fails to acknowledge the lives 'othering' obscures.

Successive waves of conquerors, invaders and migrants comprised the British people, starting with the Romans, Anglo-Saxons, Danes and Normans.[1] The subsequent millennium saw flows of Flemish weavers and Lombard bankers, religious refugees such as Huguenots in the seventeenth century and European Jews in the nineteenth and twentieth, and many others. Simultaneously, the British Isles sent forth millions who colonised for Britain the Americas, the Antipodes, Africa and Asia. Scholars trace the African and Asian presence to the earliest times, and people from the Caribbean, Africa, the Indian Ocean region and elsewhere increasingly

---

[1] Christopher Hill, 'The Norman Yoke', in *Puritanism and Revolution: Studies in Interpretation of the English Revolution of the 17th Century* (London, 1958), 50–122; William Cunningham, *Alien Immigrants to England* ((1897) London, 1969), 3. Notably, the latter was reprinted in the late 1960s, amid alarm over postcolonial migration.

passed through or settled in Britain as it became the hub of a global empire. Invoking, even celebrating this multicultural legacy to counter xenophobia, scholars have yet fully to digest its implications for who the British are.[2] Despite constant migration throughout Britain's history, particular groups have emerged as emotionally charged 'internal others' in the course of ongoing nation building and concomitant redefinitions of Britishness, processes inseparable in turn from the rhythms of colonialism and empire building.

Diverse individuals and groups have been labelled 'outsiders' in modern Britain: in various historical contexts, Irish, Jewish, German, colonised, Arab and other residents found themselves denied jobs, housing and other social resources, attacked in the streets, and subject to official surveillance and harassment. Isolating these events from their global and imperial context, explanations for hostility to 'internal others' include the assumption that excessive 'numbers' induced conflict; that migrants' cultural practices antagonised locals; and that Britain harbours 'traditions of intolerance'. These three interpretations work together to inform an implied narrative in which migration of a significant although unspecified 'number' possessing perceptible 'cultural differences' have triggered xenophobia or 'intolerance' – the latter reflected not only in episodes of overt conflict but latent in textual and other artefacts. Questions emerge: how many were too many, and, more fundamentally, too many of what?

DEFINING INTERNAL OTHERS

British culture never was homogeneous, uncontested or innocent of power, taking shape through English domination of Wales, Scotland and Ireland, often violent processes scarcely distinguishable from overseas colonisa-tion.[3] Hardly consensual, British societies remain internally diverse, crosscut by class, gender, region, religion, sexuality and other power relations, whose relative weight has altered with historical change.[4] Within any supposedly homogeneous 'community' or 'nation', individuals remain

---

[2] This despite a prolific literature on national identity, starting with Robert Colls and Philip Dodd (eds.), *Englishness: Politics and Culture, 1880–1920* (London, 1986); Linda Colley, *Britons: Forging the Nation, 1707–1837* (New Haven, 1992).

[3] Robert Bartlett, *The Making of Europe: Conquest, Colonization and Cultural Change, 950–1350* (Princeton, 1993); Hugh Kearney, *The British Isles: A History of Four Nations* (Cambridge, 1989); Michael Hechter, *Internal Colonialism: The Celtic Fringe in British National Development, 1536–1966* (Berkeley, 1975). Given space constraints, all citations remain suggestive rather than exhaustive.

[4] Raphael Samuel, *Theatres of Memory*, vol. II: *Island Stories: Unravelling Britain* (London, 1998).

silenced and marginalised: indeed, such silencing proves integral to group constitution.[5] We cannot, therefore, assume all Britons uniformly perceived overseas migrants as more 'other' or different from themselves than many native Britons: J. B. Priestley recalled that in Edwardian Bradford 'a Londoner was a stranger sight than a German'.[6] We actually know little about migrants' reception unless their presence provoked comment.

The term 'other' itself derives from anthropological and psychological analysis first applied to gender and only later to colonial relations. This should caution us that dehumanising 'otherness' remains relational rather than essential, inhering in the eyes of the beholder rather than in the 'othered'.[7] We must enquire whose gaze or viewpoint has been represented as authentically British or consensual, against whom various 'others' have been defined. The dreary predictability of 'othering' representations, of immorality and hygienic or genetic deficiency, reflect more on power relations within 'host' societies than their purported objects, rendering migrants' reception and experiences inseparable from class, gender, labour, politics, property and empire building. This critique owes much to cultural critics' challenges to the discreteness of ethnic and racial categories, and their insistence that debates about British diversity and homogeneity remain incomprehensible in isolation from economic, political and other historical processes, including Britain's imperial history.[8]

---

[5] On silencing, see Cherré Moraga, 'From a Long Line of Vendidas: Chicanas and Feminism', in Teresa de Lauretis (ed.), *Feminist Studies/Critical Studies* (Bloomington, 1986), 172–90; Uma Chakravarti, 'Whatever Happened to the Vedic *Dasi*? Orientalism, Nationalism, and a Script for the Past', in Kumkum Sangari and Sudesh Vaid (eds.), *Recasting Women: Essays in Indian Colonial History* (New Brunswick, NJ, 1990); Andrew Parker, Nancy Russo, Doris Sommer and Patricia Yeager, 'Introduction' to *Nationalisms and Sexualities* (New York, 1992); Slavenka Drakulic, *The Balkan Express: Fragments From the Other Side of War* (New York, 1994); Yasmin Ali, 'Muslim Women and the Politics of Ethnicity and Culture in Northern England', in Gita Sanghaza and Nira Yuval-Davis (eds.), *Refusing Holy Orders: Women and Fundamentalism in Britain* (London, 1992), 107–8.

[6] Quote is from Panikos Panayi, *The Enemy in Our Midst: Germans in Britain During the First World War* (New York, 1991), 20. See also Steve Rappaport on the medieval definition of 'alien', in *Worlds Within Worlds: Structures of Life in Sixteenth Century London* (Cambridge, 1989).

[7] Simone de Beauvoir, *The Second Sex* ((1952) New York, 1989). Beauvoir immediately acknowledged, however, the flexibility of alterity in comprising Jews, 'negroes', 'natives' and the 'lower class': xxiii; Edward Said, *Orientalism* (New York and London, 1978). Also see Ann Laura Stoler's challenge to psychoanalytic interpretations of race in *Race and the Education of Desire: Foucault's History of Sexuality and the Colonial Order of Things* (Durham, NC, 1995).

[8] Centre for Contemporary Cultural Studies (CCCS), *The Empire Strikes Back: Race and Racism in 70s Britain* (London, 1982). For critiques of cultural absolutism, see Paul Gilroy, *'There Ain't No Black in the Union Jack': The Cultural Politics of Race and Nation* (Chicago, 1987); Michael Banton, 'The Race Relations Problematic', *British Journal of Sociology*, 42 (1) (1991), 115.

THE PERILS OF NARRATION

Despite more than a century of scholarship on overseas migration we remain far from a complete picture. Scholars have yet substantially to reconstruct where migrants came from, how many there were and where in Britain they settled. We know much more about some groups, times and localities than others, and more about notorious episodes of violence than about community formation and internal dynamics, or even daily inter-actions between migrants and natives. We have barely engaged why some native Britons – and which ones – attacked such settlers as 'others' at some times and not others.[9] Narratives emerging from this fragmentary evidence must remain tentative, subject to revision upon further investigation.

Colour-blind source material has impeded researchers' efforts to establish objectively the size and location of Britain's black or colonised populations. Paradoxically, since racial categories remain fundamentally fictive, efforts to quantify or otherwise render them objectively threaten to restabilise the very constructs we repudiate. As the salience of 'race' may reside in the eye of the beholder, evidence about people of colour most often appears only in the most 'race'-conscious sources. The documentary record may thus remain frustratingly silent in the absence of conflict, skewing our view of past social relations and concealing those whose lives we wish most to uncover. Like women, another group often hidden in conventional historical records, just because people didn't 'see' or recall black Britons or overseas migrants does not mean they were not there. Further, we must beware the comforting but damaging projection of contemporary racial polarisation on to the past.

Modern narratives often begin with the African diaspora communities of slaves and freed people in eighteenth-century London exposed by the James Somerset affair, when a slave brought to Britain refused to return to the Caribbean, threatening the slave system under-girding British industrial and imperial expansion. Repeal of Napoleonic-era legislation initiated a period of unrestricted migration in the 1820s, coinciding with Britain's era of 'free trade imperialism' but also with a 'liberal' migration regime across Europe between 1815 and 1880.[10] Overseas

---

[9] This assessment, offered in Colin Holmes, 'Historians and Immigration', in Michael Drake (ed.), *Time, Family and Community: Perspectives on Family and Community in History* (Oxford, 1994), 165–80, holds today.

[10] Aristide Zolberg, 'International Migration Policies in a Changing World System', in William H. McNeill and Ruth S. Adams (eds.), *Human Migration: Patterns and Policies* (Bloomington, 1978), 251–4; Andreas Fahrmeir, *Foreigners and Law in Britain and German States 1789–1870* (Oxford, 2000).

migrants rendered Britain increasingly diverse between 1841, when enumeration began, and 1891. As early as 1851 foreigners outnumbered Scots and/or Welsh in Birmingham, Bristol and London.[11] From 1820 onward England and Wales lost more population through emigration than they gained through immigration.[12] These emigrants, presumably of English and Welsh origin, were replaced by Irish, Scots, colonials and foreigners, prompting the *Daily Mail* to lament in 1911 the 'scum of Europe' replacing the 'cream' of Britain 'skimmed off by emigration'.[13] Those born outside England and Wales grew from 4.1% in 1851 to 4.6%, nearly one in twenty, by 1861, and by 1871 over a million (1,020,101), approximately 4.5% of the country's twenty-two million inhabitants, over a fifth of them foreign or colonial born.[14] Of these, 98,617 came from Europe and a further 18,496 from America, with only a scattering from Asia and Africa.[15] Like other migrants they clustered in burgeoning urban areas: by 1881 51% were found in London, and 39% in forty-six 'great provincial towns'.[16] By 1911, of 36,070,492 persons enumerated in England and Wales, those born in the colonies and India totalled 161,502 and those in foreign countries, mostly northern Europe, 373,516.[17]

HOW MANY WERE TOO MANY?

Historians long dismissed colonial subjects and foreigners as unimportant due to their modest numbers, yet antagonism to the same people has been attributed to intolerably large numbers. Aggregate census figures, despite their limitations, offer some objective basis for comparing the size of migrant populations to their visibility as objects of hostile 'othering'. These figures reveal only tenuous correlation between numbers and conflict (see Table 1).

---

[11] Colin G. Pooley, 'The Residential Segregation of Migrant Communities in Mid-Victorian Liverpool', *Transactions of the Institute of British Geographers*, 2nd ser., 2 (1977), 366.

[12] Francesca Klug, '"Oh, To Be in England": The British Case Study', in Nira Yuval-Davis and Floya Anthius (eds.), *Woman-Nation-State* (London, 1989), 34 fn.12

[13] Quoted in David Feldman, *Englishmen and Jews: Social Relations and Political Culture 1840–1914* (New Haven, 1994), 361. *1911 Census Report: Administrative Areas* 1913 1 (Cd.6258), xxi.

[14] *1931 Census General Report* (London, 1950), Table LXX 'Birth-places of the Population ... 1851–1931', 169; also see *1871 Census Report: Summary Tables*, xxi.

[15] *1881 General Census Report*, pp1883 (C. 3797) LXXX, 56.

[16] *1861 General Census Report* pp1863 (3221) LIII, Pt.I, 39–40; *1891 General Census Report* pp1893–4 (C. 7222) CVI, 65.

[17] *1931 Census General Report* (London, 1950), Table LXX 'Birth-places of the Population ... 1851–1931', 169.

Table 1. *Birthplaces of the people of England and Wales 1841–1931*

	Ireland	Scotland	Foreign	Colonies	Total
1841[18]	289,404	103,238	39,244	1,088	15,914,148
1851[19]	519,959	130,087	61,708	33,688	17,927,609
1861	601,634	169,202	101,832	51,572	20,066,224
1871	566,540	213,254	139,445	70,812	22,712,266
1881	562,374	253,528	174,372	94,399	25,974,439
1891	458,315	282,271	233,008	111,627	29,002,525
1901	426,565	316,838	339,436	136,092	32,527,843
1911	375,325	321,825	373,516	161,502	36,070,492
1921	364,747	333,517	328,641	204,466	37,886,699
1931	381,089	366,486	307,570	225,684	39,952,377

Unfortunately, birthplace data tell us nothing about racial assignment, perhaps reflecting its limited salience, much less cultural practices. Yet they do reveal most groups grew steadily, jibing ill with the discontinuous record of xenophobic outbursts and suggesting we must look elsewhere for the causes of conflict. While the Irish dwarfed others at mid-century, the gap later narrowed substantially: Irish population peaked in 1861, thereafter diminishing steadily, by over 30% between 1871 and 1881 and again by 104,059 or 18.5% between 1881 and 1891.[20] Others burgeoned 1871–81, Scots by 26%, foreigners by 25% and colonial subjects – 'race' unspecified – by fully one-third, 33%. Between 1871 and 1881 Europeans increased by 9.8%, Asians by 34.4%.[21]

If sheer numbers explained the construction of Britain's 'others', we might expect to see anti-Irish hostility ebbing after 1861 at the expense of Scots, foreigners and colonials. Indeed, between 1881 and 1891 the proportion of the population born in England and Wales increased, from 957/1,000 in 1881 to 961/1,000 in 1891, which, if numbers were critical, should have reduced xenophobia. The 'foreign-born element', dismissed in 1891 as 'numerically insignificant ... much smaller than is commonly supposed',[22] shortly became the object of a vicious campaign culminating

[18] *1841 Census Enumeration Abstract I* pp1843 (496) XXII, 459; *1931 Preliminary Census Report: Tables* (London, 1931), III, Table I, 1.
[19] *1931 General Census Report* (London, 1950), Table LXX 'Birthplaces of the Population ... 1851–1931', 169.
[20] *1891 Census Report:* pp1893–4 (C. 7058) CVI, 61–2.
[21] *1881 General Census Report* IV pp1883 (3797) LXXX, 52–5.
[22] *1891 Census Report*, 60, 64, 65.

in the Aliens Act 1905. These apparently inexplicable patterns of conflict or its absence may be illuminated by the historical context of British and European empire building.

EMPIRE BUILDING CREATED INTERNAL OTHERS

Reconstructing the history of Britain's internal 'others' demands attention to global and local contexts drawing migrants to Britain, rendering some rather than others threatening to or exploitable by institutional actors or ordinary Britons. Focus on the Irish, Jews and colonised people, for example, arguably reflects their historical visibility in repeated crises of empire building, British, European and beyond, as well as racism's inextricability from imperial processes.

Premising explanations for racism on visceral 'white' responses to 'difference' risks naturalising race, placing it beyond historical analysis.[23] Colonialism 'made' 'race' in the British context, remaining inseparable from it. Discourses of racial inferiority developed as ideological justifications for European domination and privilege.[24] Absent power relations, physical appearance or cultural practices remain value-free: given the ongoing struggles colonisation provoked, such differences visibly marked the boundaries of power and privilege. Colonised people including the Irish became visible when they challenged their position within the imperial system to demand a fair share of the resources their labour produced. Resistance often involved moving physically: migrating, fleeing, escaping; shifting to more visible positions in the social as well as geographical landscape, perhaps encroaching on colonisers' prerogatives. In particular, many refused the role of cheap or enslaved labour by migrating to Britain. Racism against recent migrants remains inseparable from continuing efforts to perpetuate their relegation within the neo-imperial

---

[23] Peter Kolchin argues 'whiteness', even in the more rigid US context, has proven 'overworked', 'Whiteness Studies: The New History of Race in America', *Journal of American History*, 89 (1) (2003), 154–73. If an imperfect fit with the British case, Barbara Jeanne Fields' 'Of Rogues and Geldings', *American Historical Review*, 108 (2003), 1397–405, offers a bracing antidote to muddled thinking. Also see Thomas C. Holt, '"An Empire Over the Mind": Emancipation, Race, and Ideology in the British West Indies and the American South', in J. Morgan Kousser and James M. McPherson (eds.), *Region, Race and Reconstruction: Essays in Honor of C. Vann Woodward* (New York, 1982), esp. 303, 307, 313 fn. 47.

[24] Barbara Jeanne Fields, 'Slavery, Race and Ideology in the United States of America', *New Left Review*, 181 (1990), 95–118; Stuart Hall, 'Conclusion: The Multi-Cultural Question', in Barnor Hesse (ed.), *Un/Settled Multiculturalisms: Diaspora, Entanglements, 'Transruptions'* (London, 2000), 209–41.

world system.[25] Its amelioration awaits dismantling inequities within Britain and globally.

Recognising imperial and racial processes as inseparable from and constitutive of domestic society and history, including that of 'internal others',[26] prompts questions about similar circulation of people, artefacts and cultural practices between Britain and outside the Empire, specifically the European Continent, with which Britain has shared a long history. Britain's ongoing repeopling drew migrants from Europe and indeed elsewhere in the British Isles: colonial subjects formed but part of a continually emigrating and immigrating population.[27] Incorporating Continental migration into analyses of ongoing empire building permits integrated reinterpretation of apparently disconnected processes.

Arguably, episodes of xenophobic conflict reflected the rhythms of British and European competition for empire. Although Continental empire building lies outside the purview of this volume as a whole, it proves indispensable in understanding the periodic pulses of European migrants that crosscut circulation between colonies and metropole.[28] Colonised and Continental migrants arrived in Britain in the process of intense competition for empire among the major states of Europe, culminating in two sanguinary world wars. While Britain, France and other industrialising nations expanded beyond Europe, wars of conquest and redivision redrew boundaries on the Continent. The eighteenth-century partition of Poland erased the ancient kingdom to feed the territorial

[25] Clive Harris and Gail Lewis found post-1945 black migrants filled jobs native workers evacuated in the least stable and profitable sectors. 'Postwar Migration and the Industrial Reserve Army', and 'Black Women's Employment and the British Economy', in Winston James and Clive Harris (eds.), *Inside Babylon: The Caribbean Diaspora in Britain* (London, 1993), 9–54, 73–96.

[26] Catherine Hall, 'Gender Politics and Imperial Politics: Rethinking the Histories of Empire', in Verene Shepherd, Bridget Brereton and Barbara Bailey (eds.), *Engendering History: Caribbean Women in Historical Perspective* (New York, 1995), 49.

[27] Arthur Redford, *Labour Migration in England, 1800–1850* ((1964) Manchester, 1978), 165; Leslie Page Moch, *Moving Europeans: Migration in Western Europe since 1650* (Bloomington, 1992), 103; P. J. Lees, B. Piatek and I. Curyllo-Klag (eds. and intro.), *The British Migrant Experience, 1700–2000: An Anthology* (London, 2002).

[28] On nation building in southern Europe, see Gerard Noiriel, *The French Melting Pot: Immigration, Citizenship, and National Identity* (Minneapolis, 1996); Donna Rae Gabaccia, *Militants and Migrants: Rural Sicilians Become American Workers* (New Brunswick, NJ, 1988); Rogers Brubaker, *Citizenship and Nationhood in France and Germany* (Cambridge, MA, 1992); Vicki Caron, *Between France and Germany: The Jews of Alsace-Lorraine, 1871–1918* (Palo Alto, 1988); and on the massive eastward movement of Russians into Central Asia and Siberia in the same period, Ewa Morawska and Willfried Spohn, 'Moving Europeans in the Globalizing World: Contemporary Migrations in a Historical-Comparative Perspective (1855–1994 v. 1870–1914)', in Wang Gungwu (ed.), *Global History and Migrations* (Boulder, CO, 1997), 52 fn. 4.

aspirations of Prussia, the Romanov Empire and Austria.[29] During the Napoleonic Wars, Russia seized Finland from Sweden, and Sweden annexed Norway at Denmark's expense.[30] Between 1864 and 1871 the German Empire took shape at the expense of Denmark, Austria-Hungary and France, incorporating neighbouring states, through conquest and coercion, under Prussian domination.[31]

Pursued in the name of national unity but achieved through force, Continental empire building mirrored the violent processes simultaneously expanding the overseas empires of Britain, France, Italy and Belgium, and indeed the Spanish, Portuguese and Dutch before them.[32] State-sponsored nation building exhibited imperialistic disregard for indigenous institutions and loyalties.[33] As Italy and Germany took shape through warfare, German language and culture were imposed, if imperfectly, in the Habsburg lands and later Prussia, followed by Russification campaigns in the Romanov Empire and Turkification in the Ottoman.[34]

Nominally dynastic projects, Russian and German empire building, like that of other European powers, remained inextricable from the drive to industrialise.[35] Hegemonic nation building, integral to economic and political modernisation, created outsiders as well as insiders,

[29] Hubert Izdebski, 'Government and Self-Government in Partitioned Poland', in Michael Branch, Janet Hartley and Antoni Maczak (eds.), *Finland and Poland in the Russian Empire* (London, 1995), 77–89; Edward Thaden, *Russia's Western Borderland 1710–1870* (Princeton, 1984), vii–viii.

[30] Finland changed hands formally in 1808 by the Treaty of Tilsit. Osmo Jussila, 'How Did Finland Come under Russian Rule?', in Branch, Hartley and Maczak (eds.), *Finland and Poland in the Russian Empire*, 61. By the Treaty of Kiel in 1813 Norway was taken from Denmark and annexed by Sweden. Frank H. Aarebrot, 'Norway: Centre and Periphery in a Peripheral State', in Derek W. Urwin and Stein Rokkan (eds.), *The Politics of Territorial Identity: Studies in European Regionalism* (Beverly Hills, 1982), 85–6, 90.

[31] Gordon A. Craig, *Germany 1866–1945* (Oxford, 1978), 1–37; Derek W. Urwin, 'Germany: From Geographical Expression to Regional Accommodation', in Urwin and Rokkan (eds.), *The Politics of Territorial Identity*, 175–9.

[32] 'The Russian Empire evolved in ways that are comparable to those of other Western empires'. Daniel Brower and Edward J. Lazzerini (eds.), *Russia's Orients: Imperial Borderlands and Peoples, 1700–1917* (Bloomington, 1997), xix.

[33] J. E. O. Screen, 'The Military Relationship between Finland and Russia, 1809–1917', in Branch, Hartley and Maczak (eds.), *Finland and Poland in the Russian Empire*, 259–70, and several other essays in this volume, especially Vytautas Merkys, 'The Lithuanian National Movement: The Problems of Polonization and Russification', 271–82.

[34] Merkys, 'The Lithuanian National Movement', 274–9; Izdebski, 'Partitioned Poland', 81; Tuomo Polvinen, *Imperial Borderland: Bobrikov and the Attempted Russification of Finland, 1898–1904*, trans. Steven Huxley (London, 1995), 18, 271–2 and *passim*; Thaden, *Russia's Western Borderland*, 126, 142, 178–99, 231–3.

[35] Lenin made this connection clear in his much maligned but apparently seldom read *Imperialism: the Highest Stage of Capitalism* ((1917) New York, 1939); also see Urwin, 'From Geographical Expression to Regional Accommodation', 179; Polvinen, *Imperial Borderland*, 6, 9.

proletarianising artisans and displacing petty gentry, peasants, teachers, clergy and intellectuals.[36] Simultaneously, in spite of or perhaps because of nineteenth-century 'emancipation', Europe's Jews faced renewed persecution.[37] Large portions of the non-European world came under British formal and informal domination in the same years, rendering Britain's growing non-European population too an effect of empire building. These economic and political destabilisations and rearrangements expelled diverse populations into the global labour market, stimulating unprecedented migration, yielding sixty to seventy million transatlantic 'comings and goings' between 1850 and 1925 alone.[38] Hundreds of thousands migrated to Britain. Their history embodies tension between acknowledged contributions to the making of British society and a painful history of often violent 'othering'.

Present in Britain for centuries, Germans and Jews became threatening in this context of heightened competition between Britain and its global rivals. Germans, until 1891 the largest Continental migrant group, arrived in Britain due to Prussian empire building which simultaneously displaced, dispossessed and excluded while coercively incorporating unwilling territories and peoples.[39] Jews likewise fled Czarist pogroms stimulated by Russian nation building and empire building, outstripping Germans in number by the early twentieth century.[40] Alarm greeting their arrival not only reflected Britain's resumed drive for empire but its underlying stimulus – vulnerability to Germany and other imperial and industrial rivals expressed in renewed anxiety about the 'condition of England': Sidney Webb feared the 'country would gradually fall to the Irish and Jews'.[41]

---

[36] Theodore Hamerow, *Restoration, Revolution, Reaction: Economics and Politics in Germany, 1815–1871* (Princeton, 1958), 14–15, 246–8, 252–3, 255; Morawska and Spohn characterise these developments as the incorporation of Eastern Europe into the Atlantic world-system, in 'Moving Europeans in the Globalizing World', 52 fn.4; and see Risto Alapuro, 'Finland: An Interface Periphery', in Rokkan and Urwin, *The Politics of Territorial Identity*, 113–64, esp. 120, 115–16; Merkys, 'Lithuanian National Movement', 274, 278–9; Thaden, *Russia's Western Borderland*, 141–2, 170, 193, 198–9, 213–14, 240. On similar processes in Ireland, see Roger Swift, *Irish Migrants in Britain 1815–1914*, (Cork, 2002), 4–6.

[37] Feldman, *Englishmen and Jews*, esp. 2–3, 148–53.

[38] Zolberg, 'International Migration Policies', 266, 269. Morawska and Spohn, 'Moving Europeans in the Globalizing World', 52 fn.4; also see Aristide Zolberg, 'Global Movements, Global Walls: Responses to Migration, 1855–1925', in Wang (ed.), *Global History and Migrations*, 279–307; Eric R. Wolf, *Europe and the People Without History* (Berkeley, 1982).

[39] Holmes, 'Historians and Immigration', 166.

[40] W. J. Fishman, *Jewish Radicals: From Tsarist Stetl to London Ghetto* (New York, 1974).

[41] Feldman, *Englishmen and Jews*, 268, 275, 279; Anna Davin, 'Imperialism and Motherhood', *History Workshop Journal*, 5 (1978), 9–66. The quote from Webb is found on p. 23. Colin Holmes, *John Bull's Island: Immigration and British Society, 1871–1971* (Basingstoke, 1988), 62–4, 69.

MIGRATION, OTHERING AND EMPIRE

Despite dire titles such as *John Bull's Island* and *Bloody Foreigners*, historians agree that migrants' experiences remained mixed and contingent: episodes of intense 'othering', discrimination and violence remaining better documented than everyday coexistence or conflict.[42] 'Othering' representations lead us to expect rigid social barriers between native Britons and overseas migrants, yet historical investigation reveals practice remained fluid, indeterminate and contested, perhaps most visibly reflected in ongoing exogamy, anathema to nationalists, racists and xenophobes.[43]

Irish migration proves paradigmatic in the responses it met and the fallacies its well-developed scholarship debunks. Irish seasonal migrants had long sojourned in Britain, some 60,000–100,000 in the 1860s, but moral panic heightened in the late 1840s against the 'low Irish', proletarianised smallholders and cotters fleeing Famine. Between 1851 and 1921 one-quarter of Irish emigrants went to Britain, amounting to 3.5% of Britain's population and 8.8% of the labour force in 1861. Yet conflict and 'othering' proved neither inevitable nor universal. In the 1820s, English radicals, demanding reform in Ireland, diffused competition from Irish migrant labourers by incorporating them.[44]

Racial language developed for use against the Irish provided nineteenth-century literati with a 'vocabulary' expressing religious, class and political anxieties and justifying imperial subordination.[45] Anglo-Saxonist racial doctrine attributed British superiority to the mixture of Germanic stock ending in AD 449, yielding a 'genetic preference for individual liberty and

---

[42] Holmes, *John Bull's Island*, 56–7, 65, 84, 294–5 and *passim*; Robert Winder, *Bloody Foreigners: The Story of Immigration to Britain* (London, 2004), 4–5.

[43] Maria Lin Wong, *Chinese Liverpudlians: A History of the Chinese Community in Liverpool* (Liverpool, 1989), 38–9, 66–75; Richard Lawless, *From Ta'izz to Tyneside: An Arab Community in the North-East of England During the Early Twentieth Century* (Exeter, 1995), 174–206; Laura Tabili, 'Outsiders in the Land of Their Birth: Exogamy, Citizenship, and Identity in War and Peace', *Journal of British Studies*, 44 (2005), 796–815; on the painful ambiguities of interracial families, see Gail Lewis, 'From Deepest Kilburn', in Liz Heron (ed.), *Truth, Dare, or Promise: Girls Growing Up in the Fifties* (London, 1985), 213–36; Caroline Bressey, 'Forgotten Histories: Three Stories of Black Girls from Barnardo's Victorian Archive', *Women's History Review*, 11 (3) (2002), 351–74. Thanks to Daniel Gray for this reference.

[44] Swift, *Irish Migrants in Britain*, xix, xxii, 3–6, 8–9, 27, 29, 51–2, 73, 77, 151–2; John Belchem, 'English Working Class Radicals and the Irish 1815–50', in Roger Swift and Sheridan Gilley (eds.), *The Irish in the Victorian City* (London, 1985), 87–8.

[45] M. A. G. O'Tuathaigh, 'The Irish in Nineteenth-Century Britain: Problems of Integration', 21, and Tom Gallagher, 'A Tale of Two Cities: Communal Strife in Glasgow and Liverpool Before 1914', 120, both in Swift and Gilley (eds.), *Irish in the Victorian City*.

the rule of law'.[46] Fears of 'feckless, stupid, violent, unreliable, and drunken' Irish outbreeding natives, augmenting the indigenous 'dangerous classes' and producing 'racial deterioration', exacerbated the 'condition of England' question preoccupying British elites.[47] Despite relative diminution of overseas migration and the absolute diminution of Irish migrants, Anglo-Saxonism, Social Darwinism and other racisms intensified rather than abated due to ongoing and occasionally violent nationalist agitation explicitly challenging 'British domination' as 'the root of Ireland's problems'.[48] Thus, neither sheer numbers nor labour market competition fomented visceral conflict; rather it was fomented by political relations and elite manipulation indivisible from imperial and class agendas to 'divide and govern'.[49]

Contradictorily, nineteenth-century political borders crosscut the geographical and occupational mobility of an unprecedentedly global working class. States pursuing imperial and industrial advantage increasingly mobilised invented traditions and histories to differentiate between internal and transborder migrants, constraining the latter through legislation and other coercion.[50] Britain 'led' industrial states in restricting eastern and southern European immigration legally, responding to a xenophobic and anti-Semitic campaign by promulgating the Aliens Act 1905.[51]

JEWS AND THE CONDITION OF ENGLAND

Spurred by Czarist pogroms in 1881 and 1903, enhanced Jewish migration coincided with the late nineteenth-century crisis of the 'second' British Empire, exacerbating alarm about the 'condition of England'. Increasing

[46] The quote is from Richard Cosgrove, *Our Lady the Common Law: An Anglo-American Legal Community, 1870–1930* (New York, 1987), 70; also see 59–65, 70–7. For Macaulay's alternative chronology, see Catherine Hall's essay in this volume.

[47] Swift, *Irish Migrants in Britain*, xix, xxii, 4–6, 8–9, 29, 51, 73, 77; quote is from Sheridan and Gilley (eds.), *Irish in the Victorian City*, 5.

[48] Quote is from Swift, *Irish Migrants in Britain*, 4: also see xxii, 4–6, 80, 118–20, 149, 174; Belchem, 'English Working Class Radicals', 85–105; Gallagher, 'A Tale of Two Cities', 109–10, 112, 116, 122 and *passim*.

[49] Quote is from Belchem, 'English Working Class Radicals', 94, but this theme infuses Sheridan and Gilley (eds.), *Irish in the Victorian City*.

[50] Morawska and Spohn, 'Moving Europeans in the Globalizing World', 25–6, 32; Zolberg, 'International Migration Policies', 241, 242, 265, Cosgrove, *Our Lady the Common Law*, esp. 59–65, 70–7; Eric Hobsbawm and Terence Ranger (eds.), *The Invention of Tradition* (Cambridge, 1983).

[51] Bernard Gainer, *The Alien Invasion: The Origins of the Aliens Act, 1905* (London, 1972); David Feldman, 'The Importance of Being English: Jewish Immigration and the Decay of Liberal England', in Feldman and Gareth Stedman Jones (eds.), *Metropolis: London: Histories and Representations since 1800* (London, 1989), 56–84; Zolberg, 'International Migration Policies', 275–6.

from 9,569 in 1871 to 103,244 by 1911, Russians, including Poles, most presumed Jewish, overtook Germans as the largest foreign-born group, quintupling Britain's Jewish population from 60,000 in 1881 to 300,000 in 1914.[52] As with the Irish, trade unionists attempted to incorporate these proletarianised migrants, overwhelmed not simply by their numbers but by a xenophobic and racist campaign orchestrated for Conservative electoral advantage. The resultant Aliens Act 1905 reduced annul migration by nearly 75% between 1906 (12,481) and 1911 (3,626). Although their large numbers fuelled scare tactics, British Jewry's size and diversity, paradoxically, compelled the state to negotiate: debates about Jews' place in the nation proved integral in forming a non-racial definition of Britishness premised on relations between the individual and state institutions, institutions, ironically, on which Anglo-Saxonist ideology rested.[53] The campaign for the Act of 1905 equipped Tories and xenophobes with potent 'othering' rhetorics and administrative mechanisms subsequently turned against Chinese, German and colonised migrants, among others.

Intensified differentiation between British subjects and aliens followed, yielding the impression that whenever migrants appeared antagonism followed, and, conversely, that the absence of conflict indicated migrants' absence. Relying on conflict to detect migrants' presence has allowed the most xenophobic and racist of historical actors to stand for all Britons. Decontextualised focus on spectacular episodes of violence renders migrants perpetual victims, neglecting broader contexts and communities in which everyday relations occurred.[54] Portraying 'the British' as monolithic, stressing barriers between rather than dialogue among British cultures and peoples, isolates migrants analytically from the rest of British society and history, reproducing racists' own reified and naturalised categories. According primary agency to racists, Anglocentric emphases on 'othering' and polarisation neglects migrants' integral involvement in building Britain's fundamental institutions, including unions, radical movements, political parties, especially Labour, working-class culture, liberalism, urban and commercial culture, industry and the professions,

---

[52] *1911 Census Report* IX, Table XIV, 'Number of Foreigners of Various Nationalities', xviii; Table CVIII 'Number of Foreigners ... 1891, 1901, and 1911', 219; Feldman, *Englishmen and Jews*, I, 127–8, 148, 157. On prior Jewish migration, see Werner E. Mosse (ed.), *Second Chance: Two Centuries of German Speaking Jews in the United Kingdom* (Tübingen, 1991).

[53] Feldman, *Englishmen and Jews*, 110, 278–9, 363–4, 376–82, 384–5, 387; Zolberg, 'International Migration Policies', 275–6.

[54] Swift called such approaches 'passé', in *Irish Migrants in Britain*, xxii; while Panikos Panayi labelled them 'Anglocentric', in 'The Historiography of Immigrants and Ethnic Minorities: Britain Compared with the USA', *Ethnic and Racial Studies*, 19 (4) (1996), 829.

and modernity itself.[55] Hostility towards the poor has overshadowed substantial integration of Irish and Jewish middle-class people and professionals, including relatively affluent German Jews and literati. The well-developed literature on these groups shows malicious xenophobes did not represent consensus: relations within and between migrant groups, unsurprisingly, reflected and could be mitigated by class schisms and solidarities, regional differences, political alliances or tactics, and broad historical processes such as empire building and war.[56]

EMPIRE AND ANTI-GERMANISM

Silence about Britain's numerous and increasing German population contrasts starkly with the furore greeting Russian and Polish Jews. In 1861, imputed racial affinity rationalised large numbers of mariners from Norway, Denmark, Sweden and Germany as 'descendants of the same races as invaded England', the confected 'Anglo-Saxons'.[57] Britain's German population grew from 32,823 in 1871 to 53,324 in 1911. Germanophobia punctuated the late Victorian and Edwardian years, fuelled by geopolitical rivalry between the ascendant German Empire and a defensive, stagnating Britain, expressed through street violence during the Franco-Prussian War and the Boer War, and Edwardian 'spy fever', culminating in the world wars of the twentieth century.[58] The riots, internment and wholesale deportation of Germans and their British-born wives and children during and after the First World War reduced this population from 57,500 in 1914 to 22,258 in 1919.[59] Neither their numbers nor cultural incompatibility can explain Germans' abrupt shift from

---

[55] Colin Holmes, 'Building the Nation: The Contributions of Immigrants and Refugees to British Society', *BSA Journal* (November 1991), 725–34; Bill Williams, *The Making of Manchester Jewry, 1740–1875* (Manchester, 1976), vi–viii; Joseph Buckman, *Immigrants and the Class Struggle: The Jewish Immigrant in Leeds 1880–1914* (Manchester, 1983). Douglas Lorimer wrote, 'Our fascination with the stereotype of the Other runs the risk of denying historical agency to the objects of the racist gaze', in 'Reconstructing Victorian Racial Discourse: Images of Race, the Language of Race Relations, and the Context of Black Resistance', in Gretchen Holbrook Gerzina (ed.), *Black Victorians/Black Victoriana* (New Brunswick, NJ, 2003), 203.

[56] Holmes, *John Bull's Island*, 61, 140; Mosse, *Second Chance*; Swift and Gilley, *Irish in the Victorian City*, 5; Swift, *Irish Migrants in Britain*, xxii, 49–50, 73–80, 149; Belchem, 'English Working Class Radicals'; Gallagher, 'A Tale of Two Cities', 109–10, 112, 116, 122 and *passim*.

[57] *1861 Census Report* pp1863 (3221) LIII Pt. I, 39–40.

[58] Holmes, *John Bull's Island*, 62; Panikos Panayi, 'Anti-German Riots in Britain During the First World War', in Panayi (ed.), *Racial Violence in Britain in the Nineteenth and Twentieth Centuries* (London, 1996), 65–6.

[59] Sir E. Troup, 'Treatment of Alien Enemies'. Cabinet Papers. CAB24/55 (GT4931) n.d.c. June 1918, TNA ff. 129–32. The fullest treatment of this episode remains Panayi, *Enemy in Our Midst*.

Table 2. *Origin of major foreign-born populations*

	1861[a]	1871[b]	1881	1891	1901[c]	1911	1921	1931
Germany	21,438	32,823	37,301	50,599	49,133	53,324	12,358	14,981
United States		8,270	17,767	19,740	16,664	18,494	19,171	11,220
France	12,989	17,906	14,596	20,797	20,467	28,827	23,659	15,628
Poland and Russia	5,249	9,569	14,468	45,074	82,844	95,541	84,896	56,382
Italy	4,489	5,063	6,504	9,909	20,332	20,389	19,098	16,878
Holland			6,258	6,350	6,851	<7,643	<7,426	<5,927

Notes:

[a] *1901 Census Report, I 1904 (Cd.2174), 142.*

[b] *1871 Census Report: Population Abstracts III 1873 (.872) Table xxiii, 'Number of Natives of Foreign Countries . . . ', li.*

[c] *1911 General Census Report with Appendices 1917 (Cd.8491) Table CVIII, 'Number of Foreigners . . . ' 219.*

Sources: Colin Holmes, 'Immigrants and Refugees in Britain', in Mosse, *Second Chance*, 12; *1871 Census Report: Population Abstracts*, III, PP1873 (C.872), Table XXIII, 'Number of Natives of Foreign Countries...', li; *1901 Census Report*, PP1904 (Cd.2174) CVII, 142; *1911 General Census Report with Appendices*, PP1917–18 (Cd.8491) XXXV, Table CVIII 'Number of Foreigners...1891, 1901, and 1911', 219; *1931 General Census Report* (London, 1950), Table LXXVII, 177; see also essays by Pollinson and Newman in Mosse, *Second Chance*.

insiders to 'others' in these years, nor can the 'commonsense' equation among numbers, visibility and conflict explain the dearth of resistance to Belgians, 200,000 of whom arrived between August 1914 and spring 1915, outnumbering all the Russian and Polish Jews who arrived between 1881 and 1914.[60] Rather, long-standing Anglo-German imperial rivalry produced war, transforming Germans overnight into enemies within, racialised as 'Huns', with Belgians portrayed as their victims.

Scholarly and popular focus on the Irish, Jews and Germans begs the question of other substantial groups such as the French, Italians, Americans and Scots (see Table 2). Political economy and specifically empire building may suggest why. Although French-born residents remained among the top two or three largest groups throughout the nineteenth century, Francophobia, critical to eighteenth-century British nation building, apparently dissipated once France ceased threatening Britain's imperial dominance.[61] As Home Rule agitation posed a specifically anti-imperial threat, the Irish replaced the French and Spanish as the Roman

[60] Holmes, 'Historians and Immigration', 173.

[61] On Francophobia and imperial competition, see Colley, *Britons*.

Catholic 'other'.[62] Consistently among the top five, Italians, like the Chinese and West Indians a classic 'labour diaspora' retaining links with their homeland, attracted only sporadic concern until Axis rivalry for global dominance made them imperial enemies; its tragic consequence the 2 July 1940 drowning of half of Italian internees on the *Arandora Star*.[63] In contrast, the seamen's union and the yellow press, manipulating 'othering' images of immorality and racial inferiority, fomented panic about the minuscule presence of a few thousand Chinese.[64]

COLONISED DIASPORAS/IMPERIAL CIRCULATION

In contrast to the Irish, other colonial subjects, while present during the period of 'free trade imperialism', excited little apparent hostility and have received minimal scholarly treatment: scholars once thought they had 'disappeared' altogether.[65] Africans actually diminished from 385 in 1851 to 258 in 1861.[66] Rediscovering colonised people's ubiquity in, and contributions to, Victorian and Edwardian Britain helps destabilise the boundedness of the British nation. A surprising variety of African residents and sojourners, including skilled workers, domestic servants, students, political activists, businessmen, merchants, artists, entertainers and seafarers lived in or circulated through Britain throughout the nineteenth and twentieth centuries.[67] A web of dense and overlapping personal networks of black Britons, Africans, Afro-Caribbeans and African Americans crisscrossed Britain, the Empire, and beyond, creating a diasporic 'Black

---

[62] Swift and Gilley, *Irish in the Victorian City*, 4; Swift, *Irish Migrants in Britain*, 118–19.

[63] The phrase is from Robin Cohen, 'Diasporas, the Nation-State, and Globalisation', in Wang, *Global History and Migrations*, 129; Lucio Sponza, *Italian Immigrants in Nineteenth Century Britain: Realities and Images* (Leicester, 1988); Terry Colpi, *The Italian Factor: The Italian Community in Great Britain* (Edinburgh, 1991); Terry Colpi, 'The Impact of the Second World War on the British Italian Community', *Immigrants and Minorities*, 11 (3) (1992), 167–86.

[64] Wong, *Chinese Liverpudlians*, 78–83; Harris Joshua, Tina Wallace and Heather Booth, *To Ride the Storm: The 1980 Bristol 'Riot' and the State* (London, 1983), 17–19; Laura Tabili, *'We Ask for British Justice': Workers and Racial Difference in Late Imperial Britain* (Ithaca, 1994), 86–95.

[65] Ian Duffield, 'Skilled Workers or Marginalised Poor? The African Population of the United Kingdom, 1812–52', *Immigrants and Minorities*, 12 (3) (1993), 49–87, offers a pithy assessment of the literature up to 1993. Also see pioneering historical treatments in Kenneth Lindsay Little, *Negroes in Britain: A Study of Race Relations in an English City* ((1948) London, 1972); Michael Banton, *The Coloured Quarter: Negro Immigrants in an English City* (London, 1955), 18–36. Norma Myers, *Rediscovering the Black Past: Blacks in Britain, 1780–1830* (London, 1996); Diane Frost, *Work and Community among West African Migrant Workers in the Nineteenth Century* (Liverpool, 1999).

[66] *1881 General Census Report*, pp1883 (3797) LXXX, 52–5.

[67] Duffield, 'Skilled Workers'; David Killingray, 'Africans in the United Kingdom: An Introduction', *Immigrants and Minorities*, 12 (3) (1993), 2–27, esp. 11, 17.

Atlantic'.[68] Indians too circulated to Britain and back to Asia: by 1891 numbers of Indian and colonial subjects had risen to 111,627, attributed in part to the increased size of the Empire, yet 'greater than can thus be explained'.[69] The 1911 census estimated the Indian population at 3,891 men and 176 women, 2,531 of them lascar seamen, and 931 students.[70] Indians, Africans and other colonised subjects, present in Britain throughout centuries of colonialism, resurfaced as problematical only in the context of imperial crises. Britain's renewed late nineteenth-century drive for empire simultaneously hardened class stratification in Britain and racial stratification in the colonies, evidence of the ongoing dialectical exchange of people, ideas and cultural practices between colonies and metropoles.[71]

As for Irish labourers, class mattered: since their exploitation secured the imperial system, colonised workers in Britain destabilised imperial hierarchies more than sojourners such as students or dignitaries, who experienced random cruelty and harassment but not systemic subordination.[72] Traversing the spatial distance between metropole and colonies, colonised workers threatened the imperial appropriation that geographical separation reinforced, obscured and excused. Rendering geographical barriers permeable, thus ideological dichotomies unstable, colonised workers, in competing with native Britons for resources expropriated to the metropole, threatened the economic and political imbalances sustaining the imperial system. Their presence became problematical, thus remarked in an otherwise silent historical record.[73]

If imputed racial affinities failed to protect Germans from xenophobia during the First World War, imputed racial difference alone hardly seems sufficient to explain hostility towards and violence against Arabs and other colonised workers in 1919 and after.[74] In the 1920s and 1930s

---

[68] Jeffrey Green, *Black Edwardians: Black People in Britain 1901–1914* (London, 1998); Paul Gilroy, *The Black Atlantic: Modernity and Double Consciousness* (Cambridge, MA, 1993).

[69] *1881 General Census Report*, 55; *1891 Census*, 61; Visram, *Asians in Britain*; Michael Fisher, *Counterflows to Colonialism: Indian Travellers and Settlers in Britain, 1600–1857* (Delhi, 2004).

[70] *1911 Census Report: Birthplaces* pp1913 (Cd. 7017) LXXVIII 216.

[71] Christine Bolt, *Victorian Attitudes to Race* (London, 1971); Douglas Lorimer, *Colour, Class and the Victorians: English Attitudes to the Negro in the Mid-Nineteenth Century* (Leicester, 1978); Said, *Orientalism*; Frederick Cooper and Ann L. Stoler, 'Introduction: Tensions of Empire: Colonial Control and Visions of Rule', *American Ethnologist*, 16 (4) (1989), 600–21; Stoler, *Race and the Education of Desire*; and several essays in Henry Louis Gates (ed.), *'Race', Writing and Difference* (Chicago, 1985).

[72] Shompa Lahiri, *Indians in Britain: Anglo-Indian Encounters, Race and Identity 1880–1930* (London, 2000).

[73] Tabili, *'We Ask for British Justice'*.

[74] A useful treatment is Roy May and Robin Cohen, 'The Interaction Between Race and Colonialism: A Case Study of the Liverpool Race Riots of 1919', *Race and Class*, 14 (2) (1974), 111–26.

colonised workers preoccupied the Home Office Aliens department despite their technical status, like the Irish, as internal migrants. Neither their number, never exceeding a few thousand, nor their cultural practices, which remained diverse, explain this; rather their migration from colonies to metropole threatened the political economy of imperial extraction. Efforts to exclude colonised mariners originated not with popular 'intolerance', but with employers who wanted them confined to the colonies, cheap and unprotected by union or social wages. *Agents provocateurs* precipitated the Mill Dam riot of 1930 to destroy the Seamen's Minority Movement precisely because it organised across racial lines, threatening the unbalanced divisions of labour and compensation integral to Britain's faltering empire.[75]

SINCE 1945: WAS THE *WINDRUSH* SOMETHING NEW?

Panic about overseas migrants, prompting preoccupation with Britishness and otherness, recurred after 1945, another historical moment of vulnerability accompanying the perceived demise of Britain's imperial power. Part of a broader Cold War project aiming to forestall perceived cultural challenges associated with fears of decline, British social scientists borrowed from failed US racial paradigms, imposing a rigid outsider/insider binarism on Britain's fluid post-imperial relations. This interpretation effectively erased centuries of migration to and from the colonies as well as Europe and elsewhere, presenting colonised workers in Britain as an alarming anomaly. Popular understandings postulated discontinuity between migration to Britain, often dated spuriously to the 1948 arrival of Caribbean migrants on the *Empire Windrush*, and social homogeneity and harmony allegedly characterising previous centuries.[76]

Alarm about colonised migrants stemmed not from their modest numbers – only 2,000 per year between 1948 and 1953 – but from media hype coupled with covert state moves towards restriction. The British state manipulated distinctions between Irish, colonial and displaced European workers, a class project to divide and control working people. The state exaggerated 'numbers' of colonial migrants relative to more numerous Europeans, recruiting over 200,000 of the latter between 1945 and 1948 alone. The state favoured Europeans not only for their perceived

---

[75] Tabili, 'We Ask for British Justice'; David Byrne, 'The 1930 "Arab Riot" in South Shields: A Race Riot That Never Was', *Race and Class*, 18 (3) (1977), 261–77.

[76] Chris Waters, '"Dark Strangers" in Our Midst: Discourses of Race and Nation in Britain, 1947–1963', *Journal of British Studies*, 36 (April 1997), 207–38.

'cultural' affinities with native workers but for their lack of labour rights in Britain. Colonised workers enjoyed citizenship, thus the prerogative to seek and leave jobs as other British workers.[77]

Although Caribbean migration slackened by the late 1950s in response to Britain's depressed labour market, the Notting Hill and Nottingham riots of summer 1958 panicked the state into immigration restriction that actually stimulated migration from the colonies to 'beat the ban', while encouraging popular xenophobia and racism.[78] Subsequent state intervention has largely legitimated racial divisions through institutional racism, policing, and state and media rhetorics of cultural incompatibility.[79] Non-historians' domination of post-1945 scholarship has reinforced a sense of crisis, neglecting the constant history of circulation and cultural exchange between Britain, the Empire and beyond. Multiculturalism may appear unprecedented and alarming rather than an enriching constant of British and indeed human history. Nonetheless, as evidence of this continuing process, postwar popular culture has become synonymous with black diaspora culture embodied in music and other art forms.[80]

EMIGRATION

Emigration too remains inseparable from imperialism. Emigrants fled a society in which state redirection of resources to empire building rather than domestic consumption and redistribution robbed domestic populations of economic and other prospects.[81] Restricted until 1815 due to the Napoleonic Wars, emigration subsequently became governments' 'panacea for all social ills'.[82] Part of an exodus of millions from Europe, amounting to 'the greatest transfer of populations in the history of mankind',

[77] Kathleen Paul, *Whitewashing Britain: Race and Citizenship in the Postwar Era* (Ithaca, 1997), 119 and *passim*; Ceri Peach, *West Indian Migration to Britain: A Social Geography* (Baltimore, 1965); Paul Foot, *Immigration and Race in British Politics* (London, 1968); James Hampshire, *Citizenship and Belonging: Immigration and the Politics of Demographic Government in Postwar Britain* (Basingstoke, 2005), esp. 46, 61–2, 66, 70–4, 76.

[78] Peach, *West Indian Migration to Britain*; Foot, *Immigration and Race in British Politics*; Gilroy, *'There Ain't No Black in the Union Jack'*.

[79] A. Sivanandan, *A Different Hunger: Writings on Black Resistance* (London, 1982), esp. 99–140; Stuart Hall et al., *Policing the Crisis: Mugging, the State, and Law and Order* (London, 1978); Wendy Webster, *Imagining Home: Gender, 'Race' and National Identity, 1945–64* (London, 1998); Gail Lewis and Sarah Neal, 'Introduction: Contemporary Political Contexts, Changing Terrains, and Revisited Discourses', *Ethnic and Racial Studies*, 28 (3) (2005), 423–44.

[80] Paul Gilroy, 'One Nation Under a Groove: The Cultural Politics of Race and Racism in Britain', in Geoff Eley and Ronald Grigor Suny (eds.), *Becoming National: A Reader* (Oxford, 1996), 361.

[81] Alexander Murdoch, *British Emigration 1603–1914* (London, 2004); Lenin, *Imperialism*.

[82] Redford, *Labour Migration in England*, 172.

thirty-seven million Europeans migrated to North America, eleven million
to South America and, among Britons, 3.5 million to Australia and New
Zealand, rendering emigration indivisible from empire building.[83]

Emigrants to the Americas, Australia and elsewhere, often cast-offs
from their own society, participated, whether voluntarily or involuntarily,
in the dispossession and enslavement, even extermination, of indigenous
people, in some respects constituting the shock troops of empire.[84] Not
surprisingly, their commitment to racial subordination remained stronger
than that of metropolitan populations.[85] Settlers, occupying a 'middle
position' between indigenes and colonial states, proved most intransigent,
even when abandoned by the imperial state after 1945.[86]

Thus the emergence of 'internal others' may derive less from people's
presence or absence, their number, their cultural practices, or the inherent
viciousness and intolerance of ordinary Britons, than from structural
shifts rendering them visible or invisible, problematical or not. Only a far
more complete record of migration from the Empire and outside it can
affirm or invalidate this or other open questions. These remain most
effectively tested by enquiring into the history of overseas migration
before 1945, a project remaining far from finished. When this is complete
we may better assess the historical contexts that rendered newcomers or
long-standing residents 'internal others' at particular historical moments.
The abundant documentation that visible episodes of conflict generated
might be mined more creatively to illuminate the deeper structures and
cultures within which migrants and natives lived and interacted, uncovering the corrosive everyday cruelties twentieth-century memoirists and
oral historians report, but also accommodation and coexistence, marriage
and family, as David Nirenberg used medieval pogroms or Ellen Ross
domestic violence.[87]

[83] Klug, 'Oh, To Be in England', 34. The quote is from Moch, Moving Europeans, 147.
[84] Howard L. Malchow, Population Pressures: Emigration and Government in Late Nineteenth-Century
Britain (Palo Alto, 1979); Eric Richards, Britannia's Children: Emigration from England, Scotland,
Wales, and Ireland since 1600 (London, 2004); Stephen Constantine (ed.), Migrants and Empire:
British Settlement in the Dominions between the Wars (Manchester, 1990); on involuntary
emigration, see especially Philip Bean and Joy Melville's oral history project, Lost Children of the
Empire (London, 1989); Robert Hughes, The Fatal Shore (New York, 1987).
[85] Neville Kirk, Comrades and Cousins: Globalization, Workers and Labour Movements in Britain, the
USA and Australia from the 1880s to 1914 (London, 2003), part 3.
[86] John Springhall, Decolonization since 1945: The Collapse of European Overseas Empires (London,
2001), esp. 129, 133, 146–84; Caroline Elkins, Imperial Reckoning: The Untold Story of Britain's
Gulag in Kenya (New York, 2005).
[87] Ellen Ross, 'Fierce Questions and Taunts: Married Life in Working-Class London, 1870–1914',
Feminist Studies, 8 (1982), 575–602; David Nirenberg, Communities of Violence: Persecution of
Minorities in the Middle Ages (Princeton, 1996).

Complete analysis must account not only for migrants' agency but state and industrial impositions.[88] Future research must enquire how relations among migrants and between migrants and natives became complicated not only by cultural, religious or racial differences but further stressed or eased by economic instability, class, gender and sexual relations, imperial dynamics and local contexts. Examining these multiple dimensions of inclusion and 'otherness' may deepen our understanding that 'racial' conflict did not arrive in Britain with colonised subjects but inhered in Britain's 'imperial social formation'.[89]

A CASE STUDY: SOUTH SHIELDS 1841–1939

My ongoing research on industrial South Shields seeks to account for local and global as well as national and imperial dynamics shaping demographic diversity and migrant–native relations. A surprising volume and variety of overseas migrants passed through or settled in Victorian South Shields, even before migration became a public issue. Each census from 1841 through 1901 revealed overseas-born people living in the town, and their numbers and proportion increased steadily throughout the century. Mirroring national trends, the overseas-born population of South Shields grew, from 32 in 23,000 or .13% in 1841 to 929 in 78,391 or 1.18% in 1891.[90] In its preponderance of men South Shields' foreign-born population proved typical rather than atypical of long-distance migrants to other industrial towns. As in the country as a whole, Germans constituted the largest single group throughout the nineteenth century, followed by Norwegians, rivalled in numbers only by Arabs from the Yemen and East Africa who arrived in the twentieth century.

Overseas migrants hardly remained isolated in Victorian South Shields: census returns show most resided with or were related to native-born residents, and many enjoyed strong personal relationships with other natives. Evidence from naturalisation case files illustrates how nineteenth-century migrants became incorporated into British society through local personal networks and cultural practices such as work, marriage and kinship.[91] This contrasts with John Foster's results which showed significant

---

[88] See, for example, several essays in James and Harris, *Inside Babylon*.
[89] Mrinalini Sinha, *Colonial Masculinity: The 'Manly Englishman' and the 'Effeminate Bengali' in the Late Nineteenth Century* (Manchester, 1995).
[90] My tabulation of the 1901 census remains incomplete at this writing.
[91] Laura Tabili, '"Having Lived Close Beside Them All the Time": Negotiating National Identities Through Personal Networks', *Journal of Social History*, 39 (2) (2005), 59–80.

segregation between the Irish and natives in mid-century South Shields, measured in residential patterns and endogamy.[92] The explanation may lie in overseas migrants' relative affluence: whereas the town's workforce generally practised semi-skilled occupations threatened by the unskilled Irish, whom Victorian employers deployed as strike-breakers,[93] international migrants tended to be skilled workmen and small shopkeepers with independent means, however modest.[94] By far the largest such group, Germans constituted a recognisable community with shops, a church and a high proportion of endogamous households. In South Shields, only Jews and, in the 1920s and 1930s, Arabs, formed similarly visible communities.

Sailors, more similar in class character to the natives and Irish, made up the largest and steadily increasing occupational group by far, accounting for more than one-third of the town's male labour force in the 1840s and 20.5% of all wage earners in 1891,[95] drawn from across the globe, but mostly northern Europe, Scandinavia and, in the twentieth century, the Baltic and the Gulf of Aden. Tyneside arguably became a 'zone of contact', a borderland or frontier analogous to Gilroy's Black Atlantic: there, diverse people converged and dispersed, dissolving boundaries between Britons and 'others', and exemplifying circulation rather than unidirectional and finite movement as the characteristic pattern of human mobility.[96] As the expanding industry recruited non-British seafarers after 1851, many ports in Britain, a maritime society, likely assumed this character.

Tyneside's economy relied substantially on state expenditures for railroads, battleships and other infrastructure locally and in the overseas Empire. Thus it depended 'on the subordination of other economies' including colonial

---

[92] *Class Struggle and the Industrial Revolution: Early Industrial Capitalism in Three English Towns* (London, 1979), 128–9. Pooley found enclavement might occur involuntarily due to poverty and discrimination, or voluntarily due to cultural cohesion, manifested in institutions such as churches, in 'The Residential Segregation of Migrant Communities'.

[93] J. Carney, R. Hudson, G. Ive and J. Lewis, 'Regional Underdevelopment in Late Capitalism: A Study of the Northeast of England', in I. Masser (ed.), *Theory and Practice in Regional Science* (London, 1976), 18.

[94] That is, classes iv vs iii or ii on the Armstrong-Booth occupational scales. W. A. Armstrong, 'The Use of Information About Occupation', in E. A. Wrigley (ed.), *Nineteenth-Century Society: Essays in the Use of Quantitative Methods for the Study of Social Data* (Cambridge, 1972), 191–310, esp. tables 215f.

[95] Foster, *Class Struggle and the Industrial Revolution*, 90; J. W. House, *North-Eastern England: Population Movements and the Landscape Since the Early Nineteenth Century* (Newcastle, 1954), 60.

[96] Zolberg, 'International Migration Policies', 243, 245. On 'contact zones', see Peter Sahlins, *Boundaries: The Making of France and Spain in the Pyrenees* (Berkeley, 1989), 4–5; Mary Louise Pratt, *Imperial Eyes: Travel Writing and Transculturation* (London, 1992), 4, 6; also Gilroy, Fisher, Duffield and Green cited above.

ones, formal and informal.[97] Yet colonised people and other empires increasingly contested this privileged and ultimately precarious position.

With the new century, the town's social fluidity diminished due to deepening imperial crisis, reflected in economic contraction and intensified scrutiny of overseas migrants. Shifting state and industrial policies, driven by global competition for imperial and industrial advantage, increasingly impinged on local social relations, conflicting with the survival strategies as well as the loyalties and sensibilities of local people. The state removed discretion over naturalisation from local residents to industry and the military, and mariners became subject to increasingly intensive surveillance, policing and manipulation, segregating them from land-based society, curtailing their freedom of movement and inhibiting their incorporation into local society. The First World War, climaxing decades of Anglo-German imperial rivalry, overnight made enemy aliens of long-standing German residents and their families, subjecting them to internment, press calumny, mob violence and ultimately deportation.

Before and during the war a new group of migrants became visible in South Shields: mariners from Britain's newly acquired possessions in Aden, the Yemen and East Africa. South Shields' Arab community formed in the same decades as Britain became increasingly inhospitable to overseas migrants, including colonial subjects, due to imperial and industrial crises. Attacks on Arabs in 1919 and 1930 appear analogous to those on the Irish in the nineteenth century, stemming from a common structural position: competing with locals for unskilled labour in a depressed labour market. Yet some processes of incorporation, such as intermarriage, co-residence and naturalisation, remained available to Arabs in the 1920s and 1930s as they had to previous migrants. Migrant–native relations hardly reflected rigid 'othering' binarisms, instead responding to class positionality, economic and industrial shifts, gender and social relations, and local, national, imperial and global dynamics.

CONCLUSION

As we consider imperial influences on domestic social relations, we discover that arguments attributing hostility towards 'internal others' to

---

[97] John Foster, 'South Shields Labour Movement in the 1830's and 1840's', *North East Labour History Bulletin*, 4 (1970), 5; John Foster, 'Nineteenth Century Towns: A class dimension', in H. J. Dyos (ed.), *The Study of Urban History* (New York, 1968), 282; Anthony King, *Urbanism, Colonialism and the World-Economy: Cultural and Spatial Foundations of the World Urban System* (London, 1990), esp. 70, 74.

cultural differences, excessive numbers or endemic 'intolerance' neglect British and European empire building and imperial competition that rendered various migrants problematical. Britain's 'internal others' emerged due to their shifting positionality during recurrent crises of empire building, illustrated by the fate of Germans who had lived in Britain for decades. Domestic political advantage, class projects to divide and rule while promoting empire building, Anglo-Saxonism and other forms of racism informing the 'condition of England' question, and racialised global divisions of labour all reflected the imperatives of imperial political economy, while Britain's population circulated throughout the Empire and beyond it.

Scholarship about Britain's 'internal others' thus demands contextualisation within a broader challenge not only to the assumed homogeneity but to the geographical boundedness of British society. Britain has always been culturally diverse, and the boundaries and definitions of Britishness fluid, protean, contested and changeable over time.[98] Investigating processes that created 'others' and erased them from the historical landscape shows how repeated transformations in culture and identity and continually shifting boundaries between 'British' and 'others' responded to the broader, global context of competing empires.

[98] Samuel, *Island Stories*.

CHAPTER FOUR

At home with the Empire: the example of Ireland

Christine Kinealy

The position of Ireland within the British Empire, especially after 1801 when the United Kingdom of Great Britain and Ireland was created, divides both Irish and non-Irish historians. From this date, the political relationship between Ireland and Britain became paradoxical, with Ireland being part of the imperial parliament, yet treated by that body as a subordinate partner within the United Kingdom. Despite the new legislative framework resulting from the Union, Ireland was regarded as a colony, moreover, a dangerous one, as the intermittent rebellions attested.

The colonial association between Ireland and Britain was well established by the time of the Act of Union. It had originated in the twelfth century, although the whole country was not under English control until the early seventeenth century.[1] Even before this time, there were attempts to control Ireland's political, economic and cultural traditions through a combination of military and legislative means and to segregate natives and settlers.[2] From the thirteenth century, Ireland had possessed its own parliament, but after 1494 its policy-making had been subjugated to the English parliament. It was not until 1782 that the Irish parliament received limited legislative autonomy, although Catholics remained excluded. For some Irish nationalists, inspired by the revolutions in Colonial America and France, this concession was too little. An unsuccessful republican uprising in 1798 brought this phase of limited self-government to an end and precipitated the Act of Union. This legislation, which created the United Kingdom of Great Britain and Ireland, abolished the parliament in Dublin and brought Irish representatives into the imperial parliament in

---

[1] In 1603, Hugh O'Neill surrendered to Queen Elizabeth (who was dead). The crowning of James VI of Scotland as James I of England in the same year, created a *British* monarch.

[2] The Statutes of Kilkenny (1366) attempted to halt the Gaelicisation of the English colony by prohibiting social relations between the colonisers and the native Irish; in the fifteenth century, a ditch (pale) was built around the area of English rule. See, S. J. Connolly (ed.), *The Oxford Companion to Irish History* (Oxford, 1998), 286–7, 424–5.

London. Irish historians, however, have taken diametrically opposing views of whether or not Ireland was a colony during these centuries.[3]

The Union was not achieved by consensus, but was forced on the Irish parliament.[4] As a consequence, Ireland occupied a distinctive position within the British Empire, becoming part of the metropolitan core while simultaneously remaining a crucial component of the imperial project.[5] Regardless of the Union, visible vestiges of a colonial relationship continued. An Irish Executive, based in Dublin Castle, remained, consisting of a Viceroy (or Lord Lieutenant) assisted by a Chief Secretary and Under-Secretary, all of whom were appointed in London and answerable directly to the British Premier. The office of Viceroy survived until 1922.[6] Less visibly, but no less importantly, after 1801 the economic, political, social and cultural interests of Ireland remained secondary to those of Britain. The disastrous consequence of this mindset was most evident during the Great Famine of 1845 to 1852, when Ireland lost over one-quarter of her population.

After 1801, the Irish presence within both the United Kingdom and the imperial parliament placed Irish issues at the heart of British politics. Moreover, Ireland's standing within the Empire changed as Irish people existed 'not simply as imperial subjects, but also as players in the Empire at large: as migrants and settlers, merchants and adventurers, soldiers and administrators, doctors and missionaries'.[7] To what extent did the Irish population view themselves as part of the imperial core, and were they accepted as such? Was it possible for Ireland to be both imperial and colonial concurrently and for its people to be simultaneously colonisers and colonised?[8]

Despite the exceptional nature of the Irish colonial encounter, there were parallels with other parts of the British Empire, especially with reference to cultural stereotyping, law and order, voting rights, trade, famine and education. In each of these areas, Ireland was treated differently from the rest of the United Kingdom, having more in common with other parts of

---

[3] For opposing views see, Jane H. Ohlmeyer, 'A Laboratory for Empire?: Early Modern Ireland and English Imperialism', in Kevin Kenny, *Ireland and the British Empire* (Oxford, 2004), 28–9, and S. Ellis, 'Representations of the Past in Ireland: Whose Past and Whose Present?', *Irish Historical Studies*, 27 (1991), 294.

[4] Alvin Jackson, 'The Irish Act of Union', *History Today*, 51(1) (January 2001), 19–25.

[5] See Christine Kinealy, *A Disunited Kingdom? England, Ireland, Scotland and Wales 1800–1949* (Cambridge, 1999) and Michael Hechter, *Internal Colonialism: The Celtic Fringe in British National Development, 1536–1966* (Berkeley, 1975).

[6] Its abolition was debated in the British parliament in 1823, 1830, 1844, 1850, 1857 and 1858. See R. B. McDowell, *The Irish Administration 1801–1914* (London, 1964).

[7] Kevin Kenny, 'Ireland and the British Empire: An Introduction', in his *Ireland and the British Empire*, 4.

[8] See Keith Jeffery (ed.), *'An Irish Empire'? Aspects of Ireland and the British Empire* (Manchester, 1996).

the Empire.[9] Furthermore, Irish resistance to colonialism, including the campaign for Catholic Emancipation, the struggle for independence and the agitation for land reform, were watched by nationalist groups elsewhere.[10] Yet, by the beginning of the twentieth century, other countries within the Empire had achieved more political independence than Ireland, and they were arguing that similar rights should extend to Ireland. Thus, in 1903 and 1906, the Canadian House of Commons and the Australian Legislature respectively passed measures supporting Irish Home Rule.[11] While the Irish nationalist movement was well organised, even by European standards, concurrently, loyalism to the Union, the crown and the Empire, as embodied by the Orange Order, provided a model of allegiance for pro-Empire groups. Overall, responses to the Union within Ireland (both for and against) changed the nature of the British political landscape, while forcing a reconsideration of Britain's other colonial relationships in the nineteenth and twentieth centuries.

This chapter examines the relationship between Ireland and Britain, and between Ireland and the Empire, from the passage of the Act of Union to the Partition of Ireland in 1920. A central contention is that, even after 1801, Ireland continued to be treated as a colony by successive British administrations, albeit as a distinctive one because of its constitutional position within the United Kingdom. Furthermore, it is argued that Irish history during this period can be understood only in the context of a colonial association with Britain.

WAS IRELAND A COLONY?

The opinion that Ireland was not a colony has had powerful advocates among British and Irish historians, from Thomas Babington Macaulay in the 1840s and 1850s[12] to Roy Foster and Steven Ellis at the end of the twentieth century. Arguing from different perspectives, they have each portrayed Irish history as assimilated history, and the association with Britain and its empire as benign.[13] A number of influential historians have

---

[9] For example, Amartya Sen, *Poverty and Famine: An Essay on Entitlement and Deprivation* (Oxford, 1981).

[10] Tony Ballantyne, 'The Sinews of Empire: Ireland, India and the Construction of British Colonial Knowledge', in Terence McDonough (ed.), *Was Ireland a Colony? Economics, Politics and Culture in Nineteenth-Century Ireland* (Dublin, 2005), 145–64.

[11] Jeffery, 'Introduction', in *An Irish Empire*, 6.   [12] See Catherine Hall, Chapter 2.

[13] Ellis, 'Representations of the Past in Ireland', 288–308; R. Foster, 'History and the Irish Question', in *Paddy and Mr Punch: Connections in English and Irish History* (London, 1993), 1–20. Foster prefers to talk about England, not Britain, regarding Ireland.

denied the existence of anti-Irish racism in Britain.[14] At the beginning of
the twenty-first century, these interpretations have been championed by
Stephen Howe, who rejects the term 'colonial' as valid when applied to
nineteenth-century Ireland.[15] Such contentions, however, disregard the
fact that Ireland was not treated as an equal partner within the United
Kingdom, while successive British governments viewed her retention
within the Empire as crucial to the maintenance of the imperial project.
Moreover, as Tony Ballantyne has argued, Ireland provided imperial
administrators with an expertise and 'colonial knowledge' that they
deployed in other sites of empire, most notably India.[16]

Seeing Ireland in its wider colonial context has been championed by
some younger Irish historians, who have broadened the debate beyond the
discipline of history, most strikingly in the field of literary and cultural
criticism. The fact that the debate continues to be polarised is evident in
the collection of interdisciplinary essays, published in 2005, entitled *Was
Ireland a Colony? Economics, Politics and Culture in Nineteenth-Century
Ireland.* In the Introduction, the editor averred that:

The colonial experience of Ireland cannot be ignored in the development of a
complete understanding of the nineteenth century. Further, an account of
colonialism is broadly necessary in the realms of economics, politics, ideology
and culture.[17]

In the same volume, Terry Eagleton suggested that 'at different times and
in different places, several of those forms of colonialism have complexly
co-existed'.[18]

A combination of geographic, historic, political and economic factors
ensured that the political association between Ireland and Britain would be
unique. The longevity of their relationship, the geographical proximity of
the islands, the changing balance of power between those who supported
union with Britain and those who desired independence, the oscillation
between reform and revolution by nationalists, and the presence of large
numbers of Irish people in Britain, ensured that the relationship between
metropole and colony would be different from that of other parts of the

---

[14] Roy Foster draws heavily on the research of Sheridan Gilley; see Foster, 'We Are All Revisionists
Now', *Irish Review*, 1 (1986), 1–5.
[15] Stephen Howe, *Ireland and Empire: Colonial Legacies in Irish History and Culture* (Oxford, 2002),
32–9. Also see J. Ruane, 'Colonialism and Interpretation of Irish Historical Development', in
M. Silverman and P. H. Gulliver (eds.), *Approaching the Past: Historical Anthropology through Irish
Case Studies* (New York, 1992), 296–7.
[16] Ballantyne, 'Sinews of Empire', *Was Ireland a Colony?*, 155.
[17] *Ibid.*, Terrence McDonough, 'Introduction', vi.
[18] *Ibid.*, Terry Eagleton, 'Afterword: Ireland and Colonialism', 326, 329.

Empire. Distinction and difference within the colonial framework have been highlighted by Simon Schama who, like Howe, juxtaposed the Irish experience with that of India, although coming to a different conclusion. Schama cited the Irish Famine as a tragic example of imperial misgovernment under the guise of liberal administration. He believed that the British determination to hold on to empire at all costs, including through the use of violence, meant that opportunities for reform and a constitutional path to self-government were lost. This response, in turn, made extremism, bloodshed and separatism inevitable within the component parts of the Empire, notably in Ireland and India.[19] The process of letting go of empire proved to be ungainly, ungracious, brutal and piecemeal, while creating as many new problems as it seemed to resolve. Arguing from different perspectives, what Howe, Schama, Eagleton and others confirm is that there is no single model of colonial experience or of colonial disengagement.

LOCATING IRELAND

Placing Ireland within the historiography of Britain and the British Empire has proved problematic for some historians, especially when dealing with the nineteenth century, when Irish MPs sat in the imperial parliament. The reluctance of British historians to integrate Ireland into their studies is exemplified by Linda Colley's influential *Britons: Forging the Nation, 1707–1837*, in which she assigns to France a more central role in the creation of a British identity than Ireland, by virtue of their 'otherness'. However, if, as she also argues, British national identity was 'forged' in this period, thus uniting the peoples of England, Scotland and Wales, regardless of a legislative change in 1801, Irish people remained outside this invisible bond.[20] Given the omission of Ireland from historical definitions of Britishness, it is ironic that at the beginning of the twenty-first century the most 'volatile crucible' of British identity was located in Northern Ireland.[21]

Ireland's position in the British Empire has been similarly challenging for both Irish and non-Irish historians. At the centre of the debate is the question of whether Ireland continued to be a colony after 1801. The

---

[19] Simon Schama, *A History of Britain: The Fate of Empire 1776–2000* (New York, 2003).

[20] Linda Colley, *Britons: Forging the Nation, 1707–1837* (New Haven, 1992).

[21] Willy Maly, 'Nationalism and Revisionism: Ambivalences and Dissensus', in Scott Brewster, Virginia Crossman, Fiona Beckett and David Alderson (eds.), *Ireland in Proximity: History, Gender, Space* (London, 1999), 54; Christine Kinealy, 'The Orange Order and Representations of Britishness', in S. Caunce, E. Mazierska, S. Sydney-Smith and John Walton (eds.), *Relocating Britishness* (Manchester, 2004), 217–36.

discussion has largely followed existing ideological divisions, with conservative and revisionist historians refusing to discuss Irish history within an imperial context.[22] Consequently, key developments in Irish history, such as the Great Famine, have been written about without reference to her colonial relationship with Britain.[23] The domination of revisionism among Irish historians since the 1930s acted as an invisible censor, closing down debate in areas considered to be controversial or anti-British.[24] Brendan Bradshaw was one of the first historians to challenge the revisionist stranglehold in a controversial article first published in 1989, in which he argued that Ireland's nationalist traditions could not be separated from her colonial status. He also suggested that Ireland's uniqueness was due to her position as the only European colony.[25] In 1991, Kevin Whelan reproached revisionist historians for removing national identity and the colonial experience from Ireland's past, for their own political and ideological reasons, and appealed for a post-revisionist agenda for Irish history.[26] Revisionism, however, was not systematically challenged until the mid-1990s, when a reappraisal of the Great Famine provided a prism for re-examining the relationship between Britain and Ireland in the nineteenth century.[27] Significantly, some of the new research located the experience of the Famine in the context of Ireland's colonial status, thus opening a fresh debate about Ireland's position within the British Empire.[28] According to Tony Ballantyne, divisions among Irish historians are entrenched because:

The question of Ireland's relationship to Britain and Britain's imperial project stands at the heart of recent debates over revisionist approaches to the interpretations of the Irish past. Ireland's exact status within the empire ... [is] at the heart of competing visions of Ireland's present and future.[29]

---

[22] The revisionist approach originated in the 1930s to counter a simplistic nationalist interpretation of Irish history. It claimed to be objective and apolitical; a claim that was hard to sustain after 1969 when revisionism became overtly anti-nationalist.

[23] Roy Foster's *Modern Ireland* (London, 1988) has been described by Tim Pat Coogan as 'the bible' of revisionism.

[24] Maley, 'Nationalism', in *Ireland in Proximity*, 20–5; Christine Kinealy, 'Beyond Revisionism: Reassessing the Irish Famine', *History Ireland*, 4(4) (Winter 1995).

[25] B. Bradshaw, 'Nationalism and Historical Scholarship in Modern Ireland', in C. Brady (ed.), *Interpreting Irish History: The Debate on Historical Revisionism 1938–1994* (Dublin, 1994), 191–216.

[26] K. Whelan, 'Come All You Staunch Revisionists: Towards a Post-revisionist Agenda for Irish History', *Irish Reporter*, 2 (1991), 23–6.

[27] Revisionists generally claim that the Famine was inevitable, not a watershed in Irish development, and that the British government's response was adequate.

[28] Christine Kinealy, 'Was Ireland a Colony? The Evidence of the Great Famine', in McDonough (ed.), *Was Ireland a Colony?*, 48–67.

[29] Ballantyne, 'Sinews of Empire', in *Was Ireland a Colony?*, 145. See also, Virginia Crossman, 'Introduction', in *Ireland in Proximity*, 9.

A UNITED KINGDOM?

Even before the nineteenth century, the political relationship between Ireland and Britain differed from colonial relationships elsewhere, both in origin and in day-to-day governance. Since the Henrician Reformation in the sixteenth century, the Anglican Church had been the state church in Ireland: a situation that was upheld by the Act of Union. The Penal Laws, introduced after 1790, disadvantaged both Catholics and nonconformists.[30] After 1728, also, only Protestants could vote or be members of the Dublin parliament, making it unrepresentative of over 80 per cent of the population. At the end of the eighteenth century, most of the Penal Laws were removed, although Catholics remained unable to sit in parliament until 1829. Not all Irish Protestants supported the involvement of Britain in Irish affairs. A movement for more political independence at the end of the eighteenth century was led by Irish Protestants. The resulting 'Grattan's Parliament' came into existence in 1782. Catholics could neither vote nor sit in it and Westminster retained executive powers. Inspired by events in France, a Protestant lawyer, Theobald Wolfe Tone, formed the United Irishmen, which demanded the establishment of a democratic, non-sectarian Irish Republic. Draconian political repression by the British government precipitated a series of uprisings throughout Ireland in 1798.

The 1798 rebellion was brutally suppressed, resulting in approximately 30,000 Irish casualties. The British government then acted swiftly to change the political relationship with Ireland, no longer trusting the Protestant parliament to govern the country. The abolition of the Irish legislature was regarded as essential to safeguard not only Britain, but also her empire. Thus, the Irish Lord Lieutenant, Lord Cornwallis, declared unequivocally that 'without a union the British empire must be dissolved'.[31] This view was endorsed by the Prime Minister, William Pitt, who argued that a union would make Ireland 'more free and more happy', but, more importantly, it would 'make the empire more powerful and secure'.[32] When members of the Irish parliament refused to vote themselves out of existence, the British government combined incentives with threats to achieve its desired end. Consequently, on 1 January 1801, the United Kingdom was born. Disappointment immediately followed.

---

[30] For example, Catholics could not purchase or inherit property, build schools or churches, own a gun, vote, join the professions, etc.
[31] Patrick M. Geoghegan, *The Irish Act of Union: A Study in High Politics, 1798–1801* (Dublin, 1999), 85.
[32] *Ibid.*, 95.

Pitt had promised that Catholic Emancipation (the right to sit in parliament) and state subsidies to Catholic priests would follow but, confronted with George III's opposition, he backed down: an inauspicious
start to the new relationship and an early reminder of the uneven balance
of power. Nor were the king's interventions over. In 1807 he 'dissolved a
parliament less than one year old so as to increase the strength of a
ministry hostile to Catholic Emancipation'.[33] Clearly, Catholics were to
remain subordinate within the association.

The Act of Union completed the process of creating a unitary British
state, centred on England.[34] In 1801, 100 Irish MPs (105 after 1832) entered
the imperial parliament, where they contributed to policy-making for
Ireland, the United Kingdom and the Empire. Throughout the nineteenth
century, British politics was dominated by interactions with Ireland and, by
the 1880s, the two main political parties were distinguished and separated
by their attitude to Irish independence. Irish issues also defined or
destroyed the careers of politicians as diverse as William Pitt, Robert Peel,
William Gladstone, Randolph Churchill and David Lloyd George.

The paradoxical nature of Ireland's relationship with Britain after 1801
was evident in the legislation passed by the imperial parliament on issues
such as poor relief, education, and law and order, when Ireland was
treated distinctively from other parts of the United Kingdom, suggesting
that her colonial status had not ended. Some historians have suggested
that in areas of social legislation, Ireland 'functioned as a testing ground
for new legislation and systems of government'.[35] The varied approach
was evident in the Irish Poor Law of 1838, which treated Irish paupers
more harshly than their counterparts elsewhere in the United Kingdom.
No right to relief existed in Ireland and the poor could receive assistance
only inside the newly built workhouses.[36] These restrictions had sombre
implications during the Famine, when many workhouses became full and
no alternative relief could be offered.[37]

Even after 1801, there were attempts to subjugate Irish culture and
identity, and to impose the values of the metropole. The 1831 Education Act
provided for all instruction to be carried out through the English language,

[33] David Cannadine, 'The British Monarchy, c. 1820–1977', in Eric Hobsbawm and Terence Ranger
   (eds.), *The Invention of Tradition* (Cambridge, 1983), 108.
[34] Hechter, *Internal Colonialism*, describes it as 'internal colonialism' although his work has been
   criticised, notably by Welsh historians.
[35] Ballantyne, 'Sinews of Empire', in *Was Ireland a Colony?*, 158.
[36] 1 and 2 Vic. c. 56. An Act for the more Effectual Relief of the Destitute Poor in Ireland (1838 Poor
   Law Act).
[37] Christine Kinealy, *This Great Calamity: The Irish Famine 1845–52* (Dublin, 1994 and 2006), 106–35.

and while the school curriculum included 'British poets', neither Irish history nor the Irish language were taught. Charles Gavan Duffy, a founder of the *Nation* newspaper claimed in 1842 that while British institutions and heroes were promoted in Ireland, the state 'deliberately starved or suppressed' Irish culture.[38] Consequently, the *Nation* aimed to instil in Irish people a sense of their historical, cultural and intellectual heritage.

Politically, Irish people remained disadvantaged as a consequence of franchise restrictions. The granting of Catholic Emancipation in 1829, while giving Catholics the right to sit in parliament, simultaneously disenfranchised 40-shilling freeholders, who were mainly Catholic. In the wake of the 1832 Reform Act, while one in seven men in England could vote, the figure was one in twenty in Ireland.[39] In 1840, following an attempt to further limit the Irish franchise, O'Connell renewed his agitation for repeal of the Act of Union on the grounds that Ireland had been denied 'an extension of the franchise and full equality of rights within Britain'.[40]

Regardless of her new constitutional position, Ireland continued to be politically turbulent, thus occupying a disproportionate amount of parliamentary time. Throughout the nineteenth century, Irish politics was dominated by the demand for self-government. Yet varieties of nationalism coexisted, ranging from the republicanism of the United Irishmen and the Fenians, to the constitutional methods favoured by Daniel O'Connell and Charles Stewart Parnell. The latter approach favoured Ireland remaining within the Empire and enjoyed majority support. The unwillingness of the British parliament to allow even a limited form of Home Rule contributed to the persistence of republican nationalism, which was manifested through the rebellions of 1803, 1848, 1867 and 1916.

Nationalist agitation, and its counterpart loyalist and unionist activities, not only kept Irish issues to the forefront in Westminster, but meant that there was a high military and police presence in Ireland. Furthermore, the Irish constabulary force established in 1814 was, from the outset, armed, unlike police in the rest of the United Kingdom. Generally, in the area of law and order, Ireland was treated more harshly, with special measures being introduced, to supplement the existing criminal justice system.[41] While political agitation in Britain was mostly dealt with

---

[38] Charles Gavan Duffy, *Four Years of Irish History* (London, 1883), 82.
[39] Kinealy, *Disunited Kingdom, passim.*
[40] *Journal of the British Empire,* 17 July 1840.
[41] Insurrection Acts were in force in 1796–1802, 1807–10, 1814–18 and 1822–5. In 1833 (because of the 'Tithe War') the Suppression of Disturbances Act was introduced, providing for trial by military courts rather than magistrates. Similar measures remained in force, intermittently, up to the Partition.

under common law, in Ireland emergency legislation was introduced, in the form of draconian coercion Acts.[42] Additionally, Habeas Corpus was suspended between 1796 and 1806, between 1848 and 1849, and again from 1866 to 1869, each time coinciding with renewed republican agitation.

Full economic integration with Britain never materialised, and Ireland continued to play a subordinate role within the relationship, functioning as a peripheral region that provided cheap labour and cheap raw materials to the metropole.[43] Since the 1780s Britain had depended on Ireland as a main supplier of corn and, by the eve of the Great Famine, was receiving enough Irish corn to feed two million people annually. Vast amounts of other foodstuffs were also imported from Ireland.[44] How could a country with such a massive agricultural surplus be plunged into a devastating famine, as occurred after 1845?

FAMINE: AN IMPERIAL CALAMITY?

Within fifty years of the Act of Union being passed, a famine occurred in Ireland that was unprecedented in its longevity and impact. It resulted in the death of over one million people and the emigration of approximately two million, reducing the Irish population by almost one-third. The longer-term impact of the crisis was equally devastating, with the population dropping to only four and a half million by 1901. Neither the wealth of the United Kingdom nor the resources of the British Empire protected the Irish poor from the destructive impact of seven years of food shortages. Consequently, a famine of acute severity occurred, not merely at the centre of the Empire, but within a constituent part of the United Kingdom. The situation in Ireland dominated parliamentary debates between 1845 and 1851, while the arrival of famine refugees in cities such as Liverpool and Manchester added to the existing social problems of these areas, and increased ethnic tensions and anti-Catholic hostility.[45]

The British government's response to the Famine demonstrated that Ireland was not an equal partner within the United Kingdom and that the needs of the Irish were of less importance than those of people in the

---

[42] The government responded to the repeal agitation with the Crime and Outrage Act (1847), which was regularly renewed and, in 1848, habeas corpus was suspended. Other measures included the Prevention of Crime Act (1882–5), the Criminal Law, and the Procedure Act (1887), a permanent measure.

[43] R. Munck, *The Irish Economy: Results and Prospects* (London, 1993).

[44] Roger Scola, *Feeding the Victorian City: The Food Supply of Manchester 1780 to 1870* (Manchester, 1992).

[45] This hostility was evident during the introduction of the Ecclesiastical Titles Act in 1851.

metropole.[46] In Ireland, uniquely within the United Kingdom, no right to poor relief existed and outdoor relief was illegal. Moreover, the Irish Poor Law did not include a Law of Settlement, unlike in England, Wales and Scotland, confirming the different status of Irish paupers from British ones. The consequence was that if Irish immigrants sought relief in Britain, they could be transported back to Ireland, which deterred even the destitute from seeking assistance.[47]

Throughout the course of the Famine, despite palpable evidence of suffering and hunger, relief policies increasingly prioritised the regeneration of the Irish economy over the needs of the poor. Furthermore, the interests of the metropole were protected, even if the outcome was damaging to Ireland. After 1845, the British government refused to close the Irish ports to prevent food exports (despite requests to do so), choosing to leave the movement of food to the merchant class and the vagaries of an underdeveloped import sector and unregulated distribution network. Consequently, large amounts of foodstuffs were exported from Ireland to Britain.[48] When the Irish Viceroy, Lord Clarendon, arrived in Dublin in 1847, he was appalled by the consequences of his government's policies and privately informed the Prime Minister, Lord John Russell, that 'No-one could now venture to dispute the fact that Ireland had been sacrificed to the London corn-dealers because you were a member for the City, and that no distress would have occurred if the exportation of Irish grain had been prohibited.'[49]

Successive relief measures, including the Poor Law Extension Act of 1847 and the Rate-in-Aid Act of 1849, transferred the financial burden for intervention to Irish taxpayers, thus demonstrating that, within the metropole, the Famine was viewed as neither a British nor an imperial responsibility.[50] Increasing the tax burden on Irish landowners contributed to an escalation in evictions, adding homelessness to the problem of hunger. The process was largely unregulated, leading Clarendon to inform Russell that 'I don't think there is another legislature in Europe that would disregard such suffering as now exists in the west of Ireland, or coldly persist in a policy of extermination.'[51] British officials, who were

---

[46] Kinealy, *Disunited Kingdom, passim*.

[47] Frank Neal, *Black '47: Britain and the Famine Irish* (London, 1998).

[48] Kinealy, *Great Irish Famine*, ch. 5. There are similarities with the British government's response to the Bengal Famine of 1943–5.

[49] Clarendon to Russell, Clarendon Papers, Bodleian Library, 12 July 1847.

[50] The London *Times* spearheaded a campaign against giving support to Ireland: *Times*, 10 October 1846, 4 October 1848.

[51] Clarendon to Russell, Clarendon Papers, Bodleian Library, 28 April 1849.

appointed to enquire into continuing high mortality in County Clare in 1850, were similarly critical, averring that:

Whether as regards the plain principles or humanity or the literal text and admitted principles of the Poor Law of 1847, a neglect of public duty has taken place and has occasioned a state of things disgraceful to a civilised age and country, for which some authority ought to be held responsible and would long since have been held responsible had these things occurred in any union in England.[52]

The treatment of Ireland after 1845 dismayed even traditional supporters of Britain and the Empire. At a meeting held in Dublin in January 1847, attended by landlords and the Irish upper middle classes, it was agreed that as the Famine was an 'imperial calamity' the Exchequer should finance the relief schemes.[53] The abandonment of the Irish poor dismayed a number of British politicians and administrators. Edward Twistleton, an Englishman who was in charge of the Irish Poor Law, argued that if the Act of Union had any validity, then the Irish poor should not be treated as separate entities during a crisis.[54] The radical Irish landlord and MP for Rochdale, William Sharman Crawford, repeatedly asked for more government intervention, pointing out that Irish taxes were paid into an imperial Treasury 'and placed at the disposal of an Imperial Legislature for the general purposes of the United Kingdom', and expenditure by the Treasury should similarly be used to benefit all portions of the United Kingdom.[55] These pleas were ignored and Ireland's treatment during the Famine confirmed that, despite the Act of Union, the humanitarian needs of the Irish people were secondary to the protection of the metropole. If, as the Famine demonstrated, the Irish people were unequal partners within the United Kingdom, what was their place within the British Empire?

INTERNAL DIVISIONS

The small landowning Anglo-Irish elite who controlled Irish politics in the nineteenth century were distinguished from the majority of the population by their religion, class and allegiance to the Union. While the Protestant Ascendancy was disliked and viewed as alien within Ireland, in

---

[52] *Report of the Select Committee appointed to enquire into the administration of the Poor Law in the Kilrush Union since 19 September 1848*, BPP, 1850 (613) xi, xiii.
[53] *Freeman's Journal*, 17 January 1847.
[54] Evidence of Edward Twistleton, *Select Committee on Irish Poor Law*, 1849, xv, 699–714.
[55] Parliamentary Debates, *Hansard*, 1 March 1849.

Britain they were widely regarded with disdain and as an impediment to modernisation. Consequently, their interests were marginalised within the British parliament, as was evident by the passage of the Encumbered Estates Acts of 1848 and 1849 and various Land Acts after 1870, all of which undermined them economically, and forced the sale of their properties.[56] The granting of various tenant rights constituted a social revolution and demonstrated that Ireland was treated differently from other parts of the United Kingdom, in order to keep the Empire intact. Gladstone's justification for the first Land Act of 1870 was that 'the end of our measure is to give peace and security to Ireland and through Ireland to the Empire'.[57] Moreover, just as the Famine had done, the legislation demonstrated that even the Protestant Ascendancy class were not accepted as partners within the Union, and were only given support when the interests of Empire were at stake. Nonetheless, throughout the nineteenth century identification with Britishness and empire was increasingly asserted.

The success of the Home Rule movement between 1885 and 1914 gave rise to a new form of militant unionism, in which the populist Orange Order played a key role. A further consequence was that politics in Ireland split along nationalist/Catholic and unionist/Protestant lines.[58] Thus, by the time of the General Election of 1885 (based on the new parliamentary franchise), political allegiances in Ireland had become polarised along denominational lines.[59] By the late 1880s, largely as a result of sectarian conflict, Belfast was the most policed town in the United Kingdom and possibly the Empire. An unfortunate consequence was that the middle ground in Irish politics and the non-sectarian aspirations of earlier generations of nationalists increasingly evaporated.[60] As a result, two distinctive colonial experiences coexisted in Ireland, which Pamela Clayton has characterised as 'Rebel Ireland' and the 'Imperial Province', that is, Ulster.[61] Increasingly, the latter was associated with a form of conservative Protestantism that cut across class divides. Meanwhile, Ireland's ambiguous colonial status meant that the opposing political traditions could diametrically represent themselves either as a partner and beneficiary, or as a subjugated colony, with each side prioritising what they wanted to.[62]

---

[56] Brewster et al., 'Introduction', in *Ireland in Proximity*, 2.

[57] Jeffery, 'Introduction', in *An Irish Empire*, 4, 16.   [58] *Ibid.*

[59] B. M. Walker, *Ulster Politics: The Formative Years 1868–86* (Belfast, 1989), *passim*.

[60] *Ibid.*, 176–7.

[61] *Ibid.* Clayton, 'Two Kinds of Colony', in *Was Ireland a Colony.*, 235–48.

[62] D. Fitzpatrick, quoted in Y. Whelan, 'The Construction and Destruction of a Colonial Landscape: Monuments to British Monarchs in Dublin Before and After Independence', *Journal of Historical Geography*, 28 (4) (2002, 508–33), 511.

Between 1880 and 1921, politicians in Westminster spent a disproportionate amount of time discussing Irish affairs. The Liberal Party, led by
Gladstone, supported Parnell and Home Rule, while the Tory Party,
encouraged by Randolph Churchill, allied with the Unionists. By doing so,
they kept Ireland at the forefront of British parliamentary debate and
energised British politics. In particular, Irish independence increased the
appeal of the Tory Party to British working-class voters. For the Liberal
Party, however, their close association with Home Rule after 1880 sowed
the seeds of their ultimate demise.

Within Ireland, a version of Britishness was developing that was rooted
in the reconstruction of a series of conflicts that had taken place in Ireland
in the seventeenth century, but had been part of wider British and
European power struggles. These events, notably the Battle of the Boyne
in 1690, left an enduring legacy on both Irish and British politics. The
vision of a Protestant victory over Catholics was perpetuated by the anti-
Catholic Orange Order, which was formed in County Armagh in 1795,
partly in response to the growth of republicanism.[63] The Orange Order
spread quickly, especially when Protestants felt their interests were being
threatened. In 1832, alarmed by the granting of Catholic Emancipation,
the Orange Order announced their willingness to put down all 'Catholic'
rebellions and thus maintain 'the integrity of the Empire'.[64]

By 1803, Orange lodges had been established in Britain and were then
formed throughout the British Empire, mostly by Protestant Irishmen
serving in the British army.[65] Consequently, at the same time that Ireland
was inspiring nationalist movements throughout the Empire, she was
simultaneously exporting the ideology of the conservative, anti-Catholic
and sectarian Orange Order to the same locations. Within Britain, 'the
Irish Orange Order provided the model for ultra Tories in England who
wanted to harness working class support in defence of the Church and
the Constitution'.[66] This strategy was particularly important to the Tory
Party following the 1884 extension of the parliamentary franchise. The
impact of Irish sectarian divisions was not confined to high politics but,
according to Donald MacRaild, 'Orangeism became the very symbol of
British patriotism; once appropriated by the Tories, it recruited strongly

---

[63] Jim Smyth, 'The Men of No Popery: The Origins of the Orange Order', *History Ireland* (1995), 52.
[64] Resolution of the Grand Orange Lodge, Beresford Papers, Manuscript Room, Trinity College,
Dublin, ms.2319, 21 January 1832.
[65] *Report of Select Committee to Inquire into the Nature, Character, Extent and Tendency of Orange
Lodges*, British Parliamentary Papers, 1835, xv.
[66] Frank Neal, *Sectarian Violence: The Liverpool Experience 1819–1914: An Aspect of Anglo-Irish History*
(Manchester, 1988), x.

among Protestant workers in Liverpool and other British cities with no Ulster or Irish connections'.[67] Due to the presence of large numbers of both Catholic and Protestant immigrants in Liverpool, political divisions emulated those in Ireland, with constitutional nationalism emerging triumphant following the election of T. P. O'Connor to a Liverpool constituency in 1885. He served as an Irish Nationalist MP until 1929, outlasting the Partition of Ireland. At the same time, his opponents perpetuated and exploited sectarian tensions, enabling 'the Liverpool Conservative Party to harness Protestant fears and prejudices for political ends' beyond the Second World War.[68] Ireland, therefore, shaped British politics at both local and national levels even after 1921.

The question of Ireland's place within the Empire if Home Rule was granted was of little concern to many nationalists during this period. However, opponents of Home Rule articulated their hostility in terms of the damage that it would do to the cohesion of the British Empire, possibly acting as a spur to other imperial movements for independence.[69] This contention was marshalled to bolster the Unionist position, notably during the campaign to resist the passing of the 1912 Home Rule bill, when 'the defence of the empire' was frequently invoked.[70] Increasingly, a Unionist identity was being forged, which argued that nation, union and empire were indivisible.[71] Simultaneously, it was becoming more associated with one place: Ulster.[72]

AT HOME? THE IRISH IN BRITAIN

Despite the Act of Union, the Irish in Britain were still regarded as a threat to the political stability and economic prosperity of the metropole. In 1826, Thomas Malthus, an influential commentator on population growth, warned a parliamentary committee that Irish emigration to England, if unchecked, could have a negative impact on the British economy.[73] The

---

[67] Donald MacRaild (ed.), *The Great Famine and Beyond: Irish Migration in Britain in the Nineteenth and Twentieth Centuries* (Dublin, 2000), 142.

[68] *Ibid.*, xi.

[69] George Boyce, 'British Conservative Opinion, the Ulster Question and the Partition of Ireland 1919–21', *Irish Historical Studies*, 17 (65) (1970).

[70] Jonathan Moore, *Ulster Unionism and the British Conservative Party: A Study of a Failed Marriage* (London, 1997), 7.

[71] Mark McGovern, 'The Siege of Derry', in D. George Boyce and Roger Swift (eds.), *Problems and Perspectives in Irish History since 1800* (Dublin, 2003), 52.

[72] Kinealy, 'The Orange Order and Britishness', 25.

[73] Thomas Robert Malthus, *Essay on the Principle of Population* (first pub. 1798; Harmondsworth, 1970), 118–19.

perception of Ireland as a financial drain on Britain climaxed during the Famine years, when publications as influential as *The Times*, *Punch* and the *Illustrated London News* suggested that British taxpayers should not have to pay for Irish poor relief.[74] The cultural inferiority of Irish people was articulated by influential writers and intellectuals as diverse as J. A. Froude, Charles Dickens, Charles Kingsley and Friedrich Engels, all of whom accepted and perpetuated these racialised characterisations.[75] The written negative depictions of the Irish were reinforced by visual images in *Punch* and other widely read journals.[76] *The Times*, which argued against government intervention during the Famine, informed its readers that:

Before our merciful intervention, the Irish nation were a wretched, indolent, half-starved tribe of savages ... notwithstanding a gradual improvement upon the naked savagery, they have never approached the standard of the civilised age.[77]

In the second half of the nineteenth century, Darwin's theories of evolution gave depictions of the Irish race as inferior a patina of scientific legitimacy, evident in an article in *Punch* in 1862, which explained:

A creature manifestly between the gorilla and the negro is to be met with in some of the lowest districts of London and Liverpool ... It belongs in fact to a tribe of Irish savages ... When conversing with its kind it talks a sort of gibberish.[78]

The racialisation of Irish immigrants had far-reaching consequences, informing both populist and high politics and contributing to intermittent anti-Irish riots. The limited rights of Irish people in the United Kingdom were evident during the Famine when the deployment of the British Laws of Settlement resulted in the large-scale deportation of Irish paupers back to Ireland.[79] Despite protests from Ireland, the Laws of Settlement remained in place until 1948, when workhouses were finally closed in Northern Ireland. Palpably, Britain was not home to the Irish poor, except when their labour was considered useful. That Irish immigrants were not at home in Britain was further demonstrated in the

---

[74] *Times*, 5 January 1847, 22 September 1847.
[75] For example, Friedrich Engels, *The Condition of the Working Class in England* (Leipzig, 1845; London, 1892), 934.
[76] For more on this see Liz Curtis, *Nothing But The Same Old Story: Roots of Anti-Irish Racism* (London, 1984) and Leslie A. Williams, ed. William H. A. Williams, *Daniel O'Connell, the British Press and the Irish Famine: Killing Remarks* (Aldershot, 2003).
[77] *Times*, quoted in *Freeman's Journal*, 4 January 1847.
[78] Quoted in Roger Swift, 'The Outcast Irish in the British Victorian City: Problems and Perspectives', *Irish Historical Studies*, 25 (99) (1987), 271–2; see also, L. P. Curtis, *Apes and Angels: The Irishmen in Victorian Caricature* (London, 1971).
[79] Kinealy, *This Great Calamity*, 334–7.

debates preceding the introduction of the Second Reform Act of 1867, during which a central concern was the notion of what constituted British citizenship and who was deserving of the right to vote. According to Catherine Hall, race was foregrounded in these debates in order to justify or deny the right to British identity and citizenship. Irish people did not benefit from this approach as 'in the imagined nation as it was reconstituted in 1867, "Paddy" the racialised Irishman, stood as a potent "other" to the respectable Englishman, who had proven his worth and deserved the vote'.[80] Despite over sixty years of Union, therefore, discussions about the Irish were still racialised, with their being represented as different, dangerous and undeserving of political rights. The fact that the debate coincided with a period of Fenian agitation perpetuated a view of the Irish as untrustworthy and violent.

IMPERIAL NATIONALISM?

Irish nationalism in the early nineteenth century favoured a constitutional stance, seeking Irish independence within the framework of monarchy and empire. This approach largely reflected the views of the moderate Daniel O'Connell, who was opposed to physical force, arguing that only constitutional means should be used to gain justice for Ireland. O'Connell's success in winning Catholic Emancipation in 1829, using only peaceful tactics, was a psychological blow for the British state and resulted in Robert Peel losing his parliamentary seat. More generally, O'Connell's achievement was applauded by Catholics and political activists in both Europe and the Empire. Just as the American Revolution had done in the 1770s, it demonstrated that British imperialism was not invincible. O'Connell initially desired a repeal of the Act of Union, but between 1832 and 1840, he argued for more integration with Britain as an alternative to independence, informing the House of Commons in 1832 that:

The people of Ireland are ready to become a portion of the Empire, provided they be made so in reality and not in name alone; they are ready to become a kind of West Briton if made so in benefits and in justice; but if not, we are Irishmen again.[81]

In 1840, disappointed with the actions of successive British governments, O'Connell returned to demanding repeal. The title of his new

---

[80] Catherine Hall, in Catherine Hall, Keith McClelland and Jane Rendall, *Defining the Victorian Nation: Class, Race, Gender and the British Reform Act of 1867* (Cambridge, 2000), 220.
[81] Quoted in Liz Curtis, *The Cause of Ireland* (Belfast, 1994), 32.

association – the Loyal National Repeal Association – reflected the paradox of O'Connell's nationalism; he wanted independence for Ireland, but within an imperial context and while maintaining allegiance to the throne. O'Connell was not alone in having this limited view of Irish independence. William Smith O'Brien, a Protestant landlord and leader of the 1848 rebellion, saw no contradiction in desiring the Act of Union to be overturned, while simultaneously supporting the Empire and monarchy.[82] He also advocated more Irish emigration to the British colonies.[83] Nonetheless, the agitation for repeal after 1840 worried the British government because of its implications for the Empire. The Premier, Robert Peel, warned the House of Commons in 1843:

There is no influence, no power, no authority which the prerogatives of the crown and the existing law give to the government, which shall not be exercised for the purpose of maintaining the union; the dissolution of which would involve not merely the repeal of an act of parliament, but the dismemberment of this great empire ... Deprecating as I do all war, but above all civil war, yet there is no alternative which I do not think preferable to the dismemberment of this empire.[84]

Peel placed Ireland at the heart of the Empire, reasoning that if the demand for Irish independence was successful, there would be repercussions elsewhere. Sir James Graham, Home Secretary under Peel, was also alarmed at the spread of the repeal movement, but he regarded it as the failure of administrations since the passage of the Union to raise Ireland above the status of a colony. He believed that the country was only governed by force, and that without a strong military presence, it would be ungovernable.[85] In October 1843, he warned the Prime Minister:

An insurrection may be subdued by the sword; but a military government and free institutions cannot permanently coexist; and Ireland must at last be treated as a rebellious colony, or reconciled to Great Britain on terms which will command the hearts and the affections of her people.[86]

Response to the Great Famine divided nationalist opinion in Ireland, with many radicals viewing the tragedy as a failure of British rule. However, it was the French Revolution of February 1848 that both radicalised

[82] In 1830 Smith O'Brien published 'Considerations Relative to the East India Company's Charter' (London, 1830). He was a founder member of Edward Gibbon Wakefield's 'National Colonization Society'.

[83] Richard Davis, *Revolutionary Imperialist: William Smith O'Brien 1803–1864* (Dublin, 1998), 131–5. The title of this book reveals much about O'Brien's political stance.

[84] Sir Robert Peel, Prime Minister, to House of Commons, *Hansard*, 9 May 1841.

[85] Sir James Graham to Peel, 17 October 1843, Charles Stuart Parker, *Sir Robert Peel from his Private Papers* (London, 1899), 64.

[86] *Ibid.*, Sir James Graham to Peel, 20 October 1843, 65.

nationalist politics and moved Young Ireland from simply wanting a repeal of the Act of Union, to demanding a republic, thus ending the union with Britain. The resulting uprising took place in July 1848 in County Tipperary and was easily defeated by a small force of Irish constabulary. For a brief period, however, in the spring and early summer of 1848, British Chartists and Irish Repealers worked together in support of Irish independence – an alliance that worried the British state, which preferred to isolate Irish national demands as unrealistic and unnecessary.[87] The 1848 uprising had important long-term consequences. After 1848, Irish nationalism increasingly 'defined itself in opposition to British political culture and customs'.[88] John Belchem has suggested that in response, 'The volume and nature of anti-Irish propaganda underwent significant change once the events of 1848 demonstrated Irish "apartness". Paddy appeared in new and defamatory guise, denied his former benign and redeeming qualities.' This prejudice fed into the emergence of popular Toryism in Britain.[89] Nor was this revised view of the Irish confined to Britain as 'On both sides of the Atlantic, 1848 proved an important point of closure. ... Through the misperceptions of 1848, the "outcast" Irish were deemed incapable of political and cultural conformity.'[90]

Nonetheless, many Home Rulers, who dominated Irish nationalist politics from 1870 to 1916, were 'strongly imperial in sentiment'.[91] Overwhelmingly, they were concerned with gaining internal self-government rather than challenging the existence of the British Empire. When they engaged with the wider imperial relationship, the contradictions of the nationalist position became manifest. This was evident during the Boer War of 1899, when many militant nationalists supported the Boers and an Irish Brigade of 300 men fought on their side.[92] Constitutional nationalists, however, supported the war and approximately 25,000 Irish-born men fought on the British side. But even among militant Irish nationalists, there was little sympathy for the colonised black population of South Africa: rather, it was an attempt to fight against Britain.[93] It was not until the early twentieth century that the next phase of militant nationalism, often

[87] See John Saville, *1848: The British State and the Chartist Movement* (Cambridge, 1990).
[88] Brewster et al., 'Introduction', in *Ireland in Proximity*, 3.
[89] John Belchem, 'Nationalism, Republicanism and Exile: Irish Emigrants and the Revolution of 1848', *Past and Present*, 146 (February 1995), 103–35.
[90] *Ibid.*, 135.
[91] T. G. Fraser, 'Ireland and India', in Jeffery (ed.), *An Irish Empire*, 85.
[92] Donal P. McCracken, 'MacBride's Brigade in the Anglo-Boer War', *History Ireland*, 8 (1) (Spring 2000), 26–9.
[93] Howe, *Ireland and Empire*, 56–8.

associated with Sinn Féin, adopted a separatist and anti-imperialist position. This stance may have been to counter the Unionist claim that Home Rule was not merely an attack on the United Kingdom, but also on the Empire. Unionists were encouraged by some Conservative politicians, Andrew Bonar Law telling a meeting in Derry in 1912 that 'Once more you hold the pass for the Empire, you are a besieged city.'[94]

Within Ireland, non-sectarian, inclusive politics were undermined by the cultural revival at the end of the nineteenth century, largely portraying Irish culture as Gaelic and Catholic, thus excluding Protestant history and heritage. This development was particularly ironic as many of the principal writers of that period were Protestant and wrote in the English language. The movement rejected symbols of British culture, including sport, through the anti-English Gaelic Athletic Association. Paradoxically, at the same time that Gaelic culture was being promoted in Ireland, Irish artists were 'conquering' England, notably in the fields of visual arts and literature.[95]

The First World War was a watershed in Anglo-Irish relations. In the 1918 General Election, Sinn Féin won 73 out of 105 seats in Westminster. However, its members refused to take their parliamentary seats or to swear an oath of allegiance to the British monarch. The emergence of Sinn Féin as the largest political party in Ireland was an indication that Irish nationalism was no longer content to be part of empire. The decision by the British government in 1920 to partition Ireland confirmed that the Union had failed and that the majority of Irish people had been neither assimilated nor integrated into the United Kingdom.

AN IRISH EMPIRE?

Through emigration, transportation and missionary activities there was an Irish presence in all parts of the Empire while, 'as part of the metropolitan core of the Empire, [they] supplied many of its soldiers, settlers, administrators', demonstrating the fluidity of home and empire.[96] The Irish contribution to the Empire left a visible and enduring legacy, in the roads, bridges and buildings that they helped to design and construct. Irish men were particularly evident in the military sphere. By 1830, approximately 40 per cent of non-commissioned members of the

---

[94] Quoted in David H. Hume, 'Empire Day in Ireland', in Jeffery, *An Irish Empire*, 155.
[95] 'Conquering England: Ireland in Victorian Britain' was an exhibition at the National Portrait Gallery curated by Fintan Cullen and R. F. Foster, March to June 2005.
[96] Jeffery, 'Introduction', in *An Irish Empire*, 1.

British Army were Irish-born. Ireland also supplied the Empire with some of its leading imperial soldiers (from the Duke of Wellington to Lord Kitchener). Consequently, while parts of Ireland remained the most policed areas within the Empire, Irish soldiers and administrators were helping to extend and maintain order throughout the rest of it. The combination of imperial soldier and defender of the Union was embodied by Field-Marshal Sir Henry Wilson, from County Longford. A veteran of the Boer War, in 1918 he was appointed Chief of the Imperial General Staff. He was dismayed by Lloyd George's negotiations with Sinn Féin in 1921, cautioning that 'the surrender to the murder gang in Ireland is going to have a deplorable and very immediate effect on Palestine, Egypt and India'.[97]

Ireland's presence in the Empire also resulted from mass emigration. According to Donald Akenson, Irish emigrants represented 'ideal prefabricated collaborators' who were well placed to support the Empire.[98] However, the vast majority of Irish emigrants did not settle in the Empire, despite the economic opportunities available: between 1840 and 1920 over 80 per cent of Irish emigrants chose the United States as their new home. Moreover, wherever they settled, Irish immigrants were active participants in labour and radical movements, suggesting that their sympathy was not always with the imperial administrations. Inevitably, nationalist politics were transported overseas, most notably in the post-Famine generations that blamed Britain for their exile.[99]

END OF EMPIRE?

Ireland in the nineteenth and early twentieth centuries occupied an important middle place in terms of metropole and empire. Consequently, Ireland challenges simplistic definitions of the wider colonial experience. At the same time, it enriches an understanding of the British state as an imperial legislature. Historically, Ireland provided a prism – albeit a dangerous one – through which radicals and dissidents in other parts of the Empire judged the British state. One manifestation of this relationship was the informal links created in the component parts of the Empire, sometimes bypassing the metropole, which were particularly uncomfortable for the London administration.[100]

---

[97] Mark Coulter, 'Field-Marshal Sir Henry Wilson: Imperial Soldier, Political Failure', *History Ireland*, 13 (1) (January/February 2005), 26–9.
[98] Jeffery, 'Introduction', in *An Irish Empire*, 16.
[99] This tradition is kept alive by songs such as 'Revenge for Skibbereen'.
[100] H. Brasted, 'Indian Nationalist Development and the Influence of Irish Home Rule, 1870–1886', *Modern Asian Journal of the Asiatic Society of Bangladesh*, 22 (1977), 66–89.

The creation of the United Kingdom brought the Irish national question to the heart of Westminster politics, destroying the career of some politicians in the process. It also shaped and ultimately contributed to the destruction of the Liberal Party, thus helping to pave the way for the emergence of the Labour Party.

The changing view of Irish people towards both the Union and the Empire bequeathed a visible outlet in the erection of statues in Ireland, which reflected the changing political and cultural relationship with Britain, and thus changed from signs of loyalty to sites of contestation.[101] Yvonne Whelan contests that 'far from possessing a linear historical narrative of uncritical colonial discourse, Ireland's status as a colony was ambivalent and significantly different from for example, Calcutta, its counterpart capital of the British Indian empire'.[102] After 1921, statues of British monarchs and heroes in Ireland 'functioned not just as works of art but as constant reminders of Ireland's colonial connection with Britain'.[103] Not surprisingly, the fate of most statues in the Republic was either to be blown up by dissident groups (as with statues of William of Orange in 1929, George II in 1937, Lord Gough in 1955 and Nelson's Pillar in 1966) or sold, as happened with George I's statue in 1928. Queen Victoria's statue, however, was 'donated' to Australia in 1986.[104] Overall, the fate of these statues indicated that the new Irish Republic wanted to disassociate itself from its imperial past.

In contrast, the Northern Ireland state held on to symbols of the imperial past, although they were increasingly disliked by the nationalist community. In 1922, the identity of the new Northern Ireland state was explained by the Minister for Finance, thus:

We regard Ulster today as the key-stone of the arch of the British Empire ... Ulster has been selected as the cock-pit of strife by those whose object is the Destruction of the Empire, rather than the mere acquisition of Ulster. Here in this province the whole principle of Empire is at stake; we the people of Ulster are the children of the Empire.[105]

---

[101] Y. Whelan, 'The Construction and Destruction of a Colonial Landscape: Monuments to British Monarchs in Dublin Before and After Independence', *Journal of Historical Geography*, 28 (4) (2002), 508–33.

[102] *Ibid.*

[103] *Ibid.*, 510, 523–8.

[104] 'How the Indian Wolf Met Dingo' at http://web.mid-day.com/smd/play/2004/june/85015.htm and 'Queen Victoria Building', Sydney at http://www.10bestcityguides.com/details.process. *Cork Examiner*, 14 June 1995 and Eileen Black, *Universitas: An Exhibition Celebrating 150 Years of University College, Cork* (Belfast, 1995). William of Orange's statue was replaced by Thomas Davis, a Protestant nationalist.

[105] Quoted in D. Hume, 'Empire Day in Northern Ireland', in Jeffery, *An Irish Empire*, 159.

Empire Day, which fell on 24 May, continued to be celebrated in Protestant schools in Northern Ireland until the early 1960s.[106] Additionally, monuments and murals dedicated to the two world wars became symbols of Protestant loyalty to king and empire. However, the demise of empire forced Unionists to find other ways of defining their relationship with Britain and their identity.[107] Queen Victoria, the embodiment of empire, remained particularly visible in many public spaces in Northern Ireland, with numerous streets, a park, a bridge and a university being named after her, and her statue dominating the entrance to the City Hall in Belfast.[108] Nonetheless, the place of empire was being increasingly contested. In 2000, when the Belfast City Council attempted to relocate a small statue of Victoria to a public park, it was opposed by a Sinn Féin councillor, who argued:

There are more than enough monuments to our colonial past. Queen Victoria was known as the famine queen who was responsible for the deaths of millions of Irish people. We should be remembering the victims of the famine and not the person responsible for the deaths. Nationalists will find this offensive. It is a Unionist symbol in a predominantly nationalist area.

Wallace Browne, a Democratic Unionist Party Councillor, responded that, 'The British way of life is part of our culture. We are part of the United Kingdom and Queen Victoria is an important part of our British tradition.'[109] Fifty years after the demise of the British Empire, its visible remains continue to cause dissent in Ireland.

CONCLUSION

One hundred years of union with Britain and participation in the imperial parliament brought few tangible benefits to Ireland. The Union did not bring prosperity or save the country from a devastating famine and a dramatic decline in its population. At the time of the Union, Ireland had accounted for 50 per cent of the population of the United Kingdom; a hundred years later, it represented less than 10 per cent. In the two centuries after the Union, emigration became an integral part of Irish life. While the vast majority of emigrants went to the United States, large numbers settled in other parts of the Empire, notably Australia, Canada and New Zealand, helping to shape the development of those

[106] *Ibid.*, 153.   [107] For information on First World War murals, see http://cain.ulst.ac.uk.
[108] See website of John Cassidy, sculptor, at http://rylibweb.man.ac.uk. And website of Northern Ireland Tourist Board at http://www.geographia.com/northern-ireland.
[109] *Irish News*, 19 August 2000, http://www.irishnews.com/archive2000/19082000/Politics7.html.

countries. Within Britain, however, Irish people never achieved equal status, but remained 'other', despite being both white and British citizens.

The Union did not give political stability to Ireland, but it exacerbated religious divisions. A consequence was the Partition, which created a political fracturing that continued 100 years later. Although Northern Ireland remained within the United Kingdom after 1921, British government intervention was minimal. After 1969, however, they were forced to intercede in a way that suggested that the state had failed. Moreover, the unequal relationship between Britain and Northern Ireland raised the unpalatable question of whether this part of Ireland was still a colony. The imposition of Direct Rule from London in 1972 highlighted Northern Ireland's ambivalent status, leading John Biggs-Davidson, a Conservative politician, to protest, arguing, 'Northern Ireland is part of the Homeland, not a colony ... The effective powers of the new Irish Secretary exceed those of the Lord Deputies, Viceroys and Irish Secretaries of the past.'[110] More vehemently, writing in 1994, Anne McClintock suggested that the debates about Ireland's colonial situation, and the refusal to acknowledge its postcolonial status, arose because:

The term 'postcolonial' is, in many cases, prematurely celebratory. Ireland may, at a pinch, be 'postcolonial', but for the inhabitants of British-occupied Northern Ireland ... there might be nothing 'post' about colonialism at all.[111]

At the beginning of the twenty-first century, the Celtic Tiger, the Peace Process and the Irish cultural revival have changed the way in which Ireland and Irish people are viewed in Britain. However, Irish and British politics remain intertwined, demonstrating that the colonial past continues to shape the political present.

[110] John Biggs-Davidson, *Rock Firm for the Union: Background to the Ulster Troubles 1969–1978* (Essex, 1979), 31–2.
[111] Anne McClintock, 'The Angel of Progress: Pitfalls of the Term "postcolonialism"', in P. Williams and L. Chrisman (eds.), *Colonial Discourse and Postcolonial Theory* (New York, 1994), 294.

CHAPTER FIVE

The condition of women, women's writing and the Empire in nineteenth-century Britain

Jane Rendall[1]

In 1814 Maria Graham lamented the lack of 'mutual understanding and mutual knowledge' between the European residents and the indigenous inhabitants of India, and hoped to fill that gap with a popular introduction to Indian history, literature, science, religions and manners.[2] She had sailed to India in 1809, and on her return published her *Journal of a Residence in India* (1812) and *Letters on India* (1814). In 1814 she looked back at the *Journal* as 'liable to the reproach of European prejudice'.[3] She had been shocked to find 'Mussulman ladies ... so totally void of cultivation', and Hindus characterised by 'passive submission ... apathy and ... degrading superstition'.[4] But in the *Letters*, she used the language of eighteenth-century stadial theory, assuming a hierarchy of stages of development, and the tone was more informed, comparative and philosophical. She found in ancient Hindu civilisation 'the maxims of that pure and sound morality which is founded on the nature of man as a rational and social being'. She expressed her greatest delight in the Mahabharata as 'the pleasing light in which it places the early condition of the Hindu women, before the jealous Mahomedan maxims had shut them up in zenanas'.[5]

Graham was only the third British woman to publish her observations on India, and her work had a mixed reception in Britain.[6] The *Journal* was praised by the *Monthly Magazine*, the *Critical Review* and the *Monthly*

[1] Acknowledgements: thanks to Rosemary Raza for permission to cite her thesis, and to Rosemary Raza, Caroline Lewis and the editors of this volume for their careful reading of this article.
[2] *Letters on India* (London, 1814), 2; on Graham see Rosamund Gotch, *Maria Lady Callcott: The Creator of Little Arthur* (London, 1937); Nigel Leask, *Curiosity and the Aesthetics of Travel Writing, 1770–1840* (Oxford, 2002), 205–17.
[3] Graham, *Letters*, 85.
[4] Maria Graham, *Journal of a Residence in India* (Edinburgh, 1812), 18, 134.
[5] Graham, *Letters*, 36, 87.
[6] Her predecessors were Jane Smart, *Letter from a Lady in Madrass to Her Friends in London ...* (London, 1743) and Jemima Kindersley, *Letters from Teneriffe, Brazil, the Cape of Good Hope, and the East Indies* (London, 1777); see Rosemary Raza, 'British Women Writers on India between the Eighteenth Century and 1857', DPhil thesis, University of Oxford, 1998, 455.

Review, yet went unnoticed in the influential *Edinburgh Review*, although its editor, Francis Jeffrey, had urged her to publish. The conservative *Quarterly Review* noted the *Journal* condescendingly as the work of a young lady who went to India to find a husband, and ignored the *Letters*.[7]

In 1820 Graham sailed with her husband to South America. Mary Louise Pratt has written of her journals of these years as by a 'social exploratress', constantly commenting on social and reforming institutions and political conflicts.[8] Yet Maria Graham's most popular work, published under the name of Maria Callcott, was *Little Arthur's History of England* (1835), a patriotic history for children, which sold 80,000 copies in the course of the next century. Nowhere did it acknowledge the imperial dimensions of English, or British, power. Graham was a sharp and intelligent observer, who had challenged the limits of women's writing on the Empire. Her shift by the 1830s reflected the invisibility of the Empire in British historical thinking. Yet in representing India to a British readership, ambitiously, reflectively, and clearly from a female perspective, she indicated new possibilities for women's writing. Those new possibilities were inseparable from the observation of culturally diverse gender relations, and consequently from the debate about gender relations at home.

Maria Graham's writings raise issues relevant to the impact of Britain's imperial role on discourses of femininity in nineteenth-century Britain. First, she wrote in the immediate context of the global conflicts of 1793–1815. Much recent work has been done on the gendered nature of eighteenth-century British imperialism, as on nineteenth-century anti-slavery and missionary movements, and late nineteenth-century imperialism.[9] Yet the significance in terms of gender relations of the extensive early nineteenth-century territorial expansion of the Empire, simultaneously with the rapid growth of commercial activity and missionary commitment, remains to be examined. In *Britons* (1992), Linda Colley suggested the growth of a British national consciousness, and the agency of middle-class women as patriots in these years, though referring only briefly to the extent of British imperial acquisitions. Elsewhere she recognised the ambiguous situation of Ireland, as 'the laboratory of the British empire'; in what follows, Ireland's semi-colonial status following the Act of Union of 1801 will be assumed.[10]

---

[7] *Quarterly Review*, 8 (December 1812), 406; *Monthly Magazine*, 34 (1812), 632–50; *Critical Review*, 3 (April 1813), 337–46; *Monthly Review*, 77 (1815), 258–71; Maria Graham to unknown correspondent, 28 March 1812, National Library of Scotland MS 3610 f. 46.

[8] Mary Louise Pratt, *Imperial Eyes: Travel Writing and Transculturation* (London, 1992), 155–71.

[9] See Introduction, Chapter 1.

[10] Colley, 'Britishness and Otherness: An Argument', *Journal of British Studies*, 31 (1992), 309–30, here 327.

Secondly, Graham's writing suggests the gendered nature of representations of social, cultural and religious differences. The stadial theory of the Scottish Enlightenment, constructing a hierarchy of four stages of civilisation – nomadic (or 'savage'), pastoral (or 'barbarian'), agricultural and commercial – defined by their material condition but also by their manners, culture and political structures, was immensely influential. That framework legitimated British cultural superiority, and provided a way of classifying the variety of societies encountered in British imperial expansion.[11] A hierarchy of gender relations was at its heart. William Alexander wrote that the condition of women in any country indicated 'the exact point in the scale of civil society to which the people of such country have arrived'.[12] These writers used figures of womanhood to differentiate from savage, or barbarian, or despotic societies, that polite and refined form of domesticity, the companionate marriage, to which they themselves aspired. William Robertson, writing of the drudgery of the Native American woman in North America suggested that 'to despise and to degrade the female sex, is the characteristic of the savage state in every part of the globe'.[13] They also employed orientalist tropes, following Montesquieu, in paralleling political despotism in the East with the despotism of the harem and polygamy.[14]

There were clearly connections between that vocabulary and the different explanations offered for the physical varieties of humanity: culture, climate, polygenesis. Even within the prevalent view that humanity constituted one species, the idea of a hierarchy of races within that species was becoming accepted. By the end of the eighteenth century the use of the language of fixed racial difference was increasing, although coexisting with emphases on climatic, material and cultural influences. Whichever perspective was taken, such language was gendered; women were regarded as contributing to the physical shaping of races, through their nursing practices and the form which sexual relationships took.[15]

[11] Christopher Bayly, *Imperial Meridian: The British Empire and the World 1780–1830* (London, 1989), 151–2.

[12] William Alexander, *The History of Women, From the Earliest Antiquity to the Present Time*, 2 vols. (1782 edn, repr. Bath, 1995), vol. II, 151.

[13] William Robertson, *History of America* (1777), in *The Works of William Robertson DD*, 12 vols. (London, 1817), vol. IV, 103.

[14] *Ibid.*, 225; Alexander, *History of Women*, vol. I, 284–97; Pauline Kra, 'Montesquieu and Women', in Samia Spencer (ed.), *French Women and the Age of Enlightenment* (Bloomington, 1984), 272–84.

[15] Roxanne Wheeler, *The Complexion of Race: Categories of Difference in Eighteenth-Century British Culture* (Philadelphia, 2000), 248–50; Silvia Sebastiani, '"Race", Women and Progress in the Scottish Enlightenment', in Sarah Knott and Barbara Taylor (eds.), *Women, Gender and Enlightenment* (London, 2005), 75–96.

These representations were part of the construction of white British middle-class femininity in the early nineteenth century. From the mid-1770s onwards, representations of savage and 'Eastern' women were used to signal the superiority of white British femininity by differentiating it from its 'others' in the prescriptive literature addressed to young women.[16] But in Catherine Macaulay's *Letters on Education* (1790) and Mary Wollstonecraft's *Vindication of the Rights of Woman* (1791), these images were employed with a feminist purpose, with the harem coming to symbolise the tyrannical oppression of women. As Joyce Zonona suggests, these tropes were already 'a fully developed cultural code implicitly shared with their readers', a code which for Macaulay and Wollstonecraft marked the distance which British civilisation still had to travel.[17]

In the early nineteenth century, the appeal of comparative history was declining. The reaction against the radicalism of the French Revolution, the growing strength of evangelical religious practice and the distinctive aspirations of the middling sections of society, all appeared to strengthen the assumption that the domestic household should be viewed as the natural and divinely ordained setting for women's lives. Discourses of domesticity can be read as confining, in that they regulated gender relations along fixed lines. Yet they could also enable middle-class women's moral and social influence, through participation in the moral life of the household, the exercise of sociability, and the growth of religious and philanthropic activity.

The growth of the apparently confining language of 'separate spheres' has to be considered in the context of the massive expansion of print culture, in which women shared both as readers and as writers. Women's reading was, commercially, highly significant, yet the figure of the female reader was a focus for anxiety and surveillance, signalled both in literary representations of women's reading, and in advice manuals on the appropriate kinds of reading. That anxiety recognised the significance of reading as shaping subjectivities and as a means of socialisation, whether through the imaginative fulfilment of desire or as the act through which one might become part of a wider community. As Kate Flint indicates, reading could be an act of conformity or of questioning.[18]

---

[16] Mary Catherine Moran, 'From Rudeness to Refinement: Gender, Genre and Scottish Enlightenment Discourse', PhD dissertation, Johns Hopkins University, 1999, 234–43.

[17] Joyce Zonona, 'The Sultan and the Slave: Feminist Orientalism and the Structure of *Jane Eyre*', *Signs*, 18 (1993), 592–617; Clare Midgley, 'Anti-slavery and the Roots of Imperial Feminism', in Midgley (ed.), *Gender and Imperialism* (Manchester, 1998), 161–80.

[18] Kate Flint, *The Woman Reader 1837–1914* (Oxford, 1993), 38–43; Jacqueline Pearson, *Women's Reading in Britain 1750–1835: A Dangerous Recreation* (Cambridge, 1999), 14–21.

Women were of course not only readers but also writers, although their scope was limited by the genres deemed appropriate for them. The gendered boundaries of genre were increasingly patrolled by such shapers of cultural opinion as the editors of the influential periodicals founded in this period, including the *Edinburgh Review* and the *Quarterly Review*. While poetry, the novel and the moral tale were recognised as appropriate fields for women writers, there were clear limits to women's writing about the directly political. The *Quarterly Review* rebuked Graham in 1824 for not realising that 'she was unqualified to write *political* disquisitions on Brazil'.[19]

Yet such constraints could be evaded and the most apparently limited horizon extended to the reading and writing of the colonial experience. In January 1813, Jane Austen's reading, shared with her mother and the local Chawton book club, included Sir John Carr's *Descriptive Travels in the Southern and Eastern Parts of Spain* (1811) and Charles Pasley's *Essay on the Military Policy and Institutions of the British Empire* (1810). These she compared with Thomas Clarkson's *History . . . of the Abolition of the African Slave Trade . . .* (1808) and Claudius Buchanan's *Christian Researches in Asia* (1811). Others might have encountered Carr's *Travels* and Buchanan's *Christian Researches* through extracts in the *Lady's Magazine* for 1811.[20] For the literatures of war and empire, travel and mission, appear in the everyday reading of literate women, not only in literature and periodicals for the general reader but in those addressed specifically to them.[21]

Women writers and readers responded to the growth of a new territorial empire through a variety of discourses: a patriotic understanding of imperial destiny, an emphasis on the mission of Christian civilisation, a vision of an empire of commerce and exchange, or one of potential opportunity for both philanthropists and emigrants. Such responses were not merely passive, as empire came to be a constitutive element in the rewriting of nineteenth-century femininity and feminism. As Cora Kaplan indicates below, postcolonial criticism has re-read canonical novels such as *Mansfield Park* (1814) and *Jane Eyre* (1847) as colonial encounters, yet these still remain to be located in the broader context of women's reading and writing practices.

---

[19] William Jacob, 'Travels to Brazil', *Quarterly Review*, 31 (December 1824), 1–25, here 14.

[20] Jane Austen, *Selected Letters*, ed. Vivien Jones (Oxford, 2004), 133, quoted in Vivien Jones, 'Reading for England: Austen, Taste and Female Patriotism', *European Romantic Review*, 16 (April 2005), 223–32.

[21] See David Finkelstein and Douglas M. Peers, 'Introduction', to Finkelstein and Peers (eds.), *Negotiating India in the Nineteenth-Century Media* (Basingstoke, 2000), 1–22.

Writing about empire employed overlapping discourses about gender, cultural difference and race, inextricably involved in the imaginative construction of gender identities which were also imperial identities. References to the 'savage' or the 'Eastern' woman were not necessarily explicitly directed towards British imperial territories. But they gradually took on a more immediate relevance in the expanding territories of the British Empire. A culturally superior femininity entrenched in women's domestic power and moral influence would work for the benefit of the Empire. A recurrent theme is that of British women's mission, and sacrifice of self, in the cause of the civilisation of the 'savage', 'barbarian' and unenlightened societies which Britain ruled.[22] Such sacrifice might demand new kinds of discipline, courage and authority from women, qualities also needed at home in the simultaneous mission to the British working class.

In what follows I focus mainly on white women who wrote for a white readership, though the former black slave Mary Prince also appears, as does Mrs Meer Hassan Ali, a white woman married to a Muslim man from Lucknow. These women drew upon the hierarchies of culture and race, as well as class, in developing their own varied – never monolithic – discourses of femininity and women's roles. If they assumed the benefits of white British 'civilisation', their interpretations of that might vary sharply. In the early years of the nineteenth century most limited themselves to approved genres, including imaginative writing, educational treatises, moral tales and missionary discourses. An increasing number, like Graham, published journals of their travels and a few others engaged directly with political issues through journalism and history.

Even at the beginning of this period, women writers debated the future of the British Empire, in poetry and the novel. Exceptionally, Anna Barbauld, in 1812, anticipated first the spread of British cultural imperialism, and then its decline and collapse. She addressed 'my Country, name beloved, revered':

> Wide spreads thy race, from Ganges to the pole,
> O'er half the western world thy accents roll. . . .
> Thy stores of knowledge the new states shall know
> And think thy thoughts, and with thy fancy glow;

In the Empire's days of glory, she forecast in the streets of London the 'turban'd Moslem, bearded Jew / And woolly Afric, met the brown Hindu'. But 'arts, arms and wealth destroy the fruit they bring', and the

---

[22] Deirdre David, *Rule Britannia: Women, Empire and Victorian Writing* (Ithaca, 1995), 5–7.

future lay with the North American empire. Reviewers, almost unanimously, found the poem 'culpably subversive of national morale'.[23] Anne Grant's lengthy poetic response *Eighteen Hundred and Thirteen* (1814) celebrated Britain's victory and Britain's empire in nationalist terms.[24]

The most popular female poet of the early nineteenth century, Felicia Hemans, whose immense success is today forgotten, wrote of the centrality of domestic affections to national unity and to an imperial future. She appealed to chivalric themes across a variety of historical and geographical settings and themes, including war, politics and murder as well as the celebration of home and the domestic affections. She has been viewed as 'the undisputed representative poet of Victorian imperial and domestic ideology'.[25] Modern criticism suggests a more ambivalent view of her poetry, not as simply glorifying the expansion of nation and empire, but as recognising the conflict and suffering it brought.[26]

Women writers explored the revaluation of the private and the domestic, in the national interest and in fulfilment of an imperial destiny, from the 1790s onwards through the novel. Their contribution in representing national cultures within the British isles has been widely recognised, but the novel was also a means of imagining and debating the British Empire; Balachandra Rajan suggests that 'the novel about India was originated by women'.[27] For the Scottish writer Elizabeth Hamilton, that empire was to be a Christian one. Her mildly anti-Jacobin novel, *Translation of the Letters of the Hindoo Rajah* (1796), drew on the writing of her brother Charles, an East India Company officer and a scholar of Indian languages and history. She represented a feminised version of Hindu India sympathetically, as an ancient civilisation overrun by tyrannical Muslim invaders. In *The Memoirs of Agrippina* (1804), Hamilton wrote of the weaknesses of the Roman Empire, its arrogance and reliance on the system of slavery. Only a Christian empire could overcome

[23] Anna Letitia Barbauld, 'Eighteen Hundred and Eleven', in William McCarthy and Elizabeth Kraft (eds.), *The Poems of Anna Letitia Barbauld* (Athens, 1994), 155, 157, 160–1, 310 quoted in Tim Fulford and Peter J. Kitson, 'Romanticism and Colonialism: Texts, Contexts, Issues', in Fulford and Kitson (eds.), *Romanticism and Colonialism: Writing and Empire 1780–1830* (Cambridge, 1998), 4–5, 7.

[24] Anne Grant, *Eighteen Hundred and Thirteen* (Edinburgh, 1814).

[25] Norma Clarke, *Ambitious Heights – Writing, Friendship, Love: The Jewsbury Sisters, Felicia Hemans and Jane Carlyle* (London, 1990), 45; Kelly, *Women, Writing and Revolution*, 183–9.

[26] Susan J. Wolfson, 'Introduction' to *Felicia Hemans: Selected Poems, Letters, Reception Materials* (Princeton, 2000).

[27] Balachandra Rajan, *Under Western Eyes: India from Milton to Macaulay* (Durham, NC, 1999), 123; Kelly, *Women, Writing and Revolution*, 173–91. For a list of British women's novels of India, see Raza, 'British Women Writers on India', 465.

differences of culture and race, as it assumed the mission of benevolence and enlightenment.[28]

Women also wrote as educationalists, whether directly on the philosophy and practice of education, or through the didactic moral tale. Hamilton was committed to improving the educational practice of mothers, by drawing on the insights of both philosophers and historians. In the 1810 edition of her *Letters on the Elementary Principles of Education* she wrote of a mother's role in shaping the national character, arguing that women's powers were capable of developing to meet the maternal responsibilities of every stage of society. In her view, it was the task of

the Christian and the patriot, to raise the female mind to a sense of the dignity of a situation, which enables it not only to effect the happiness or misery of individuals, but to influence the character of nations, and ameliorate the condition of the human race.[29]

The most powerful identification of Christianity with the progress of civilisation came from the evangelical Christian impulse, which rested upon a sense of sinfulness, and the possibility of salvation through conversion, and the disciplining of the self within the community of the family. With that impulse came a sense of mission and a drive to regenerate and save corrupt and unchristian worlds, in Britain and beyond. From the 1790s onwards, in opposition to radical ideas, evangelical writers paid particular attention to the role of women within British society. The evangelical writer Hannah More wrote tracts, moral tales and ballads to counter radicalism and effect the moral reformation of the working population of Britain. But she also stressed the significance of women's role in a new kind of empire. In orientalist terms, she suggested that the use of women's influence for vanity or pleasure was characteristic of those victims to 'luxury, caprice and despotism', excluded from 'light, and liberty, and knowledge', by 'the laws and religion of the voluptuous prophet of Arabia'. She called on women of the upper and middle classes to demonstrate a 'firm and feminine patriotism', and contrasted the pagan Roman Empire and a modern British empire distinguished by Christian humility, as well as by Christian refusal to coexist with other faiths.[30]

From the 1790s onwards, the number of missionary societies associated with the evangelical movement grew steadily across Protestant denominations.

---

[28] Elizabeth Hamilton, *Translation of the Letters of a Hindoo Rajah*, ed. Pamela Perkins and Shannon Russell (Peterborough, ON, 1999); Kelly, *Women, Writing and Revolution*, 129–43, 269–73; Rajan, *Under Western Eyes*, 124–8.

[29] *Letters on the Elementary Principles of Education*, 5th edn, 2 vols. (London, 1810), vol. I, 2–9, 21.

[30] Hannah More, *Strictures on the Modern System of Female Education* . . . , 2 vols. (London, 1799), vol. I, 3, 77–8, 251–2.

Susan Thorne has shown how central was the missionary enterprise to the formation of middle-class identity in Britain. Its objects included the conversion and moral reform of indigenous peoples in colonised territories, of the Irish peasantry and of the 'heathen' working class at home.[31] Gender was central to this enterprise, as the happy condition and moral influence of the domestic and monogamous woman was contrasted with the lives of degraded 'savage' women or women of the zenanas of India. Anna Johnston has argued that 'missionary texts constitute a distinct genre of missionary discourse, a genre that has an unmistakeable, though ambivalent, relationship with imperial discourses as a whole'. Such texts informed the essential support and sponsorship given by mission enthusiasts at home.[32]

Yet the representation of gender presented missionary writers with difficulties. Most missionaries were male, with women accepted only as their wives; they encountered in colonial societies very different kinds of gender relations, and also relied on their wives to take a far greater public role than might have been expected. The pioneering Hannah Kilham visited the Gambia in 1822–3, and Sierra Leone in 1827 and 1830–2, against some male resistance, publishing her letters and reports in the *Missionary Register*, the periodical of the Church Missionary Society. But only with the foundation of the Society for the Promotion of Female Education in the East, in 1834, were single woman missionaries sent out regularly. The Society's women founders responded to a powerful appeal by an American missionary for missionaries to aid women in China, but immediately decided to extend their mission to India, where girls' schools, orphanages and teacher training, as well as missions to zenanas, became their major concern. By 1838 they also sent teachers and missionaries to South Africa, and from 1853 published the monthly *Female Missionary Intelligencer*.[33]

The British domestic audience read of such work through missionary travel writing, missionary periodicals, exemplary biographies and didactic tales, produced in great quantity.[34] Alison Twells has shown how, in

---

[31] Susan Thorne, '"The Conversion of Englishmen and the Conversion of the World Inseparable": Missionary Imperialism and the Language of Class in Early Industrial Britain', in Frederick Cooper and Ann Stoler (eds.), *Tensions of Empire: Colonial Cultures in a Bourgeois World* (Berkeley, 1997), 238–62.

[32] Anna Johnston, *Missionary Writing and Empire, 1800–1860* (Cambridge, 2003), 202 and *passim*.

[33] Margaret Donaldson, '"The Cultivation of the Heart and the Moulding of the Will ...": The Missionary Contribution of the Society for Promoting Female Education in China, India and the East', in W. J. Sheils and Diana Wood (eds.), *Women in the Church*, Studies in Church History, 27 (Oxford, 1990), 429–42.

[34] Johnston, *Missionary Writing*, 32–4.

Sheffield, evangelical families read of the voyages of London Missionary Society missionaries George Bennet and Daniel Tyerman to the South Pacific, New Zealand and elsewhere from 1821 to 1829. Through their letters, reprinted in the *Sheffield Iris*, and their *Voyages and Travels* (1831), the adoption of new patterns of marriage and gender relations in the South Pacific was publicised.[35] Families might also read the lives of exemplary women missionaries like Margaret Wilson or Louisa Mundy in India, and Margaret Mary Clough in Ceylon, through their letters and journals, reprinted in periodicals, memoirs or anthologies such as Mary Weitbrecht's *Female Missionaries in India ...* (1843).[36] The central importance of the mission to Indian women was stressed, as was, by implication, the inability of male missionaries to undertake the work of education and visiting the zenanas. These texts created 'a form of self-writing in which the woman subject emerged as heroic'.[37] They also indicated the strength of evangelical campaigning on behalf of Indian women, and especially Indian mothers, and against the practice of sati.[38]

The same sense of mission could be conveyed through moral tales and tales for children. The outstanding writer of Indian tales for children was Mary Sherwood, who accompanied her army officer husband to India and spent ten years there, greatly influenced by the missionary Henry Martyn. Her stories and tracts included *The History of Little Henry and his Bearer* (1814), *The Ayah and Lady* (1816), *The Indian Pilgrim* (1818) and many others. All were reprinted many times, especially for Sunday School use. Other, less travelled, writers, like the popular Barbara Hofland, followed her example in stories of India such as *The Young Cadet* (1828) and *The Captives in India* (1834). And a bestselling family novel by another immensely popular, if now unread, writer, Charlotte Yonge's *The Daisy Chain* (1856), is pervaded by a similar sense of mission,

[35] Alison Twells, '"A Christian and Civilised Land": The British Middle Class and the Civilising Mission, 1820–42', in Alan Kidd and David Nicholls (eds.), *Gender, Civic Culture and Consumerism: Middle-class Identity in Britain, 1800–1940* (Manchester, 1999), 47–64, and 'Happy English Children: Class, Ethnicity and the Making of Missionary Women, 1800–1850', *Women's Studies International Forum*, 21 (1998), 235–45; for Birmingham, see Catherine Hall, *Civilising Subjects: Metropole and Colony in the English Imagination, 1830–1867* (Cambridge, 2002), 301–6.

[36] *Extracts from the Journal and Correspondence of the Late Mrs M. M. Clough, Wife of the Rev. Benjamin Clough, Missionary in Ceylon* (London, 1829); George Mundy, *Memoir of Mrs Louisa Mundy, of the London Missionary Society's Mission, at Chinsurah, Bengal ...* (London, 1845); John Wilson (ed.), *Memoir of Mrs Margaret Wilson* (Edinburgh, 1838).

[37] Linda Peterson, 'Women Writers and Self-writing', in Joanne Shattock (ed.), *Women and Literature in Britain 1800–1900* (Cambridge, 2001), 209–30, here 223–4; Johnston, *Missionary Writing*, 82–3.

[38] Clare Midgley, 'Female Emancipation in an Imperial Frame: English Women and the Campaign Against *Sati* (Widow-burning) in India, 1813–30', *Women's History Review*, 9 (2000), 95–122; Hall, *Civilising Subjects*, 303–5.

simultaneously to the impoverished local hamlet of Cocksmoor and to the Loyalty Islands of the South Pacific. The heroine, Ethel, sacrificed her own academic ambitions to care for her family and support her brother Norman, who in turn abandoned his brilliant career to become a missionary. The profits of the novel were devoted to building a missionary college in New Zealand.[39]

There are close associations between such literature and the anti-slavery movement in Britain, which was powerfully promoted by women as a philanthropic mission. From the late 1780s Hannah More, with other women writers, participated actively in the anti-slavery movement. Their poetry and tracts frequently foregrounded the slave mother, and the separation of the slave family, as did More in *The Sorrows of Yamba; or, a Negro Woman's Lament* (1795), and Mary Sherwood in *Dazee, The Re-Captured Negro* (1821).[40] Barbara Hofland's *Matilda; or The Barbadoes Girl* (1816) illustrated the corrupting effects of slavery on slaveowners. *The History of Mary Prince* (1831), the only autobiographical narrative by a black woman slave from the West Indies, was published in London through the agency of Thomas Pringle, secretary of the Anti-Slavery Society. The product of an unequal collaboration, it was transcribed from Prince's dictation by her amanuensis Susanna Strickland, and is a text which tells the story of a life of cruel suffering, struggle and industry intended to appeal to an abolitionist readership, yet also including some elements of Prince's resistance. In its representation of white slaveowning women it challenged and confused assumptions about the domestic civility of middle-class white women in colonial contexts.[41] From 1838 the energy of British women's abolitionism was to be directed towards North America, but it remained profoundly influential on the growth of British feminism.

The belief in the dynamic force of women's moral influence was to be widely adapted to the secular purposes of education, philanthropy and civilisation, at home and overseas. The imperial mission was not always directly related to the acquisition of territorial power or to conversion. Civilisation could also be a question of commerce and settlement. The early nineteenth century saw two major perspectives on the political

[39] Talia Schaffer, 'Taming the Tropics: Charlotte Yonge takes on Melanesia', *Victorian Studies*, 47 (2005), 204–14.

[40] Clare Midgley, *Women Against Slavery: The British Campaigns, 1780–1870* (London, 1992), 29–35, 93–103; Moira Ferguson, *Subject to Others: British Women Writers and Colonial Slavery, 1670–1834* (London, 1992), 218–20, 249–71.

[41] Gillian Whitlock, *The Intimate Empire: Reading Women's Autobiography* (London, 2000), ch. 1; Moira Ferguson (ed.), *The History of Mary Prince, A West Indian Slave, Narrated by Herself* (Ann Arbor, 1997), Introduction.

economy of empire. One, still following Adam Smith, saw Britain exercising an informal economic dominance throughout the world, through industrial strength rather than colonial possessions. The other, associated with Edward Gibbon Wakefield, adapted Malthus' critique of industrial expansion and population growth to suggest continuing prosperity for Britain would require colonisation and emigration to create secure markets and outlets for population.

Women writers engaged with these issues, initially mainly through moral and didactic tales. The writer Mary Leman Grimstone spent four years from 1826 to 1829 in Tasmania, then Van Dieman's Land and still a penal colony.[42] In 1832 she wrote of that experience in her short story 'The Settlers of Van Dieman's Land'. Her settlers created a new, prosperous and ordered estate in a remote area; but the story was about 'woman's power and woman's privilege to put her hand to the moral regeneration of the world' as Marion, the heroine, visited the most degraded convicts, and cared for the child of Alice Brien, transported from Ireland for a trifling theft, degraded and seduced. The child, Patrick, was to grow up worthy to marry Marion's own daughter, Lucy.[43]

In Harriet Martineau's didactic tales in the *Illustrations of Political Economy* (1832–4) she attempted to construct a framework for a progressive liberal civilisation, and women's place within it. Following the political economy of James Mill, she opposed trading monopolies, sympathised with Wakefield's programme for colonial reform and asserted the civilising powers of commerce.[44] In the early 1830s these principles informed her didactic fiction and here as elsewhere she advocated progressive improvement through the acquisition of knowledge, by women as well as men. 'Homes Abroad' (1832) traced the improving fortunes of young rural emigrants to Van Dieman's Land. Martineau supported well-organised voluntary, but not penal, emigration, and emphasised the extreme savagery of the indigenous inhabitants.[45] In 'Life in the Wilds' (1832), she wrote of a small British settlement in southern Africa, attacked by Bushmen in an understandable response to colonial brutalities, and reduced 'from

---

[42] Michael Roe, 'Mary Leman Grimstone (1800–1850?): For Women's Rights and Tasmanian Patriotism', *Tasmanian Historical Research Association, Papers and Proceedings*, 36 (March 1989), 9–32.

[43] Grimstone, 'The Settlers of Van Dieman's Land', *La Belle Assemblée*, 1 n.s. (November 1832), 227–31.

[44] R. K. Webb, *Harriet Martineau: A Radical Victorian* (London, 1960), 339; Claudia Orazem, *Political Economy and Fiction in the Early Works of Harriet Martineau* (Frankfort, 1999), ch. 3; Catherine Hall, 'Imperial Careering at Home: Harriet Martineau on Empire', in Alan Lester and David Lambert (eds.), *Colonial Lives across the British Empire: Imperial Careering in the Long Nineteenth Century* (Cambridge, 2006).

[45] Martineau, 'Homes Abroad', in *Illustrations of Political Economy*, 9 vols. (London, 1832), vol. IV.

a state of advanced civilisation to a primitive condition'.[46] The settlers, both men and women, used their intellectual capital to establish a suitable division of labour and generate the economic growth which could justify imperialism. 'Ireland' (1832) illustrated the exploitation of the Irish poor through the land system, though not by individual landlords, at the same time as women's domination by father and husband. The clever young Dora Sullivan did her best, by leaving school and working, to save her family from both the disastrous impositions of landlords and the mis-judgements of her father and husband. Ultimately evicted and charged with involvement with the Whiteboys, one of many secret societies seeking to redress rural grievances, she was convicted and transported. Here Martineau stressed the need for economic growth through agricultural improvement, eliminating political and religious grievances, reducing population through emigration, and, most permanently, education. Dora embodied the possibility of such changes.[47]

In the 1840s and 1850s, in radical periodicals like the *People's Journal* and *Eliza Cook's Journal*, Mary Leman Grimstone and Eliza Meteyard appealed to artisan family values and discussed women's work and responsibilities. In 1846–7, Grimstone, by then an Owenite and a fem-inist, reprinted her 'Settlers of Van Dieman's Land' in the *People's Journal*, with other tales of Tasmania, 'The Heroine of the Huon' and 'Kate of Kildare: A Wife's Trials and Triumphs'.[48] Eliza Meteyard wrote of the possibilities for emigration for women in *Eliza Cook's Journal*. She prefixed to her story, 'Lucy Dean, the Noble Needlewoman' (1850), the words of Wakefield:

In trade, navigation, war and politics – in all business of a public nature, except works of benevolence and colonization – the stronger sex alone take an active part; but in colonization, women have a part so important that all depends on their participation in the work.[49]

Lucy Dean, an impoverished needlewoman, found work, prosperity and a husband in the mining districts of Australia, and returned to establish, with her benefactor, the saintly Mary Austen, an emigration scheme for

[46] 'Life in the Wilds', in Deborah Logan (ed.), *Harriet Martineau's Writing on the British Empire*, 5 vols. (London, 2004), vol. I, 14.

[47] 'Ireland', in *ibid.*, vol. IV, 5–69.

[48] Grimstone, 'Heroine of the Huon' and 'Van Dieman's Land, A Passage of Domestic History', *People's Journal*, 1 (1846), 50–2 and 289–92; 'Kate of Kildare: A Wife's Trials and Triumphs', *People's Journal*, 2 (1847), 249–51, 255–6.

[49] Edward Gibbon Wakefield, *A View of the Art of Colonization* (London, 1849), 155, quoted in 'Silverpen' (Eliza Meteyard), 'Lucy Dean: The Noble Needlewoman', *Eliza Cook's Journal*, 46–51 (March–April 1850), 312–16, 329–31, 340–3, 360–4, 376–9, 393–5, here 312.

the 'slaves of the needle' emphasising the opportunities open to them in the 'new world'.[50] Mary Austen was probably based upon Caroline Chisholm, the pioneer of early female emigration, as was Dickens' Mrs Jellyby in *Bleak House* (1852–3).[51]

From the 1820s onwards, many white middle- and upper-class British women followed Maria Graham in writing of their travels. Most took particular notice of indigenous women, and of women in colonial societies. Their work, directed to a British audience, tended to define and authorise the writer as imperial subject, and to contribute to a wider debate around the condition of women in Britain. Gillian Whitlock has noted that, because of the extent of emigration in the 1830s, 'Upper Canada emerged as an extraordinary site of autobiographic writing'.[52] Susanna Strickland, Mary Prince's amanuensis, emigrated there with her husband, John Moodie, in 1832, joining other family members including her sister Catherine Parr Traill. Traill's handbook for emigrants, *The Backwoods of Canada* (1836) was followed by the publication of a series of autobiographical sketches written between 1832 and 1839 by Susanna and John Moodie, *Roughing it in the Bush* (1852). These works tended to construct the domestic woman in a new setting, drawing different distinctions to maintain a certain gentility. To the Moodies it was not the indigenous population that was marked out as the racial 'other' but the 'lively savages from the Emerald Isle', Irish men and, worse, Irish women.[53]

The literary critic Anna Jameson joined her husband, the Attorney General for Upper Canada, in 1836. She used her travel diary to confront old prejudices, doubting whether the Native American woman was 'that absolute slave, drudge, and non-entity in the community' so frequently described. She suggested that the lives of Native American women, among whom prostitution was unknown, might be favourably compared, not to those of middle- and upper-class British women, but to maids of all work and factory girls. She argued:

The true importance and real dignity of woman is everywhere, in savage and civilised communities, regulated by her capacity for being useful; or, in other words, that her condition is decided by the share she takes in providing for her own subsistence and the well-being of society as a productive labourer.[54]

---

[50] Helen Rogers, *Women and the People: Authority, Authorship and the Radical Tradition in Nineteenth-Century England* (Aldershot, 2000), 124–49; Sally Mitchell, *The Fallen Angel: Chastity, Class, and Women's Reading, 1835–1880* (Bowling Green, KY, 1981), 29–30.

[51] Mitchell, *The Fallen Angel*, 42.   [52] Whitlock, *Intimate Empire*, 46.

[53] Quoted in *ibid.*, 67.

[54] Anna Jameson, *Winter Studies and Summer Rambles in Canada*, 3 vols. (London, 1838), vol. III, 75, 311.

Returning to Britain, Jameson found her arguments widely recognised as a contribution to discussion on the rights of women.

As the numbers of British women travelling to India increased, so too did their published journals and autobiographical writings. The accounts of Emma Roberts, Mrs Meer Hassan Ali, Marianne Postans and Fanny Parks, among many others published by 1850, helped to popularise knowledge of Indian manners and customs.[55] They became informants on Indian domestic life, sometimes offering more accurate reports of secluded women's lives, sometimes responding to the role assigned to women in Hinduism and in Islam, sometimes helping to shape the continuing discussion of racial attributes.[56] Their works were widely reviewed in Britain and admired for the 'feminine' quality of their observations, even if it was sometimes suggested that their comments might come close to 'blue-stockingism'.[57]

There were orientalist elements in the representations of secluded women in these works. Emma Roberts stressed female imprisonment within Anglo-Indian society, offering only a distant perspective on the 'imprisoned women' of Benares.[58] Marianne Postans referred to 'the useless, degrading and demoralizing condition' of the women she met, yet also the gender solidarity she found in the zenana, and the business acumen of some women.[59] Mrs Meer Hassan Ali was welcomed with great kindness into her husband's family, and learnt from them much about Muslim faith and practice. She recognised and attempted to moderate the prejudices of her British readers, finding the Muslim women she met 'obedient wives, dutiful daughters, affectionate mothers, kind mistresses, sincere friends, and liberal benefactresses to the distressed poor'.[60] Fanny Parks' sensationalist title promised 'Revelations of the Zenana'. She described the zenana of her friend Colonel William Gardner, who married

---

[55] Emma Roberts, *Scenes and Characteristics of Hindostan* ... , 3 vols. (London, 1835); Mrs Meer Hassan Ali, *Observations on the Mussulmauns of India* ... (London, 1835); Marianne Postans, *Cutch, or Random Sketches, Taken During a Residence in One of the Northern Provinces of Western India* ... (London, 1839) and *Western India in 1838*, 2 vols. (London, 1839); Fanny Parks, *Wanderings of a Pilgrim in Search of the Picturesque* ... *with Revelations of Life in the Zenana*, 2 vols. (London, 1850). For a full bibliography and discussion see Raza, 'British Women Writers on India', 269–301, 455–8 and *passim*; see also Rosemary Raza, *In Their Own Words: British Women Writers on India 1740–1857* (Delhi, 2006).

[56] See Raza, *In Their Own Words*, 270–301; Indira Ghose, *Women Travellers in Colonial India* (Delhi, 1998); Leask, *Curiosity and the Aesthetics of Travel Writing*, 203–42.

[57] *Monthly Review*, 1 (1839), 2, quoted in Raza, 'British Women Writers on India', 300.

[58] Roberts, *Scenes and Characteristics*, vol. I, 239, quoted in Leask, *Curiosity and the Aesthetics of Travel Writing*, 226.

[59] Ghose, *Women Travellers*, 66–7; Postans, *Western India*, vol. II, 94–5, 102, 123.

[60] Ali, *Observations*, 313–14.

an Indian princess of Cambay, and others to whom he introduced her. Her discussion is sometimes admiring, occasionally voyeuristic, even homo-erotic, and her views on the position of Hindu and Muslim women were linked to criticisms of women's role in Britain. One reported conversation with a royal Mahratta widow compared the lives of Hindu widows with those of English wives: 'how completely *by law* they are the slaves of their husbands and how little hope there is of redress'.[61] Observing the gender relations of such a culturally different world had become inseparably intertwined with the awareness of a debate on such themes in Britain.

The poetry, novels, moral tales and travel writing discussed above were all widely reviewed in the British periodical press. Within this press, in the first half of the nineteenth century, women also addressed imperial affairs and feminist issues, some years before the establishment of feminist periodicals; much further research is needed in this area.[62] Two out-standing radical women journalists shared an awareness of the significance of Britain's imperial role for women: Harriet Martineau and Christian Isobel Johnstone. Martineau's extensive career as a journalist included wide-ranging contributions on the British Empire from 1832 onwards. In that year she wrote on the need for more information for free emigrants to Van Dieman's Land, on the potential for British colonisation to bring economic improvement in India, and on the future administration of the free labour of newly emancipated slaves in the West Indies.[63]

Johnstone, editor of *Tait's Edinburgh Magazine* from 1834 to 1846 and the only woman to edit a major Victorian periodical before the 1860s, wrote around a fifth of its articles, actively sought other women, including Martineau, as contributors and personally reviewed new women writers of the 1830s and 40s.[64] She took up a strongly anti-slavery position, assessed the potential of the Australian colonies for emigration, sympathised with Irish poverty and identified the wrongs done to indi-genous peoples in both Australia and South Africa.[65] In reviewing the

---

[61] Leask, *Curiosity and the Aesthetics of Travel Writing*, 237–8; Parks, *Wanderings of a Pilgrim*, vol. II, 8.

[62] Barbara Caine, 'Feminism, Journalism and Public Debate', in Shattock (ed.), *Women and Literature*, 99–117.

[63] Martineau, 'Van Dieman's Land' and 'Rajah Rammohun Roy on the Government and Religion of India', *Monthly Repository*, 6 (1832), 372–80 and 609–15; 'What Shall We Do with the West Indies?', *New Monthly Magazine*, 34 (May 1832), 409–13.

[64] Alexis Easley, *First-Person Anonymous: Women Writers and the Victorian Print Media, 1830–70* (Aldershot, 2004), 61–72.

[65] See Johnstone's articles in *Tait's Edinburgh Magazine* (all references are to o.s.), 'British Emigrant Colonies: New South Wales', 5 (1834), 401–19; 'Martineau's *Society in America*', 8 (July 1837), 404–24; 'Wrongs of the Caffre Nation', 8 (August 1837), 515–23; 'Abolition of Negro Apprenticeship', 9 (March 1838), 135–48; 'Alexander's *Discoveries in . . . Africa*', 9 (November 1838), 727–39; 'South

travel writers discussed above she commented particularly on their approach to the condition of women, and took especial note of Anna Jameson's view that the situation of Native American women might be no worse than that of working women in Britain.[66]

By the mid-nineteenth century, feminists who shared the political outlook of Johnstone and Martineau were drawing on the Enlightenment narrative of women's history to argue the case for women's suffrage. In her 1841 review of works on the situation of women by Martineau, Jameson and others, Margaret Mylne contrasted the freedom of the unveiled English woman with the imprisonment of the 'poor Turk confined to the harem' and argued that economic progress tended to equalise the condition of the sexes.[67] Marion Reid's *A Plea for Woman* (1843) contrasted the progress modern civilisation brought to women's place as 'the menial slave to her lord' in 'savage nations' or 'alternately his slave and his plaything' in 'barbarous states'. But, recognising the continuing 'subjugation of the sex' in the modern West, her goal remained the achievement of perfect liberty and equal rights for all adults.[68] Harriet Taylor's essay 'The Enfranchisement of Women' endorsed this. Taylor wrote of women in primitive tribes as 'the slaves of men for the purposes of labour', in Australia as well as among Native Americans, and of the 'habits of submission' of both the women and the men of Asia. If Christianity and commerce had achieved some changes in the past, further improvement required women's direct intervention. Like Reid, Taylor called for women's equality, not for them to act as 'a sentimental priesthood'.[69] But the feminism of the later nineteenth century united Enlightenment concepts of progress with its own version of woman's mission to civilise.

By 1850 what George Stocking has called the 'problem of civilisation' had been transformed, to reflect assumptions integral to middle-class reforming culture: free trade; representative government; middle-class domesticity and sexual restraint; Protestant Christianity.[70] But, increasingly,

---

Australia, and Penal Colonies', 9 (December 1838), 776–89; 'Australian Emigration', 10 (March 1839), 168–76; 'Moffat's *Missionary Labours in Southern Africa*', 13 (August and September 1842), 528–44, 597–604; 'Quaker Mission to South Africa', 15 (October 1844), 630–3.

[66] 'Miss Martineau's *Political Economy*', 1 (August 1832), 612–18; 'Anglo-Indian Society', 6 (October 1835), 683–93; 'Mrs Postans' *Cutch; or . . . Western India*' , 9 (January 1839), 28–35; 'Jameson's *Winter and Summer in Canada*', 10 (February 1839), 69–80, here 69.

[67] P.M.Y. (Margaret Mylne), 'Woman and Her Social Position', *Westminster Review*, 35 (1841), 24–52, here 32 and 35.

[68] Marion Reid, *A Plea for Woman* (Edinburgh, 1988), 2, 24.

[69] Harriet Taylor, 'The Enfranchisement of Women', *Westminster Review*, 55 (July 1851), 289–311, here 302–11.

[70] George Stocking, *Victorian Anthropology* (New York, 1987), 30–6.

empire was being defined in more sharply racial terms. By the late 1840s the notion of the Anglo-Saxon 'race' was a familiar one, and the existence of biologically determined racial differences was asserted in works such as Thomas Carlyle's 'Occasional Discourse on the Nigger Question' (1849) and Robert Knox's *Races of Men* (1850). The Indian rebellion of 1857 shocked British confidence, and the sensational reports of sexual violence against British women strengthened the sense of a crisis in imperial authority, countered by the establishment of the Indian Empire and an emphasis on the coercive and military foundations of British rule.[71] At the same time, historians were writing for the nation (as Maria Graham had for children) an English (not British) political narrative of a providentially favoured country, uniquely progressing towards greater freedom, as discussed above by Catherine Hall. Such history coexisted with an evolutionary anthropology, which appropriated the assumptions of progress and provided another means of justifying the civilising mission. These imperial concerns were incorporated into writing addressed to women. Kathryn Ledbetter has demonstrated how between 1847 and 1863 such a conservative periodical as the *Lady's Newspaper* not only discussed women's emigration but published news of colonial politics and violent military confrontations, including those in India.[72]

Harriet Martineau's later writing and journalism demonstrated her changing understanding of imperial responsibilities. She reached her widest audience in her leaders for the *Daily News*, from 1852 to 1866. The first six were on emigration to Australia, a subject on which she had lectured to her neighbours in Ambleside. She urged that not only working women but educated women should be encouraged to go, to earn their own dowries or livings.[73] Nevertheless she was much more interested in Ireland, the West Indies and, above all, India, especially from 1857. Though in her *History of British India* (1857) she wrote of Hindu civilisation as once 'nearly at the head of human civilisation for a thousand years before our own', and criticised British ignorance of India, she also wrote of 'the bottomless chasm which yawns between the interior nature

---

[71] Jenny Sharpe, *Allegories of Empire: The Figure of Woman in the Colonial Text* (Minneapolis, 1993), 58–85.

[72] Kathryn Ledbetter, 'Bonnets and Rebellions: Imperialism in the *Lady's Newspaper*', *Victorian Periodicals Review*, 37 (2004), 252–72; Nupur Chaudhuri, 'Race, Gender and Nation in *Englishwoman's Domestic Magazine* and *Queen*, 1850–1900', in Finkelstein and Peers (eds.), *Negotiating India*, 51–62.

[73] *Daily News*, 8 June 1852, in Elisabeth Sanders Arbuckle (ed.), *Harriet Martineau in the London Daily News: Selected Contributions, 1852–66* (New York, 1994), 4–8; R. K. Webb, 'Harriet Martineau's Contributions to the London *Daily News*', in *ibid.*, 317–430.

of the Asiatic and the European races', and saw 'strenuous military action' as the next inevitable stage in the imperial mission.[74] Her articles in the *Daily News* adopted a sentimental nationalism in focusing on the 'unparalleled atrocities' committed against English women and children in India in 1857.[75]

Narratives of progress, united to a Christian and civilising mission, were to strengthen the claims of white middle-class women to exercise philanthropy and authority towards the Empire as well as the nation. However, the early writings of the women's movements were cautiously conformist. The first feminist periodical, the *English Woman's Journal*, published from 1858 to 1864, limited itself to issues of education, employment and philanthropy rather than confronting the central political institutions of the nation. Although its editors were not evangelical, it was committed to a mission of moral and social improvement, to both middle- and working-class women, and it actively supported abolitionism There is, surprisingly, virtually nothing on India in its pages in these years, although its many articles on Algeria, and occasionally on Turkey, display a predictable orientalism.

However, emigration by educated women to the colonies of settlement, for gainful employment, was a constant theme. The editor of the *Journal*, Bessie Parkes, described 'judicious, well-conducted and morally guarded emigration to our colonies' as the key to the surplus of educated women in Britain.[76] Maria Rye founded the Female Middle Class Emigration Society in 1862 to promote the emigration of single educated women. The *Journal* frequently reprinted letters from emigrants and articles from correspondents on the conditions to be encountered in the colonies.[77] And considerable attention was paid to middle- and upper-class women's philanthropy in Ireland. S. Meredith, from Cork, wrote of the philanthropic work of Protestant ladies' committees, in the aftermath of the famine of 1846–7, in overseeing the labour of women and girls in producing muslin, crochet work and lace, and their entrepreneurial

---

[74] Martineau, *History of British Rule in India*, in Logan (ed.), *Martineau's Writings on the British Empire*, vol. V, 17, 142, 168.

[75] *Daily News*, 5 and 12 September 1857, quoted in Logan, 'Introduction', in *ibid.*, vol. V, xiii–xiv.

[76] *Transactions of the National Association for the Promotion of Social Science* (1860), 818, quoted in A. James Hammerton, *Emigrant Gentlewomen: Genteel Poverty and Female Emigration, 1830–1914* (London, 1979), 126–37.

[77] Maria Rye and Bessie Parkes, 'Stray Letters on the Emigration Question', *English Woman's Journal* (*EWJ*), 8 (December 1861), 237–44; 'Stray Letters on Emigration', *EWJ*, 9 (April 1862), 109–10; 'Letters on Australia and New Zealand', *EWJ*, 9 (August 1862), 407–10; 'Middle-class Female Emigration Impartially Considered . . .', *EWJ*, 10 (October 1862), 73–84.

initiatives to provide work for destitute women. This emphasis on the responsibilities of 'a well-developed female power' of philanthropy was in tune with the *Journal*'s mission. But Meredith also wrote of the differences between the pauper women of England and Ireland. Only 'intelligent female supervision' could help 'the hindrances of ignorance and poverty, found so much more in the south than the north of Ireland'.[78]

From the 1860s the women's suffrage movement focused more directly on the parliamentary institutions of the imperial nation state, in a period of growing male enfranchisement and party mobilisation. Its supporters, women and men, were in the 1860s and 70s mainly radicals and liberals from urban provincial elites, often Protestant nonconformists, united in their opposition to aristocratic dominance of central institutions. They shared a background of activism in abolitionism, campaigns for free trade, and the common interests of nonconformist Protestantism and philanthropy. Though resistant to the militarist and aristocratic aspects of the British state, these suffragists still drew upon the discourses of civilisation, the gendered histories of progress discussed above, in their writings and speeches.[79]

By the late nineteenth century, leading figures in the women's movement had developed their own nationalist and imperialist rhetoric, incorporating Britain's progressive civilising mission. Antoinette Burton's work has demonstrated the significance of the imperial mission to India for late nineteenth-century feminism. The periodicals of the British women's movement, especially the *Englishwoman's Review*, regularly reported on the situation of women in other countries across the world, in the column 'Foreign Notes and News', which by 1891 had become 'Colonial and Foreign News'. This included much detailed material on the situation of women, and progress of women's movements, in all European countries, North America and the colonies of white settlement, and on 'the status of women in uncivilised nations', particularly in India, though with reference to many societies across the world. There were debates and differences within the *Review*, though even those who evaluated most positively the condition of Indian women suggested that their education was a task to which English women should commit themselves.

---

[78] 'Female Industrial Employments in the South of Ireland', *EWJ*, 1 (July 1858), 332–8; S. C. Meredith, 'Cultivation of Female Industry in Ireland', *EWJ*, 9 (July 1862), 304–12 and 10 (September 1862), 30–9.

[79] Jane Rendall, 'Citizenship, Culture and Civilisation: The Languages of British Suffragists 1866–74', in Melanie Nolan and Caroline Daley (eds.), *Suffrage and Beyond: International Feminist Perspectives* (Auckland, 1994), 127–50.

Readers would find much in the *Review* on British women's support for
that education, as in, for example, Lady Dufferin's Fund for Female
Medical Aid. The case for medical aid justified both British women's
training in medicine and their mission to extend such training to Indian
women. Indian women's successes were reported briefly. The career of the
educated and Christian Pandita Ramabai was followed in more detail, in
ways which reflected credit on British influence. Burton suggests that the
most significant effect of the *Review* and the feminist press was the sense
of community created among its readership, an 'imagined community'
defining itself in relationship to a civilising and imperial mission to
India.[80] The *Englishwoman's Review* also reported in considerable detail
the progress of women's political demands and their ultimate successes in
New Zealand and the Australian states, contributing again to the 'imagined community' of international white feminism, still primarily Protestant. Ireland figured very prominently in the *Review*, though the
periodical was clearly identified with the unionist interest. In its response
to the formation of the Ladies Land League in 1881, the *Review* sympathised with women of the Protestant Irish gentry defending themselves
against the threat of violence.[81] However, by the end of the nineteenth
century the divisions among British feminists, liberal, radical and socialist, over imperial issues, notably Home Rule for Ireland and the Boer
War, were also apparent throughout the varied feminist press.

The nineteenth-century British women's movement was shaped by
discourses of femininity, which while emphasising the private and the
domestic also stressed women's wider moral responsibilities. From the
late eighteenth century onwards, white upper- and middle-class British
women legitimised their claims for empowerment in print, on the
grounds of their philanthropic, civilising and educational responsibilities,
in the Empire as well as in Ireland and at home. These civilising projects
were by the second half of the nineteenth century to be incorporated
within women's demands for a formal place in the imperial nation state,
demands which for the most part also rested on a gendered sense of
responsibility and, also, in differing degrees, on a collective and historic
identity with the unity of the Empire.

[80] Burton, *Burdens of History*, 97–126.
[81] Margaret Ward, 'Gendering the Union: Imperial Feminism and the Ladies' Land League',
Women's History Review, 10 (2001), 71–92, here 76.

CHAPTER SIX

Sexuality and empire

Philippa Levine

South Asian women arriving at London's airports in the late 1970s were shocked to find that they might be required to undergo a test to determine whether they had prior sexual experience. These 'virginity tests' were one of the more notorious measures pioneered to weed out 'genuine' from 'dishonest' migrants of South Asian origin. Women arriving as fiancées of South Asian men already in Britain were the targets of this practice which rested on a slew of assumptions about gender and sexuality that we can trace back with little effort to colonial days. The immigration service's position was that South Asian women entering Britain as brides would be virgins, and testing them would thus identify fake applicants for entry. While public protests and well-organised women's campaigning saw this controversial test quickly abandoned, it points nonetheless, and in vivid manner, to how ideas and assumptions about colonial sexuality found expression in Britain.[1] Examples such as this not only demonstrate the effects of its colonial past within Britain, but also reveal just how central a role sexuality has played in shaping that complex legacy.

Despite the shaping of modern Western societies around the parallel binaries of public and private and of male and female, the allegedly private world of sexuality has constantly blurred those always unstable boundaries. Fears around sexuality derive as much from the challenge this instability offers to a simple division of male and female worlds as they do from the religious proscriptions and prescriptions which have linked procreation and sexuality so tightly. Moreover, this inability to make distinctions effective and fixed lies at the heart of the relationship between sexuality and colonialism, and offers a window on to why sexuality was so prominent among the anxieties associated with imperialism. Ann Laura Stoler has convincingly argued that discourses of sexuality traced through imperial routes 'have mapped the moral parameters of European nations', establishing a deep connection that traces the effects of empire

---

[1] See, for example, the articles reprinted in *The Spare Rib Reader*, ed. Marsha Rowe (Harmondsworth, 1981), 501–3.

at its very centre, and which suggests the pliability of sexual values and practices.[2]

Sexuality is a sometimes slippery and certainly a much contested term. Here I take it to signify not a biological category, but a social and cultural one, a set of infinitely flexible practices for making sense of desire. In the Christian-imbued environment of imperial Britain, desire was something to be restrained and controlled lest it overwhelm its metaphoric opposite: reason. The regimes of bodily discipline produced in the imperial era (regulating age of consent and marriage, sexual partnering, auto-eroticism and much, much more) suggest the centrality of sexuality in both public and private realms. Robert Young's point that British literature in the imperial period was endlessly concerned with interracial sexual liaisons points us to the racial character of these bodily disciplines, while Anne McClintock's work illuminates their gendered specificities.[3] This potent coming together of some of the most anxiety-ridden social questions of the day (around race, gender and sex) produced a distinctive attention to colonial sexualities (real and imagined, bodily and fantastical) with significant implications within Britain.

Fears and laws around sexuality almost invariably focused on the control of women, and it is in this association of women and sexuality that colonial thinking about sexuality was shaped. Whether it was a fear of the sexualised woman who had stepped beyond male authority or whether, conversely, it was a fear that the traditionally meek woman would be sexually violated by lawless and lustful colonials, these anxieties made sex a key site of imperial fear, concern and action. Such colonially imbued apprehensiveness was not limited to far-flung outposts, but had considerable and tenacious purchase within Britain as well.

In the decades after the Second World War, and at the height of British decolonisation, British immigration was concerned largely with questions of labour, and the typical colonial immigrant was depicted as a wage-earning man, either single or with a family left behind in his place of origin. Immigration law, while increasingly preoccupied with controlling how many 'non-whites'[4] entered the country, devolved largely on the apportioning of work-specific vouchers. Men, as the primary

---

[2] Ann L. Stoler, *Race and the Education of Desire: Foucault's History of Sexuality and the Colonial Order of Things* (Durham, NC, 1995), 7.

[3] Robert J. C. Young, *Colonial Desire: Hybridity in Theory, Culture and Race* (London, 1995), 2–3; Anne McClintock, *Imperial Leather: Race, Gender and Sexuality in the Colonial Context* (New York, 1995), 5.

[4] This homogenising language – of white and 'non-white' – reflects the lamentable tendency so common in both colonial and postcolonial periods to lump together a significant diversity of peoples, linked largely by their experience of a coercive colonialism. Its use is, I think, significant,

migrants, were the principal targets of immigration control. In the 1970s, the balance began to shift as these men, now established in Britain, sought to bring in their kin. The focus of immigration law moved towards 'secondary' migration, the entrance into Britain of women from colonies and former colonies – as wives and as brides. Upholding a vision of traditional sexual roles which allotted men to the labour force and women to domesticity, the immigration service paid increasing attention to family settlement. Following the uproar over virginity testing, a new rule, the 'primary purpose' rule, was introduced in 1980 and enshrined in the 1981 British Nationality Act. Its intent was to assess whether a marriage was merely a ruse for attaining otherwise unallowable residence rights in Britain. The new rule gave immigration officials the power to define what constituted a real marriage; cultural differences in what a marriage was and what it looked like were swamped by the views and opinions of those charged with 'protecting' British boundaries. Profound double standards ensued; South Asian women engaged to be married had to be virgins, a requirement attached to no other women in late twentieth-century Britain.

This reading of South Asian culture as conservative and restrictive to women followed a long-standing colonial path of deeming Indian as well as other colonial cultures as narrowly confining women, and therefore as backward and unmodern. This view highlighted some critical assumptions about colonial sexuality that coloured domestic policy. Critically it tended to treat as a homogeneous mass South Asian immigrants from markedly different regions and cultures. Many South Asians who came to England after the 1960s knew little more of India than the officials assessing them. Never resident in India, they came to Britain after being expelled from former British colonies in Africa. The embracing of a nationalist Pan-Africanism in those countries left no room for the long-settled Indian communities, now regarded as an unwelcome legacy of colonial days.

British immigration officials saw this imaginary Indian monoculture as more controlling of female sexuality than British society, an assumption highlighting the link between colonialism and sexuality. From at least the eighteenth century, scientists and philosophers had associated a society's civilisational capacity with its treatment of women.[5] James Mill's is only the most famous of many similar utterances: 'Among rude people, the women are generally degraded; among civilised people they are exalted.'[6]

---

for it reveals the ways in which colonising powers stripped the colonised of their specificities, and by extension, of their humanity.

[5] See Jane Rendall's chapter in this volume.

[6] James Mill, *History of British India* (1818), 2 vols. (New York, 1968), 309–10.

The more brutal the treatment of women, went colonial thinking, the more primitive the society. But brutality could take many guises and a tight rein on female sexuality (the virginal bride) was only one variant on a theme of extraordinary malleability. Primitive societies were seen to cloister women and to routinise unchastity, both evidence of uncivilised behaviours. Nineteenth-century accounts of colonial societies are full of tales of Aboriginal men selling their womenfolk to Japanese pearl divers for the season, and of 'castes' in India in which prostitution was the occupation demanded of women.[7] These dread stories existed alongside equally breathless tales of women captive in harems and in purdah, unable to walk alone or without heavy clothing to hide them from the public eye.[8] A fear that Britons would be affected or infected by foreign immorality haunts the literature as early as the eighteenth century, and, I would argue, continues to influence the anti-immigration sentiments that emerged so powerfully in postwar Britain. That women, and women's sexuality most critically, became central to an immigration policy avowedly centred on labour availability, is more than mere accident: it cements the critical links between sexuality and politics. And in this instance it also lays bare how much colonial attitudes continued to haunt postcolonial Britain.

Reconciling the contrasting attitudes of colonial conservatism and colonial over-sexedness is not as difficult as it might seem at first glance: these were stereotypes, albeit highly polarised ones, which functioned to separate British rationality from the allegedly passionate unreason and unruliness of colonials; their lack of reason in the sexual arena mirrored colonial incapacity for self-rule. It is by no means insignificant that when commentators talked of colonial sexualities, it was seldom of white Australians and Canadians, but of peoples of colour, separated from white settlers by temperament and physical features, and by distinctive attitudes to sexuality and to nudity. Sexuality was a deep measure for the British of colonial otherness. The settler colonies in general were regarded as slightly inferior versions of Britain itself, where British values and social structures could, among settler populations, be successfully replicated. Yet fears around colonial sexuality nonetheless followed, more particularly where settler populations lived in tropical climates and among 'native' peoples. There was a constant concern, official and otherwise, about how

---

[7] For multiple examples see Philippa Levine, *Prostitution, Race and Politics: Policing Venereal Disease in the British Empire* (New York, 2003).

[8] Janaki Nair, 'Uncovering the Zenana: Visions of Indian Womanhood in Englishwomen's Writings, 1813–1940', *Journal of Women's History*, 2 (1) (1990), 8–34.

far the habits and morals associated with the allegedly libidinous tropics would rub off on the new residents. In northern Australia and in South Africa, in particular, these anxieties bubbled beneath the surface constantly, rising occasionally to a greater visibility, mostly over questions of labour and of sexuality. Some of the Australian colonial legislatures in the 1890s debated whether female age of consent laws should mirror those recently passed in Britain, since many believed that the age of menarche came earlier to youngsters raised in warmer climes.[9] Such ideas grew directly from notions of colonial sexuality forged in Britain and dependent on a vision of colonial sexual 'otherness'.

As early as the seventeenth century, in Britain and in Europe, the display of Africans and other 'exotics' was commercially successful. So-called pygmies, Zulu warriors, women with large buttocks all joined the display for profit that also exhibited those with spectacular medical conditions such as elephantiasis.[10] It was a craze that brought considerable gain to entrepreneurs in Britain, continental Europe and the United States.[11] The best known of these human exhibits was Sara (also called Saartjie by her Dutch masters at the Cape) Baartman who was shown in Britain and in France from 1810 and, sporadically, until her early death in 1816. Shrewdly advertised as the 'Hottentot Venus', Baartman's sexual characteristics were thus marketed and signalled up front as the attraction; engravings, cartoons and prints from the period emphasise that she was presented in scanty dress designed to draw attention to her breasts, genitals and buttocks.[12] Baartman's display is in a sense a commercialised culmination of some centuries' worth of sexual fascination with female colonial sexuality. Rumours regarding South African sexual difference from Europeans can be traced back at least to the seventeenth century.

---

[9] Ross Barber, 'The Criminal Law Amendment Act of 1891 and the "Age of Consent" Issue in Queensland', *Australia and New Zealand Journal of Criminology*, 10 (1977), 95–113; *Queensland Parliamentary Debates* 1887 (LII), 1889 (LVIII), 1891 (CXIII).

[10] Richard D. Altick, *The Shows of London* (Cambridge, 1978); Susan Stewart, *On Longing* (Durham, 1993); Rosemarie Garland Thomson (ed.), *Freakery: Cultural Spectacles of the Extraordinary Body* (New York, 1996).

[11] Bernth Lindfors, '"The Hottentot Venus" and Other African Attractions in Nineteenth-Century England', *Australasian Drama Studies*, 1 (2) (1983), 83–104; Anne Fausto-Sterling, 'Gender, Race, and Nation: The Comparative Anatomy of "Hottentot" Women in Europe, 1815–17', in Kimberley Wallace (ed.), *Skin Deep, Spirit Strong: The Black Female Body in American Culture* (Ann Arbor, 2002), 78.

[12] Z. S. Strother, 'Display of the Body Hottentot', in Bernth Lindfors (ed.), *Africans on Stage: Studies in Ethnological Show Business* (Bloomington, 1999), 25. See, too, Sander L. Gilman 'Black Bodies, White Bodies: Toward an Iconography of Female Sexuality in Late Nineteenth-Century Art, Medicine, and Literature', in Henry Louis Gates (ed.), *'Race', Writing and Difference* (Chicago, 1986), 223–61.

The term 'Hottentot' used to describe the Khoisan peoples of the Cape of Good Hope has an even longer lineage but, according to Linda Merians, an interest in their genitalia dates only from the late seventeenth century.[13] The earliest interest of Europeans in the Khoisan was prompted not by the women, but by the practice among Khoisan men of removing one testicle. The 1797 edition of the *Encyclopaedia Britannica* lists the Hottentots as among the class of 'Monsters', 'having one testicle extirpated'.[14] In the 1842 edition, the interest in the men has disappeared, but the 'protuberances' of the women are noted as common.[15]

Colonial sexualities were thus pathologised in part through an excessive attention to the physical aspects of colonial peoples, most especially their genitals, and partly through the association of lechery with primitiveness. Yvette Abrahams sees Baartman's exhibition in Europe as 'the turning point toward exhibiting the savage as raw sexuality'.[16] The primary reading of colonised peoples through their sexuality reinforced existing hierarchies. The suspicion that 'primitive' peoples would sport equally primitive genitalia lay at the heart of the fascination with the ill-fated Baartman.[17] Her alleged labial apron, hanging down almost like a flaccid penis, raised not only the spectre of the masculinised woman whose sexual organs were not easily distinguishable from those of men, but, equally critically, of a wholly different sexuality, separate from that of the West. A prominent, unrefined, outsized set of genitals could thus signify the larger coarseness of the 'primitive', too preoccupied with the world of the flesh to muster much concern for the reason of the West. The colonial world was fecund and lush, it was highly charged and over-abundant, and even where it was settled by Britons the local environment had to be tamed if it was not to overcome the frail but essential ties to civilisation. This critical separation of passion and reason, of the sexual and the rational, made colonial sexualities always something to be feared and to be leashed.

The sexuality and sexual behaviour of colonial women of colour was always prominent in the accounts of travellers. Certainly dress styles and more relaxed attitudes to the body contributed to British attention to

[13] Linda E. Merians, *Envisioning the Worst: Representations of 'Hottentots' in Early-modern England* (Newark, London and Cranbury, 2001), 130.

[14] 'Man', *Encyclopaedia Britannica*, 3rd edn (1797), vol. X, 508.

[15] 'Africa', *ibid.*, 7th edn, (1842), vol. II, 226.

[16] Yvette Abrahams, 'Images of Sara Bartman: Sexuality, Race and Gender in Early Nineteenth-Century Britain', in Ruth Roach Pierson and Nupur Chaudhuri (eds.), *Nation, Empire, Colony: Historicizing Gender and Race* (Bloomington, 1998), 227.

[17] T. Denean Sharpley-Whiting, *Black Venus: Sexualized Savages, Primal Fears, and Primitive Narratives in French* (Durham, 1999), 29.

these matters, but more was at work than the titillation offered observers
more used to the clothed female body. As Jennifer Morgan has argued,
'Europe had a long tradition of identifying others through the monstrous
physiognomy and sexual behavior of women', a foil against which proper,
ordered, civilised whiteness – in this case, Englishness – could be measured.[18] The complex ways in which nature was figured as female and thus
controllable and exploitable were deeply significant here, blending not
always consciously with the associations between colonialism and conquest that grew so rapidly from the eighteenth century.[19] It is no small
coincidence that European philosophy in the eighteenth century stressed
the potency of classificatory knowledge as the means to control nature
at much the same moment as European colonialism expanded its grip
on the world. Colonial sources and resources were crucial to both commercial and intellectual enterprises; Anne Fausto-Sterling argues that
scientific interest in Sara Baartman's body was shaped by colonial
expansion, which from its beginnings had been preoccupied with sexual
difference. And Baartman's body was also a site of both commercial and
intellectual exploitation within a frame only made possible by the impact
of imperialism in the region of her birth.[20] Paula Giddings notes that
interest in Baartman's body coincided with debates over slavery and the
slave trade, an association which further underscores the link between
colonialism and the 'monstrous' reading of colonial sexuality.[21] Likewise,
the Cape was, at the time of Baartman's initial showing in London, one
of Britain's newest colonies (1806), and one where missionary activism had
gained special protective status for the Khoisan in light of Dutch brutality.
These were bodies that could be held in colonial power, sometimes for
profit, sometimes for protection – and they were highly sexualised bodies,
as the long-standing attention to 'Hottentot' genitalia suggests.

   The contrast invoked by Baartman's display in London and in Paris
was between civilisation and barbarism, between reason and passion,
between beauty and monstrosity. Sexuality crystallised all of these factors,
acting as a cipher for critiques of the colonial, also already feminised in

---

[18] Jennifer L. Morgan, ' "Some Could Suckle over Their Shoulder": Male Travelers, Female Bodies,
   and the Gendering of Racial Ideology, 1500–1770', *William and Mary Quarterly*, 54 (1) (3rd ser.)
   (1997), 170.
[19] Carolyn Merchant, *The Death of Nature: Women, Ecology, and the Scientific Revolution* (San
   Francisco, 1980).
[20] Fausto-Sterling, 'Gender, Race, and Nation', 67.
[21] Paula Giddings, 'The Last Taboo', in Toni Morrison (ed.), *Race-ing Justice, En-Gendering Power:
   Essays on Anita Hill, Clarence Thomas and the Construction of Social Reality* (New York, 1992), 444
   and 445.

Western eyes by the fact of conquest. Throughout the colonial period, in Britain as well as in the colonies, sexuality, then, was the literal subject of an endlessly mapped metaphor for the necessity of colonial rule. But how did this operate in Britain itself? Clearly, the exhibiting of women like Baartman reinforced a notion of sexual difference between the British and those they colonised, a difference with a critical aesthetic quality. Whether we turn to the pages of late eighteenth- and nineteenth-century natural history or to the sketches made by the minor civil servant Arthur Munby in the 1870s, what becomes apparent is a widespread concern in Britain with the relationship between race, sexuality and beauty. The colonised were depicted as ugly by comparison with the refinements of European features. They were simian more than human in their resemblance. Munby's sketches of the Wigan pitbrow lasses are extraordinary in this regard, and though I would be wary of seeing Munby as an archetype of British maleness in the Victorian era, the seemingly unconscious reproduction of this aesthetic in his realist drawings is worth some attention.[22] Griselda Pollock maintains that Munby's portraits of begrimed northern women labouring at the English coalface are 'so other than the white femininity they opposed, they can only be imagined in the racist stereotypes created by an imperial bourgeoisie for its colonised other'.[23] Yet, as Pollock reminds us, Munby's written descriptions emphasise the humane and sociable qualities of women figured in his drawings as part-animal, part-African. It was in the ways that Munby imagined this nexus of class, race and gender that many in Britain understood empire *as* sexuality, in which everything about and in the colonies took on a sexualised quality.

Munby famously, although at the time secretly, married maidservant Hannah Cullwick in 1873. Their life together suggests the deep links between an eroticised colonialism and nineteenth-century sexual fantasies. Photographs of Hannah, naked and posed as a slave, the use of 'Massa' (master) as her endearment for Munby, the 'slave straps' Cullwick wore around her wrist and neck for him (and which in 1864 got her fired from a job) closely link their sexual fantasies to the world of colonial slavery as they imagined it. Blackness, mastery, submission, loyalty all

---

[22] For details of Munby's life, see Derek Hudson, *Man of Two Worlds: The Life and Diaries of Arthur J. Munby* (London, 1972), and Leonore Davidoff, 'Class and Gender in Victorian England', in Judith L. Newton, Mary P. Ryan and Judith R. Walkowitz (eds.), *Sex and Class in Women's History* (London, 1983), 17–71.

[23] Griselda Pollock, 'The Dangers of Proximity: The Spaces of Sexuality and Surveillance in Word and Image', *Discourse* 16 (2) (1993–4), 42.

figure in this sexual play, although as Carol Mavor rightly reminds us the choice of sexual play was, in this relationship, often mutual.[24] Certainly Munby, a keen photographer, also took pictures of Cullwick in many other poses – but when she posed as a man, as an angel or as a 'lady' she was fully clothed and also cleaned, no trace of 'black' about her.

William Sharpe, writing in 1879 on *The Cause of Colour Among Races*, argued that darkened skin, which he declared ugly, was the result of civilisational deterioration. His fear that similar degeneration was now 'common in the very heart of our European civilization' brought the fears so central to this notion literally to the centre of the Empire.[25] It was a commonplace of the period to see the poor as akin to savages, a parallel much more common in the age of high imperialism than in earlier eras. And such correspondence rested more often than not on sexual analogies: race was frequently defined through and around sex, as much as, and sometimes more than, via such visible signifiers as skin colour. Depictions of Cullwick in these various guises neatly demonstrate this reading of sexual difference through race.

Working-class women were also regarded as closer to the colonised – in their sexual habits, sexual preferences, allegedly greater libido and apparent lack of modesty. In a variety of settings, as we shall see, British authorities thought it prudent to maintain as wide a separation as possible between working-class British women and colonial men, lest they cross forbidden racial and sexual boundaries. This was a policy adhered to in both colonial and domestic sites. But since so many more white women were located in Britain, this was a question of particular concern at home.

One of the most common arenas in which we find this anxiety over colonial sexuality expressed at home is in discussions around prostitution. It was a nineteenth-century commonplace that large numbers of Britain's, and especially London's, sex workers were foreigners. Equally, the innocents of rural England were said to be easy prey for foreign traffickers, mostly figured as east-European Jews or Frenchmen. Alongside these xenophobic imaginings of commercialised sexuality as an un-British phenomenon was a growing debate about the effects of colonial prostitution regimes on and within Britain. This was of particular concern in the later nineteenth and early twentieth centuries as more soldiers were posted to colonies where a military brothel system, official or otherwise,

---

[24] Carol Mavor, *Pleasures Taken: Performances of Sexuality and Loss in Victorian Photographs* (Durham, 1995), esp. 86.
[25] William Sharpe, *The Cause of Colour Among Races, and the Evolution of Physical Beauty* (London, 1879), esp. 12–13.

gave them easy and regulated access to the purchase of heterosexual sex.[26] The champions of regulated colonial prostitution argued that without British oversight, the men would contract tropical versions of sexually transmissible diseases far more dangerous than domestic varieties, equating tropical and colonial sexuality with a greater element of peril. Others saw a different risk: that men's sexual associations with non-white women would damage or undo their Britishness. Though emphasising different aspects of the supposed sexual hazards involved, fears of colonial sexuality in this arena rested on what the colonies might import into Britain to unsettle domestic sexualities.

These distinctions shaped by colonialism operated within the British sex trade too, and not only in the desire to present prostitution as a foreign import. Commentators in the nineteenth century charged that only the Irish among Britain's prostitutes were willing to entertain as clients the black colonial seamen who docked at Britain's port cities. Liverpool doctor Frederick Lowndes describes three streets in Liverpool's dock area where Irish prostitutes worked in what Lowndes called 'black men's brothels'.[27] The double bind of colonialism is vividly apparent in his claim, which probably had some truth to it. Prostitutes certainly did seek status – and higher earnings – through their clients, and servicing black sailors would have raised neither a woman's standing in white eyes nor her income. It is quite likely that Irish women in cities such as Liverpool and London, already subject to English prejudice, needed such clients to make ends meet, and took them precisely because neither they nor their black clients were welcome elsewhere.

Colonial attitudes to the Irish had for centuries equated them with savagery. They had been drawn as different in kind from Britons, and thus a 'race' suited to colonisation. A black clientele in sex work may well have seemed natural to those for whom colonial subjection equalled difference. The severe famine in the 1840s, which prompted substantial Irish migration to England, must surely have underlined existing prejudices that saw the Irish as different and lesser. The political economists of the nineteenth century, mindful of Irish Catholicism, declared the Irish an improvident people whose overpopulation was to blame for the

---

[26] Kenneth Ballhatchet, *Race, Sex and Class Under the British Raj: Imperial Attitudes and Policies and their Critics, 1793–1905* (London, 1980); Levine, *Prostitution, Race, and Politics*; David J. Pivar, 'The Military, Prostitution, and Colonial Peoples: India and the Philippines, 1885–1917', *Journal of Sex Research*, 17 (3) (1981), 256–69; Douglas M. Peers, 'Privates off Parade: Regimenting Sexuality in the Nineteenth-Century Indian Empire', *International History Review*, 20 (4) (1998), 823–54.

[27] Frederick W. Lowndes, *Prostitution and Syphilis in Liverpool, and the Working of the Contagious Diseases Acts at Aldershot, Chatham, Plymouth and Devonport* (London, 1876), 8.

famine.[28] Excess population, of course, rested on a concomitant belief in sexual excess, an absolutely typical reading of colonial sexualities more generally. Non-Protestant, other than white, subject peoples were frequently and enthusiastically defined by and through their fecund and unseemly sexuality which many feared would penetrate and wreck rational, temperate, moderate Britain.

Anne McClintock sees the prostitute as 'the metropolitan analogue of African promiscuity', a troubling reminder of the need to control sexuality, especially female and colonial sexualities.[29] McClintock's argument is grounded in a broader literature which explores the African presence as representative of abnormality and indeed monstrosity in European and American discourse, yet it is too broad a generalisation to satisfy.[30] If we extend the argument more broadly, the point remains viable, for the association of promiscuity and colonial society was a constant theme in Britain. We can also see such parallels at repressive work in the related arena of what was popularly called the 'white slave trade' in the late nineteenth and early twentieth centuries. The term had been coined in the mid-nineteenth century to draw attention to the dreadful conditions of women mill and textile workers, which protesters claimed were akin to those endured by plantation slaves, but came instead to connote sexual enslavement. Thoroughly imbued with a narrative of the innocent girl victims of unscrupulous sex traders, the white slave trade panic grew in to a huge political issue by the early twentieth century. Despite a striking paucity of hard evidence and few successful prosecutions, the woeful tale of the uninitiated girl lured into sex work by harsh profiteers became a dramatic commonplace of journalism, fiction, morality literature, theatre and education. It acquired a distinctively colonial face not only when white women occasionally turned up in colonial brothels, but also in white settler colonies where non-British migrants were regarded as likely slave traders of local white girls.[31] In British Columbia, in western Canada, for example, early twentieth-century ordinances prohibited Chinese men from employing white women in their businesses, restricting alike women's employment opportunities and Chinese business

---

[28] Patrick Brantlinger, *Dark Vanishings: Discourse on the Extinction of Primitive Races, 1800–1930* (Ithaca, 2003), ch. 5, esp. 108–9.

[29] McClintock, *Imperial Leather*, 56.

[30] Toni Morrison, *Playing in the Dark: Whiteness and the Literary Imagination* (Cambridge, MA, 1992) and Jan Niederven Pieterse, *White on Black: Images of Africa and Blacks in Western Popular Culture* (New Haven, 1992); Morgan, 'Some Could Suckle'.

[31] Philippa Levine, 'The White Slave Trade and the British Empire', *Criminal Justice History*, 17 (2002), 133–46.

growth.[32] The link to Britain was virtually seamless. In the race riots that rocked Cardiff in 1919, one instigator of the violence claimed to have seen 'little white girls, some no more than thirteen years old, running out' of the houses of Chinese men.[33] The white slave trade narrative, with its bifurcated vision of passive and innocent girls ensnared by aggressive and amoral desires – profits on the part of their keepers, sexual arousal on the part of their clients – secured a tale of colonial and foreign sexuality as preying on feminine British innocence.

In the British context, the control of colonial sexuality was exercised well beyond the quite narrow community of prostitution. The lives of colonials resident in Britain were by the early twentieth century closely managed. With the exception of the Jews and the Irish, migrants entering Britain prior to the 1970s were predominantly male.[34] This was so for Europeans and non-Europeans alike, but women were an even smaller percentage of colonial migrants of colour than of white migrants, reflecting the gendered economic opportunities in Britain. While the numbers of migrant men of colour remained quite small, especially before the 1950s, there was nonetheless a constant rumbling disquiet about their potential and actual relations with white women. Ian Spencer notes the widespread suspicion in Britain that West Indian men lived largely off the earnings of women prostitutes.[35] Such a myth neatly coincided, of course, with the strong belief that British prostitution was controlled by foreigners. The Chief Constable of the Metropolitan Police's Criminal Investigation Division, F. S. Bullock, reported rather proudly in 1907 that the men who ran the sex trade 'are, almost without exception of foreign nationality, and their occupation is repugnant to men of English race'.[36] The assumption was self-fulfilling; the returns of the Marlborough Street police court in London in 1917 show that virtually all of the defendants charged with brothel-keeping were foreign.[37]

But while prostitution could be read as an unnatural and un-British state forced upon vulnerable innocents, interracial liaisons between

---

[32] Constance Backhouse, *Colour-coded: A Legal History of Racism in Canada, 1900–1950* (Toronto, 1999).

[33] Joanne M. Cayford, 'In Search of "John Chinaman": Press Representations of the Chinese in Cardiff, 1906–1911', *Llafur: Journal of Welsh Labour History*, 5 (4) (1991), 46, quoting Edward Tupper.

[34] Panikos Panayi, *Immigration, Ethnicity and Racism in Britain, 1815–1945* (Manchester, 1994), 58.

[35] Ian R. G. Spencer, *British Immigration Policy since 1939: The Making of Multi-Racial Britain* (London, 1997), 79, 111.

[36] National Archives, London (hereinafter NA). MEPO2/558. PP (Cd. 3453) Misc. No. 2 (1907). *Correspondence Respecting the International Conference on the White Slave Traffic Held in Paris, October 1906*, Annex 1.

[37] NA. HO45/10837/331148 (19).

British women and colonial men living in Britain were harder to gloss. As we shall see, such relationships helped spark the widespread race riots of 1919, but the antipathy to mixed-race sexual intimacies went well beyond popular anger, and had a long history. Paul Edwards and James Walvin have found pamphlet evidence of public antipathy to sexual associations between British women and black men in late eighteenth-century Britain.[38] Accounts of city slums in Britain frequently alluded to interracial intimacy; women associated with migrant colonial men were 'degraded, even below the degradation of such a neighbourhood'.[39] Laura Tabili's work on the white British wives of Somali men reveals the anxieties which surrounded these relationships, and illuminates the fault lines of the colonial state in its dealing with sexuality.[40] The colonially inflected association of British womanhood with sexual restraint and propriety unravelled when women took as sexual partners men identified (by their colonial taint) as overly sexed and un-British. Such partnerings not only reimagined British female sexuality, but implied active choice on the part of women, another cause for colonial and patriarchal alarm.

Relations between white women and men of colour were always regarded with greater unease than the relationships white men had with colonised women. The latter were frequently written off as an inevitable by-product of normative male sexuality. This distinctive double standard, which, in essence, licensed white male heterosexuality to seek out any and all avenues of desire, reinforces the associations between sexuality and race never far from the surface in the imperial context. Ideas about, opinions of and studies in colonial sexuality invariably referenced and rested upon racial considerations. That these considerations were also always gendered in ways that permitted and indeed naturalised greater (hetero)sexual freedom for men is equally critical in unpacking the hierarchies which governed the era of British colonialism, itself an enterprise conceived as fundamentally and naturally masculine. Gender divisions thus worked to reinforce colonial hierarchies. Colonial conquest, symbolised by white men's sexual relations with colonised women, could not be safely reversed. White women choosing relationships with colonial men implied danger to

---

[38] Paul Edwards and James Walvin, *Black Personalities in the Era of the Slave Trade* (Baton Rouge, 1983), 20.

[39] Thomas Archer, *The Pauper, the Thief and the Convict: Sketches of Some of their Homes, Haunts and Habits* (London, 1865), 133, quoted in John Marriott, 'In Darkest England: The Poor, the Crowd and Race in the Nineteenth-Century Metropolis', in Phil Cohen (ed.), *New Ethnicities, Old Racisms?* (London, 1999), 89.

[40] Laura Tabili, 'Empire is the Enemy of Love: Edith Noor's Progress and Other Stories', *Gender and History*, 17 (1) (2005), 5–28.

the colonial state and to white men's supremacy. Such liaisons had to be signalled as deviant and disorderly, while white men sleeping with women of colour was seen merely as a natural extension of their residence in the colonies, and certainly as greatly preferable to the prospect of male–male sexual encounters which would wholly have undone the colonial hier- archies so carefully constructed and constrained by these gendered orders.

Within Britain, interracial relationships between white women and colonial men of colour were reasonably commonplace. Unions between mostly poor, white British women and black colonial subjects were regarded by the Colonial Office as 'very undesirable'.[41] This disapproval is part of the long-standing debate over the immigration of men from the overseas colonies into Britain. While in the late twentieth century the principal fear was that their presence would lead to an increase in the migrant population, at the start of the century it was fears that such male migrants would 'steal' local women away that prompted attention. In both instances, tellingly, sexual anxieties lay at the base of policy decisions as well as of public reaction.

Throughout the period of colonialism, men (far more than women) had drifted from the British colonies into Britain itself, sometimes remaining for long periods. Many had arrived as workers aboard ships, and British shipping firms often actively recruited in the colonies for menial workers for shipboard labour. They were a cheap source of labour, and less likely than Britons to have been exposed to organised trade unionism. During the First World War, colonial workers staffed the merchant ships as British sailors joined up or were conscripted into the Navy. Others came to Britain to work in the factories where the increased demands of wartime welcomed their labour, alongside that of local women. When war-driven manufacturing contracted in late 1918, colonial workers found themselves, like British women, out of work. Many moved to the port cities of Britain, hoping to find shipboard work that might earn them a passage home, or at least a wage. Others, having entered into relationships with local women, were committed to staying in Britain. Both paths fuelled resentment. In the first six months of 1919, Britain experienced a series of race riots frequently catalysed by sexual compe- tition, and which can be understood only against the backdrop of British exploitation of this colonial male workforce. In Cardiff most notoriously, but also in South Shields in February, in Salford in March, in London in April, in Liverpool in the early summer and in Glasgow in June, violence

---

[41] NA. CO535/72/4296, quoted in Tabili, 8, n. 16.

erupted in working-class areas.[42] Houses were sacked and burned, black men were chased and attacked, and white women known to have black partners were assailed for their choice. The riots were not focused exclusively on interracial sexual liaisons; broader racism as well as economic antagonism also kindled these hostilities, but sex was always central. Neil Evans has found that in South Wales '[C]ompetition for jobs, homes, and women were the crucial factors in 1919.'[43] And Bill Schwarz notes that 'all pretence of English civility collapsed at the point when black men were seen to be with white women'.[44]

The year 1919 was the culmination of a longer-term resentment which wartime conditions helped exacerbate. The widespread use in the war of colonial soldiers, in combat and more commonly as labour crews, had spurred attention to the association of local women with visiting soldiers and sailors.[45] Colonial soldiers were a common sight in Britain in the war years, although only those from the Dominions could move freely among the local populace. There was widespread resentment that the better-paid Canadian, New Zealand and Australian servicemen could treat women more generously than could their British counterparts, and there was a parallel alarm at the high rates of sexually transmissible infections among this Dominion soldiery.[46] It was, in fact, a major source of strain between British and colonial politicians, frequently under discussion at the Imperial Conferences in London during the war years.[47] Yet sexual relations between men from the Dominions and British women raised far less public ire than did interracial sexual liaisons. Throughout the war, newspapers reported breathlessly on white women consorting with men of colour, and police and Home Office records abound with reports of violent incidents catalysed by such relations. In London's East End in July

---

[42] Neil Evans, 'The South Wales Race Riots of 1919', *Llafur*, 3 (1) (1980), 5–29; Jacqueline Jenkinson, 'The Glasgow Race Disturbances of 1919', *Immigrants and Minorities*, 4 (2) (1985), 43–67; Jenkinson, 'The Black Community of Salford and Hull, 1919–21', *Immigrants and Minorities*, 7 (2) (1988), 166–83; Michael Rowe, 'Sex, "Race" and Riot in Liverpool, 1919', *Immigrants and Minorities*, 19 (2) (2000), 53–70.

[43] Evans, 'South Wales Race Riots', 22.

[44] Bill Schwarz, 'Black Metropolis, White England', in Mica Nava and Alan O'Shea (eds.), *Modern Times: Reflections on a Century of English Modernity* (London, 1996), 197.

[45] Angela Woollacott, '"Khaki Fever" and Its Control: Gender, Class, Age and Sexual Morality on the British Homefront in the First World War', *Journal of Contemporary History*, 29 (1994), 325–47; Susan R. Grayzel, *Women's Identities At War: Gender, Motherhood and Politics in Britain and France during the First World War* (Chapel Hill, 1999), ch. 4.

[46] Philippa Levine, 'Battle Colors: Race, Sex, and Colonial Soldiery in World War I', *Journal of Women's History*, 9 (4) (1998), 111.

[47] Levine, *Prostitution, Race, and Politics*, 163.

1917, 'a gang of youths' attacked lodging houses where black men lived, 'in consequence of the infatuation of the white girls for the black men in the district'.[48] The trouble escalated the next night when 'a crowd of about a thousand people assembled' in front of the boarding houses. One local man and one black man were each fined £1.

It was not only working-class sexual resentment, however, which manifested itself in wartime. The First World War, with its enormous hunger for conscripts, its new technologies and its home front, focused a new kind of attention on gendered bodies. The intense interest, in early twentieth-century Britain, in 'national efficiency' as a bulwark against imperial decline emphasised the male body's fitness for military service and the female body's fitness for reproduction.[49] This intensification of normative gender roles heightened the fears around contaminating sexualities, sometimes with startling consequences. The War Office, for example, imposed an extraordinary set of rules on the nursing of wounded Indian soldiers convalescing in Britain, rules never applied to Dominion convalescents. Indian soldiers were not only segregated in racially exclusive settings, but those British nurses who staffed the Indian hospitals were permitted no bodily contact with their patients. Male orderlies and army medical personnel were required to undertake physical tasks such as the dressing of wounds.[50] The nurses were, by military fiat, only to 'see to the cleanliness and orderliness of the ward'.[51] Those responsible for policing the sexuality of young British women painted a picture of unruly and bold girls in constant sexual pursuit of uniformed men. The women's patrols organised by the National Union of Women Workers reported in 1918 on women's excitement when it was rumoured that German prisoners of war were to be lodged nearby.[52] Yet in such cases no rules were issued to parallel those dictating that Indian soldiers could not be nursed by white women, could not venture outside the grounds of the hospital and could not talk to local women.

This squeamishness carried over into the Second World War where, notes Sonya Rose, '[T]he outrage over young women's morals intensified

[48] *The Times*, 3 July 1917, 5.
[49] Anna Davin, 'Imperialism and Motherhood', *History Workshop Journal*, 5 (1978), 9–65.
[50] Jeffrey Greenhut, 'Race, Sex, and War: The Impact of Race and Sex on Morale and Health Services for the Indian Corps on the Western Front, 1914', *Military Affairs*, 45 (2) (1981), 71–4; Levine, *Prostitution, Race, and Politics*, 154–5.
[51] Oriental and India Office Collection, British Library, London. L/MIL/7/17316. Reference Paper. Military. 28 October 1914? H. A. Charles.
[52] Imperial War Museum, London. Women's Work Collection. Emp 42 1/4. Women's Patrol Committee reports. The location under discussion is, sadly, not revealed.

when the soldiers whom they dated were black.'[53] In World War II the issue was more about race than about colonialism, yet many of the themes already visited here re-emerged strongly in the war years.[54] Sonya Rose shows how British moral outrage contrasted loose black male morals with the innocence and simplicity of young English girls led astray.[55] In earlier years when colonial questions were more prominent, and in a war with significant and long-term colonial implications, these racial observances were profoundly about the workings and hierarchies of colonial rule and the ever-present need to establish, ground and maintain a sense of difference that was racial, sexual and political. The conflation of race and sex, and perhaps most particularly in the kinds of moral panics that fed the white slave trade alarm and the early twentieth-century race riots, was a colonial question, one exacerbated by fears around miscegenation and reproduction.

Assumptions about the nature and uncouthness of colonial sexualities – always too much, always potentially, if not actually, out of control – threatened the border between respectability and looseness, between Britain and its subject peoples. After all, if the qualities of Britishness were identified with the conquering and holding of the Empire, then sexual mixing with the necessarily inferior subjects of that empire would surely dilute British strength and destabilise British imperialism. It was in this vein that much of the alarm over miscegenation took root, for the fear of mixed-race progeny was composed of more than a mere abhorrence of racial mixing. At least from the late eighteenth century, prominent scientists had wondered whether the progeny of mixed-race parents might, like mules, prove sterile.[56] Others had stressed less the prospect of infertility than the potential for degeneration, the inheritance of the weaker or lesser characteristics of each parent. Tied in to this assumption was the belief that those willing to cross racial lines in their sexual encounters were themselves already of poor stock; ironically, that argument tended to emphasise those whose sexual relations were permanent, rather than the

---

[53] Sonya O. Rose, 'Girls and GIs: Race, Sex, and Diplomacy in Second World War Britain', *International History Review*, 19 (1) (1997), 152.

[54] David Reynolds, 'The Churchill Government and the Black Troops in Britain During World War II', *Transactions of the Royal Historical Society*, 5th ser., 35 (1985), 113–33; Graham A. Smith, 'Jim Crow on the Homefront (1942–1945)', *New Community*, 8 (3) (1980), 317–28; Christopher Thorne, 'Britain and the Black GIs: Racial Issues and Anglo-American Relations in 1942', *New Community*, 3 (3) (1974), 262–71.

[55] Sonya O. Rose, *Which People's War? National Identity and Citizenship in Wartime Britain 1939–1945* (Oxford, 2003), esp. 255.

[56] Sander L. Gilman, *Difference and Pathology: Stereotypes of Sexuality, Race, and Madness* (Ithaca, 1985), 107.

more temporary liaisons of convenience colonising men often formed when abroad. Where colonial interracial sexual relationships were at issue, promiscuity was, ironically, a better option than fidelity and child-raising! Over the course of the nineteenth century, colonial officialdom moved from a cautious encouragement of sexual liaisons with locals (although only those of white men and colonial women, and never vice versa) to increasing prohibition of such relations.[57] In the early years of empire, such relations were seen as a valuable route in to local cultures; in later years, they were regarded as threatening colonial prowess and promoting political instability.

Concubinage had been seen in the early years of colonialism as a barrier against homosexuality, and the spectre of male–male sex haunted discussions of sexuality, race and colonialism. British officials kept tabs on influential colonial men thought to engage in same-sex practices, and homosexuality was frequently seen as foreign or colonial in origin. It was both a metaphor for weakness and the sign of racial unfitness. Paul Fussell and Cynthia Enloe in particular have established beyond question the multiple and sometimes complex associations between war and sexuality.[58] As a project critically sustained and produced by military force, colonialism could hardly not be read in sexual terms. But the erotics of war raised also the question of same-sex desire, for wars have historically been homosocial engagements deeply reliant on camaraderie, trust and intimacy among men. Empire building and wars, as dominantly male environments, were thus danger zones not only for mortality but for morality, for normative heterosexuality. It was only by configuring homosexual preference or practice as colonially produced, as a colonial 'vice' with no parallel in the civilian or domestic realm, that the fiction of British sexual normativity could be upheld. By channelling discussions of homosexuality through reference to savagery and primitiveness, it could be symbolically, although never realistically, kept at bay. One of the great fears aroused by colonial sexualities more generally was that they would somehow unleash same-sex desires, especially between men, undermining national tropes that figured heterosexuality and masculinity as definitively British.

Sexuality was a complex canvas upon which the politics of colonialism could be drawn. It was a malleable and an invaluable tool, which helped regulate sexual behaviour and define proper and improper masculinity

[57] Ronald Hyam, 'Concubinage and the Colonial Service: The Crewe Circular (1909)', *Journal of Imperial and Commonwealth History*, 14 (3) (1986), 170–86.

[58] Paul Fussell, *The Great War and Modern Memory* (Oxford, 1975); Cynthia Enloe, *The Morning After: Sexual Politics at the End of the Cold War* (Berkeley, 1993).

and femininity, proper and improper sexual practices. And yet such orderings were always in danger of unravelling, and perhaps nowhere more so than in the evocation of the colonial within the realm of sexual fantasy, an arena always outside and resistant to control. In pornographic fiction and photographs, in mainstream art and literature, the colonial world became a canvas upon which was written every kind of sexual fantasy – homosexual as well as heterosexual, interracial and much else besides. Outside governing boundaries, often avowedly hostile to prevailing respectabilities, sexual fantasy nonetheless recognised the erotic lure of the colonial world for Britons living in an imperial age. The selling of Sara Baartman's body to the paying public is a potent example of this allure. From the eighteenth century onwards, and whether as caricature or as titillation, the Empire represented for cartoonists and artists, photographers and writers, publishers and performers a means of expressing sexual desire, innovation and daring as well as commerce. The imperial site shown 'at home' was a place where otherwise inexpressible desires could be manifested.

And it is through desire and its frightening connotations for imperial rule that we can perhaps best appreciate how sexuality, perhaps more than any other arena, illuminates Simon Gikandi's point about British imperial ambivalence: pride in imperial conquest and ownership seldom extended to an actual colonial presence in Britain which was frequently seen as threatening.[59] After all, sexual relationships involving colonials and locals would likely result in a more permanent colonial population as well as its reproduction. Yet such fears also drove home the inescapable fact that there never was such a thing as 'colonial sexuality', a point perhaps most glaringly apparent in its sheer malleability in political discourse as in the pages of pornography. There was, in the face of colonials in Britain communing with locals, no easily drawn boundary between colonial and domestic sexuality, between British restraint and colonial overindulgence. Always a construct of the imperial imagination, it was nonetheless of potent, inevitable and endless consequence in Britain as abroad, and it functioned as much to consolidate British definitions of self and sexuality as to mark the alleged weaknesses of colonials. If anxieties about sexuality within Britain could, in effect, be shifted to colonial margins, explained away as racially and ethnically other and not British, then the dangers of sexual desire might be better contained.

[59] Simon Gikandi, *Maps of Englishness: Writing Identity in the Culture of Colonialism* (New York, 1996), 4ff.

Colonial sexualities were a key component in British understandings, and indeed misunderstandings, of the imperial world. Empire and sexuality were linked, and inextricably, by the multiple ways in which representations and definitions of what it meant to be British, or to be colonial, annexed sexuality. The critical distinctions anxiously drawn between British and colonial sexualities, the ever-urgent need to enforce a separation between these apparent and incommensurable opposites, made sexuality inevitable and always central to the understandings as well as the practices of empire. Ann Stoler's multiple explorations of the ways in which colonial regimes around sexuality (and other 'undesirable' behaviours) moulded the precepts of European bourgeois morality are central to this discussion.[60] Sexuality, always an effect of practices in time, always a construct, is thus in the British arena an effect of empire, a category built and shaped by imperial concerns, never stable, always in danger of breaking out of its confines, ever to be watched and guarded.

I began this exploration of the contours of colonial sexuality as they played out in Britain with a discussion of the sexualised and gendered nature of British immigration law. This is also a fitting theme on which to end, for it seems to me that the politics of sexuality finally cannot be divorced from the debates about nationhood and citizenship which have so centrally shaped immigration policy, certainly from the early twentieth century on. The particular laws around immigration which have concerned me here have defined not only what kinds of sexuality (heterosexual, monogamous, respectable) were allowable for immigrant women but have also enshrined a vision of masculinity as heterosexual, wage-earning and family-oriented. While public debate often focused on the failure of immigrants to fulfil this directive for their existence, we can see in this vision a desire for and definition of ideal citizenship within the parameters of a particular vision of both British and colonial sexuality. Immigration law, as it affected those from present or former British colonies, privileged the stabilising and hopefully anglicising effects of marriage, creating families whose focus would coincide with British values, rendering them eligible for citizenship rather than mere subject-hood. While early colonial immigration to Britain had eerily mirrored the singularly male movement of colonising Britons out to imperial sites, later policies once more echoed the Empire in seeking to encourage stability through safe and respectable sexual liaisons, even while only

---

[60] See, among others, her recent collection of essays, *Carnal Knowledge and Imperial Power: Race and the Intimate in Colonial Rule* (Berkeley, 2002).

reluctantly permitting further colonial inflow. The change in imperial temperament that saw domestication in the Empire and the discouragement of promiscuity and mixed-race intimacy came 'home' in the postwar period, a pattern strongly suggestive of a continued fear of the colonial and his or her potentially disruptive values and behaviours. The effort to create colonial families in the British image, and thus to tame the rampant sexualities still associated with the colonial world, suggests how powerfully the spectre of this construct of 'colonial sexuality' figured, even as British colonial power dissolved.

CHAPTER SEVEN

Religion and empire at home

Susan Thorne

Organised religion was one of the most powerful sources of inspiration and sites of association in Victorian Britain. Few historians who work on the nineteenth century today would object to G. Kitson Clark's revisionist insistence in 1962 that 'in no other century, except the seventeenth and perhaps the twelfth, did the claims of religion occupy so large a part of the nation's life, or did men speaking in the name of religion contrive to exercise so much power'.[1] While contemporaries were alarmed that 'only' half of Britain's adult population attended church or chapel services on a regular basis, this far exceeded the social catchments of all other institutions in Victorian political culture. Moreover, most of the adults who were not regular churchgoers had probably been exposed to organised religion as children. Virtually every working-class child attended Britain's massively popular Sunday Schools at one point or another.[2]

Victorian religious practice was, furthermore, a very public and political praxis. In fact, Victorian public opinion was 'educated from the pulpit'.[3]

---

[1] G. S. R. Kitson Clark, *The Making of Victorian England* (Cambridge, 1962), 20–4. Feminist historians have been particularly influential in recent discussions of the social and political coordinates of organised religion in the nineteenth century. For fascinating introductions to this now burgeoning literature, see Joan Wallach Scott, 'Women in *The Making of the English Working Class*', in *Gender and the Politics of History* (New York, 1988), Jacqueline deVries, 'Rediscovering Christianity after the Postmodern Turn', *Feminist Studies*, 31 (1) (2005). See also Hugh McLeod, *Class and Religion in the Late Victorian City* (Hamden, CT, 1974), Stephen Yeo, *Religion and Voluntary Organisations in Crisis* (London, 1976), Deborah M. Valenze, *Prophetic Sons and Daughters: Female Preaching and Popular Religion in Industrial England* (Princeton, 1985), Leonore Davidoff and Catherine Hall, *Family Fortunes: Men and Women of the English Middle Class, 1780–1850* (London, 1987), Theodore Koditschek, *Class Formation and Urban Industrial Society* (Cambridge, 1990), Mark Smith, *Religion in Industrial Society: Oldham and Saddleworth 1740–1865* (Oxford, 1994), Callum G. Brown, *Religion and Society in Scotland Since 1707* (Edinburgh, 1997), Joy Dixon, *Divine Feminine: Theosophy and Feminism in England* (Baltimore, 2001), Pamela J. Walker, *Pulling the Devil's Kingdom Down: The Salvation Army in Victorian Britain* (Berkeley, 2001).

[2] Thomas Laqueur, *Religion and Respectability: Sunday Schools and Working-Class Culture 1780–1850* (New Haven, 1976).

[3] Olive Anderson, 'Women Preachers in Mid-Victorian Britain: Some Reflexions on Feminism, Popular Religion and Social Change', *Historical Journal*, 12 (3) (1969), 467.

This does not mean that religious Victorians spoke with a unified political voice. To the contrary, theological and sectarian differences were among the most important fault lines informing the nation's party political divide. While Nonconformists were nearly unanimous in their support for the Liberal Party, at least before 1886, Anglicans were as ardent if not quite as unified in their support for the Conservative Party.[4] Religion, then, was less a unitary influence on Victorian politics than a terrain of struggle, one of if not the most potent source of discord in Victorian political culture, a key axis around which political difference at home was organised.

Religion was no less potent a force in Victorian political culture because of the contingent and contested nature of its influence. Religious calculations pervaded Victorian political discussion: the repeal of the Test and Corporation Acts, Catholic Emancipation and disestablishment are but the most obvious examples. Even if not especially those who advocated the separation of church and state, namely, Nonconformist promoters of disestablishment, invoked religious not political justifications. Less obvious but equally religious in their inspiration as well as their support base were the abolition of slavery, the temperance crusade, the opposition to compulsory vaccination, sanitation reform, the Eastern Question, the campaigns against the Contagious Diseases Acts, compulsory state education and Irish Home Rule.[5]

The Empire was no exception to this Victorian political rule. Victorians at home learned much of what they knew about the colonies and their inhabitants in church and chapel pews. In fact, the influence of missionary intelligence about the Empire at home was one of the distinguishing features of Victorian imperial culture. The nineteenth century was the 'great age' of British Protestant missions; and most British missionaries worked in regions of the world that were or would soon fall under Britain's colonial jurisdiction. These missionaries, in turn, enjoyed access to a more broadly based audience than any other colonial lobby. As a result, the missionary movement would become a crucial conduit

---

[4] Nonconformist chapels, in particular, provided the organisational channels of communication between parliamentary representatives and their grass-roots supporters that distinguish the modern political party from the early modern parliamentary faction. See J. R. Vincent, *The Formation of the Liberal Party, 1857–1868* (London, 1966).

[5] G. I. T. Machin, *Politics and the Churches in Great Britain, 1832–1868* (Oxford, 1977), G. I. T. Machin, *Politics and the Churches in Great Britain, 1869 to 1921* (Oxford, 1987), Brian Harrison, *Drink and the Victorians: The Temperance Question in England, 1815–1872* (London, 1971), Patricia Hollis (ed.), *Pressure from Without in Early Victorian England* (London, 1974), D. W. Bebbington, *The Nonconformist Conscience: Chapel and Politics, 1870–1914* (London, 1982), Clare Midgley, *Women Against Slavery: The British Campaigns, 1780–1870* (London, 1992).

through which political intelligence and cultural influences as well as people travelled between the British Empire and its Victorian home front. The influence of the Empire brought home by the foreign missionary movement is the subject of this essay.

As the preceding references vibrantly attest, scholarly discussions of Victorian political culture have been enriched by our recognition that religion and politics were effectively inextricable in the Victorian imaginary. It is all the more interesting that religion and empire, by contrast, figure in imperial historiography as alternative categories of analysis.[6] If missionaries were complicit in imperialism, then their religion is close to irrelevant.[7] If, however, missionaries were truly motivated by their religious beliefs, then imperial considerations are largely irrelevant to their story.[8]

The missionary position in and on the Empire was certainly complex. Even when missionaries sought to 'colonise consciousness', they were frequently frustrated by indigenous converts' ability to adapt the Christian faith to their own ends.[9] Conversely, missionaries' very presence in the colonies disrupted the cultural unity on which white supremacy depended. Missionaries were a 'dominated fraction of the dominant class', contemptuously dismissed as troublesome fanatics in many quarters of the colonial community.[10] Missionaries in their turn struck back at other Europeans, colonial officials as well as military, commercial and settler interests, exposing exploitation and abuse of colonised peoples alongside their fellow Europeans' other sins.[11]

---

[6] Andrew Porter, *Religion Versus Empire?: British Protestant Missionaries and Overseas Expansion, 1700–1914* (Manchester, 2004).

[7] Stephen Neill, *Colonialism and Christian Missions* (New York, 1966) and Emmanuel Ayankanmi Ayandele, *The Missionary Impact on Modern Nigeria, 1842–1914: A Political and Social Analysis* (London, 1966).

[8] F. Stuart Piggin, *Making Evangelical Missionaries, 1789–1858: The Social Background, Motives, and the Training of British Protestant Missionaries to India* (Abingdon, 1984), Brian Stanley, *The Bible and the Flag: Protestant Missions and British Imperialism in the Nineteenth and Twentieth Centuries* (Leicester, 1990).

[9] Jean Comaroff and John L. Comaroff, *Of Revelation and Revolution*, 2 vols. (Chicago, 1991–7), Jeffrey Cox, *Imperial Fault Lines: Christianity and Colonial Power in India, 1818–1940* (Stanford, 2002).

[10] John Comaroff, 'Images of Empire, Contests of Conscience: Models of Colonial Domination in South Africa', in Frederick Cooper and Ann Laura Stoler (eds.), *Tensions of Empire: Colonial Cultures in a Bourgeois World* (Berkeley, 1997), 163–97.

[11] The global literature on British missions alone is far deeper than I can possibly gesture towards here, but my personal favourites include Peter van der Veer, *Imperial Encounters: Religion and Modernity in India and Britain* (Princeton, 2001), Comaroff and Comaroff, *Of Revelation and Revolution*, Paul Stuart Landau, *The Realm of the Word: Language, Gender, and Christianity in a Southern African Kingdom* (Portsmouth, 1995), Elizabeth Elbourne, *Blood Ground: Colonialism, Missions, and the Contest for Christianity in the Cape Colony and Britain, 1799–1853* (Montreal, 2002), Cox, *Imperial Fault Lines*, Emilia Viotti da Costa, *Crowns of Glory, Tears of Blood: The Demerara Slave Rebellion of*

This complexity has been invoked as evidence that the history of religious missions and the British Empire have been falsely conjoined. How can missionaries be complicit in colonialism when they were among the Empire's most vocal critics? Even those missionaries who supported imperialism could not have wielded much influence over its course due to their marginal position in the colonial community. Moreover, on those relatively rare occasions that missionaries actively lobbied for colonial intervention, their motivations were usually genuinely religious. The kingdom they sought was of God and not man; missionaries sacrificed wealth, health, their own lives as well as the lives, health or company of beloved family members. Missionary motivations were primarily theological – and not nationalist or racialist – in nature.[12]

There is much truth in the above. Missionary motivation and sacrifice are certainly inexplicable if abstracted from the theological inspiration of the missionary vocation. However, theology itself is not a trans-historical *a priori*. Human translations of the divine are always mediated by the historical context of the believer. Theological interpretations of the Word acquire – or lose – their purchase or appeal in circumstances not of theologians' choosing. The history of religious human beings can no more be contained within theological parameters than it can be understood outside them. And the Empire influenced and was influenced by missionary belief and practice.

This chapter will therefore try to take theology seriously without taking it at its word.[13] It focuses on what Victorian Christians referred to as the 'reflux benefit' or influence of foreign missions on British audiences *at home*. It will argue that empire figured prominently among the contexts that gave birth to the modern missionary impulse that was so central to the Victorian faith. Religious missions, in turn, played an important role in bringing the Empire *home*. In the course of their fund-raising efforts, missionary societies disseminated information about colonised peoples and encouraged if not required reflection on the Empire's *raison d'être*,

---

1823 (New York, 1994), Mary Turner, *Slaves and Missionaries: The Disintegration of Jamaican Slave Society, 1787–1834* (Urbana, 1982), Catherine Hall, *Civilising Subjects: Metropole and Colony in the English Imagination, 1830–1867* (Cambridge and Chicago, 2002).

[12] See Porter, *Religion Versus Empire?*, Andrew Porter, 'Religion, Missionary Enthusiasm, and Empire', in Wm. Roger Louis (ed.), *The Oxford History of the British Empire*, 5 vols. (Oxford, 1998–9), vol. III: *The Nineteenth Century*, ed. Andrew Porter (1999), and Andrew Porter, 'Religion and Empire: British Expansion in the Long Nineteenth Century, 1780–1914', *Journal of Imperial and Commonwealth History*, 20 (3) (1992).

[13] Barbara J. Fields, 'Ideology and Race in American History', in J. Morgan Kousser and James M. McPherson (eds.), *Region, Race, and Reconstruction* (New York, 1982).

the legitimacy of British rule. While missionary 'friends of the native' frequently condemned colonial practice, their very efforts along these lines helped to sacralise an imperial ideal.

The connections between religion and Empire described below are of a very different order than the easily discounted charge that British missionaries were being essentially or primarily *imperialistic*.[14] On the one hand, imperial developments constituted a crucial influence on the institutional form as well as the theological content of the religious beliefs and practices so important on the Empire's Victorian home front. The missionary movement, in turn, insured the Empire's vital importance in the popular Victorian worldview. Missionaries' widely publicised faith-based criticisms of colonial policy incited vituperative responses in the British media. Outside the already heavily populated corridors of evangelicalism, missions helped to keep the Empire in public view. Victorian periodicals, newspapers and novels responded to missionary critics of empire by attacking missions in their turn as a destabilising influence, subversive of a colonial rule whose legitimacy was staunchly upheld. Such conversations were far from the only such occasion on which empire was discussed in British political culture. However, they were among the most broadly consumed, thanks to the prominence of organised religion in Victorian political culture. In terms of the numbers of Britons exposed to missionary depictions of colonial life as well as the emotive power of the associations incited among its enemies as well as friends, the missionary movement helped to insure *that*, if not *how*, the Empire would matter at home in one of the world's most religious as well as imperious nations.

THE BIRTH OF MODERN MISSIONS

The Biblical mandate for foreign missions is found in the risen Christ's admonition to the apostles to 'go ye into all the world and preach the gospel to every creature'.[15] The pre-eminence of this directive in the evangelical tradition for the past two centuries obscures its early modern provenance. British Protestants showed little interest in spreading the gospel prior to the eighteenth century; the theology of the Reformation and the trauma of centuries of religious warfare provided little incentive to proselytise. Calvinists believed that salvation was predestined for an

---

[14] Bernard Porter, *The Absent-Minded Imperialists: Empire, Society, and Culture in Britain* (Oxford, 2004).
[15] Mark 16: 15, King James Version.

elect minority, while the Anglican establishment exhibited an insular nationalism from its Henrician inception. Thus the early Anglican missions, the Society for the Propagation of the Gospel (SPG), founded in 1701, and the Society for the Promotion of Christian Knowledge (SPCK), founded in 1699, worked *within* the boundaries of British settlement. Their prime directive was to maintain the spiritual health of British settlers, and secondarily to minister to the natives who lived within the settlement's immediate proximity. Neither Puritan reformers nor Church defenders were encouraged much less compelled to bestow the gospel gift throughout Stuart England's rapidly expanding world.[16]

Theology in the form of the Evangelical Revival propelled the modern missionary project to the centre of Britain's religious stage. Modern Protestant missions were distinguished from their predecessors by their global ambitions. Their expansive vision was an outgrowth of evangelical theology's Arminian challenge to Calvinist predestination and Anglican insular nationalism alike. Evangelical theology, however, is not sufficient to explain the birth of modern missions. John Wesley's heart was 'strangely warmed' in 1738.[17] Interestingly enough, Wesley experienced his own conversion in the immediate aftermath of his dismal failure to convert the Native Americans he ministered to while working for the Society for the Propagation of the Gospel in colonial Georgia. Wesley's conversion was not in itself sufficient inspiration for modern missions. The missionary societies that were responsible for the global assault on heathenism during the nineteenth century would not take institutional shape until the 1790s, on the eve of Wesley's death.[18]

What else must we take into consideration when accounting for the specifically *missionary* articulation of evangelical faith that distinguishes nineteenth-century proselytising as well as philanthropy from their eighteenth-century counterparts? Modern missions differed from the proselytising practices of the eighteenth century in their institutional form. By contrast to early missionary organisations such as the SPG or SPCK,

---

[16] John Eliot's work among the Iroquois in Massachusetts was exceptional in this regard. D. W. Bebbington, *Evangelicalism in Modern Britain: A History from the 1730s to the 1980s* (London and Boston, 1989), 40.

[17] His was not the first awakening. Welsh schoolmaster Howel Harris and curate Daniel Rowland, along with Oxford undergraduate George Whitefield, are credited with coming first to this faith in England in 1735, while a religious revival along similar theological lines was breaking out in colonial Massachusetts at the very same time. It was John Wesley, however, whose organisational brilliance spread the word to audiences unrivalled, at least in Britain, in social breadth as well as numbers.

[18] The Baptist Missionary Society was established in 1792, the London Missionary Society in 1795, the Church Missionary Society in 1799 and the Wesleyan Methodist Missionary Society in 1813.

which depended on gentry and royal patronage, modern missionary societies were voluntary organisations, funded by the small gifts of large numbers of people. And their ambitions were, as I've said, global in nature. Their outreach and their organisation alike depended on a new social geography as well as theology. The very existence of such missionary institutions assumed an identifiable and communal boundary between the saved and the damned. Nineteenth-century missionary societies appealed for support from communities that took their own salvation for granted, at least relative to those people missionaries were being *sent out* to save.

This is a very different spatial distribution of sin and salvation than that which motivated the early Wesleyan movement. Circuit riders, unlike missionaries, preached without making qualitative distinctions between communities far and near. Their targets included regular churchgoers; in fact, their audience consisted largely of those who considered themselves Christian but who were worried about their own salvation. In this setting, sin resided within every listener. The operative word for evangelical practice in this period was *revival*.

Modern *missions*, by contrast, targeted heathens outside the churches. Their sponsors were increasingly confident in their own salvation. This was a significant change in the emotional and social experience of British evangelicalism. Some of this difference may have been the result of evangelicalism's later eighteenth-century revival of Old Dissent, where it served more to moderate Calvinism than entirely to dislodge it. Calvinists were obviously more confident in their own election than Wesleyans, but from the 1780s on, they became more hopeful for the prospects of grace outside their own communities. This evangelical broadening of Calvinist horizons was initially manifested in a burst of itinerant preaching. Many of those involved would later play a leading role in the establishment of foreign missionary societies.[19]

Why though did foreign missions in particular capture the imagination and win the vast majority of the financial support on offer from the larger Victorian public? Part of the answer lies with the imperial developments associated with what historians have referred to as the rise of a second British Empire. Eighteenth-century philanthropy was more humanitarian than religious; the focus was on the material needs rather than the spiritual condition of its beneficiaries. Orphanages, Magdalen Societies and the like addressed the first British Empire's ever pressing need for sailors, soldiers

[19] Deryck W. Lovegrove, *Established Church, Sectarian People: Itinerancy and the Transformation of English Dissent, 1780–1830* (Cambridge, 1988), Elbourne, *Blood Ground*, esp. ch. 1.

and settlers. The loss of the American colonies not only diminished considerably the colonial demand for British bodies; the decline in opportunities for emigration was sufficiently significant as to raise the contrary spectre of overpopulation at home. It was, of course, in 1790 that Thomas Malthus argued that foundling hospitals and other institutions that saved the lives of the poor simply exacerbated the causes of poverty, chief among which was overbreeding.[20]

By contrast to its humanitarian predecessor, missionary philanthropy ministered to souls and not to bodies, at least during the first half of the nineteenth century. It responded to human suffering without the pressure of population on the home front, where missionaries were initially dispatched. The growing emphasis on missionary philanthropy at home was also serviceable to the nascent industrial economy. As E. P. Thompson suggested long ago, the evangelical cross had the power to transform pre-industrial labourers into a more productive proletariat, workers being the 'moral machinery' on which the emergent factory system depended.[21] None of which is to suggest that missionaries or their supporters were consciously or even unconsciously motivated by demographic or industrial factors. It is, rather, to suggest the mission cause owed the scale of its popular support, at least in part, to its fortuitous exemption from criticisms that discouraged support for rival claims on the philanthropic purse.

Home missions were first in the field, but they were not as popular as the foreign missionary cause, and the foreign field would remain pre-eminent for at least the first half of the nineteenth century. Why then did foreign missions assume their paramount position in the evangelical charitable pantheon? Elie Halévy has suggested that the Methodist Revolution more generally and particularly its foreign missionary emphasis saved Great Britain from a revolution like the one that was, simultaneously, occurring in France.[22] There are, certainly, parallels worth noting here. The enormous fascination with the South Sea voyages of Captain Cook no doubt contributed to the exuberant farewells to the first missionary parties to those exotic untouched (and not yet colonised) regions of the world.[23] In this and other ways, foreign missions may have

---

[20] Donna Andrew, *Philanthropy and Police: London Charity in the Eighteenth Century* (Princeton, 1989).

[21] E. P. Thompson, *The Making of the English Working Class* (New York, 1963), ch. XI: 'The Transforming Power of the Cross'.

[22] Bernard Semmel, *The Methodist Revolution* (New York, 1973); for a contrary view see Frederic Stuart Piggin, 'Halévy Revisited: The Origins of the Wesleyan Methodist Missionary Society: An Examination of Semmel's Thesis', *Journal of Imperial and Commonwealth History*, 9 (1) (1980).

[23] Kathleen Wilson, *The Island Race: Englishness, Empire and Gender in the Eighteenth Century* (London, 2003).

benefited from a social imperial affect, enjoying relatively more toleration than their home missionary counterparts from understandably wary elites. As Catherine Hall persuasively demonstrates, imperial preoccupations including those fomented by the missionary lobby suffused the provincial heartland of the industrial revolution. The political disabilities suffered by non-landed wealth prior to 1832 could have been as politically dangerous in Britain as they were in France. Missions may have functioned as a medium through which the industrial bourgeoisie acquired a spiritual if not an economic interest in the British Empire.

Indeed artisans (who like the bourgeoisie would play a revolutionary role in France) comprised the vast bulk of evangelical converts throughout the eighteenth century. With rare exceptions (like the Countess of Huntington) the landed classes would not convert until after the French Revolution. In fact, they subjected evangelicals to considerable discrimination, both within the Church of England and outside it in Dissent. Evangelical Churchmen were expelled from their universities and denied ordination, and it was very difficult for the ordained to find livings.

The foreign missionary cause reflected and reinforced the temporary rapprochement between evangelical Dissent with Evangelical Anglicans and Methodists. At its founding the London Missionary Society was an ecumenical body drawing on Evangelical Churchmen, Methodists and Presbyterians, as well as the Independents or Congregationalists on whom it would eventually depend. This cooperation did not end when Evangelical Anglicans founded the Church Missionary Society in 1799. With varying political inflections, foreign missions were promoted in a language that implicitly questioned the capacity of the ruling classes to govern, at home as well as abroad. Insisting that foreign missions were not designed to bring 'predatory hordes of savages into the habits and refinements of civil and social life', for 'if they be viewed as the principal object of our exertions, even ancient Rome, or Greece, might peradventure have sent out better Missionaries than ourselves'. The 'object which far transcends them all ... [is] the preaching of the gospel of the blessed Lord ... without which even Athens herself, in the meridian of her literary and philosophical glory, was in total darkness'.[24] Remarks such as these called

[24] Rev. William Borrows, 'Salvation by Christ, the Grand Object of Christian Missions', London Missionary Society, 1820, Yale Divinity School, Special Collections. The Rev. John Angell James seemed to have the Utilitarians in mind when he remonstrated before an assembly of missionary supporters in 1819 against those 'men without Christ [who] are in the very depths of misery, though they may stand in other respects, upon the very summits of civilization, literature and science, and for such an opinion we can plead the authority of the great Apostle [Paul] of the Gentiles who bewailed a city of *philosophers*, with more intense and piercing grief, that any of us

into question the classically educated and religiously apathetic aristocracy's own claims to virtue, making it clear that the primary qualification for wielding worldly authority was an evangelical rebirth.

However, when it came to parliamentary politics, evangelicals were divided along party political lines that would remain in force during most of the nineteenth century. The American Revolution separated Dissenting critics of the government from Methodists who under John Wesley's direction held themselves aloof from direct involvement. Dissenters were more supportive of the colonists than other evangelicals; but even they were mainly concerned to adjudicate colonial complaints in order to preserve the imperial bond. Dissenters blamed the Anglican gentry's leadership for the first major setback in the nation's colonial advance. In their view, the willingness or perhaps the ability to engage in such urgently needed diplomacy escaped the nation's governing classes, who then botched the military prosecution of a potentially avoidable war.

It was in this spirit that Dissenters initially championed the French Revolution as the just desserts of a corrupt and inept *ancien régime*. The radicalism of the Dissenting voice is easily overlooked today; it is important to remember that Dissenting intellectuals were the frequent victims of Church and King mobs. As the French Revolution took its Jacobin turn, however, even propertied Dissenters were increasingly cowed into at least passive acquiescence for counter-revolutionary moves that constrained their own freedom of action. The counter-revolutionary reaction was fearless and thorough. Even religious assemblies were suspect and home missions were widely feared for gathering and giving voice to the labouring poor. In their struggle to navigate between the dangerous shoals of plebeian radicalism, on the one side, and gentry Anglicanism on the other, evangelicals embraced the foreign mission cause as the more desirable setting in which to exercise their new theological understanding of the Biblical mandate to carry the gospel message.

This is not to say that evangelical missionaries were welcomed in the Empire. To the contrary, they were widely viewed as a destabilising presence in colonies always at least partially dependent on indigenous collaboration, particularly during the first half of the nineteenth century. The first missionaries were dispatched to Pacific islands not yet under European jurisdiction. However, such opportunities would become

---

ever did a horde of idolatrous *savages*'. Rev. J. A. James, 'The Attractions of the Cross: A Sermon Preached Before the London Missionary Society at Surrey Chapel, May 12, 1819', London Missionary Society, Yale Divinity School, Special Collections.

increasingly rare over the course of the nineteenth century, and the missionary project would inevitably become a colonial concern. Colonial administrators as well as European settlers were often hostile to missionary initiatives, and they actively sought to close down missionary operations.[25] Missionaries were barred from entering India until admitted by Act of Parliament in 1813. The powerful slaveowning lobby also objected to missionaries' presence in the plantation colonies of the Caribbean and South America.[26] While most though not all British missionaries worked in the Empire, they were not necessarily *of* it.

'THE CHARACTERISTIC FEATURE OF RELIGION'

These tensions in the Empire were profoundly politicising. The dismissive indifference to empire too often attributed to Victorian political culture today would certainly not have been characteristic of evangelicals who paid rapt attention to missionary reports that were enclosed within each denomination's monthly magazines and other missives. And these reports frequently reflect upon local colonial conditions. Missionaries found that religious advance itself required political engagement in the Empire as it did at home. Even those missionaries who wanted to avoid colonial politics, to remain politically above its fray, were simply not able to do so. The Empire would loom large as a result in the propaganda that the missionary movement disseminated to mobilise its highly politicised evangelical supporters at home.

This is not to say that the missionary movement conveyed consistent political directives to the evangelical public. Missionary perspectives on the general direction of colonial policy varied over denominational space and mission field as well as over time. The medium, however, was more important over the long term than the content of particular messages. The scale of missionary communication on the Victorian home front was without contemporary rival, prior to the rise of a mass media. Financial pressures insured that the channels of communication between the colonial mission field and British church or chapel were as free flowing as possible. Missionaries spent exhausting furloughs touring provincial churches to raise money and recruit volunteers to support their work abroad. In addition, missionary societies published a voluminous body of printed material appealing for funds and volunteers in support of their

---

[25] Porter, 'Religion, Missionary Enthusiasms, and Empire'.
[26] Costa, *Crowns of Glory, Tears of Blood: The Demerara Slave Rebellion of 1823*, Turner, *Slaves and Missionaries: The Disintegration of Jamaican Slave Society, 1787–1834*.

efforts to share the gospel message with the world's heathen peoples. By these and other means, the foreign missionary movement constituted an institutional channel through which representations of colonised people and sometimes colonised people themselves were displayed to British audiences on a scale unrivalled by any other source emanating from the colonies.[27]

The missionary movement thus encouraged Victorian evangelicals to think about colonised people on a regular basis; indeed to direct one's attention to the welfare of suffering heathendom was the pious evangelical's prime theological directive. Contemptuous contemporaries provide ample testimony about the obsessive character of the evangelical public's 'interest' in foreign mission fields. Missionary supporters at home were dismissed as maniacs obsessed with foreign affairs, condemned for being more familiar with and sympathetic to the heathen savages of the colonies than with suffering fellow-countrymen. For evangelicalism's influential critics within the English intelligentsia, foreign missionaries and especially their home supporters embodied all that was self-righteous and hypocritical, effeminate and ineffectual, cloyingly sentimental and culturally illiterate, about the evangelical bourgeoisie.

Dickens most famously caricatured the missionary public in his indictment of the 'telescopic philanthropy' of Mrs Jellyby and Mrs Pardiggle in *Bleak House*.[28] These unnatural women and their emasculated husbands neglected 'their own' to care for Hottentots and other thick-lipped savages in places they would never see. What enraged Dickens was precisely the extent to which colonised people if not the Empire itself mattered to evangelicals. The depths to which Dickens sank (i.e. attacking the character of someone's mother or an average man's manhood is pretty crude even by today's standard) is suggestive of the imaginative ideological labour required to keep colonised people in their proper place – out of empathy's sight and unworthy of cultured attention. *Something* matters here and it mattered a great deal at that.

---

[27] F. K. Prochaska, 'Little Vessels: Children in the Nineteenth-Century English Missionary Movement', *Journal of Imperial and Commonwealth History*, 6 (2) (1978), Alison Twells, 'The Heathen at Home and Overseas: The Middle Class and the Civilizing Mission, Sheffield 1790–1840' (DPhil, University of York, 1998), Alison Fletcher, '"With My Precious Salvation and My Umbrella": The London Missionary Society in Early and Mid-Victorian Britain' (PhD, Johns Hopkins University, 2003), Annie E. Coombes, *Reinventing Africa: Museums, Material Culture, and Popular Imagination in Late Victorian and Edwardian England* (New Haven, 1994).

[28] George Eliot similarly condemned the evangelical Bulstrode, the villain of *Middlemarch*, as one of those 'whose charity increases directly as the square of the distance'.

At stake in these Victorian culture wars was the very distinction between home and away, the affective, moral and cultural distance separating foreign mission fields from their British home front. These ostensibly spatial boundaries were – and remain – contested cultural constructs.[29] What was conversion, after all, but an attempt to bridge the divide between metropole and colony, not only by transforming the heathen races of the colonies and beyond into fellow Christian subjects but also by insuring that evangelicals at home would recognise colonial converts and potential converts as deserving recipients of philanthropic largesse?

It is highly revealing in this regard that foreign missions were not just one among the many charitable appeals that cluttered the Victorian evangelical stage. Missions were widely viewed by the Victorian faithful and their critics alike as the single most important expression of the Christian faith in action. As one contemporary put it in 1845, the 'missionary spirit' was 'the characteristic feature of religion',[30] and the religious public attended to their message and their needs with unrivalled dedication. Foreign missionary organisations were the institutional foundations on which Nonconformist religious sects became centralised denominations. And the missionary contribution to the form as well as content of Victorian religious practice was amply rewarded in turn. Foreign missions received the lion's share of the charitable donations for which Victorian Christians remain rightfully renowned, enabling missionary operations in virtually every corner of the British Empire and beyond. By the end of the nineteenth century, British churches were sponsoring a missionary field force of 10,000 missionary operatives, financed to the tune of two million pounds a year, about what the British government was then spending on civil-service salaries.[31] Whatever else they may have been, the foreign mission field and its inhabitants represented much more than 'ornaments' on evangelical mantles.[32]

Foreign missions did not displace 'domestic' concerns as Dickens seemed to fear, nor did evangelical spirituality preclude more worldly ambitions. In fact, foreign missions were a domestic 'event' as it were. During the first half of the nineteenth century ordinary people enjoyed few opportunities for association outside regular church or chapel

[29] Martin W. Lewis and Kären E. Wigen, *The Myth of Continents: A Critique of Metageography* (Berkeley, 1997).
[30] Rev. Arthur Tidman, LMS Annual Meeting, 1845; quoted in Richard Lovett, *The History of the London Missionary Society, 1795–1895*, 2 vols. (Oxford, 1899), vol. II, 675.
[31] Porter, 'Religion and Empire', 372.
[32] David Cannadine, *Ornamentalism: How the British Saw Their Empire* (New York, 2001).

meetings. The latter divided the community along sectarian lines. Missionary meetings by contrast were enormously popular, drawing audiences from across the denominational spectrum and even from outside the already extensive church- and chapel-going public. The arrival of missionary deputations was eagerly anticipated and widely advertised. And the public meetings convened to hear their inspiring stories (and to pass the collection plate) would be remembered for years if not decades as major events.[33]

Beyond their considerable entertainment and potentially educational value, these meetings were also an occasion for the performance of social relations of power vital to the making of the provincial middle class at home. Missions thereby provided substantial British audiences with a direct investment in or, conversely, a bitter resentment of the larger mission cause. While the audiences reached by evangelical organisations were probably the largest and most socially diverse of any Victorian institution, the meetings themselves were far from democratic. The staging of missionary meetings enabled the provincial middle class to display its religious virtue and its global vision before enthralled provincial audiences. In voluntary associations such as these, money talked; the role of pious plebeians was to watch and listen. What they saw were visiting missionary heroes, many of whom hailed from lowly social origins themselves, flanked by local notables on the podium.

The wider world to which missionary speakers gestured invited the most humble listeners to contribute their mite if not their life to the global struggle against heathenism.[34] However, the Christian mission on which the evangelical nation had embarked was clearly led by the missionary movement's bourgeois benefactors. The foreign missionary movement constituted an influential site at which empire was imagined in relation to modernity and through which the modernising classes fashioned themselves in relation to the colonies. The bourgeois revolution in values that constituted industrialisation's cultural counterpoint was the foundation of the missionary vision to bring the entire world to Christ. Far from an instrument of the colonial state, the missionary movement, particularly in its Dissenting guises, aimed to remake the Empire in its own godly image.[35]

Missionary imperial godliness bore the distinctively modern markings of political economy, anticipating the quasi-religious faith in globalisation

[33] Fletcher, 'The London Missionary Society in Early and Mid-Victorian Britain'.
[34] Prochaska, 'Little Vessels'.
[35] Susan Thorne, *Congregational Missions and the Making of an Imperial Culture in Nineteenth-Century England* (Stanford, 1999).

so widespread today. Missionaries spearheaded the enormously popular campaign against colonial slavery, for example, that culminated in the abolition of slavery throughout the British Empire in 1834. Missionary opposition to slavery, unfortunately, cannot be attributed to theological imperatives. Evangelicals had countenanced slavery for at least two generations and Christians for at least two centuries. Missionaries tried initially to do the same. However, New World slavery's distinctively modern features frustrated their efforts. Caribbean slave plantations were not governed according to the paternalistic social relations that characterised slave societies in pre-modern Europe or Islam. At least according to Eric Wolf, the West Indian plantation looked forward instead; in its manner of centralised production under close supervision and in its effort to maximise the amount of surplus labour that could be extracted, it anticipated the factory system.[36] The difference, however, was not that this labour force could be worked to death and often was, at least until the abolition of the slave trade in 1807. Factory reformers bitterly complained that abolitionists were indifferent to the working-class suffering at home.[37] The problem with slavery for evangelicals was not the human suffering it caused but its failure to provide sufficient incentive to labour. Slavery's dependence on coercion instead of wages was not just wrong, it was economically irrational. Following Adam Smith, evangelicals insisted that slavery was an expensive form of labour and that abolition would serve the economic interests of *all* concerned.[38]

While violence was never sufficient to contain the enslaved, the near absolute conditions of their hyper-exploitation were sufficient to render the missionary message less useful in the plantation colonies than at home where employers sometimes valued evangelical workers' temperate and disciplined natures. Colonial planters, by contrast, believed that the missionary message was subversive of plantation labour relations for the grossly simple fact that conversion acknowledged the slave's basic humanity, something West Indian whites were not willing to concede. Planter elites were therefore implacable opponents of even the most conciliatory missionary efforts. However much missionaries sought to make their peace with slavery (as their home-based employers initially

---

[36] Sidney Mintz, *Sweetness and Power: The Place of Sugar in Modern History* (New York, 1985). See also C. L. R. James, *The Black Jacobins* (New York, 1989), Paul Gilroy, *The Black Atlantic: Modernity and Double Consciousness* (Cambridge, 1993).

[37] Patricia Hollis, 'Anti-Slavery and British Working-Class Radicalism in the Years of Reform', in Christine Bolt and Seymour Drescher (eds.), *Anti-Slavery, Religion and Reform* (Folkestone, Kent, 1980).

[38] David Brion Davis, *The Problem of Slavery in the Age of Revolution 1770–1823* (Ithaca, 1975).

encouraged them to do), they found it impossible to work with the planters or their parliamentary representatives. Freeing slave bodies thus became a prerequisite of saving slave souls. And missionaries were the anti-slavery movement's closest observers on the colonial ground. Their testimony lent divine imprimatur to the colonial state's eventual emancipation of those enslaved in and by the British Empire.

However, the evangelical assault on slavery was also infused with equally abiding faith in the new science of political economy. Slavery was to be replaced by a very specific kind of freedom, the freedom to labour for wages in the global capitalist marketplace. This article of faith was challenged by colonial subjects' determination to define freedom for themselves. Resistance throughout the Empire at mid-century – most notably in South Africa, New Zealand and India – paralleled the refusal of the freed people in the Caribbean to confine their freedom to wage labour, a refusal that culminated in the rebellion in Morant Bay in 1865.[39] Evangelicals professed a profound disillusionment with colonial populations who failed to show their gratitude for the many gifts they had received from their missionary friends.

At the very least, this disillusionment passively acquiesced in the widespread hardening of racial attitudes during the second half of the nineteenth century. It was easier to question the humanity of rebellious colonial subjects than to repudiate profitable assumptions that the invisible hand governing market relations was divinely ordained. While missionaries may not have succumbed en masse to this new racism's allure (if character is biologically fixed, then conversion would be pointless), neither were they in a position to effectively contest it.

THE AGE OF EMPIRE

The missionary vision of empire during the first half of the nineteenth century was predicated on an implicitly if not consistently anti-racist universalism. It was not uncommon for missionaries or their children to marry native converts during the opening decades of the nineteenth century.[40] The interracial intimacies that distinguished missionaries' colonial encounters from those of most other Europeans, however, did not preclude racial discrimination on mission stations. Missionaries had always been constrained by their professional self-interest in their

---

[39] Freda Harcourt, 'Disraeli's Imperialism, 1866–1868: A Question of Timing', *Historical Journal*, 23 (1) (1980).
[40] Elbourne, *Blood Ground*.

mission's perpetuation, and many would drag their feet when it came to devolving authority to indigenous converts. Unfortunately, missionaries' reluctance to promote or adequately remunerate their native Christian converts would increase not diminish as the nineteenth century wore on.[41] Even the Church Missionary Society, which had led the way in such initiatives during the administration of Henry Venn, retreated from these policies after his death in 1873, culminating in the forced retirement of the first Bishop of the Niger Territories, Samuel Crowther (c. 1806–91), in 1890. The Church would not appoint another African to such a high position until 1951.[42]

The reasons for this retreat from the 'ideal of the self-governing church' during the last third of the nineteenth century were, of course, complex. Theology was certainly a factor in the missionary movement's mounting dissatisfaction with the native agency on which its operations depended. The eighteenth-century revival was a religion of the heart, but it was also rooted in Enlightenment rationalism. Evangelicals insisted that their faith was the result of observed experience of God's grace, they followed scientific advances with rapt attention and they were devotees of Lockeian empiricism. Reason, they believed 'must conclude in favour of the existence of a God who could reveal his will'.[43] The Enlightened origins of the evangelical movement had its corollary in the prominence of missionaries among the founding fathers of so many of the academic disciplines subsequently charged with the 'science' of colonial governance. These disciplines include anthropology and comparative religion, linguistics and sociology, as well as the area studies. (Interestingly, the foundations of political science alone are innocent of missionary influence, at least so far as I am aware.) As Peter van der Veer has argued, imperial logic has always contrasted a West governed by reason to a motley rest ruled by religion.[44] This article of Western faith is reflected in the disciplinary division of labour. Some people's history is studied in history departments; other's presumably without history are studied in anthropology departments. This was the academy's contribution to the cultural divide on which imperial power was predicated. (It is probably no coincidence that the distance between home and away, metropole and colony, is being called

---

[41] According to Alison Fletcher, LMS missionaries were thwarted by provincial supporters and the Society's Board of Directors, who often supported converts against missionaries during the 1830s and 1840s; Fletcher, 'The London Missionary Society in Early and Mid-Victorian Britain'.
[42] Porter, *Religion Versus Empire?*, Andrew Porter, 'Cambridge, Keswick, and Late-Nineteenth-Century Attitudes to Africa', *Journal of Imperial and Commonwealth History*, 5 (1) (1976).
[43] Bebbington, *Evangelicalism in Modern Britain*, 57–60.
[44] van der Veer, *Imperial Encounters*.

into question in projects such as ours at a moment when interdisciplinarity is all the rage.)

The tide began to turn against Enlightenment rationality in some evangelical quarters during the 1840s. The influence of Romanticism found theological expression in a new Biblical literalism and in premillenarian predictions of Christ's imminent second coming. Interestingly, Edward Irving, one of the leading proponents of this 'heightened supernaturalism', was a friend of Thomas Carlyle, a bitter critic of the anti-slavery movement and chief defender of John Eyre, the Governor of Jamaica, impeached for the brutality with which he put down the Morant Bay rebellion of 1865.[45] The new fundamentalists repudiated evangelicalism's prior emphasis on good works in favour of an almost exclusive reliance on faith. Foreign missions occupied an intermediary place between the two ends of this spectrum. Missionary outreach was not opposed for its own sake. To the contrary, this movement inspired the proliferation of faith missions during the second half of the nineteenth century, the most notable of which was the China Inland Mission founded by J. Hudson Taylor in 1865. These faith missions diverged from their older mainstream or modern predecessors in their rejection of organised outreach to home supporters. Faith missions relied instead on faith in God (and their missionaries' often-considerable private means) to fund their operations abroad.

This impulse travelled to the United States, where it found fertile soil, returning to Britain a generation later in the holiness revival led by Americans Robert and Hannah Pearsall Smith who arrived in 1874. The first Convention 'for the promotion of Scriptural holiness' was held in 1875 in the quintessentially romantic setting of the Lake District village of Keswick. In addition to its emphasis on personal holiness through spiritual mastery, the Keswick Conventions urged the rapid evangelisa- tion of the world as a precipitant of Christ's second coming. The Keswick spirit brought new recruits into foreign missionary service. University graduates, laymen and women with varying kinds of professional exper- tise, displaced the humble artisans and ordained clergy of the pioneering era. Like their precursors in the faith missions, these university mis- sionaries were disdainful of the uninformed masses in the pews at home as well as abroad. God would fund their missionary operations; they did not need to appeal to British widows for their mites and they looked askance at the shortcomings of native Christians and their churches.[46]

[45] Bebbington, *Evangelicalism in Modern Britain*, 79.
[46] Porter, 'Cambridge, Keswick, and Late-Nineteenth-Century Attitudes to Africa'.

The existence of a theological rationale for the missionary retreat from convert self-governance does not, however, remove this development from the larger history of racist thought of which it was a part. Perfectionism certainly diminished Christians' toleration of sin. However, they applied their high standards unevenly to say the least. Faith missionaries were far more interested in the splinters in the eyes of native Christians than in the logs blinding their own. Of course, native Christians were not perfect; some no doubt engaged in scandalous behaviour. So did many European missionaries, as a cursory reading of their private correspondence makes abundantly clear. However, no one drew from this a parallel conclusion that Europeans were not fit to minister. Invoking the failure of individuals in order to discriminate against a collective is never an objective response to abstract standards. Unfortunately, the propensity for such ethnic profiling grew dramatically during the second half of the nineteenth century. European missionaries' growing insistence upon the necessity of white control over missionary administration was ultimately driven by the pursuit of professional power, not by disinterested piety. This is underscored by the fact that not all missionaries succumbed. There were exceptions, such as Frank Lenwood, Robert Ashton, Henry Budden and his daughter Mary, who served with the LMS in north India. Their outraged refusal to participate in missionary conspiracies to block the advancement of their native Christian brethren testifies far more readily to theological inspiration than does their colleagues' collective capitulation to racialised self-aggrandisement.[47]

Exceptions like the Buddens remind us that where individuals are concerned, you just never know. The fact that the Buddens were exceptional, however, also proved the rule. The political tide had turned against race liberals, at least for the time being. For a variety of reasons, missionaries found it easier to indulge in racial discrimination during the new imperial age. Jumping on the racialist bandwagon was not sufficient, however, to avert declining missionary incomes. The missionary movement's influence at home receded during the second half of the nineteenth century. Patrick Dunae has shown how soldiers and explorers displace missionary heroes in boys' literature during the 1880s.[48] Catherine Hall has charted the erosion of the missionary lobby's influence even within the evangelical corridors of evangelical Dissent. No longer do

---

[47] Rhonda Anne Semple, *Missionary Women: Gender, Professionalism and the Victorian Idea of Christian Mission* (Rochester, NY, 2003).

[48] Patrick A. Dunae, 'Boys' Literature and the Idea of Empire, 1870–1914', *Victorian Studies*, 24 (1) (1980).

foreign missions enjoy first claims on the evangelical purse. Foreign missions do not disappear, of course, but they are overtaken by rival causes. In terms of foreign policy, the evangelical community's attention shifts back to the colonies of white settlement. Nonconformity's foreign policy during the second half of the nineteenth century increasingly focuses on the cause of white rights to national self-determination – e.g. Italy, Hungary, Ireland and South Africa.[49]

THE RISE OF PROFESSIONAL SOCIETY

The mainline missionary societies retained the modernising thrust that had characterised evangelicalism from the outset. Their emphasis shifted, however, from the free market liberalism of the first half of the nineteenth century to a cult of expertise. The salvation of heathen souls would increasingly be pursued through programmes designed to improve health, education and welfare. This social gospel was no less 'religious' than its more evangelical predecessor was. Religious motives were uppermost in the minds of its practitioners who were every bit as willing to sacrifice their all in God's service as their faith mission counterparts. Where they diverged was in the method by which they carried the gospel message. The widespread apathy towards organised religion in Britain was a subject of mounting concern during the second half of the nineteenth century, reflected in the growing support for home missions at the inevitable expense of their foreign counterparts. Foreign missions remained one of the favoured beneficiaries of evangelical largesse but their share was considerably less than the foreign field enjoyed during the early nineteenth century. Home missions achieved an urgency of purpose with the rise of a potentially anti-clerical socialism, encouraging some among the missionary minded to rethink methods that had failed to convert the British working classes. Advocates of a more social gospel reminded evangelicals that Christ himself had healed the sick, taught the ignorant and fed the hungry. The church need not stand by while its secular enemies took credit for what were essentially Christian values.[50]

Foreign missionary advocates of the social gospel argued that its precepts could be applied in the foreign field 'almost as it stands'. This quote is from Frederick Booth-Tucker's *Darkest India: A Supplement to General*

---

[49] See especially Hall, *Civilising Subjects*. Although note that Nonconformists would be divided on many of these issues; Birmingham's R. W. Dale, for example, left the Liberal Party over the Irish Question. The LMS chose not to discuss the Boer War so as not to offend pro-Boer sensibilities.
[50] Dale Johnson, *The Changing Shape of English Nonconformity, 1825–1925* (New York, 1999).

Booth's 'In Darkest England and the Way Out' (1890). The reciprocal influence of the domestic and foreign fields of missionary endeavour upon one another is evident in the title of this Salvation Army tract. The Salvation Army had modelled its original campaign on David Livingstone's assault on heathenism in 'darkest Africa', hence the title of its founding text. The Salvationists found the social gospel methods they evolved *in darkest England* readily applicable in the furthest reaches of the British Empire, as their ministry to India's 'criminal' castes seemed to represent.[51]

In terms of the politics of empire as well as the domestic politics of class for that matter, the social gospel contained contradictory potentials. The social gospel was, at the very least, an alternative to scientific racism. The inferiority of subaltern peoples in the colonies as well as at home was accepted, but its causes were attributed to environment not nature. The solution lay in social reforms designed to improve a corrupting environment.[52]

Some social gospellers in the Empire as at home, however, were sufficiently affected by their engagement with social problems to embrace political solutions of an anti-colonial and/or socialist nature. Fundamentalist fears about the social gospel trajectory were fully realised during the LMS's Bangalore Controversy, involving missionary removal of the name of Jesus from their literature because it aroused needless offence. And the Society's own Frank Lenwood, who served as the Society's Secretary during the interwar period, would resign after the publication of *Jesus, Lord or Leader?* in which he questioned the divinity of Christ.[53]

Social gospel practice also encouraged professional specialisation. While this closed down opportunities for the labouring classes to follow Christ in ministry in foreign mission fields, it vastly increased the opportunities available to educated laypersons, and particularly to single women. The earlier dependence on preaching the Word had excluded women from professional employment as missionaries, though

---

[51] 'The gospel of social salvation, which has so electrified all classes in England, can be adopted on this country [India] almost as it stands.' Cited in Cox, *Imperial Fault Line*. See also Walker, *Pulling the Devil's Kingdom Down*.

[52] These developments in the mission field exacerbated the growing tensions between liberal proponents of the social gospel and evangelical fundamentalists at home. See Thorne, *Congregational Missions*. On the professionalisation of social work, see Martha Vicinus, *Independent Women: Work and Community for Single Women, 1850–1920* (Chicago, 1985), and Anna Davin, 'Imperialism and Motherhood', *History Workshop Journal*, 5 (1978), and Robert James Scally, *The Origins of the Lloyd George Coalition: The Politics of Social-Imperialism, 1900–1918* (Princeton, 1975).

[53] Thorne, *Congregational Missions*.

many women did the work of missionaries in the guise of dependent wives and daughters. The social gospel, however, rested on practices that had become the 'natural' preserve of respectable women: teaching, caring for the sick, providing for the poor. By the end of the nineteenth century, women outnumbered their male counterparts. The latter were almost as concerned, perhaps more in some instances, to block women's advance in missionary administration, as they were to contain competition from native workers.[54]

The professionalisation of foreign missionary work encouraged a more circumspect relation to the colonial state. Missionary services were increasingly secular in nature that directly impinged on the colonial social order. Missionaries were more likely to see themselves as providing important social services for which they sometimes received official remuneration. Understandably enough, previously marginalised missionaries were sometimes eager to publicise this newfound official approval. Even when critical of colonial policy they increasingly couched their criticisms of policy from within the belly of the beast as it were. Excesses had to be curtailed *because* the British Empire was divinely ordained. Abuses of power were assailed as exceptions to a beneficent rule that contradicted and even threatened the Empire's otherwise rightful claim to divine approval.

IRON CAGES

In the final analysis (or at least the second half of the twentieth century), the missionary movement chose God over mammon, Christ over nation, accommodating itself to the rise of colonial nationalism with surprising rapidity. Indeed, some missionaries were active supporters of nationalist movements, echoing their forefathers' opposition to slavery a century before. Unfortunately, by this point missionaries' influence on popular culture on their British home front had waned beyond all recognition. The interwar period saw a dramatic reduction in church and chapel attendance that would snowball after the Second World War. The centre of Christianity had begun its dramatic migration from global north to south, from Europe to its (former) colonies.

As I hope I have made clear, the nineteenth century presents a very different picture than is visible today. Ultimately, however righteous, missionary ideals then constituted a double-edged sword that the defenders of

---

[54] Semple, *Missionary Women.*

empire were able to wield more successfully at home. The more passionately missionaries condemned colonial practice in light of sacred ideals, the more Britain's imperial mission would be associated with the intentions of the divine. The point for our purposes here is less the missionary failure to realise the gospel's universal promise than what that promise incited.

Foreign missionary organisations not only carried the Christian religion throughout the British Empire. More importantly for our purposes, they also brought that empire home. The centrality of organised religion in British political culture, its unrivalled social reach and its hegemonic status as cultural practice insured that missionary utterances enjoyed a wider and more authoritative hearing than those of perhaps any other colonial lobby. However laughable to critics like Dickens or Carlyle, the missionary propaganda disseminated in provincial assemblies, magic lantern shows and missionary exhibitions would insure that 'many a small tradesman or rustic knows more of African or Polynesian life than London journalists'.[55] The visions of Africa and Polynesia disseminated by the missionary movement were bathed in the stream of the most closely held of Victorian values. It was precisely because of the ubiquity and depth of their religious faith that the evangelicals were preoccupied with the foreign mission field, where they found imperial considerations if not conclusions simply unavoidable. The missionary project didn't just place the Empire under the skin of religious Victorians, to use Geoff Eley's evocative phrase; the Victorian evangelical's own eternal salvation was rendered dependent upon it.[56] While the form that the Empire should take was subject to considerable dispute, evangelicals found it theologically impossible to avoid engagement of the most intense nature. The Empire's status at home was thus far more than ornamental in this most religious of modern worlds.

---

[55] *London Quarterly Review*, 7 (1856), 239. This was true in the United States as well; Daniel H. Bays and Grant Wacker (eds.), *The Foreign Missionary Enterprise at Home: Explorations in North American Cultural History* (Tuscaloosa and London, 2003), 2.

[56] Geoff Eley, 'Beneath the Skin: Or: How to Forget About the Empire without Really Trying', *Journal of Colonialism and Colonial History*, 3 (1) (2002).

CHAPTER EIGHT

Metropolitan desires and colonial connections: reflections on consumption and empire

Joanna de Groot

There is now a body of writing and debate on the *constitutive* role of colonial and imperial elements in the material and cultural as well as political history of the United Kingdom, and on the interactions of material, political and cultural developments in that constitutive process.[1] This work has been helped by the growth of studies by economic and social historians of consumption as a dynamic *agent* in processes of material change since the eighteenth century, rather than just an *effect* of changes in production or marketing. Interest in histories of consumption in relation to those changes has converged with interest in such histories as a feature of social and cultural change signalled in publications like the volume edited by Brewer and Porter, *Consumption and the World of Goods*, and those edited by Berg on luxury.[2] Earlier studies of demand, retailing and spreading use or ownership of different products, tended to focus on providers (from large enterprises to corner shopkeepers) rather than customers. Now studies of income levels or standards of living are allied to analyses of the views, values and preferences which have influenced decisions to buy or use particular goods.[3] This convergence is part of the opening up of the study of consumption across a much broader

---

[1] See Chapter 1, above.

[2] J. Brewer and R. Porter (eds.), *Consumption and the World of Goods* (London, 1993); M. Berg and H. Clifford (eds.), *Consumers and Luxury: Consumer Cultures in Europe 1650–1850* (Manchester, 1999); M. Berg and E. Eger (eds.), *Luxury in the Eighteenth Century* (London, 2002); D. Miller (ed.), *Acknowledging Consumption: A Review of New Studies* (London, 1995).

[3] See for example L. Weatherill, *Consumer Behaviour and Material Culture in Britain 1660–1760* (London, 1988); C. Shammas, *The Pre-industrial Consumer in England and America* (Oxford, 1990); S. Mintz, *Sweetness and Power: The Place of Sugar in Modern History* (Harmondsworth, 1985); B. Lemire, *Fashions Favourite: The Cotton Trade and the Consumer in Britain, 1660–1800* (Oxford, 1991); E. Kowaleski-Wallace, *Consuming Subjects: Women, Shopping, and Business in the Eighteenth Century* (New York, 1997); W. H. Fraser, *The Coming of the Mass Market 1850–1914* (London, 1981); R. Williams, *Dreamworlds: Mass Consumption in Late Nineteenth Century France* (Berkeley, 1982); J. Burnett, *Plenty and Want: A Social History of Food in England from 1815 to the Present* (London, 1989) and *Liquid Pleasures: A Social History of Drink in Modern Britain* (London, 1999); J. Giles, *The Parlour and the Suburb: Domestic Identities, Class, Femininity and Modernity* (London, 2004), ch. 3.

front. From considering it as a discrete area of practical human activity, historians, social scientists, and cultural theorists have enlarged the range of approaches used to understand it, shifting attention from acts of consumption to the persons ('consumers') undertaking them, and developing different insights and methods of enquiry. They draw on work on gender, ethnicity, consciousness and identity within social and cultural studies of both past and present.

Recent studies open three important new perspectives on the history of consumption. Firstly, that history has been extended chronologically. Many scholars have applied the notion of 'consumer society' fairly specifically to the developed capitalistic societies of western Europe and North America in the twentieth century, and recent texts still discuss it in that framework.[4] However, since the 1980s historians have explored the role of consumption in earlier periods. Their work suggests that the involvement of wider and more diverse social groups in the purchase of goods available in a range of markets was a significant feature in the history of parts of western Europe and its Atlantic colonies from the eighteenth century. Rather than being exclusive to restricted elites, these activities can be shown to have spread to less privileged or affluent groups. Although there are, as Styles notes, real dangers in unreflective use of notions of 'consumer society/revolution', the available evidence for quantitative and qualitative shifts in participation in consumption alters our understanding of its history.[5] From the emergence of new styles of household, urban and family life to the establishment of new patterns of global exchange there is evidence of growing means and opportunity for commercialised consumption among those with modest incomes or status. While heeding warnings about overuse of the term 'consumer revolution' – 'before frequent repetition secures for it a place in that used-car lot of explanatory vehicles reserved for historical concepts that break down directly after purchase by the passing scholar'[6] – this evidence indicates an important shift. Significantly for the discussions in this book, much of it relates to 'colonial' products.

Secondly, consumption is now studied in a more holistic and active way. Recognising that products have both physical and social properties, so that for example food, in Barthes' phrase, 'has a constant tendency to

---

[4] R. Bocock, *Consumption* (London, 1993); D. Miller, *Consumption* (London, 2001).
[5] J. Styles, 'Manufacturing, Consumption, and Design in Eighteenth Century England', in Brewer and Porter, *Consumption*, 530–5.
[6] J. deVries, 'Between Purchasing Power and the World of Goods: Understanding the Household Economy in Early Modern Europe', in Brewer and Porter, *Consumption*, 107.

transform itself into a situation', historians of consumption now consider the use and exchange of products from that perspective.[7] As Brewer and Porter observe, their task is to 'investigate in the most comprehensive way the links connecting this material culture ... to the political and social systems with which it has become symbiotic', and to consider its 'value in interpreting the central transformations in the histories of Europe and America over the last several centuries, not just in economic history or the history of material culture, but across a far wider spectrum of human affairs'.[8] Such a task implies a number of 're-visionings' of the notion of consumption. It considers consuming activities not just as outcomes of movements in prices and incomes, but as embedded in the whole range of economic activity. It repositions consumption as an *active* element in the complex processes of material change, interacting with labour, skill and entrepreneurship, physical and financial resources, and forms of organisation of investment and production. It attends to relationships between the exchange, purchase and use of goods and the social relations, cultural forms and political institutions shaping those activities, and therefore to the interaction of material, political and cultural aspects of past human experience. To consider the role of corner shops in the evolution of working-class or immigrant communities and households in Salford or east London, or of clothing and entertainment in ethnic, gender, class and youth cultures in Birmingham, Manchester or Lewisham, illumines larger political and social histories of those topics.[9] Histories of the politics and economics of famine and agriculture in nineteenth-century Ireland have opened up similar stories of colonial and consumer activities.[10] This approach to consumption has imperial and global dimensions, whether in the role of eighteenth-century coffee houses in making the masculinised spaces of 'modern' political and commercial activity, or of exotic and racialised images in marketing everyday twentieth-century products.

Thirdly, extended and interactive approaches to the study of consumption and its histories have been deepened by the use of multi- or

---

[7] See B. Fine, 'From Political Economy to Consumption', in D. Miller (ed.), *Acknowledging Consumption* (London, 1995), 144; R. Barthes, 'Towards a Psychology of Consumption' (1961), repr. in R. Forster and O. Ranum (eds.), *Food and Drink in History* (Baltimore, 1979), 15.

[8] J. Brewer and R. Porter (eds.), 'Introduction', in *Consumption*, 3–4.

[9] deVries 'Between Purchasing Power and the World of Goods', 85–132; C. Chinn, *They Worked All Their Lives: Women of the Urban Poor in England 1880–1939* (Manchester, 1988) and *Poverty Amidst Prosperity: The Urban Poor in England 1834–1914* (Manchester, 1995); A. Davies, *Workers' Worlds: Cultures and Communities in Manchester and Salford 1880–1939* (Manchester, 1992); L. Young, *Middle Class Culture in the Nineteenth Century* (London, 2003); A. Kidd and D. Nicholls (eds.), *Gender, Civic Culture and Consumerism: Middle Class Identity in Britain 1800–1940* (Manchester, 1999).

[10] See C. Kinealy's chapter in this volume.

cross-disciplinary insights. One of the most important effects of this has been to consider consumption as not only meeting particular *needs*, but as expressing social and cultural *meanings*. The work of Bourdieu on the establishment of social boundaries and identities through the use of material goods or space, and that of Barthes on leisure and material culture, bring theoretical and cultural readings to supplement anthropological work on the symbolic social meanings which humans attach to acquiring, using and exchanging material objects.[11] While acts of consumption have physical and practical dimensions, they also express values, identities and the contests around them. Langer argues that the capacity to create and meet needs for symbolic meaning in the world is as much part of the human condition as the capacity to satisfy bodily needs for food, warmth and shelter, or personal needs for security, intimacy and learning. De Certeau draws attention to the *productive work* of those who see, hear or read the media, choose goods in a shop, adopt religious rituals or respond to teachers, seeing them as opportunities for subaltern agency within dominant economic, cultural or political structures.[12] Consuming behaviours can be understood as cultural practices or languages involving human creativity as well as material activities. Histories of the tea room as a place for respectable public female and family consumption, or the political role of tobacco smoking ('smoke-filled rooms'), or the sugar boycott as a strand in anti-slavery campaigns, are enriched by this perspective. Signalling respectability and social hierarchy around a tea table, or the desirability of goods by association with patriotism, virtue and status, or political agency and shared identity by using particular products, were integral to the whole process of consumption with its global and colonial dimensions. Such enlarged views of consumption show how it involves human agency rather than just being a symptom or effect of other actions, and that it has political and cultural, as well as material, bases.

This more developed view of consumption has obvious relevance for histories of empire, and in particular for the notion of the Empire in Britain. British imperial history, while partly a story of competition between European states and its associated strategic interests, and of

---

[11] P. Bourdieu, *Outline of a Theory of Practice*, trans. R. Nice (Cambridge, 1977); R. Barthes, *Empire of Signs* (London, 1983) and *The Fashion System* (New York, 1983); see also M. Douglas and B. Isherwood (eds.), *The World of Goods: Towards an Anthropology of Consumption* (rev. edn) (London, 1996); A. Appadurai (ed.), *The Social Life of Things* (Cambridge, 1986).

[12] S. Langer, *Philosophy in a New Key* (Cambridge, MA, 1951), 45, 53; M. de Certeau, *The Practice of Everyday Life*, trans. S. Randall (Berkeley, 1984), xii–xiii. Like Bourdieu, who used reflections about Kabyle culture in French-ruled Algeria, de Certeau draws on *colonial* relationships in Latin America to develop his propositions.

overseas settlement and investment, has equally importantly been a history of the role of commerce and imported products *within* Britain. The role of spices and textiles in the earliest imperial ventures, of consumer goods from colonial plantations (tobacco, sugar, coffee) since the eighteenth century, of tea, wheat and cocoa since the nineteenth century, and of Antipodean meat and butter as well as petrol from the British mandate in Iraq in the twentieth century, established direct links between consumption and empire. More indirectly, consumer products like textiles, soap and clothing since the nineteenth century or bicycle and car tyres in the twentieth century made extensive use of materials produced in colonial settings (Indian and Egyptian cotton, Australian and South African wool, West African palm oil, Malaysian rubber). While access to any of these varied significantly across time, place and social groups, the well-documented growth in the use of consumer goods within British society from the eighteenth century onwards had a large 'colonial' dimension.

One paradox explored in this chapter is how the powerful everyday presence of colonial products in metropolitan lives was both pervasive (the role of sugar, tea or tobacco in mass consumption) and invisible (the unseen commercial and exploitative structures of colonial power or labour which delivered the products). Sometimes contrasts and links between locations of colonial production and domestic consumption became powerful images in the marketing of some consumer goods. Similarly, contradictions created by the entangled commitments of British colonialism to commerce, dominance and progress became politicised around sugar and slavery, free trade, tariffs on consumer goods and competition between 'empire-produced' and other imports. The meanings of everyday activities like dressing, eating or cleaning were part of experiences and ideas of home, community, family and gender roles and differences, but also had powerful, if implicit, associations with patriotism (the use of 'empire' goods) and exotic pleasures (the glamour of familiar tropical or oriental products). As the image of milk and cocoa *together* in Cadbury's Dairy Milk chocolate advertising suggests, it is the *combination* of the domestic (indigenous rural purity) with the colonial (tropical exotic flavour) which had cultural power and impact.

INTERACTIONS OF COLONIES AND METROPOLE

In the colonial dynamic of histories of consumption the creation and movement of products became a constitutive element in relationships between the British and the areas of conquest, settlement and commercial or political control which they established beyond Europe, contributing to new forms of culture and consciousness. By tracking the entry of consumer goods with colonial origins into general use in the UK, it is possible to explore the processes whereby the British developed both intimate and extended links with a growing number of colonies, links based on interactions between capital and consumption. New household and workplace habits shaped, and were shaped by, the evolution of plantation slavery and European settlement in the Atlantic colonies, the structuring of the East India Company's trade and territorial expansion in Asia, and the growing influence and institutionalisation of these developments in the commercial, financial, social and political lives of people in Britain.

The qualitative shift in British consumption patterns from the eighteenth century onward involved the expanded and regular use of imported products by various income groups. During the eighteenth century, tobacco, sugar and tea, originally specialised luxury products, became articles in widespread use (using Shammas' benchmark of use by over 25 per cent of the adult population).[13] Tobacco exports from British colonial settlements to the UK rose from around 30 million lb in 1700 to about 76 million lb in 1800. Consumption of sugar produced on colonial plantations was 4 lb per head in the 1690s and 24 lb per head by the 1790s. The annual consumption of tea imported through the largest British eighteenth-century colonial trading enterprise, the East India Company, rose from about 0.5 lb per head in the 1730s to over 2 lb per head in the 1790s. Evidence for a steady fall in prices, and for the growing dominance of these products in the sales of grocers across the country, suggests that tea and sugar consumption was spreading across the social spectrum. Both moralising commentators and analytical observers of lower-class diet in the later eighteenth century reflected on the growing presence of these commodities.[14] Commitments to profitable production and trade in these products lay at the core of the development of the Atlantic colonies of settlement, and also of the territorial and political construction of the colonies of commerce in the Indian subcontinent, and later Hong Kong, West Africa and south-east Asia. Other areas of food production for UK consumers (wheat, meat, fruit, dairy produce) played a role in the

---

[13] C. Shammas, 'Changes in English and Anglo-American Consumption from 1550–1800', in Brewer and Porter, *Consumption*, 177–205: 179, 199, 202 n. 5.

[14] See Mintz, *Sweetness and Power*, ch. 3; J. Goodman, *Tobacco in History* (London, 1993); Shammas, *Pre-industrial Consumer*, J. Hanway, *Letters on the Importance of the Rising Generation of the Labouring Part of our Fellow Subjects* (London, 1767); D. Forbes, *Some Consideration on the Present State of Scotland* (Edinburgh, 1794), 7; Sir F. Morton Eden, *The State of the Poor* (London, 1797), vol. I, 496–7; D. MacPherson, *The History of the European Commerce with India* (London, 1812), 132.

development of colonies of European settlement in Australasia, South Africa and Canada in the nineteenth and twentieth centuries. By 1913 UK consumers obtained 80% of their wheat and 45% of their meat and dairy produce from foreign, including colonial, sources.[15]

Alongside this shift in food consumption there was comparable expansion in the market for cotton and cotton-based textiles, initially fabrics imported from India, and then, following restrictions on those imports, English-made calico, fustian and cotton using imported raw materials. The appeal of light, fast-dyed, colourful, washable Indian cottons spread across the social spectrum, generating a demand which continued after their importation was banned from the 1720s. British manufacturers of dyes and textiles applied themselves to the production of equivalent goods to meet these established preferences and desires. Lemire's work shows how the ownership of these fabrics was not confined to an affluent minority, and how the challenge of Indian textiles stimulated productive innovations in the UK as textile production and printing emulated and replaced eastern imports, in an expanding market. As she says, 'East Indian textiles were an archetype of popular consumer merchandise ... [which] permanently changed the dynamics of textile production and sale ... altering forever western decor and western dress.'[16]

This initial transformation of consumption to include significant quantities of colonial goods continued and diversified. The emergence of an independent USA removed the main sources of tobacco and raw cotton production from the British colonial orbit, although the importance of India as a supplementary source for cotton played an important role in the British relationship to India into the twentieth century (Indian raw cotton being 15–20 per cent of Indian exports between the 1870s and the 1930s). Cotton production was also significant in British involvement in Egypt from the 1820s, which became actual governance there (and in the Sudan, another source of cotton) between the 1880s and the Second World War. The levelling off of *per capita* tobacco consumption at around 2 lb annually during the nineteenth century changed with the rapid expansion of a new smokers' product, the cigarette, which grew faster in the UK than elsewhere from the 1880s. This marked a

---

[15] R. Floud and D. McCloskey, *The Economic History of Britain* (Cambridge, 1994), vol. I, 303.
[16] Lemire, *Fashion's Favourite*, 94–108, and 'Fashioning Cottons: Asian Trade, Domestic Industry and Consumer Demand 1660–1780', in D. Jenkins, *Cambridge History of Western Textiles* (Cambridge, 2003), 493–512; S. Chapman and S. Chassagne, *European Textile Printers in the Eighteenth Century* (London, 1981); M. Berg, 'Manufacturing the Orient: Asian Commodities and European Industry 1500–1800', in *Prodotti e technicie d'oltramare nelle economie Europee* (Prato, 1997).

gender shift in tobacco use, as women took to cigarettes, as well as a general rise in tobacco consumption, which took 4% of consumer spending in 1939 compared to 2% in 1913. It is notable that it was in the later nineteenth and twentieth centuries that 'colonial' sources of tobacco in Egypt and 'Rhodesia' were actively developed to supplement US sources. In the latter case, vigorous campaigns to promote an 'empire grown' product developed between the two world wars, like similar promotions of Kenyan coffee or Australian butter.[17]

These processes need to be situated in the global material structures through which they functioned. Circuits of capital, exchange and consumption depended upon and influenced one another. Machinery made in Glasgow supported sugar refining in the West Indies and sugar and syrup consumption in the UK, just as the tools, guns and chains produced in the English Midlands supported the capture, transport and control of slave labour upon which sugar production depended. During the nineteenth century these circuits were expanded and elaborated, whether through use of UK finance and technology to build the railways to transport Canadian wheat, Egyptian cotton, South African fruit and wool or Indian tea for UK consumption, or the 'informal' dominance of UK investment and trading interests in Argentinian meat production, Iranian oil and Anatolian opium. They were supported by financial and commercial systems linking the stages of the circuit through investment and credit, and by the ship building on which trade depended, and which was a key industry in the UK in modern times. Historians have traced complex relations between demand for consumer goods, formal and informal imperial power, and the modernising of manufacture, trade and finance which underpinned the industrial and commercial transformations in the UK after 1700.[18]

---

[17] On cotton see P. Nightingale, *Trade and Empire in Western India 1784–1806* (Cambridge, 1970); P. Harnetty, *Imperialism and Free Trade: Lancashire and India in the 19th Century* (Manchester, 1972); A. Silver, *Manchester Men and Indian Cotton* (Manchester, 1966); R. Owen, *Cotton and the Egyptian Economy 1820–1914* (Oxford, 1969); on tobacco see Goodman, *Tobacco in History*; M. Havinden, *Colonialism and Development: Britain and its Tropical Colonies 1850–1960* (London, 1993); S. Constantine, *The Making of British Colonial Policy 1914–1940* (London, 1984) and '"Bringing the Empire Alive": The Empire Marketing Board and Imperial Propaganda, 1926–33', in J. MacKenzie (ed.), *Imperialism and Popular Culture* (Manchester, 1986), 192–231; B. Alford, *W. D. and H. O. Wills and the Development of the UK Tobacco Industry* (London, 1973); see also A. Ramamurthy, *Imperial Persuaders: Images of Africa and Asia in British Advertising* (Manchester, 2003).

[18] See P. O'Brien and S. Engerman, 'Exports and the Growth of the British Economy', in B. Solow (ed.), *Slavery and the Rise of the Atlantic System* (Cambridge, 1991); R. Davis, *The Industrial Revolution and English Overseas Trade* (Leicester, 1979); D. Richardson, 'The Slave Trade, Sugar, and Economic Growth', in B. Solow and S. Engerman (eds.), *British Capitalism and Caribbean Slavery* (Cambridge, 1987); R. Austen and W. Smith, 'Private Tooth Decay as Public Economic

Most pervasive of these developments were those associated with sugar and tea. The emergence of beet sugar and the ending of slavery on West Indian sugar plantations placed older colonial structures of production and trade in a new competitive situation, further modified by the rise of colonial production centres elsewhere (Natal, Australia, Mauritius). Similarly the shifting patterns of British imperial power in India, as the commercial monopoly of the East India Company was replaced and its political authority brought under government control and abolished in 1857, had their effects on the provision of tea for UK consumers. The tea trade with China was opened to competition from 1834, while continuing and growing demand for tea encouraged the development of production in India and Sri Lanka. By 1900 'Assam' and 'Ceylon' teas accounted for over 90% of UK tea imports, and those from China 10%, reversing the proportions of thirty years earlier and embedding tea consumption in the structures of imperial authority, investment and trade. *Per capita* sugar consumption rose from around 18 lb annually in the first decade of the nineteenth century to 50 lb in the 1850s, 90 lb by the end of the century, and 100 lb in the later 1930s, while *per capita* tea consumption rose from 2 lb annually in the early nineteenth century to 6 lb at its end, and 8 lb by 1940.[19]

Such quantitative markers indicate more complex processes and relationships embedding colonial consumption in Britain. Just as the potential for mass consumption could be realised only through the creation of retail and marketing networks reaching more and more communities, so actual consumption practices involved the reshaping of everyday life. Evidence that tea-and-bread-based meals flavoured with sweet products (sugar, jam, syrup) became predominant in poorer people's diets in the nineteenth century also shows the accessibility of the products in question. This was the effect both of cheaper production and transport, brought about by the restructuring of labour, investment, taxation and transport in the colonies and the UK, and of the evolution of new forms of retailing in British slums and suburbs.[20] At one end of

Virtue: The Slave-Sugar Triangle, Consumerism, and European Industrialisation', *Social Science History*, 14 (1990), 95–115.

[19] On sugar see N. Deer, *The History of Sugar* (London, 1949–50); Mintz, *Sweetness and Power*; on tea see D. Forrest, *Tea for the British* (London, 1973) and *A Hundred Years of Ceylon Tea* (London, 1967); P. Griffiths, *History of the Indian Tea Industry* (London, 1967).

[20] On diet see S. Rowntree, *Poverty: A Study of Town Life* (London, 1901) and *Poverty and Progress* (London, 1941); M. Pember Reeves, *Round About a Pound a Week* (London, 1913); J. B. Orr, *Food, Health, and Income* (London, 1937); Burnett, *Plenty and Want* and *Liquid Pleasures*; D. Oddy and D. Miller, *The Making of the Modern British Diet* (London, 1976); on retailing see P. Mathias, *Retailing Revolution* (London, 1967); J. Benson and G. Shaw (eds.), *The Evolution of Retail Systems c. 1800–1914* (Leicester, 1992); J. Benson, *The Rise of Consumer Society in Britain 1880–1980*

the process the flow of colonial products into consumer baskets was characterised by consolidation, oligopoly and vertical integration in the nineteenth and twentieth centuries. At the other end distribution and selling linked small shops into marketing networks in which the 'brand name' (Players and Wills cigarettes, Keiller and Crosse and Blackwell jams, Brooke Bond and Lipton teas, Tate and Lyle sugar and syrup) was associated with affordable and accessible products sold in affordable quantities. By 1911 branches of the Co-op and chain stores accounted for 16% of all shops, rising to 19% by 1939.[21] The imperial connections of the burgeoning retail grocery trade ran through chains like Lipton's and the Home and Colonial Trading Association, which established over 100 shops and 4,000 agencies based on tea and margarine sales between its founding in 1885 and the end of the century.

These developments in the material fabric of daily life had wider social roles and meanings. The sweetened cup of tea which came to play a central role in British diets also shaped patterns of work and social activity, and many public and private rituals. The tea break and the tea shop, like drinking tea at family events such as Christmas or funerals, and at gatherings of neighbours, clubs or charity organisations, became established forms of social interaction, workplace life and personal refreshment. They offered a surge of warmth and calories which alleviated distress, lubricated social events and provided a focus for respectable leisure and entertainment, or welcome breaks in daily work. The social significance of tea consumption included tea drinking as an aid to temperance, invitations to 'tea' as settings for social exchange, emulation and competition, tea as part of employees' wages, or as the 'break' or canteen provision offered by employers, and 'tea' as the term for the meal at the end of the working day in many working-class homes. The role of tobacco smoking in work breaks, leisure time or sociable settings, and the use of 'sweets' as rewards and incentives for children, similarly gave acts of material consumption personal, social and moral meanings. Just as there were complex structures of production and distribution behind the corner shops and grocery stores which provided daily access to colonial consumer goods, so consumption was enmeshed with family, social and household relationships. Women's decisions about weekly budgeting, contact with neighbours ('borrowing a cup of sugar') or sociability, and

(London, 1994); J. Jefferys, *Retail Trading in Britain 1850–1950* (Cambridge, 1954); Fraser, *The Coming of the Mass Market.*
[21] Benson, *The Rise of Consumer Society in Britain*, 62.

the association of pubs and music halls with smoking, like that of the tea shop with modest and respectable public eating and drinking, were quite particular classed and gendered consumer practices.

The histories of these products which became everyday components of British lives are paralleled by others which established similar, if less pervasive, links between British consumers and empire. West African palm oil and cocoa in soaps, candles, drinks and confectionery, Australian wool on women's knitting needles, Malaysian rubber for tyres, clothes and condoms, New Zealand butter, or Kenyan coffee competing with that from Brazil, are instances of such links. Furthermore 'the Empire' itself became a consumer product. The readership for narratives of imperial travel, conquest, adventure and settlement, which began with educated elites in the eighteenth century, spread to wider middle-class audiences during the nineteenth century, and to literature aimed at children by its end.[22] Kipling, Rider Haggard and Henty are just iconic and successful examples of a whole spectrum of 'empire writing' in fiction, journalism, verse and travel narrative, as well as missionary journals, pamphlets and lantern shows.[23] Depictions of glamorous, comic or threatening figures of colonial people ('wily' or sexy orientals, 'unfortunate' slaves, loyal or dangerous Indians, 'sambos', Zulu warriors) in plays, cartoons, panto-mime, music hall and other forms of entertainment brought a whole cast of imperial characters for purchase and consumption in the mainstream of British culture.

Similar images were used by advertisers to market actual colonial goods and to associate pride in empire with other products, for example by attaching the term 'empire' to those products. Just as British tobacco

[22] On travel see D. Spurr, *The Rhetoric of Empire: Colonial Discourse in Journalism, Travel Writing, and Imperial Administration* (Durham, NC, 1993); M. Pratt, *Imperial Eyes: Travel Writing and Transculturation* (London, 1992); L. Franey, *Victorian Travel Writing and Imperial Violence* (London, 2003); E. Said, *Orientalism* (London, 1978); on fiction see P. Brantlinger, *Rule of Darkness: British Literature and Imperialism* (Ithaca, 1988); D. Bivona, *Desire and Contradiction: Imperial Visions and Domestic Debates in Victorian Literature* (Manchester, 1990) and *British Imperial Literature 1870–1940: Writing and the Administration of Empire* (Cambridge, 1998); on children's literature see M. Logan, *Narrating Africa: George Henty and the Fiction of Empire* (New York, 1999); J. Richards (ed.), *Imperialism and Juvenile Literature* (Manchester, 1989); J. Bristow, *Empire Boys* (London, 1991).

[23] A. Johnston, *Missionary Writing and Empire, 1800–1860* (Cambridge, 2003); C. Hall, 'Missionary Stories: Gender and Ethnicity in England in the 1830s and 1840s', in her *White, Male, and Middle Class* (Cambridge, 1992) and '"From Greenland's Icy Mountains ... to Afric's Golden Sand": Ethnicity, Race and Nation in Mid-Nineteenth-Century England', *Gender and History*, 5 (1993), 212–30; S. Thorne, *Congregational Missions and the Making of an Imperial Culture in Nineteenth-Century England* (Stanford, 1999) and '"The Conversion of Englishmen and the Conversion of the World Inseparable": Missionary Imperialism and the Language of Class in Early Industrial Britain', in F. Cooper and A. Stoler (eds.), *Tensions of Empire* (Berkeley, 1997).

traders signalled their reorganisation to confront American competition at the start of the twentieth century by allying in the Imperial Tobacco Company, so other entrepreneurs marketed empire typewriters, or used images and stories of empire to sell Eno's Salts, Pear's Soap, Beecham's Pills or Bovril.[24] Between the 1880s and the 1930s, railway companies named locomotives after dominions, colonies and other imperial references, as well as after royal personages, military heroes, classical and Shakespearian characters, and famous battles. Railways, which were a key feature in the expansion and manifestation of power 'out' in the Empire, had imperial associations 'at home' in Britain.[25] The popular name 'Empire' for music halls, theatres, dance halls and cinemas between the 1880s and 1930s signalled the new and self-conscious public cultural presence of an imperial identity accompanying new political concerns with empire in the era of Boer and Afghan Wars, Irish and Indian nationalism, and the rhetoric of Disraeli, Chamberlain and Churchill. Empire 'sold' aids to pleasure and self-improvement, everyday products and high ideals, newspapers and medicines, pride in modern technology, fun and fantasy. It literally and figuratively marked the growth of 'modern' consumer practices from the development of new working-class diets to the commercialisation of services and leisure, and the marketing of culture and politics.

INTERACTIONS OF THE 'MATERIAL' AND THE 'CULTURAL'

The visible presence of 'imperial' images and references across a spectrum of consumption wider than that of particular colonial products suggests that the 'consumption of empire' was a matter of more than material histories of the flow of West Indian sugar, Assam tea, Rhodesian tobacco, Middle Eastern petroleum or Australian wool into British households. As noticed already, the use of colonial products met a variety of needs and social relations as well as satisfying dietary and other practical demands. It therefore makes sense to examine consumption as a set of practices in which cultural meaning and creativity combine with material interests and social exchanges. Such practices involved the expression or manipulation of choice, desire and aspiration, and played a part in the shaping of human relationships and identities and of social structures and institutions, as well as satisfying hunger and other material needs. A fuller

---

[24] See D. and G. Hindley, *Advertising in Victorian England 1837–1901* (London, 1972); Alford, *W. D. and H. O. Wills*, 258–77.

[25] H. Casserley, *British Locomotive Names of the Twentieth Century* (London, 1963), 19–20, 21, 58, 79–80, 97, 122. I thank Peter Breeze for this reference.

analysis of the 'consumption of empire' should approach it as a composite of material and cultural elements with combined, uneven and shifting interactions.

These interactions and their imperial dimensions can be explored through specific examples. The adoption of new consumer products with colonial origins (sugar, tea, cotton clothing) in Britain during the eighteenth and nineteenth centuries produced lively comment on the spread of those products to poorer, less privileged sections of society, and anxious satirical depictions of the new phenomenon of upper- and middle-class women presiding over social events centred on the consumption of tea. For some (including tea enthusiasts like Dr Johnson), new lower-class consumption patterns expressed a dubious spirit of equality and emulation, unravelling old distinctions of rank and status based on the 'proper' restriction of access to 'luxuries' which, from the mid-eighteenth century, were being used by 'the common people'. For others, the expense and time involved in the preparation of meals consisting of sweetened tea with bread and butter and the time taken up in 'defamation and malicious tea-table chat' undermined lower-class industry and economy – and lower-class girls' attractiveness ('the very chambermaids have lost their bloom by drinking tea'). For yet others the appearance of new diet patterns among the poor was evidence of their difficulties amid the challenges of a commercial capitalistic society with its competing interests of trade, taxation, production and social stability.[26]

In the comments of analysts like Young and Eden in the late eighteenth century, of political and medical commentators and statisticians in the mid-nineteenth century, and of social observers in the twentieth century, the association of tea and sugar with the changing and distinctive patterns of working-class life was a dominant theme. It could be seen as a marker of the boundary between relative and absolute poverty, as a measure of dietary preference ('the acquired habits and tastes of the people'), as women and children's compensation for protein and fat that went to male wage earners, or as a snatched moment of comfort with a calorie boost during a working day.[27] Modern historians argue that the adoption

---

[26] J. Hanway, 'Essay on Tea', in his *Journal of Eight Days Journey* (London, 1767); D. Davies, *The Case of the Labourers in Husbandry* (London, 1795), 35–9.

[27] Arthur Young, *A Farmer's Tour Through the East of England* (London 1771), vol. II, 180–1, vol. IV, 352; Eden, *The State of the Poor*, 496–7, 770; Engels, *The Condition of the Working Class in England in 1844*; Burnett, *Plenty and Want*, 56–9, looks at the 1840's budget analyses of W. Neild; E. Smith, *Practical Dietaries for Families, Schools and the Labouring Classes* (London, 1875), 99; Rowntree, *Poverty*; Pember Reeves, *Round About a Pound*, 103; J. B. Orr, *Food, Health, and Income* (London, 1936); W. Crawford and C. Broadley, *The People's Food* (London 1938).

of sweetened tea at the core of the diet was significant in the transformation of household labour, in growing reliance on bought commodities rather than self-produced goods, and the imperial twist to state policies of taxation, protection and free trade affecting the prices of colonial goods. New patterns of waged work in market-driven production, and the need for working families and households to organise labour and meals around the different working patterns of women, men and children, made the easily produced and rapid infusion of energy, sweetness and warmth which it provided attractive. In a context where the ingredients grew cheaper in relation to other food products, and where there was growing reliance on purchased rather than time-consumingly self-produced goods, it was a welcome part of the diet. Interestingly, the use of statistics on the lower-class turn to tea and sugar in historians' debates on standards of living in the later eighteenth and nineteenth centuries has constructed them as part of the definition of a 'better' life.[28]

Unlike the role of cups of tea in the domestic rituals of middle-class and elite consumption, the growth of working-class consumption was associated with work and wages. From employers' use of sugar and tea as forms of payment, to the institution of tea-breaks and canteens in twentieth-century workplaces (bargained over by employers and workers), and tea brought to workplaces in cans and flasks, it played its role in shaping wage workers' lives. Those lives also shaped and were shaped by the development of urban communities, where by 1900 the sale of colonial commodities structured both local retailers and major providers (Liptons, the Co-op, Brooke Bond, Tate and Lyle) straddling national and colonial commerce and corner shops and modest grocery stores.[29] Beyond that, the provision and preparation of tea and sugar, supplemented later by sugar-fuelled jams, treacle and condensed milk as calorific flavourings for starch-based diets, shaped the domestic practices of working women in their entwined roles as carers, budget managers and earners. The establishment of 'tea' as the meal eaten on return from work, the use of 'sweets' as rewards or treats for children, daily calculations of money, credit or neighbourly support available to ensure supplies of these key goods, shaped gender cultures and divisions of labour, parent–child

---

[28] deVries, 'Between Purchasing Power'; Mintz, *Sweetness and Power* and in Brewer and Porter (eds.), *Consumption*; Burnett, *Liquid Pleasures* and *Plenty and Want*; Oddy and Miller, *The Making of the Modern British Diet*; J. Mokyr, 'Is There Still Life in the Pessimist Case? Consumption During the Industrial Revolution', *Journal of Economic History*, 48 (1988).

[29] Fraser, *Coming of the Mass Market*; Mathias, *Retail Revolution*; Benson, *Rise of Consumer Society*.

relations and neighbourhood reputations.[30] Like accounts of gender and consumption, workplace experience and the collective practices of religion, leisure and politics, appreciation of the colonial presence of the cup of tea, the 'smoke' and the jam sandwich enriches the analysis of working-class cultures and communities.

Nor was working people's tea consumption just a money matter. One witness to the 1830 Select Committee on the East India Company's tea monopoly observed, 'the best consumers of tea in this country ... are the servants in your own houses, for they drink black tea at 6 shillings and 8 shillings a pound when you may drink it in many instances at a shilling or two less'. Preference and taste influenced less well-off consumers, as was recognised by agents buying tea in Canton for British tea dealers and needing to be told that 'the strong tarry Pekoe flavour is going out of favour in London now but they still keep up their flavour in Leith'.[31] The powerful association between tea and temperance, established from the 1830s, flavoured the culture of colonial consumption with moral improvement and plebeian self-respect. It mirrored early nineteenth-century debates over slave-grown sugar and late nineteenth-century arguments over the role of alcohol selling in colonial West Africa.[32]

Just as expanding consumption of tea, sugar and cotton clothing during the eighteenth century stimulated anxieties about social mobility and emulation by the 'lower sort', so it produced a parallel and entwined set of concerns with gender roles and boundaries. A 1758 pamphlet attacked the use of tea and sugar by 'persons of an inferior rank and mean abilities ... of the lowest class' who 'vainly imitate their betters', citing 'tradesmen and wives and country dames', and 'every gammer [elderly

---

[30] Ross, *Love and Toil*; Roberts, *A Ragged Schooling*; A. Davin, 'Imperialism and Motherhood', *History Workshop Journal*, 5 (1978), 9–66; Pember Reeves, *Round About a Pound*; M. Llewelyn Davies (ed.), *Life As We Have Known It by Co-operative Working Women* (London, 1931); Women's Co-operative Guild, *Maternity: Letters from Working Women* (London, 1915).

[31] Report of the House of Commons Select Committee on the East India Company, 1830, vol. I, 53 (Mr Layton); William Melrose (Canton) to Mr Simpson (Leith), 1846, in H. and L. Mui, *William Melrose in China 1845–1855* (Edinburgh, 1973).

[32] B. Harrison, *Drink and the Victorians: The Temperance Question in England, 1815–1872* (rev. edn) (Keele, 1994); L. Shiman, *The Crusade Against Drink in Victorian England* (Basingstoke, 1988); A. Reade, *Short Anecdotes on Temperance* and *Tea and Tea Drinking* (London, 1884); C. Midgley, *Women Against Slavery* (London, 1992); C. Sussman, *Consuming Anxieties: Consumer Protest, Gender, and British Society, 1713–1833* (Stanford, 2000); M. Kingsley, 'The Liquor Trade in West Africa's *Fortnightly Review* (April 1898), 537–60; A. Olorunfemi, 'The liquor traffic dilemma in British West Africa', *International Journal of African Historical Studies*, vol. 17, 1984, 229–41; W. Ofonagoro, *Trade and Imperialism in Southern Nigeria* (New York, 1979); D. Birkett, *Mary Kingsley: Imperial Adventuress* (London, 1992); M. Crowder, *West Africa under Colonial Rule* (London, 1968).

woman]' in 'every cottage', and linking consumption of these goods to the gender as well as the class order.[33] Simon Mason associated tea-drinking among 'the lower set' with the wives of labouring men, who 'to be fashionable and imitate their superiors' spend men's wages on tea, and instead of attending to their children, spinning or knitting, indulge in 'canvassing over the affairs of the whole town, making free with the good name and reputation of their superiors'. Here tea consumption trans-gresses both class and gender status quo as women imitate their 'betters' and neglect their 'proper' roles as wives and mothers.[34] Jonas Hanway's criticisms of the spread of tea-drinking down the social scale associated tea with effeminate and inferior peoples (the Chinese), who were con-trasted with the 'wise and warlike' British nation, and saw a danger that those British qualities would be emasculated – an early instance of the racialisation of gender images and the gendering of racial hierarchy.[35] The link of British tea consumption to British interests in the East India Company's management of the China tea trade (like links between slave trading and the sugar colonies) gave it a homely as well as public and global setting.

These polemics from the initial stages in the spread of tea-drinking already link changes in daily diet to the changing social roles, relations and identities which were part of emergent commercial and market-led changes in work and family life, and continued through the next century and a half. They were also associated with the growth of British global colonial and commercial power and its impact on the emergence of 'polite' urban life, and of workforces and consumers whose experiences were shaped by ties to distant markets. The demands of colonial trade and settlement, of finance and shipping, and of networks of production and distribution, which made and moved Jamaican sugar, Birmingham metal goods, Chinese tea, enslaved Africans or Lancashire fustians, in pedlars' packs or East India Company fleets, were met by people and institutions adapted to these activities. In doing so they created not only goods and services but also new social, public and household worlds and cultures. The eighteenth-century coffee houses where commercial and political issues were explored and contested by urban men in a changing 'public' sphere – like the eighteenth- and nineteenth-century tea tables where abolitionists and missionaries linked domestic consumption and

[33] Quoted in D. Pigott, *Two Centuries: The Story of David Lloyd Pigott and Company of London, Tea and Coffee Merchants* (London, 1960), 4.
[34] S. Mason, *The Good and Bad Effects of Tea Considered* (London, 1745).   [35] *Ibid.*

women's agency to the moral and political challenges of imperial power –
were constituents of these worlds and cultures. Debates in educated,
dissenting and elite circles about the benefits and dangers of consumption
('luxury') often focused on the moral and social meanings of exotic and
increasingly widespread colonial imports, linking them to controversy
over colonial expansion itself, and to the 'imperial' characterisation of
'British' identity. Material goods and productive activity were infused
with a range of cultural and political meanings.

Like the spectacle of lower-class emulation of the tea-drinking habits of
their 'betters', the development of 'respectable' tea-drinking as part of a
new social sphere, based in households and supervised by women, generated reactions which developed particular gendered and spatial meanings for colonial consumption. Pope's image of Queen Anne taking tea
and counsel at Hampton Court, and the elite patrons of Ranelagh
Gardens, were early versions of the practice, but it rapidly became
associated with life in an expanding number of prosperous households.
When Addison in *The Spectator* recommended that 'all well-regulated
families ... set aside an hour every morning for tea and bread and butter', accompanied by reading of that paper which should 'be looked upon
as a part of the tea equipage', he evoked a household scene combining
colonial consumption, domestic virtue and self-improvement.[36] It set a
template (breakfast with the newspaper) which configured middle-class
life, spreading to other groups and taking changing forms in later periods.

This scene included both harmony and tension. The establishment of
the women-centred tea table for breakfast and for entertainment and
refreshment in the home in the evenings or afternoons became a focus for
the depiction and construction of gender and familial norms, identities
and differences, and for contests over them. It brought men and women
together in a new social setting, providing new opportunities for women
to organise and participate in gatherings which combined proper
domesticity, distinct from the masculinised spaces of political and commercial activity 'in public', with a social activity linking home and family
to broader social networks. In doing so, notions of women and femininity
were ambiguously constructed in new 'domestic' discourses and practices
which defined 'differences' from men and 'masculinity' in ways which
both constrained and empowered actual women. The spectacle of women
gathering either to supervise gatherings of men and women, or to talk
among themselves over those increasingly pervasive cups of tea, provoked

---

[36] *The Spectator*, ed. D. Bond, 5 vols. (Oxford, 1965), vol. I, no. 10, 44–5.

debate, satire and questioning. Was it a source of beneficial civilising and domesticating influences, of dangerously weakening unmanly and frivolous habits or of subversive possibilities for challenge to accepted roles and practices? It is notable that references to tea exemplified these questions. Eighteenth-century commentators focused on tea consumption to convey concerns about the emergence of new social groupings and practices, whether lower-class use of wages to emulate others, or women expressing subversive judgements of husbands. There is also evidence for men being drawn into the new forms of homely sociability centred around tea tables during the nineteenth century.[37] Just as the household or public gathering to drink tea affirmed sociability among kin or professional and entrepreneurial networks, or among supporters of particular causes (anti-slavery, philanthropy, Chartism), it might also shape new kinds of familial manliness.[38]

However, tea-drinking also produced male discomfort with the restrictive or 'weakening' claims of domesticity. In the 1870s and 1880s writers spoke of how 'the acceptance gained by the rite of five-o'-clock tea is the symbol of the ascendancy of the softer over the sterner sex' – a restriction on masculine privilege and autonomy, from which male clubs, or work in the Empire, where 'there is no ... having people fool around you with a cup of tea' offered escape.[39] Whether or not this relationship between the domestic and the masculine shifted over time, as Tosh suggests, there was certainly cultural tension between the positive associations of manliness with men's presence at the tea table showing proper concern with family and respectability and its negative associations with female inferiority. The denigration of the social exchanges which accompanied tea-drinking as 'gossip' about trivia, laden with petty spite and competitiveness, or female emotionalism, was the obverse of positive perceptions of those exchanges as part of a civilising and moralising process in which virtue and reputation were tested, and conduct and values appropriately regulated. As the satirical and advice literature of the eighteenth century was replaced by fictional portrayals of tea-drinking gatherings, moral approval or censure of female conduct and influence in

[37] L. Davidoff and C. Hall, *Family Fortunes: Men and Women of the English Middle Class, 1780–1850* (London, 1987), 436–45; P. Levine, 'The Humanising Influences of Five O'clock Tea', *Victorian Studies*, 33 (1990); J. Tosh, *A Man's Place* (New Haven, 1999), 23, 124.

[38] E. Yeo, 'Culture and Constraint in Working Class Movements', in E. and S. Yeo, *Popular Culture and Class Conflict* (Brighton, 1981); *Northern Star*, 29 September 1838, 8; 4 January 1840, 4; 20 February 1841, 1; 14 January 1843, 1.

[39] T. H. Escott, *England and its People, Polity, and Pursuits* (London, 1879), vol. I, 17; B. Wilson quoted in R. Hyam, *Britain's Imperial Century* (London, 1974), 138; see Tosh, *A Man's Place*, ch. 8.

the home or in society more generally was expressed in depictions of tea-party scenes in Dickens sketches or *Punch* cartoons.

Movements in the consumption of colonial groceries from elite gatherings to the homes of the middling sort, and from wage workers' payment to daily use in working-class households did not end there. At the end of the nineteenth century the development of the tea shop established a new location for public consumption, suitable for respectable family and female use and modest, affordable pleasure and relaxation for shoppers and others on urban streets. They were distinct from the pubs, clubs and eating places associated with the provision of refreshment for manual workers during their working day, with elite masculine gatherings and restaurants for the affluent, or with 'unrespectable' lower-class sociability. Interestingly, they served colonial products and also deployed other colonial associations, making early appearances as stalls at the colonial exhibitions of the 1880s. The *Times* commentator on the Colonial and Indian Exhibition of 1886 noted how 'weary afternoon visitors and dangling couples enjoy their tea all the more because it is served to them by white-robed Sinhalese with their jet-black heads coronetted with a cross-comb'.[40] When the successful tobacconists Salmon and Gluckstein embarked on selling cups of tea to a wide public, which gave rise to the ubiquitous Lyons Corner Houses of the early twentieth century, their first venture was with an associate, Joseph Lyons, who ran a refreshment stall at the Liverpool colonial exhibition of 1887, an experiment repeated at a similar exhibition in Glasgow in 1888. The prelude to the opening of their first tea shop in 1894 was an 1893 catering contract with the Imperial Institution and an agreement with the Ceylon tea producers for a £300 subsidy for supplying and advertising Ceylon tea 'and none other'. At the Liverpool exhibition too were sold the first cups of 'Kardomah' tea, whose exotic name became that of a chain of cafeterias.[41] The use of Indian, Chinese and other 'oriental' images in the sale of tea, whether as a grocery or as refreshment, continued to reproduce cultural constructions of its colonial character.

A significant feature of the new chains of tea shops (Lyons, Kardomah, ABC) founded from the 1880s on was their combination of affordability, menu and ambience, aimed at those of modest means who sought refreshment as part of a new pattern of urban activity which was neither

---

[40] *Times*, 18 August 1886, p. 13, column 6.
[41] Forrest, *Tea for the British*, 182–5 and *A Hundred Years of Ceylon Tea*, 172, 199–200; E. Rappoport, *Shopping for Pleasure* (Princeton, 2000), 102–5.

that of the sophisticated (and suspect) *flaneur*, nor of boisterous street life and manual labour. 'The natural habitat of the teashop was … in the less exclusive shopping streets … and in those business and commercial quarters where lady "typewriters" and other feminine staff were already making their presence felt.'[42] The ABC shops, started in 1884, were often situated near the transport which took commuting office workers and shoppers to and from home. The provision of two-penny cups of tea and 'light' food in a setting with 'waitress service' and modestly attractive decor met the needs and tastes of women and families on shopping excursions, and of the new 'pink collar' workforce of female shop and office staff. The tea-shop atmosphere of propriety and restraint matched lifestyles developing among wider sections of the urban population, and was associated with the larger white- and pink-collar workforce, the growth of suburban communities and widespread aspirations to respectability. This shift can be compared to shifts in attitudes to female tobacco smoking as 'fast' or 'lower class' to being first daring and bohemian, and then acceptable and even stylish (modelled by Hollywood stars) by the mid-twentieth century. Tobacco use also became a marker of generational tension and self-definition as adolescent challenges to parental or social authority were expressed by illicit smoking. Access to this colonial product was a mode of youthful self-assertion from the 1890s, when youth organisations were proffered as a 'healthy' alternative for unruly boys loitering with cigarettes in their mouths, to the 1950s and 1960s, when the media demonised 'rebellious' cigarette-smoking youth.

Aspirations embodying conventions of family and female proper conduct were themselves being modified by changing patterns of education, expectation and occupation for women. On the one hand approval for married women occupying themselves with household and family responsibilities and in domestic spaces was influential among class-conscious skilled workers and new service workers, as well as more 'middle-class' people. On the other hand the experiences and interests of young women who might be teachers, telephone operators, shop assistants or office workers, and who, when married, looked to provide their households with furnishings, clothing or crockery from the new kinds of shops catering to their modest budgets, produced new practices. The tea shop could be an appropriate setting for such women, who were more at home in various urban spaces than their fore-sisters, while looking to sustain feminine respectability in new and proper public social

---

[42] *Ibid.*, 184.

consumption. As late nineteenth-century male radicals in Halifax com-
memorated surviving Chartists with tea and food at the Temperance
Hotel, their daughters before the First World War visited tea shops with
workmates, with children, after a shopping trip or as a sociable treat.[43]

The story of tea-drinking is a many-sided narrative of the embedding
of social practices and cultural meanings in the physical consumption of a
product which emerged from a network of material processes linking
peasant labour in 'the East' to slave or free producers of West Indian
sugar, British entrepreneurs and shopkeepers, and consumers in kitchens,
workshops, cafés and drawing rooms. As Sidney Mintz eloquently shows,
the spread of sugar as the normal sweetener of 'bitter' drinks in the
eighteenth and nineteenth centuries, as a key ingredient in widely eaten
biscuits, jams and tinned goods from the later nineteenth century, and as
a cheap pleasure in twentieth-century confectionery, is a story with
similar features.[44] The consumption of colonial products like tobacco,
rubber, tinned 'tropical' fruit and cocoa products similarly made material
contributions to everyday culture and embedded colonial meanings as
well as colonial trade in ordinary lives. Beyond that there is the presence
of goods brought back from the Empire to ornament British homes,
whether the carpets, shawls and brasses in the houses of the prosperous
and privileged or smaller objects which soldiers, sailors and missionaries
could afford to bring to their families. This moves discussion into the
arena of cultural consumption through images, ideas and entertainment,
which connect material choice both to social meanings and to cultural
practice more specifically defined, and to the market for 'imperial' culture, as well as the use of 'empire' to market goods.

INTERACTIONS OF THE EXOTIC AND THE EVERYDAY

When colonial goods first entered British markets, their 'exotic' character
gave them prestige associated with elite consumption and luxury. Their
glamorous provenance from faraway, unfamiliar and hence mysterious
societies, known through legend and colourful reportage, was part of their
attraction and value which was translated into a means of marketing. The
process whereby products like tobacco, tea, sugar and Indian textiles

---

[43] B. Wilson, *Struggles of an Old Chartist* (1887) in D. Vincent (ed.), *Testaments of Radicalism*
(London, 1977), 241–2; diary of Ruth Slate, 7 February 1907, 19 and 29 April 1908, 19 August 1908,
in T. Thompson (ed.), *Dear Girl: The Diaries and Letters of Two Working Women* (London, 1987),
99, 116, 127.
[44] Mintz, *Sweetness and Power*.

became available as well as attractive involved extending those exotic associations in to the field of public advertising and selling. On the streets of eighteenth-century London, displays of shop signboards associated 'blackamoors' with sugar, coffee and tobacco, Chinamen with tea and groceries, 'Sultans' and 'Turks' with coffee and textiles, and 'Sultanesses' and 'Indian Queens' with textiles and China goods.[45] The expansion of consumption and the search for new markets were entwined with the imaging of increasingly familiar products as appealingly exotic but potentially accessible commodities for purchase and possession.

This predictable linking of the marketing of products to images with recognised connections to their West Indian, Chinese or Indian origins did not exhaust their potential. The glamour of exotic images was used to sell a wider range of products, so that 'Indian Queens' were used to advertise card makers' shops, 'Turks' for stationers, and 'blackamoors' for sign-painters and coat shops. The commercialisation of the exotic and the exoticisation of consumption spread beyond the trade in specifically exotic goods, just as terms like chintz, taffeta, muslin, calico, dimity and ging-ham, originally names for particular Asian fabrics, entered the everyday language of making and buying/selling textiles in Britain. One strand in the development of modern commodity culture was the evocation of the exotic as desirable, accessible and an effective lever of marketing and consumer demand. From oriental depictions selling eighteenth-century textiles, to eastern and African images used to market confectionery, soap and medicine, as well as colonial products, in the twentieth century the colonial entered the repertoire of commercial and public representation. Some of the accepted images of people and places in India, the West Indies, the Middle East and Africa (Fry's Turkish Delight, Robertson's 'golliwog' jam label) owe their familiarity to wide commercial use. The public and visible character of this repertoire gave it a more general role in bringing the colonial exotic into everyday ideas and experience in Britain, and added further dimensions to the interplay of commerce and culture. The influence and transmission of the imperial images used to sell products were not confined to those who bought or sold them, since they became part of a shared visual culture in the streets and media.

The role of such images is often depicted as the creation of naturalised, fixed and essentialised representations which establish 'difference' by repeating and transmitting particular forms and ideas, creating imperial, often racialised, 'knowledges'. These processes can also be seen as relations

---

[45] A. Heal, *The Signboards of Old London Shops* (London, 1947).

of power, linking material and political dominance to the making and maintenance of ideas and images.[46] Critiques of over-homogeneous and totalising versions of these arguments focus on the complexity and instability of meaning and representation in general, and, in the context of race and empire, examining cultural practices in specific contexts.[47] Other issues emerge when these broad questions are brought in to discussions of the role of images in consumer culture and in successful marketing of specific commodities. Some studies treat advertising as 'a capitalist form of representation', constitutive both of capitalism – through its intimate relationship to commodification and commerce – and of representation, through its verbal and visual forms. For some analysts, advertising is 'parasitic work' compared to the 'useful work' of production, while for others it actively forms cultures of capitalism, connecting commodities and desires as well as influencing markets.[48] Other debates focus on discourse and signification, seeing advertising as a distinctive mode of making meanings which organise knowledge, perception and understanding of the world, interacting with the world of consumption and with other areas of cultural production.[49] The former line of enquiry emphasises how exotic representations of everyday products obscure the 'real' conditions of production and exchange joining them to the consumer, while the latter examines how such representations give commodities some of their inherent character. Images of elegant sari-clad tea pickers and orderly tea plantations on tea packets and posters might conceal the character of labour conditions in Sri Lanka or the role of retail chains and oligopoly; they equally gave the familiar domestic consumption of tea imperial and exotic associations, underlining popular views of the Empire and its peoples found elsewhere. The Lipton slogan 'from the tea garden to the teapot', accompanying the image, projected an illusory vertical integration

---

[46] See J. Pieterse, *White on Black: Images of Africa and Blacks in Western Popular Culture* (New Haven, 1992); A. McClintock, *Imperial Leather* (London, 1995); Said, *Orientalism*; M. Alloula, *The Colonial Harem* (Manchester, 1986); A. Coombes, *Reinventing Africa: Museums, Material Culture and Popular Imagination in Late Victorian and Edwardian England* (New Haven, 1994); T. Richards, *The Commodity Culture of Victorian England: Advertising and Spectacle 1851–1914* (London, 1991).

[47] See Ahmad et al., *Commodity Culture*; McClintock, *Imperial Leather*, ch. 5; Ramamurthy, *Imperial Persuaders*.

[48] Richards, *Commodity Culture*; Ramamurthy, *Imperial Persuaders*; S. Jhally, *The Codes of Advertising: Fetishism and the Political Economy of Meaning in Consumer Society* (London, 1987).

[49] R. Barthes, *Mythologies* (London, 1973), *The Empire of Signs* (London, 1983); Richards, *Commodity Culture*; G. Debord, *The Society of the Spectacle* (New York, 1974); J. Baudrillard, *For a Critique of the Political Economy of the Sign* (London, 1983), *The System of Objects* (London, 1996).

of the tea trade (most tea sold by Lipton was not grown on its estates), refiguring it as a domesticated colonial exchange.[50]

The addition of visual to verbal advertising in the later nineteenth century intensified the process whereby images of 'exotic' colonial peoples entered the circuit of everyday British culture. If the street signs, coffeehouse names and traders' cards of eighteenth-century London, like the stylish engravings of Chinese men offering tea used by tea dealers elsewhere, spoke of urban sophistication, commerce and refinement, nineteenth-century posters and newspaper advertisements had wider audiences and references. The use of black women and babies to advertise the new commercial soaps, like that of 'orientals' to market tea and coffee, had imperial as well as exotic and ethnic characteristics, as traders, producers and advertisers reached new mass markets of potential purchasers. Images of white people washing black children dramatised the improving and morally 'cleansing' mission of empire in relation to the cleansing role of soap, itself part of the 'improving' aspirations of groups of Britons.

While Ramamurthy's reading of late nineteenth-century soap advertisements focuses on racial stereotyping as a feature of imperial control of colonies (in this case West Africa),[51] it is equally worth noting how these images of 'Africans' played a role in shaping British perceptions of their 'imperial' selves. They were part of a web of popular song, children's toys and pantomime and cartoon characters which positioned 'white' British people as powerful, responsible, improving and regulating in relation to 'black' colonial subjects. Similarly the pantomime figures of Aladdin and Widow Twankey, a name derived from an old term for a Chinese tea sold in Britain (twankay), linked the world of seasonal popular entertainment with an imperial exotic repertoire in which 'Chinamen' and 'negros' were still used to sell tea in the Edwardian period. 'Loyal Indian servants' offering refreshment to officers on coffee-essence labels, and supposed testimonies from explorers in Malaya, doctors in Kenya and soldiers in Afghanistan about the restorative powers of Eno's Salts for both Britons and locals, signified the strength and virtue of British culture, identity and imperial mission.

CONCLUSIONS

The world where Cadbury's chocolate and Brooke Bond tea were part of everyday British experience, and tobacco firms attracted boys to smoking

---

[50] Ramamurthy, *Imperial Persuaders*, 107, 111, illustrating advertisements in *The Graphic* from 1892 and 1896.

[51] Ramamurthy, *Imperial Persuaders*, ch. 2.

with cigarette cards depicting 'Heroes of the Transvaal War' or 'Maori chiefs',[52] was very different from the eighteenth-century world of coffee houses and tea tables. There were, however, connecting threads of consumption, the exotic and the shaping of racialised/ethnicised cultures and social relations in Britain. For historians of 'empire in the metropole', study of the interweaving of these threads with each other and with threads of urbanisation, political reform or gender and class formations reveals how intimate and domestic activities interacted with global structures of power and exchange. While the connections were in some ways invisible, or actively concealed, the persistence of exotic imagery in everyday consumer settings affirmed them, and translated the harsh aspects of imperial dominance into picturesque and pleasing forms. The consumability of empire in foods, entertainment, political gatherings or advertising, involved both pleasure and practical need, and cultural meanings as well as monetary calculations. Whether unreflective (as in daily routines) or politically and culturally self-conscious (for abolitionists, free traders, temperance reformers, imperial preference campaigners), consumption placed 'British' homes in an imperial world.

[52] A. Cruse, *Cigarette Card Cavalcade* (London, 1948), 54–7, 70, figs. 83–4.

CHAPTER NINE

Imagining empire: history, fantasy and literature

Cora Kaplan

How did imaginative literature make the Empire both vivid and legible to readers in Britain? In what ways did the language and narratives of fiction, poetry and other popular genres – from travel writing to anti-slavery polemic – represent the everyday relations of metropole and colony, of domestic and imperial subjects? What sort of dreams and nightmares did they evoke? In thinking about the shifting role which literary production has played in the imaginative construction of the Empire at home across two centuries this chapter will argue for the uses of literature by historians, by drawing on two exemplary instances from discrete historical periods – the critical decades leading up to and following the abolition of colonial slavery in 1834 and the years from the 1950s through to the millennium. In the first and much more detailed case, it will explore some of the ways in which the colonial connection was imagined in fiction and in anti-slavery writing up to and after the abolition of colonial slavery. The British campaign to end slavery was never free of hierarchical distinctions – historians and critics have long noted the ordering of peoples and cultures immanent in the imaginative and polemical literature associated with it. Less recognised perhaps is that in the two decades following abolition literary texts also played a central role in a retrospective critique of the Christian humanitarianism and/or liberal universalism that had inspired an earlier radical moment. After abolition, the ambiguity of the status of ex-slaves and the future of the colonies made more, not less, urgent the fashioning by white British writers of geopolitical and racially distinct hierarchies, reordering both domestic and colonial spaces, subjects and cultures. Postcolonial writers of the past half century, rewriting the history of British slavery, its overthrow and its long-term effects in fiction and poetry, have been acutely aware of this disturbing trajectory. The understanding of its legacies for twentieth-century Atlantic societies experiencing the effects of decolonisation and the movement of populations from the former colonies to the metropole is nowhere more evident than in their powerful imaginative rendering of the postwar Caribbean emigration to

Britain. My chapter ends with a coda – a very brief exploration of four key novels of emigration by Samuel Selvon, George Lamming, Caryl Phillips and Andrea Levy – written between the mid-1950s and the noughts of the new millennium, narratives which would profoundly disrupt both prior definitions of, and fixed divisions between, 'home' and 'empire'.

Few literary critics today would deny the importance of historicising literary studies and theorising that process. But if one were to turn the question around, asking whether, and in what ways, historians should go about integrating the literary, the answer is rarely straightforward. And while many historians, particularly social and cultural historians, use literary example as a matter of course, it is telling that there is no analogous verb to 'historicise' that sums up the articulation of literary texts to historical narrative, an absence that is perhaps indicative of a certain level of unease with its presence there at all. Indeed both integrative moves raise interesting and, by their very nature, unresolved issues within and across the disciplines about causality, evidence, referentiality, aesthetics and authorship.

Even so the literary can be a creative resource for the writing of history, especially if it ventures beyond the illustrative model that is the most typical use of the literary for historians – the dramatisation for the reader of a case already made through other more factually based materials. Offered a more dynamical role, literature can point towards new historical questions, rather than simply glossing existing ones. I want to suggest, perhaps provocatively, that literary texts are not only, or even primarily, a body of evidence that supplements or supports social and political history, although of course they may quite properly and usefully act in that way, but should be of most interest to historians because of their very generic specificity, the ways in which they give free – and freely acknowledged – reign to the space of imagination and of fantasy, a discursive mode where both the utopian and dystopian sides of imperial relations can be elaborated. I am using fantasy here not in its common-sense definition as something private or essentially sexual, 'the dirty tricks of the mind', but in its psychoanalytic sense as many cultural critics do, and as Jacqueline Rose has defined it in *States of Fantasy* (1996) – something not 'antagonistic to social reality' but 'its precondition or psychic glue', something that 'plays a central, constitutive role in the modern world of states and nations'. If we follow Rose we might also emphasise the way in which fantasies of nationhood, of identities, both serve to bar memories and to re-elaborate memories struggling to 'be heard'.[1] It is by reading literature historically with

---

[1] Jacqueline Rose, *States of Fantasy* (Oxford, 1996), 5.

attention to the register of fantasy – the hopeful and fearful projections of the political and social relations of metropole and colony – that historians as well as critics can best trace the shifting imaginative terms of that connection.

***

'Did you not hear me ask him about the slave trade last night?'
'I did – and was in hopes the question would be followed up by others. It would have pleased your uncle to be inquired of farther.'
'And I longed to do it – but there was such a dead silence!'[2]

This brief exchange between Fanny Price and her cousin Edmund Bertram from Jane Austen's *Mansfield Park* (1814) has become a much disputed literary moment in a wide-ranging debate about the writing of empire in imaginative literature, a debate certainly not initiated but energetically renewed in Edward Said's *Culture and Imperialism* (1993), a study which extends Benedict Anderson's argument about the novel as a key element in nineteenth-century nation building to the relation of empire. In this study Said uses Austen's 'casual references to Antigua', where Mansfield's patriarch, Sir Thomas Bertram, owns estates, to construct a genealogy of fictional texts from Austen through Jean Rhys in which a 'usable colony' like Antigua becomes a resource 'to be visited, talked about, described, or appreciated for domestic reasons, for local metropolitan benefit'.[3] Like Chinua Achebe's eloquent critique (1977) of the imperialist trajectory in Conrad's *Heart of Darkness* and Gayatri Chakravorty Spivak's provocative essay on *Jane Eyre* in 'Three Women's Texts and a Critique of Imperialism' (1985),[4] Said challenged readings of *Mansfield Park* that were so fully embedded in a metropolitan perspective that the colonial or imperial reference went unremarked. He asked that critics historicise rather than 'jettison' Austen. They should begin 'to deal with as much of the evidence as possible, fully and actually, to read what is there or not there, above all, to see complementarity and interdependence instead of isolated, venerated, or formalised experience that excludes and forbids the hybridizing intrusions of human history'.[5] Critics have responded to this call by placing the moment of *Mansfield Park*'s likely composition in relation to the debate on colonial slavery and

---

[2] Jane Austen, *Mansfield Park*, ed. Claudia L. Johnson (New York, 1998), 136.
[3] Edward Said, *Culture and Imperialism* (New York, 1993), 93 and see 80–97.
[4] Chinua Achebe, 'An Image of Africa: Racism in Conrad's *Heart of Darkness*', *Massachusetts Review*, 18 (1977), 782–94; Gayatri Chakravorty Spivak, 'Three Women's Texts and a Critique of Imperialism', in Henry Louis Gates (ed.), *'Race', Writing, and Difference* (Chicago, 1985), 262–80.
[5] Said, *Culture and Imperialism*, 96.

exploring Austen's family connections with Britain's overseas empire. (Her father, the Reverend George Austen, was a principal trustee of slaveholding estates in Antigua owned by James Langford Nibbs who became godfather to Jane's brother James.)[6] They have also gone back to the novel to rethink Austen's treatment of the problematic figure of Sir Thomas Bertram, exploring in great detail the social and ethical implications of his multiple roles, as father, uncle, domestic patriarch, master of Mansfield Park and slaveowner.[7]

Yet for literary critics, and not only Austen specialists, the reclamation of Austen's own ethical position and that of her heroine in terms of modern political sensibilities is a factor even in the most sophisticated analyses of *Mansfield Park*. Austen's iconic and fetishised place in any account of the origins of the modern novel and of female authorship only intensifies this effect. However it is one that historians might well ignore in favour of the wider point made by Said, Southam, Lew and others about the undoubted fact that the novel is implicated, and deliberately so, in questions relating to empire and slavery, metropole and colony. The interest of *Mansfield Park* for historians might be, as Southam suggests, in the radical ambiguity of the relationship between home and empire for the Austen family, for the fictional Bertrams and for England in 1811–14. Rather than impugning or defending Austen or her characters, historians might dig deeper into the implications of the narrative aporia posed by Fanny's question and the social silence that ensues. Its twofold lack of overt narrative consequence – for the novel repeats the dinner-table silence by not allowing Fanny to ask her question again, in spite of her cousin Edmund's encouragement – leads back to the question about what gets left in and out of discourse. Its structure as an incident follows the psychoanalytic form of negation, a wish brought to consciousness, but spoken only to be immediately denied. Freud argues interestingly that this seemingly perverse action is in fact a half-move towards bringing an issue to consciousness, for it represents 'a kind of intellectual acceptance of the repressed, while at the same time what is essential to the repression persists'.[8] Reading *Mansfield Park* and the moment of its production in these terms, as a psychic effect 'constituent of social reality', makes both historical and psychological sense of a novel whose main thrust is the

---

[6] See Brian Southam, 'The Silence of the Bertrams', *Times Literary Supplement*, 17 February 1995.
[7] See Joseph Lew, ' "That Abominable Traffic": *Mansfield Park* and the Dynamics of Slavery', in Beth Fowkes Tobin (ed.), *History, Gender and Eighteenth Century Literature* (Athens, GA, 1994), 271–300.
[8] Cited in J. Laplanche and J.-B. Pontalis, *The Language of Psychoanalysis* (London, 1983), 263.

reform and moralisation of the metropole, but which paradoxically chooses to highlight without being willing to explore one of its central ethical contradictions.[9] The economic dependence of England on a slave economy was an issue vividly present in anti-slave-trade polemic and poetry of the period leading up to 1807, but one that, as was clear by the time of *Mansfield Park*'s composition, such partial legislation could not resolve, but only deepen.

Considering Austen's novel in relation to the anti-slavery poetry and prose of the period 1788–1807 gives it one kind of resonance, while reading it as a precursor to the critical mass of anti-slavery writing of the 1820s in the lead-up to abolition gives it another. If *Mansfield Park*'s agonistic 'silence' is precisely historically situated, then did an earlier period find speaking of the relationship between metropole and colony less problematic? If we work backwards, focusing on the first set of dates, *Mansfield Park*'s fragmentary allusions to the slavery debate and Sir Thomas's West Indian plantations might be compared to the much more overt treatment offered in Amelia Anderson Opie's *Adeline Mowbray* (1805). Opie was a friend of William Godwin and Mary Wollstonecraft and in the early nineties shared many of their views; her novel however was a *roman-à-clef* about Godwin and Mary Wollstonecraft's experimentation with 'free' love, but, as Opie's own social politics altered in line with the late nineties' rejection of feminism and republicanism, so her novel evoked the seductive appeal of radical social ideas for an idealistic but wrongly educated young woman while mounting a blistering attack on them. Anti-slavery sentiment crossed political lines, and *Adeline Mowbray* makes it clear how humanitarianism and hierarchy would come, for many, to be integrated in the English imagination at the beginning of the nineteenth century. Playing on the negative representations of the West Indies, certainly the dominant metropolitan view of colonial life in the eighteenth and nineteenth centuries, Jamaica is represented as a source of unearned wealth accrued through the evils of chattel slavery, a haven for European rogues of all kinds, including unfaithful, absconding husbands. The degeneration of European society in the metropole and the colony are narratively, if not quite causally, linked. England – as in Austen's fiction

---

[9] Said suggests that the silence emanates from the fact that 'one world could not be connected with the other' and argues that a 'postcolonial consciousness' would come to see 'works like *Mansfield Park*' as 'in the main ... resisting or avoiding that other setting, which their formal inclusiveness, historical honesty, and prophetic suggestiveness cannot completely hide': *Culture and Imperialism*, 96. This passage, and others in his discussion, leans towards an ethical defence of canonical authors that goes beyond existing evidence.

but more melodramatically – is a breeding ground for louche masculinity – regency rakes and common cads who can interpret Adeline's principled refusal to marry her lover only as a free invitation for them to make crude sexual advances to her. But after Adeline's philosopher lover, Glenmurray, dies she is increasingly imperilled by the harassment her tarnished reputation provokes and rashly marries a perfidious friend of his, Berrendale, whose deceased first wife was a Jamaican colonial. Berrendale, like Sir Thomas, leaves his English household to attend to his financial interests in Jamaica, but unlike Mansfield's master he dies there after bigamously marrying another rich European woman. The problematic movement of imperial men between metropole and colony is present in both Opie and Austen, but in the former the social anarchy of the slaveholding colony is foregrounded. In its negative representation of Jamaica, so typical in metropolitan writing, *Adeline Mowbray* throws light on the refusal of *Mansfield Park* to paint Antigua in similar terms – indeed we might see Austen's novel, in contrast, not as actively contesting, but perhaps implicitly resisting, such stereotypes.

However, *Adeline Mowbray*'s much more discursively elaborated account of the human and economic traffic between home and empire centres on the presence in England of nominally free persons of colour. A key figure in the novel is a mulatto ex-slave from Jamaica, Savanna, whose ailing husband William – whose race the novel never specifies – Adeline saves from debtor's prison. In gratitude, Savanna becomes Adeline's devoted servant and her outspoken champion. Adeline's altruistic behaviour in rescuing Savanna's husband – she uses money that should have purchased the dying Glenmurray a longed-for pineapple – is presented as evidence of her altruism. The forfeit of the tropical luxury of the pineapple, associated with slavery, for the well-being of an ex-slave, underlines the novel's anti-slavery message. Adeline's sympathy is motivated in large part not by Savanna's colour, which, virtuously colour blind, she 'had not recollected', but by the ugly sentiments it aroused – 'a circumstance which made her an object of greater interest to Adeline', an interest intensified by the racist slurs – 'black bitch' – directed at her unoffending person, slurs that have a corollary with Adeline's own treatment by England's male population.[10] Opie frames Adeline and the reader's sympathy with Savanna's plight in terms of the integrity of the mulatto's family, which includes a young son known to the reader only as 'the tawny boy', but in order that Savanna's fidelity to Adeline should be

---

[10] Amelia Opie, *Adeline Mowbray*, ed. Shelly King and John B. Pierce (Oxford, 1999), 138.

absolute, Opie takes care to disperse them: the son is taken up by an English benefactor, and Savanna's husband William finds a place as a manservant to a gentleman en route to Jamaica. This cavalier narrative separation from her chosen partner and biological child permits Savanna's attention to be almost wholly focused on her mistress who comes to depend on her servant as 'the only person in the world ... who loves me with sincere and faithful affection'.[11] Savanna leaves Adeline for a short time only, to visit her husband in Jamaica; here she is briefly recaptured by her former owner, but returns to England to serve her mistress, and, after Adeline's death, her orphaned daughter.[12]

Published in 1805, two years before the abolition of the slave trade, *Adeline Mowbray* sets up deliberate parallels between the social rebel Adeline and the more sexually conventional but outspoken ex-slave Savanna. Savanna's married state and distaste for the adulterous relationships she observes silently confront the stereotype of mulatto West Indians as sexually promiscuous almost by virtue of their mixed-race status, just as Opie's portrait of Adeline makes her an essentially feminine and nurturing woman in spite of her heterodox views, a far cry from the cruel contemporary caricature of Wollstonecraft as a 'hyena in petticoats'. But the fate that the novel invents for the independent women it has created underlines the intimate relationship between the conservative turn in English gender politics from the late 1790s, in which a domestic, maternalist rhetoric supplants the idea of female autonomy and equality, and the hierarchical and familial nature of much anti-slavery discourse. The so-called 'love' between Savanna and Adeline is structured through debt and dependence – when the servant extravagantly promises to return from Jamaica and 'die wid' her mistress, Adeline reminds Savanna in a deliberate if shocking turn of phrase which equates subaltern gratitude with slavery that 'you have given me the right to claim your life as mine; nor can I allow you to throw away my property in fruitless lamentations'.[13] And just as Adeline, in the final pages of the novel suddenly (and for modern readers, unconvincingly) renounces and repents of her youthful, principled rejection of marriage – so Savanna seems to escape involuntary servitude in Jamaica only to re-enslave herself

---

[11] *Ibid.*, 188.

[12] For an excellent analysis of empire and abolitionism in *Adeline Mowbray* see Carol Howard, ' "The Story of the Pineapple": Sentimental Abolitionism and Moral Motherhood in Amelia Opie's *Adeline Mowbray*', *Studies in the Novel*, 30 (1998), 355–76.

[13] Opie, *Adeline Mowbray*, 194. For a reading that sees a more radical imperative in the novel's maternalism, see Roxanne Eberle, 'Amelia Opie's *Adeline Mowbray*: Diverting the Libertine Gaze; or, The Vindication of a Fallen Woman', *Studies in the Novel*, 26 (1994), 121–52.

through a debt of gratitude that has no term of payment and which supplants her freely chosen familial ties.

Read in the register of fantasy, *Adeline Mowbray* not only highlights an anxiety about the status of free blacks that would percolate through the anti-slavery writing of the twenties and surfaces in fiction and poetry *after* 1834, but ties that anxiety closely to a conservative, post-revolutionary agenda for women. In the narrative resolution of Adeline and Savanna's parallel, linked but distinct histories we can see the rejection of the right to individual autonomy that the republicanism, abolitionism and feminism from the late 1780s through the mid-nineties briefly fostered. Adeline's threat to social order is seemingly the more extreme, since perhaps she has potentially the most ideological and social power – her detailed repentance of her youthful radicalism does not avert an authorial death sentence. But the novel takes equivalent steps to curtail Savanna's liberty in Britain, and in doing so pre-emptively defends itself against the notion of black autonomy for free persons of colour – whether in the metropole or in the colonies – disarming and containing these figures within an English familial order and economy before they become dangerous or threatening.

Neither *Adeline Mowbray* nor *Mansfield Park* is primarily *about* slavery or empire, yet the insistent inclusion of its themes and anxieties in texts whose main thrust is the reformation of English society is neither accidental nor trivial. It provides evidence for the argument made throughout this volume about the centrality rather than the marginality of the relations of empire to the British imagination. And in Opie's creation of the feisty figure of Savanna we see the emergence of a condensed, gendered representation of those anxieties about black autonomy that would become a recurring motif in nineteenth-century British writing about home and empire. The imagined black female subject of African descent who arrives on British soil is almost always a paradoxical figure, signalling both the humanitarian and the repressive impulses of that society, defining, if you will, the limits of both.

For if we move backwards in time once again to 1803, to Wordsworth's two resonant sonnets 'To Toussaint L'Ouverture' and 'September 1, 1802', both published first in February 1803 in the *Morning Post*, we encounter an earlier representation of this figure, now paired with a heroic masculine counterpart. The first sonnet is a celebratory, but prematurely elegiac, tribute to St Domingue's revolutionary black leader whose betrayal, capture and imprisonment by Napoleon provided Wordsworth with a further instance of his disillusion with Bonaparte, aligning Toussaint with poetic liberty, the powers of 'air, earth and skies' and the immortality of 'Man's unconquerable mind'.[14] The second, equally motivated by Wordsworth's belief that France had rejected the humanitarian universalism that was part of his hopes for the early moments of the French Revolution and for Bonaparte's ascent to power, tells the story of an anonymous Negro woman encountered by William and his sister Dorothy as they travelled back from France in September 1802. She like 'all others of that race' had been summarily ejected from the country by the statute of 2 July 1802, which forbade people of colour from entering the continental territories of France and warned that any residing there without government approval would be expelled. Published initially as 'The Banished Negroes', this poem was frequently revised between its first publication and 1845. In its first form the woman is a figure of utter abjection – 'silent', 'fearing blame'. 'Dejected, meek, yea pitiably tame' unable even to 'murmur' 'at the unfeeling Ordinance'; she is a feminine counterpart to the safely incarcerated Toussaint of 1803.[15] The defeat and abjection of men and women of African descent at the hands of the French provide the occasion for poetics and pity, emphasising also Wordsworth's reawakened patriotism through the representation of Britain as a more racially tolerant nation. By the 1820s, however, Toussaint is long dead, Haiti's black leadership is in deep trouble and the campaign to abolish slavery in British colonies is in full swing. Wordsworth's mid-life anxieties about postcolonial Haiti were expressed as early as 1821 in a comic poem, composed with his sister-in-law Sara Hutchinson, which mocked, in egregiously racist terms, the supposed pretensions of the widow of the deposed and dead King of Haiti, Henri Christophe, who with her children were guests of the Wordsworths' friends, the British abolitionist Thomas Clarkson and his wife Catherine, with whom they had close ties. The poem, a parody of Ben Jonson's 'Queen and Huntress, Chaste and Fair', suggests that the very idea of a 'Queen and Negress, chaste and fair' is a double oxymoron, and that her presence in a 'British chair' in Clarkson's household – indeed in Britain at all, it is implied – is more than a little ridiculous, matter out of place. The poem, injudiciously sent to the Clarksons by Dorothy Wordsworth, caused considerable offence, and forced a very grudging half-apology from the Wordsworth household about their joke on 'poor fallen royalty'.[16] The shift in Wordsworth's sentiments

[14] William Wordsworth, *'Poems in Two Volumes', and Other Poems, 1800–1807*, ed. Jared Curtis (Ithaca, 1983), 160–1.

[15] *Ibid.*, 161–2. For discussion of 'The Banished Negroes' see Judith W. Page, *Wordsworth and the Cultivation of Women* (Berkeley, 1994), 67–76.

[16] Dorothy Wordsworth to Catherine Clarkson, 24 October 1821 and D. W. to C. C., 16 January 1822. *The Letters of William and Dorothy Wordsworth*, ed. Alan G. Hill (Oxford, 1978), vol. III, 87–91. See my longer discussion of sonnet and parody in 'Black Heroes/White Writers: Toussaint L'Ouverture

are apparent in both this graphic 'private' composition and in his 1827 revisions of 'The Banished Negroes', now retitled, 'September 1, 1802'. Where the unnamed woman of the 1803 sonnet was already so humbled as to present no possible threat to England as a refugee, Christophe's royal widow is not considered such an object of pity, and must be rendered harmless through ridicule. And by 1827 the 'woman' passenger had become a less dignified 'female'; at once less passive and more unstable, she might also be threatening if she weren't presented as tragic-comic. Unlike the Queen of Haiti she does not require the poet's parodic scorn since he now sets her up as an object of self-derision, the contrast between her hope-lessness and mad 'eyes' 'burning independent of the mind, / Joined with the lustre of her rich attire / To mock the outcast'.[17]

The undoubted presence of black women in England in eighteenth- and nineteenth-century Britain, some of them ex-slaves who became servants, grounds the figure of Savanna in history. Dorothy and William Wordsworth are unlikely to have invented the unnamed woman on the cross-Channel boat, however embroidered her character became over the years, and Christophe's widow and her children were real enough. But the questions they pose for the history of empire cannot be framed or answered by tracing their supposed models or actual prove-nance. Symbolic figures, they represent at once the humane and eman-cipatory impulses in British liberal thought and its domestic and imperial fear of social anarchy, an anarchy that is displaced and projected as racialised female excess, defined here as a desire for independence as much as unrestrained sexuality. What becomes ideologically excluded from virtuous European femininity – a radical autonomy of mind and beha-viour, whose dangerous bottom line is the will and capacity to rebel – is relocated in the figure of the black woman. Women of mixed race, however virtuous, like the fictional Savanna, are also the visible evidence of transgressive European male behaviour, so that their intrusion in to the metropolitan space is an unwelcome reminder of the inevitable perme-ability of social and moral borders between empire and 'home'.[18]

I have suggested above that modern literary criticism's disciplinary inclination to repudiate, rationalise or reclaim the imperial politics of canonical authors often obscures the wider historical significance of

---

and the Literary Imagination', *History Workshop Journal*, 46 (1998), 33–62, also Debbie Lee, *Slavery and the Romantic Imagination* (Philadelphia, 2002), 202–7 and Marcus Wood, 'Slavery and Romantic Poetry', in *Slavery, Empathy and Pornography* (Oxford, 2002), 233–9.
[17] Wordsworth, *'Poems in Two Volumes'*, 162–3.
[18] The French statute went so far as to outlaw intermarriage between races.

imaginative literature. Different but not unrelated issues affect the interpretation of other key texts of empire. In the case of early black diasporan literature, memoir and slave narrative in particular, the problem of the authenticity of factual detail and narrative voice has, in the first instance, been the leading concern of historians and critics. The current debate about the veracity of Olauda Equiano's *Interesting Narrative* (1789) is a case in point.[19] Similar concerns dog the discussion of *The History of Mary Prince, A West Indian Slave, Related by Herself* (1831), one of the earliest accounts of slavery by a black woman, and which in its length, detail and rhetorical power remains a uniquely important document.[20] Mary Prince's published narrative was dictated to Susanna Strickland while Mary was a servant in the London house of the Scottish poet Thomas Pringle, the secretary of the Anti-Slavery Society from 1827 and responsible in that role for much of the huge output of abolitionist propaganda in the last years of the campaign to abolish slavery. Part of this propaganda campaign, and tailored by Strickland and Pringle for a white British audience, the *History* excluded elements of Prince's life which would damage its case, for example Prince's long liaison with a Captain Abbott, together with other evidence of her sexuality prior to conversion and marriage. Presented to parliament on behalf of the anti-slavery lobby, the *History* rapidly went through three editions in that year, subsequently becoming the subject of two bitter legal disputes between Pringle and the *History*'s detractors, including Wood himself.

Many of the same strictures that shaped *Adeline Mowbray*'s depiction of Savanna, hover over Mary Prince's *History*, which emphasised her innate modesty, her probity and her Christian conversion by the Moravians as the moral elements which support her story. Like Savanna in her confrontations on Adeline's behalf with the abusive Berrendale, but in defence of herself against Mr and Mrs Woods, the owners she accompanied to London, and in her critique of slavery to her reading public, Mary is heard by her sympathetic readers as speaking truth to power – according to Pringle, 'in her own words as far as possible'. While

[19] See Vincent Carretta, *Equiano the African: Biography of a Self-made Man* (Athens, GA, 2005). Carretta has strong evidence that Equiano was born in Carolina and never visited Africa. David Dabydeen argues for the historical significance of the fictional elements of the text in his review of Carretta, *The Guardian*, 3 December 2005.

[20] Mary Prince, *The History of Mary Prince, A West Indian Slave, Related by Herself*, ed. and intr. Moira Ferguson, rev. edn (Ann Arbor, 1997). My discussion of the historical context of the production and reception of the *History* is indebted to Ferguson's introduction to this edition and the section on Prince in her monograph *Subject to Others: British Women Writers and Colonial Slavery, 1670–1834* (New York, 1992), 281–98.

it is clear that the *History* was pruned and shaped for its intended audience, containing what amounts to a checklist of the everyday sadism that
the Anti-Slavery Society conventionally highlighted in its attack on
slavery, Mary is depicted as an unwilling and never passive victim, a
survivor. The *History* represents her as an entrepreneurial, resourceful and
strategically resistant woman throughout her life, in opposition to Mr and
Mrs Wood of Antigua who are painted, as Moira Ferguson says, as
'typical representations of the anti-emancipationist plantocracy'.²¹ Prince's *History* closes with an unambiguous assertion that 'all slaves want to
be free', and anyone 'buckra' or slave who says otherwise are liars. The
advantages of freedom that she says she hopes for in her *History* are
modest and class bound but remarkably free of the kind of dependent
attachment or speechless abjection found in Opie or Wordsworth: chief
among them is the pragmatic right to 'give warning' to a bad master and
'hire' to a better one. 'We don't mind hard work, if we had proper
treatment, and proper wages like English servants.'²²

Mary in this guise, as a gutsy, independent woman, capable not only of
agency but of a sharp, effective critique of the cruelty and hypocrisy of
slaveholding whites, is just the kind of black heroine for our own times, a
woman that twentieth- and twenty-first-century historians and critics
wish to discover, and much of the excellent and nuanced research on and
discussion of the *History* has attempted to rescue and separate this 'true'
character, so much to our taste, from the confines of the Anti-Slavery
Society's bowdlerising editorship. But this desire to find an objective
correlative to our modern idea of resistant subjectivity creates a problem:
the more Moira Ferguson, the *History*'s first unsurpassed modern editor
and analyst, and others that follow her meticulously analyse the historical
evidence and pursue with subtlety and skill the stylistic, rhetorical and
ideological clues that will differentiate Mary's 'own' language and desires
from that of her anti-slavery minders, the more the search for the real
Mary Prince seems oddly to duplicate, albeit in modern anti-racist terms,
the dispute over authenticity, character and motive from the 1830s, as if it
were still necessary to prove, through this process, the independent
humanity of non-white subjects.

If, however, we step back from the attempt to unpick the distinct
strands of white and black anti-slavery discourse, admitting that we can
never quite disentangle them, another and perhaps more illuminating
mise-en-scène appears. The surviving documents published with the text of

²¹ Prince, *The History of Mary Prince*, 'Introduction', 1.   ²² *Ibid.*, 94.

the *History*, which include extracts from the court cases, letters etc., suggest that all parties involved in Prince's story – herself, her previous owners and current employers, the Pringles – were impelled to defend, and in doing so rhetorically to construct, their characters both as individuals and as types: slave, slaveowners, abolitionists. Rather than allowing us to judge the 'truth' of Mary's story, the thicket of charges and countercharges involving the idealisation and the defamation of all three of the leading players, reveals the fictional nature of each of these identities, and the melodramatic conventions to which they must adhere.

In his 'Supplement' published with his narrative, Pringle emphasises his personal knowledge of Mary's character as he observed it in his household, shoring up the conventionally virtuous elements of her self-portrait but with a clever touch of tactical realism. He comments on her relatively untutored Christian piety and her capacity for 'strong attachments', adding that she felt 'deep, but unobtrusive, gratitude for real kindness shown her', a formulation that attempts to confirm her capacity for attachment to whites, a sentiment under-represented in the *History*.[23] Her virtues, her 'discretion and fidelity', her 'quickness of observation', her '*decency* and *propriety* of conduct – and her *delicacy* even in trifling minutiae', were, Pringle says, specially remarked 'by the females' of his family; they outweighed her observed 'faults' which were 'a somewhat violent and hasty temper, and considerable share of natural pride and self-importance'.[24] But even as Pringle carefully defends Mary against her would-be defamers he seems to reach a point where his patience with the whole enterprise of devising a persona acceptable to his pious audience seems to run out:

But after all, Mary's character, important though its exculpation be to her, is not really the point of chief practical interest in this case. Suppose all Mr Wood's defamatory allegations to be true – suppose him to be able to rake up against her out of the records of the Antigua police, or from the veracious testimony of his brother colonists, twenty stories as bad or worse than what he insinuates – suppose the whole of her own statement to be false, and even the whole of her conduct since she came under our observation here to be a tissue of hypocrisy; – suppose all this – and leave the negro woman as black in character as in complexion, – yet it would not affect the main facts – which are these.[25]

And here Pringle details the dilemma in which Mary Prince found herself, because Wood, 'not daring in England to punish this woman arbitrarily, as he would have done in the West Indies', gave her the Hobson's choice of submitting to 'intolerable usage' in England or an

---

[23] *Ibid.*, 115.   [24] *Ibid.*   [25] *Ibid.*, 116.

immediate return to slavery in Antigua.[26] Pringle makes no attempt to reverse the moral associations of colour, yet in arguing that the 'blackness' or 'whiteness' of Mary's character is irrelevant to the ethics of her case – ethics which are grounded in the absolute wrongness not only of chattel slavery and its effects, but of the kind of extra-legal arbitrary power of employers – he comes dangerously close not only to collapsing the carefully edited narrative he has fostered, but of admitting to the self-conscious level of fabrication at the heart of much anti-slavery discourse, which seeks always to produce an appropriately idealised subject to support its claim for authenticity. Pringle's 'outburst', which concedes for the sake of argument that the accusations against Mary of wicked slaveholders might be supported by evidence, is as rhetorically strategic as the rest of his 'Supplement' which aims to meet the pro-slavery attacks through a range of counter-arguments that in themselves may be contradictory.

The *Anti-Slavery Reporter* detailed many cases of the abuse of women slaves in the West Indies. Mary Prince's story is explosive because it situates the abuse of slavery in Britain itself, dramatically reducing for its readers geopolitical and emotional distance between metropole and slave colony, locating slavery's refugees and their problems at empire's own doorstep. It was by then a cliché, articulated in Pringle's poetry as well as in much abolitionist literature – see for example the introduction to Harriet Martineau's *Demerara* published in the same year as Prince's *History* – that the 'bitter draught' of slavery taints the character of slaveholder and slave, but it was more comfortable to position one as a 'demon' of 'avarice, rage or lust' and the other as a sinking 'victim'.[27] Mary's supposed 'violent temper' and 'pride' may be noted as character 'flaws' in a female servant in Pringle's supplement, but overall the documents do underline the necessity and capacity to resist abuse even for subaltern women. An essential element in liberal ideas of personhood, the innate longing for liberty – as opposed to acute pain at separation from child, partner or 'home' or horror at sexual abuse – is more frequently and easily ascribed to male slaves; when women are allowed to speak in such 'masculine' terms their testimony suggests both their extremity and their transgression of social norms.[28] Unlike the self-immolating or infanticidal black female subject of

---

[26] *Ibid.*, 117.

[27] Mary Prince, *The History of Mary Prince*, ed. Sara Salih (London, 2000), 'Appendix One', 97.

[28] See, in particular, Elizabeth Barrett Browning, 'The Runaway Slave at Pilgrim's Point', *The Poetry of Slavery*, ed. Marcus Wood (Oxford, 2003), 356–63. Published in 1848 in the Boston Anti-Slavery annual, *The Liberty Bell*, its Promethian black female speaker combines the masculine and feminine characteristics of the rebel slave subject in abolitionist literature.

Romantic and Victorian poetry, Mary Prince is presented – perhaps as much by Pringle and Strickland as by herself: we cannot know – as someone demanding a better life, perhaps even in Britain, not salvation through death. In this fantasmatic guise, she represents a paradox, an implicit threat to social order, as well as a case of injustice for the British state to answer.

In the decade in which the fragile anti-slavery consensus that enabled abolition fragments, and in which the economic and social autonomy of the free population is heavily criticised in the metropole, racial thinking takes on a new life.[29] No longer tied to the crime of chattel slavery, but an easy rationale for the lesser humanity of non-white subjects, racism, overtly or subliminally influenced by widely disseminated popular racial science, becomes a common strand in political and social commentary. Two related fictions by women writers from the late 1840s rework the figure of the black woman and the unhappy relationship between metropole and West Indian colony. Charlotte Brontë's *Jane Eyre* (1847) is the novel which most fully represents the ideological turn in post-abolition British culture. Empire dominates its plot, and no leading character can evade its reach: orphan Jane's employer and suitor Edward Fairfax Rochester is a younger son sent out to Jamaica to marry money and becomes tied, almost fatally, to a mad, bad colonial heiress whose family, the Masons, reproduce the cliché about the moral and physical degeneration of colonial Europeans. Jane's cousin, the cold and ambitious St John Rivers, becomes a missionary in India, and dies there. Near the end of the novel impoverished Jane learns that she has inherited her Madeira uncle's fortune, made in the triangular trade. As in *Adeline Mowbray* and *Mary Prince*, empire in *Jane Eyre* gets a poor press. It is at best a necessary evil in Brontë's novel, at worst a source of moral and physical contagion, its climate and environment – in Rochester's graphic imagery of Jamaica presided over by a 'broad and red' moon with a 'bloody glance' – as a crazed, racialised woman.[30]

Yet, and here we might remember the significant silence in *Mansfield Park*, race and especially slavery, classical and oriental as well as trans-atlantic, are only metaphorically and metonymically figured in the novel, heavily structuring its language and controlling its affect but not overtly part of its story. The novel's rough time-span covers the transition from

[29] See Catherine Hall, *Civilising Subjects: Metropole and Colony in the English Imagination, 1830–1867* (Cambridge, 2002), ch. 6, 338–79.
[30] Charlotte Brontë, *Jane Eyre*, Norton Critical Edition (New York, 1987), 271.

slavery to freedom in Jamaica, but these events are, strangely, never highlighted. The child Jane, in her rage and fantasies of revenge against her appalling Aunt Reed and her cousins, aligns herself mentally with 'any other rebel slave'.[31] Her story of childhood abuse by family and institutions, her gradual conversion to a more Christian – if still rebellious – character, her attempted seduction and betrayal by Rochester and her escape from his household and rescue by her clergyman cousin who finds her employment, have an eerie resemblance to the ordering of slave narrative – bearing some relationship even to Mary Prince's *History*. Jane's slave imaginary is, we might say, that of an earlier abolitionist moment, committed to the view that all humans 'want to be free', but interpreted by the mediating voice of the adult Jane who tells the story, as an innocent's imperative that always threatens the family and polity with anarchic violence. This dangerous if necessary imaginary is therefore compromised and conditioned by post-abolitionist racial thinking. On the other side we have the novel's more unforgiving and racially problematic representation of a white creole with a violent temper, unspeakable 'giant propensities' and 'pygmy intellect',[32] Bertha Mason, brought to England by Rochester in the hold of a ship, transformed from pale beauty to an animalistic figure with a 'fearful blackened inflation of the lineaments',[33] incarcerated murderously mad in Thornfield's attic. Bertha escapes to threaten Jane, eventually burning down the house, built – like Mansfield Park we might hazard, but the novel will stubbornly not say – on the economics of slavery. Bertha Mason is a grotesque condensation of white colonial degenerate and subhuman racial other – she is figured finally as an anomalous beast of indeterminate gender. (In her representation there is an echo too of a familiar type in anti-slavery literature normally represented by the vengeful male slaves determined to slaughter their white masters.) Bertha is never a fully realised character in the novel; she functions more as a nightmarish representation of the evil dynamic of master/slave feminised and undead – Jane compares her to a 'vampyre' – colonialism's immoral social and economic legacy returned to haunt and wreak what havoc it could in the metropole.

And yet, for all its deep immersion in the tropes and narrative of empire, *Jane Eyre* is not 'about' these questions, but 'about' Jane's very English progress from abused orphan to rich, happily married mother: something it seems she cannot do without the novel's imaginative engagement with empire. The novel's closing fantasy, related but distinct

---

[31] *Ibid.*, 9.   [32] *Ibid.*, 269.   [33] *Ibid.*, 249.

to those imagined in *Adeline Mowbray* and *Mansfield Park*, is that Britain could magically evade and reject the negative aspects of slavery's legacy, retreating, as Jane and the crippled and blinded Rochester do, to some 'green heart of England' for repair and regeneration, while sending St John Rivers out to India as a sacrificial agent for and a victim of the Christianising ethical impulse of empire.

These very limited comments on a complex novel are intended as a symptomatic reading of *Jane Eyre*, a twenty-first-century historical and cultural reflection directed at wider questions about the shifting, uneven and contradictory terms of racial and imperial thinking in Britain in the 1840s.[34] The novel's manifest investment in the context of empire together with its evasions and incoherence about it provide, I would offer, a suggestive line of historical enquiry about the soured sense, in some parts of British society in this decade, that abolition had let loose a Pandora's Box of problems that the metropole could not solve, a naive idealism gone wrong.

That the shadowy figure of a black woman, at once childlike, abused, heroically resistant, monstrous, mad, vengeful, dead and magically vindicated, is part of the representation of both Jane and Bertha is reinforced in a novel published only a few years later by a young novelist, Dinah Mulock Craik. *Olive*[35] boldly borrows from and recasts the themes of empire and race in *Jane Eyre*, outing its racial subtext by giving literal embodiment to what is figuratively rendered in Brontë's novel. The heroine, Olive Rothesay, is an angelic, artistically talented but crippled daughter of a misalliance between an Englishwoman and a Scotsman with estates in the West Indies. Angus Rothesay is an adulterer with a bitter, discarded quadroon mistress, Celia Manners, who follows him to England and dies in poverty there, and her virtually white illegitimate daughter Christal, proud, beautiful and flirtatious. Christal's mixed-racial inheritance is revealed to her only as an adult, knowledge that makes her attack her half-sister Olive in a temporary but racially coded fit of insanity. Christal retreats to a religious order, a move which places her safely outside the civil society her status and temperament would disrupt. In a seemingly reciprocal development, Olive's deformity disappears and

---

[34] For longer discussions of the role of empire in *Jane Eyre*, see Spivak, 'Three Women's Texts'; Susan Meyer, *Imperialism at Home: Race and Victorian Women's Fiction* (Ithaca, 1996), 60–95; Cora Kaplan, ' "A Heterogeneous Thing": Female Childhood and the Rise of Racial Thinking in Victorian Britain', in Diana Fuss (ed.), *Human, All Too Human* (London and New York, 1996), 169–202.

[35] Dinah Mulock Craik, *Olive*, ed. and intro. Cora Kaplan (Oxford, 1999).

she marries the man she loves. Craik's attitudes towards empire are as ambivalent as Brontë's, but her views on race in *Olive* are at once more simply humanitarian and more explicitly grounded in biology than in *Jane Eyre*. The close pairing of these two novels and their relation to the earlier texts I have discussed, suggest how intimately connected, in the political and literary imagination of Britain in the first half of the empire, were the relations of metropole and colony and the dangers of female and non-white autonomy.

CODA

A discursive figure, a trope such as the one I have been tracing – the invasive and disturbing presence of a woman of African or partly African descent on English soil – emerges, I have been arguing, at particular historical moments, giving narrative shape and virtual embodiment to temporarily specific constellations of hopes, fears and anxieties. The activity of condensation and projection that go in to their articulation turns the question back to history as to why such associations should take place: why these, and not others? Why is the menacing racialised figure in Brontë and Craik female and not male? Why is this figure in Wordsworth, Opie, Brontë and Craik so metonymically tied to the political and moral integrity of the metropole's relationship to the Empire on the one hand and, in the latter three texts, the imperilled and disputed status of femininity – of every class and ethnicity – within it? Why is this nineteenth-century figure – and here Mary Prince's *History* is a key text – doomed to oscillate between perfect victim and transgressive agent? The answers are not obvious, but the questions remain compelling.

What does seem to be true is that gender continues to be a primary part of the post-imperial imaginary, working overtime, one might say, to embody the hopes, disillusion and feeling tone of the period of decolonisation and of its aftermath: the experience of emigration from ex-colony to England. For when the Empire writes back, it transfigures the affective and social implications of the relations between the metropole and its former Caribbean colonies, redefining identities and place – and the space between. The first wave of novels written about that immigrant experience is very focused on the experience and feelings of male immigrants. In what is now the best-known and loved text, Sam Selvon's *The Lonely Londoners* (1956), women are altogether marginal figures. A nameless cast of white women who become casual lovers of the men seem largely to exist as sexual partners, answering a mutual desire and need, but also exploited and exploiting. The few black women – Lewis' abused wife, Agnes, Tolroy's mother and Tanty Bessie – seem unwanted burdens in the men's new life, whose fragile infrastructure is based on a homosocial network that depends, and in some sense thrives, on the initial absence of women and family ties. George Lamming's brilliantly bitter *The Emigrants* (1954) includes a few women on his fictional voyage from the Caribbean to England, but either these women play a subsidiary role in the story of the encounter with English life – taken on as partners to deflect the all-encompassing loneliness of voluntary exile – or they represent more fully the general perils of emigration in a disturbingly negative and misogynist register: Queenie becomes a prostitute who sleeps with women, and the socially aspirant, near white Miss Bis sheds her old identity, changes her name and her style, transforming herself in to a wholly amoral figure, not only sexually perverse but capable of murder, the worst sort of rootless cosmopolitan.[36]

These two remarkable novels are most interesting in what they have to say about the masculine imaginary in these first decades of postwar immigration: what they also reveal is a radical ambivalence about the relocation of a family-based community in England – one which might be, although always with a sense of difference and alienation, 'home'. As if conscious of this absence in the 1950s' fiction of Caribbean immigration, the writer Caryl Phillips, born in St Kitts in 1958 and brought up in Leeds, retells the story, putting a woman at the centre in his first major work of fiction. *The Final Passage* (1985), written in the heyday of Thatcher's reign, is a sympathetic but wholly bleak account of a clever young woman, Leila, in a troubled cross-class marriage, emigrating with her baby son and husband to a cold and 'overcast' racist London. Leila's passage is paid for by her mother who has gone before her and whose hopes were set on England, but the 'passage' proves fatal for the mother who dies defeated in a London hospital, telling Leila 'London is not my home'.[37] It is nearly fatal too for the deserted, bereaved and pregnant Leila who, isolated and nearly mad, plans to return to the Caribbean where at least she has one close friend, but not for her more working-class husband Michael, who, like the men in Lamming and Selvon's fiction, rise above the anomie and hostility of England, hoping still to advance themselves and to escape from marriage and fatherhood. Phillips' novel

[36] For a very subtle analysis of Miss Bis's complex role in *The Emigrants* see A. J. Simoes da Silva, *The Luxury of Nationalist Despair: George Lamming's Fiction as Decolonizing Project* (Amsterdam, 2000), 111–23.
[37] Caryl Phillips, *The Final Passage* (London, 1985), 124.

highlights the uneven and antagonistic relations of gender that, together with the climate and xenophobic culture of Britain, make emigration such a different and difficult experience for men and women. In all three men's novels Britain is represented as an anti-domestic space for Caribbean emigrants, signalling, for men at least, something more than a desire to leave the limited economic and cultural opportunities of the Caribbean. The imagined marginality or failure to thrive of emigrant women in Britain is a sign of both the metropole's ingrained racism and xenophobia, its inhospitability which takes the form of a resolute resistance to the establishment and reproduction of an immigrant community: the negative pole of diaspora – and a more intractable incommensurability of the expectations and desires of men and women.

Two decades later, Andrea Levy's Whitbread award-winning novel *Small Island* (2004) returns to that first generation of postwar immigrants, revisiting not just their experience but the highly gendered imagined worlds of Selvon, Lamming and Phillips which have by now become part of the cultural memory of those early years of arrival. Levy, Phillips' contemporary, the only one of these four novelists to be born in Britain, rewrites, in a more hopeful but never sentimental key, their narratives of the encounter with England. London with its 'no coloureds' signs is not significantly altered in Levy's fictional world, but she makes room for a more emotionally positive encounter between black men and white women, and gives her white characters, both the sympathetic Queenie and her racist husband Bernard, a generous and rounded fictional treatment. In *Small Island*, a description that might now just as aptly be applied to England as to Jamaica, the emigrating couple, Hortense and her husband Gilbert – as ill matched a pair in terms of class, complexion and expectations of England as Michael and Leila in *The Final Passage* – find that emigration makes, not breaks, their marriage; they adopt the illegitimate, mixed-race child of their landlady and friend Queenie and move to Finsbury Park, accepting with an optimism without illusions the racially freighted and divided metropole. Levy's rendering of that experience is not without its own fatalism. By making Queenie give up her child because she hasn't got 'the guts' for 'that fight' against everyday racism, the novel seems to exclude from the positive possibilities it foreshadows the complex and often positive history of cross-racial partnerships and families in this period, one of the many distinctive characteristics of today's British population.[38] Nevertheless, in

---

[38] Andrea Levy, *Small Island* (London, 2004), 521.

Levy's historical imaginary, from the perspective of the new millennium and several generations on from the late forties and fifties, Britain, unwelcoming and difficult as it was, could and would be made 'home' to the mixed and merged descendants of the former colonies.[39]

In these two long periods, 1800–50 and 1950–2005, I have been pursuing through literary sources the shifts and changes in the social and political imaginary of empire and home, suggesting that in the fantasmatic register in which literature operates an alternative history opens up, with a complicated narrative of its own, but one that is at the same time constitutive of the social real, representing most eloquently and sometimes scarily its affective dimensions. If historians can draw that poetic register into their 'everyday' discussions, both the story and the interpretation of empire's resonance in Britain will be greatly enriched.

[39] See Zadie Smith, *White Teeth* (London, 2000) for a more optimistic representation of this inheritance.

CHAPTER TEN

New narratives of imperial politics in the nineteenth century

Antoinette Burton

Parliament cares about India little more than the Cabinet. The English people, too, are very slow and very careless about everything that does not immediately affect them. They cannot be excited to any effort of India except under the pressure of some great calamity, and when that calamity is removed they fall back into their usual state of apathy.
(John Bright, 1860[1])

The sentiment of empire is innate in every Briton.
(William Gladstone, 1878[2])

The trouble with the English is that their history happened overseas, so they don't know what it means.
(Salman Rushdie, 1989[3])

For historians of the nineteenth century, the question is, arguably, not whether empire had an impact on domestic life and experience, but how. The realm of high politics is a domain where those influences are most evident, though the role of imperialism in shaping it has received comparatively little attention. If historians have been slow to see and to recognise the impact of empire on 'domestic' history, Britons who followed high politics from the 1830s until just after Queen Victoria's death in 1901 could not have ignored the ways in which imperial questions impinged upon and helped to shape Victorian democracy across the nineteenth century. Swing rioters and other 'criminals' were exiled to Australia; opium debates made their way to the floor of the House; and Irishmen and women together with former Caribbean slaves were involved in Chartist agitations – whose spokesmen drew in turn on metaphors of slavery to

---

[1] Quoted in Mary Cumpston, 'Some Early Indian Nationalists and their Allies in the British Parliament, 1851–1906', *English Historical Review*, 76 (1961), 280.
[2] William Ewart Gladstone, 'England's Mission', *Nineteenth Century*, 4 (1878), 560–84.
[3] Quoted in Homi K. Bhabha, 'Dissemination: Time, Narrative and the Margins of the Modern State', in Bhabha (ed.), *Nation and Narration* (London, 1990), 317.

inform their political demands.[4] White English middle-class women entered debates about citizenship through their interest in the plight of slaves and colonial peoples – an interest that laid the groundwork for Victorian feminism.[5] Whether the issue was abolition or the extension of democracy to the new middle classes, parliamentary statesmen and social reformers understood the linkages between domestic concerns and imperial problems, in part because they viewed empire as a constitutive part of national character, national life and national political culture.

Political reform at the highest level was carried out in the context of tremendous public debate about imperial questions. As Catherine Hall has shown, the years leading up to the passage of the Great Reform Act – which did away with 'rotten' boroughs and expanded the electorate by approximately 60 per cent across the United Kingdom in 1832 – were preceded by elaborate discussions of citizenship in a variety of 'colonial' contexts.[6] Ireland was one. Although Britons did not typically use the word 'colony' for Ireland at the time, in Hall's view it was a colony 'in that Irish Catholics in Ireland were treated as a conquered people and English Protestants in Ireland acted as colonial settlers'.[7] Religious difference carried with it overtones of racial difference, and Irish Catholics were politically disenfranchised as well as culturally subordinated. Daniel O'Connell's work with the Catholic Association and especially his speeches to parliament placed civil rights for the Catholic Irish at the heart of political debate and made it clear that the peace and stability of the whole of the United Kingdom was in peril if political emancipation at the periphery closest in was not forthcoming. Unrest in Upper and Lower Canada in this period added to the sense that the Empire was in crisis.[8] Jamaica was another very visible colonial context in which debates about political reform occurred in the 1830s. Parliament was preoccupied with events in Jamaica in the two years leading up to the passage of the 1832 Reform Act, especially in the wake of the December 1831 Christmas

---

[4] For the latter see Richard Oastler, 'Slavery in Yorkshire', in Rosemary Mundhenk and Luann Fletcher (eds.), *Victorian Prose: An Anthology* (New York, 1999), 9–11.

[5] See Clare Midgley, *Women Against Slavery: The British Campaigns, 1780–1870* (London, 1992) and Antoinette Burton, *Burdens of History: British Feminists, Indian Women and Imperial Culture, 1865–1915* (Chapel Hill, 1994).

[6] Catherine Hall, 'The Rule of Difference: Gender, Class and Empire in the Making of the 1832 Reform Act', in Ida Blom, Karen Hagemann and Catherine Hall (eds.), *Gendered Nations: Nationalisms and Gender Order in the Long Nineteenth Century* (Oxford, 2000), 107–35.

[7] *Ibid.*, 112. See also Stephen Howe, *Ireland and Empire: Colonial Legacies in Irish History and Culture* (Oxford, 2000).

[8] See Lord Durham, 'Report on the Affairs of British North America (1839)', in Arthur Berridale Keith, *Selected Speeches and Documents in British Colonial Policy, 1763–1917* (Oxford, 1929).

rebellion, in which free black men and women sought to overthrow slavery and were brutally repressed.[9] As in Ireland, the language of civil rights and the threat to private property in Jamaica set the stage for a quite conservative Reform Bill in 1832, one which enfranchised about 400,000 men in the UK but which left the majority of British men and all British women without the parliamentary vote.

The 1830s was a decade characterised by 'liberal' reforms shaped by imperial pressures, including the Act that abolished slavery in 1833. Indeed, for all the allusions to their connections across the whole of the nineteenth century in scholarship from the 1940s onwards, the direct and indirect connections between imperialism and the slave trade have yet to be fully documented.[10] In any case, some of the men involved at the highest levels of domestic reform were also involved in promoting legislation that would have a huge impact on colonisers and colonised alike. One such man was Thomas Babington Macaulay, who famously supported the 1832 Act by arguing that Britain must 'reform to preserve'.[11] Just three years later he took quite a different tack when he suggested that Government of India funds for Instruction in Arabic and Sanskrit should not be pre- served – and offered the equally famous opinion that 'we must at present do our best to form … a class of persons, Indian in blood and colour, but English in taste, in opinions, in morals, and in intellect'.[12] Debates about citizenship and belonging in the nation-empire persisted into the 1840s, once again with Ireland and Jamaica at the fore. O'Connell continued to press for Irish freedoms, while two of the century's most famous men of letters, Thomas Carlyle and John Stuart Mill, engaged in heated public debate about the impact of the West Indian 'Negro ques- tion' on issues such as labour, virtue and civilisation. Nor was empire merely debated at the rhetorical level. British imperial ambitions extended to China and Afghanistan in the 1840s. Contests with Russia over the limits of British imperial interests led to a war in the Crimea (1853–5), which in turn led some commentators like Richard Cobden to reflect on the extent to which imperial ambition could, or should, define national

---

[9] Hall, 'The Rule of Difference,' 118–19 and Tom Holt, *The Problem of Freedom: Race, Labor, and Politics in Jamaica and Britain, 1832–1938* (Baltimore, 1992).

[10] Eric Williams, *Capitalism and Slavery* (Chapel Hill, NC, 1944/1994).

[11] Thomas Babington Macaulay, 'A Speech Delivered to the House of Commons, 2nd March 1831', in *The Works of Lord Macaulay: Speeches, Poems and Miscellaneous Writings* (London, 1898), 407–26.

[12] Thomas Babington Macaulay, *Macaulay's Minutes Of Education in India in the Years 1835, 1836, and 1837 and Now First Collected From Records in The Department of Public Instruction* (London, 1862).

greatness.[13] Others, like William Greg in 1851, posed an equally provocative question about the financial viability of empire: 'Shall We Retain Our Colonies?'[14] Though it was not the only uprising to threaten British imperial stability before mid-century or after, the Indian Mutiny (sometimes called the Rebellion) of 1857 has become the most famous. Karl Marx, writing from New York, declared it a 'catastrophe' and chastised the colonial state for its 'abominations' against the rebels.[15] Nonetheless, the Mutiny brought images of empire home to Britons like no other event of the century – thereby revealing the fragility of British imperial rule to a generation of Victorians for whom the power of the Raj had appeared untouchable.[16]

The generation of British politicians that oversaw the passage of the Second Reform Act (1867) was equally preoccupied with imperial questions – again in Jamaica, where the Morant Bay rebellion of 1865 exerted enormous pressure on discussions both in and outside parliament about who could count as a Briton and how race shaped the definition of a citizen.[17] And once again, Ireland played an important role at this political juncture as well: in 1867 the Fenians sought justice through violent means and an Irish Republic was briefly declared.[18] That year also witnessed the British North America Act, which provided for the federation of Upper and Lower Canada, New Brunswick and Nova Scotia, thus rearranging Britain's long-standing relationship with one of its chief white settler colonies.[19] More so than in 1832, imperial power was visible in the legislation that enfranchised 400,000 more British men, some of them labourers, in 1867. The polity to which they gained entrance was decidedly white, male and middle-class, despite attempts by English women to gain access to the vote through voluntary associations, parliamentary petitions and direct confrontation at the hustings.[20] Perhaps surprisingly, Victorian feminists were no less wedded to empire than their male counterparts. As they made their case for the right to participate in the political nation, they invoked colonial women and other orientalist images almost casually as part of their case for emancipation.[21] In this

[13] Richard Cobden, *Russia and the Eastern Question* (Cleveland, OH, 1854).
[14] William Greg, 'Shall We Retain Our Colonies?', *The Edinburgh Review* (April 1851), 475–98.
[15] Karl Marx and Friedrich Engels, *The First Indian War of Independence, 1857–59* (Moscow, 1975), 82.
[16] See www.adam-matthew-publications.co.uk (Cultural Contacts: Mutiny Writings).
[17] See Catherine Hall, Keith McClelland and Jane Rendall, *Defining the Victorian Nation: Class, Race, Gender and the British Reform Act of 1867* (Cambridge, 2000).
[18] See John Newsinger, *Fenianism in Mid-Victorian Britain* (London, 1994).
[19] Auberon Herbert, 'The Canadian Confederation', *Fortnightly Review*, 7 (April 1867), 480–90.
[20] See Hall et al., *Defining the Victorian Nation*, ch. 3.
[21] Millicent Garrett Fawcett, 'The Women's Suffrage Bill', *Fortnightly Review*, 51 (March 1889), 555–67 and Burton, *Burdens of History*.

sense they were little different from the leaders of both of Britain's political parties in the Victorian era. William Gladstone and Benjamin Disraeli (prime ministers and political adversaries) each used British imperialism, its limits and possibilities, as a platform for party unity and ideological sparring.[22] Although the Tory Party became known as the party of empire, many Liberals embraced imperialism as the inevitable if not wholly desirable burden of geopolitical power, especially after the siege of Khartoum and the death of General Gordon (1884–5).[23]

The third and final Reform Act of the century (1884) did little to alter the basically conservative character of Victorian democracy except by enfranchising agricultural labourers. But parliamentary debates in its wake – especially those about Ireland and India – kept empire visible at home. Though it had been a consistent feature of political life since at least the 1870s, the question of Irish self-determination came to a head at this same moment, with the defeat of a Home Rule bill in 1886 ensuring an almost permanent end to Liberal Party power until the twentieth century.[24] The Indian National Congress, founded in 1885, also made a variety of political claims on the idea of English democracy.[25] Despite its links with Irish nationalists, it fell short of demanding Home Rule at this stage. One of its first Presidents, Dadhabai Naoroji, was elected MP for Central Finsbury in 1892, bringing the question of Indian self-representation directly into the 'Mother of all Parliaments'.[26]

As Bernard Semmel documented in astonishing detail nearly forty years ago, the discourses and policies of social imperialism provided the major ideological backdrop for British politics from the fin de siècle until the Great War.[27] The so-called Khaki election of 1900 provided an opportunity for many political constituencies to comment on the nature and direction of imperial policy. George Bernard Shaw's confidence in the invincibility of the British Empire was to be sorely tested by the Boer War (1899–1902), which many Britons supported as a 'holy war' intended to protect the 'native races' of its South African Empire from the

---

[22] Benjamin Disraeli, 'Conservative and Liberal Principles', in T. E. Kebbel (ed.), *Selected Speeches of the Right Honourable the Earl of Beaconsfield*, vol. II (London, 1882), 523–35 and Gladstone, 'England's Mission'.

[23] For an excellent account of this through documents, see Barbara Harlow and Mia Carter (eds.), *Imperialism and Orientalism: A Documentary Sourcebook* (Oxford, 1999), ch. 8.

[24] William Gladstone, *The Irish Question* (New York, 1886).

[25] W. C. Bonnerjee (ed.), *Indian Politics* (Madras, 1898).

[26] See Antoinette Burton, 'Tongues Untied: Lord Salisbury's "Black Man" and the Boundaries of Imperial Democracy', *Comparative Studies in Society and History*, 43 (2) (2000), 632–59.

[27] Bernard Semmel, *Imperialism and Social Reform: English Social-Imperial Thought, 1895–1914* (London, 1960; repr. New York, 1969), 2.

depredations of lesser civilisations like the Afrikaans-speaking Dutch settlers who posed a threat to Britain's ambitions on the African continent at large.[28] This kind of competitive whiteness signalled an intensified awareness of racial identities at the turn of the century. Indeed, racial exclusion was the precondition of nation formation as well as empire building, as is evident in the creation of an all-white citizenship policy alongside the foundation of Australia in 1901.[29] By the time J. A. Hobson wrote in his famous treatise, *Imperialism* (1902), that 'colonialism, in its best sense, is a natural overflow of nationality; its test is the power of colonists to transplant the civilization they represent to the new natural and social environment in which they find themselves', empire was so natural a fact of life in Britain that it has taken historians until very recently to rediscover its many influences and effects at home.[30]

What I have sketched above should not, of course, be taken as any kind of definitive new narrative. It represents one of many possibilities enabled by students of imperial political culture, many of whom are now refocusing our attention on the role of Britain's white settler colonies (South Africa, Canada, Australia, New Zealand) in the metropole in ways that recontextualise and may in the end mitigate our emphasis on the role of India and Africa, long considered the dominant colonial influences at home and in the Empire.[31] This work, together with the explosion of visual culture projects in a variety of British metropolitan and provincial museums in recent years, provides the basis for a number of different, and perhaps even competing, paradigms for the study of imperial Britain in the nineteenth and twentieth centuries.[32] The challenges of periodisation

[28] For more on the Boer War see Andrew Porter, *The Origins of the South African War: Joseph Chamberlain and the Diplomacy of Imperialism 1895–99* (Manchester, 1980).

[29] The formal beginnings of the Australian nation were also very much a white supremacist masculine affair, despite the role of women in its creation; see Patricia Grimshaw, Marilyn Lake, Ann McGrath and Marian Quartly, *Creating a Nation* (Ringwood, Victoria, 1994).

[30] J. A. Hobson, *Imperialism: A Study* (London, 1902).

[31] See for example Pamela Scully, *Liberating the Family? Gender and British Slave Emancipation in the Rural Western Cape, S. Africa, 1823–1854* (Portsmouth, NH, 1997); Adele Perry, *On the Edge of Empire: Gender, Race, and the Making of British Columbia, 1849–1871* (Toronto, 2000); Cecilia Morgan, '"A Wigwam to Westminster": Performing Mohawk Identities in Imperial Britain, 1890s–1900s', *Gender and History*, 15 (2) (2003), 319–41; and Angela Woollacott, *To Try Her Fortune in London: Australian Women, Colonialism, and Modernity* (Oxford, 2001).

[32] See for example the Merseyside Maritime Museum's collections on slavery at http://www. liverpoolmuseums.org.uk/maritime/slavery/slavery.asp; press coverage of plans for a museum of slavery in Liverpool in 2007: http://www.guardian.co.uk/arts/news/story/0,11711,905368,00.html; and Durba Ghosh, 'Exhibiting Asia in Britain: Commerce, Consumption, and Globalization', provided courtesy of the author. For two rather different narratives of imperial culture at home that I have tried to work out, see Antoinette Burton, 'Women and "Domestic" Imperial Culture: The Case of Victorian Britain', in Marilyn J. Boxer and Jean H. Quataert (eds.), *Connecting*

nonetheless remain, beginning with the very term 'Victorian' which technically binds us to the years 1837–1901. Few surveys, whether in the form of textbooks or course syllabi, cleave to either that beginning or end date. In my primary source reader, *Politics and Empire in Victorian Britain*, I suggest as one alternative 1829 to 1905 – on the grounds that book-ending the period with Catholic Emancipation on one side and the Alien Act on the other restores questions of religion and race to the dominant narratives of both national *and* imperial histories, offering a flexible alternative to both the Whig interpretation and the *Oxford History of the British Empire* one.[33] And yet there are still 'political' events and formations that have left little trace on even alternative narratives of the Victorian period. Fully fledged wars in Afghanistan, China and the Transvaal before the 1890s, and lesser but equally significant eruptions and/or rebellions in Canada, South Asia and Africa across the century, impinged on national consciousness and high politics in ways that have yet to be fully explored by historians of the period – even though Victorians themselves left evidence of the politicising influence of faraway battles in distant imperial lands.[34] Incidents like the Don Pacifico affair (where a Portuguese Jew born in Gibraltar tried to claim British citizenship and sparked an international incident) and events like the Crimean War (in which Britain sought to contain Russia's territorial ambitions in order to protect its Indian empire) also brought imperial questions before the popular and the official mind in ways that have yet to be fully historicised, let alone reconciled with accounts of Britain's 'imperial century'. Whether military in the strictest sense or not, such high-profile imperial episodes helped to gender citizenship as masculine and to underscore it as presumptively white, the very public work of Florence Nightingale (the famous 'Lady with the Lamp') and Mary Seacole (a mixed-race nurse who was also in the Crimea) notwithstanding.[35] Taking seriously the intersections between military ideology and 'domestic' policy will likely further erode the distinctions between 'home' and 'empire' and may also give rise to a chronology which interrupts the canonical recourse to the Crystal Palace and the 1857 Mutiny as the twin embodiments of

---

Spheres: Women in a Globalizing World, 1500 to the Present, 2nd edn (Oxford, 2000), 174–84 and my online essay, with primary text links, 'The Visible Empire at Home, 1832–1905', *Empire On-Line*: www.adam-matthew-publications.co.uk.

[33] Antoinette Burton (ed.), *Politics and Empire in Victorian Britain* (Palgrave, 2001).

[34] *Pace* Michael Davitt's boyhood recollection of hawking newspapers which featured coverage of the Maori Wars and the US Civil War. *Life and Progress in Australasia* (London, 1898), 344.

[35] Mary Seacole, *Wonderful Adventures of Mrs Seacole in Many Lands* (London, 1858).

'mid-Victorian' political culture.[36] Nor has the articulation of political economy and political culture in national, regional or local landscapes been as fully attended to as it might be. The story of the unequal competition between the Lancashire and Indian cotton mills at the height of the industrial revolution is, for example, among the most celebrated and yet perhaps least well-integrated instances of Sinha's 'combined but uneven development' – one with arguably world-historical ramifications, if Mahatma Gandhi's embrace and mobilisation of *swadeshi* in the next century is taken as one indirect, *longue durée* effect of India's comparative eclipse with respect to industrial 'progress'.[37]

COLONIAL CIRCUITRY AND THE POLITICS OF SOCIAL IMPERIALISM

Despite the purchase of Bernard Semmel's argument that imperialism was a constituent feature of reform politics in the two decades before World War I, histories of British labour, British socialism and British progressivism at the turn of the century have not fully countenanced the impact of empire on those movements. The great exception to this is, of course, Anna Davin's germinal 1978 article, 'Imperialism and Motherhood', which made a persuasive case for the influence of the post-Boer War political climate on the creation of a eugenicist programme of social reform and state intervention that targeted Britain's poor and, arguably, laid the groundwork for the twentieth-century welfare state.[38] While Davin's piece was remarkable as much for connecting the dots between an imperial war and state-sponsored social programmes as it was for its emphasis on the role of women and gender in shaping those connections, it has not proven unusual in identifying the Anglo-Boer conflict as the take-off point for reformers' engagements with imperialism in the post-'scramble-for-Africa' period. Indeed, Britain's pyrrhic victory in South

---

[36] This is true despite the proliferation of imaginative new work on both events. See Jenny Sharpe, *Allegories of Empire: The Figure of Woman in the Colonial Text* (Minneapolis, 1993); Nancy Paxton, *Writing Under the Raj: Gender, Race and Rape in the British Imagination, 1830–1857* (New Brunswick, 1999); Jeffery Auerbach, *The Great Exhibition of 1851: A Nation on Display* (New Haven, 1999); Peter Hoffenberg, *An Empire on Display: English, Indian and Australian Exhibitions from the Crystal Palace to the Great War* (California, 2001); Louise Purbrick (ed.), *The Great Exhibition of 1851: New Interdisciplinary Essays* (Manchester, 2002); and Lara Kriegel, 'The Pudding and the Palace: Labor, Print Cultures and Imperial Britain in 1851', in Burton, *After the Imperial Turn*, 230–45.

[37] See Rajnarayan Chandavarkar, *The Origins of Industrial Capital in India: Business Strategies and the Working Classes in Bombay, 1900–1940* (Cambridge, 1994).

[38] Anna Davin, 'Imperialism and Motherhood', in Cooper and Stoler (eds.), *Tensions of Empire: Colonial Cultures in a Bourgeois World* (Berkeley, 1997), 87–151.

Africa tends to be the point of departure for past and present work on the history of the left and empire, as if progressives' interest in imperial questions was limited to the duration of that struggle or even its aftermath, or could be reduced to an anatomy of who supported and who rejected the government's aims and military campaigns in the Transvaal.[39] There is, in other words, a back-story about empire and progressive politics before the onset of the Boer War that remains to be told. Meanwhile, the insularity of later nineteenth-century liberal-left political culture from imperial influences in extant British historiography remains one of the most remarkable features of British studies after the imperial turn.[40]

To be sure, social reform histories, and especially those interested in the late Victorian and Edwardian origins of the welfare state, have long taken a transnational approach with respect to European influences, in part because of the internationalist character of fin-de-siècle socialism, in part because of the attraction of continental models (such as Bismarck's Germany) for social insurance and other reform schemes.[41] But given the tremendous mobility of reformers and politicians – a mobility of people matched by the cross-pollination of ideas and policy-making, as Ian Tyrell and Daniel T. Rodgers have shown in the Atlantic context – the geographical ambit of that internationalism must be extended to include the colonies, which many contemporaries frankly admired as a social laboratory for progressive political and social reform projects.[42] The white settler colonies, especially Australia and New Zealand, were singled out for scrutiny in the 1890s when a series of socio-economic crises and liberal government responses there produced a variety of progressive outcomes, including the passage of a women's suffrage Act in New Zealand in 1893.[43] If feminists the world over could not resist shaming modern

---

[39] See Richard Price, *An Imperial War and the British Working Class* (London, 1972); Henry Pelling, *Popular Politics and Society in Late Victorian Britain* (London, 1968), ch. 5 and Paul Ward, *Red Flag and Union Jack: Englishness, Patriotism and the British Left, 1881–1924*, Royal Historical Society Studies in History (Woodbridge, 1998), ch. 4.

[40] See Antoinette Burton, *After the Imperial Turn: Thinking With and Through the Nation* (Durham, NC, 2003).

[41] Susan Pedersen, *Family, Dependence and the Origins of the Welfare State: Britain and France, 1914–1945* (Cambridge, 1993); Seth Koven and Sonya Michel (eds.), *Mothers of a New World: Maternalist Politics and the Origins of Welfare States* (London, 1993).

[42] Ian Tyrell, *Woman's World, Woman's Empire: The Woman's Christian Temperance Union in International Perspective, 1880–1930* (Chapel Hill, 1991); Daniel T. Rodgers, *Atlantic Crossings: Social Politics in a Progressive Age* (Cambridge, MA, 1998); and Paul Kramer, 'Empires, Exceptions, and Anglo-Saxons: Race and Rule Between the British and United States Empires, 1880–1910', *Journal of American History*, 88 (4) (2002), www.historycooperative.org/journals/jah/88.4/kramer.html.

[43] Patricia Grimshaw, *Women's Suffrage in Zealand* (Auckland, 1972). For the long life of this phenomenon in feminist circles see Fiona Paisley, 'Performing "New Zealand": Maori and Pakeha

Euro-American democracies for being upstaged by such an Antipodean success story, they were by no means alone in pointing to Australia and especially New Zealand as the place where the true future of democracy might be glimpsed.[44]

Although space does not permit me to rehearse this in detail, I would not like to reproduce the historiographical emphasis on the 1890s where metropolitan attention to the Antipodes is concerned. Quite apart from the sustained interest in New Zealand in the 1860s and 1870s in the wake of the Maori Wars, the periodical press in Britain was attentive to political dynamics and developments in the Antipodes, Canada, South Africa and of course the United States in a concentrated way at least from the 1880s, using all these places as sites for evaluating the successes and failures of Anglo-Saxon values and 'colonial' projects. The Antipodes were an especially attractive destination for political ethnographers, not least because the vexed histories of their settlement offered a myriad of comparisons with 'English' form and practices, whether political, social, economic or cultural. The familiarity of Australia and New Zealand – their presumptive whiteness and their apparently recognisable Englishness, especially in the context of decimated aboriginal populations, whose virtual extinction was alternately bemoaned or ignored, and Chinese labourers, whose access to the nation was being restricted – was also an attraction, though one that could reveal the vexed nature of 'identification' with fellow Anglo-Saxons. To take only the most famous example, Charles Dilke's *Greater Britain* (1868) surveyed the white settler colonies past and present, combining travelogue with political commentary in ways that put 'Australasia' on the map in enduring ways. *Greater Britain* (and its successor, *The Problem of Greater Britain* (1890)) was undoubtedly a species of imperial apologia, but in it the young Dilke professed his admiration for the fact that what he saw in Australia was very much like what Britain was destined to become in the wake of manhood suffrage. He described the colony of Victoria as

The most interesting place I have been in, since it probably presents an accurate view 'in little' of the state of society which will exist in England after manhood suffrage is carried, but before the nation as a whole has become completely democratic. Democracy – like Mormonism – would be nothing if found among Frenchmen, or niggers, but is at first sight very terrible when it wears an

Delegates at the Pan-Pacific Women's Conference, Hawai'i, 1934', *New Zealand Journal of History*, 38 (1) (2004), 22–38.

[44] For a full accounting of this phenomenon see Michael Bassett, *The State in New Zealand 1840–1984: Socialism without Doctrines?* (Auckland, 1998), esp. 9–11.

English broad-cloth suit, and smiles on you, from between a pair of Yorkshire cheeks.[45]

Dilke's ambivalence about the image of the future he caught sight of in Australia was echoed by many of the well-known or well-heeled Victorians who travelled to Australia and New Zealand in the last three decades of the nineteenth century to engage in the hard work of that uniquely Victorian genre: reform-minded tourism. Of particular interest here are those radicals and progressives who sought out the Antipodes in the 1890s and after, for what political events and legislative experiments there could tell them about democracy and progress in action, especially of the socialist variety. The Irish MP Michael Davitt, the SDF leader H. M. Hyndman, the Labour Party organiser and future Prime Minister Ramsay MacDonald (with his wife Margaret) and the Fabians Sidney and Beatrice Webb are just a few among the many fin-de-siècle reformers who travelled to 'the Democratic communities of the South Seas' in search of 'socialism without doctrines'.[46]

What impact did such travels have on metropolitan politics in the making? First and foremost, they brought knowledge about colonial conditions into the discursive space of reform circles and advertised specific legislative innovations that were of great interest especially to radical reformers in the age of Chamberlain and Rosebery. So, for example, Michael Davitt's 1898 travelogue, *Life and Progress in Australasia*, trumpeted the passage of the Industrial Conciliation and Arbitration Act of 1894 in New Zealand as part of a series of government interventions covering 'almost every risk to life, limb, health and interest of the industrial classes'. In his view New Zealand was 'the most progressive country in the world today', surpassing even Australia in its emphasis on state responsibility for the problems engendered by a modernising industrial democracy.[47] The case of the Webbs is equally instructive. Although their diaries are notorious for the general snobbery and contempt they exhibited over what they viewed as the 'vulgar' Australians and New Zealanders (not to mention Americans) they encountered on their 1898 tour, Sidney Webb's public pronouncements were

---

[45] Quoted in John Rickard, 'The Anti-Sweating Movement in Britain and Victoria: The Politics of Empire and Social Reform', *Historical Studies: Australia and New Zealand*, 18 (1979), 596.
[46] This phrase was coined by Andre Métin in his book of the same name, *Le Socialisme sans doctrines: Australie and Nouvelle Zélande* (Paris, 1901).
[47] Davitt, *Life and Progress*, 366, 373.

much more positive. In an interview in the *Echo* in 1898 he was quoted as saying:

We have got to wake up to the fact that Australia must be taken seriously, and studied, not as an infant community just out of the gold-diggings stage, but as an adult Anglo-Saxon Democracy, full of interest and instruction to the political world. We have a vast amount to learn from Australia, especially in the sphere of government. Our statesmen are always running over to the United States, which is essentially a foreign country, as unlike England as Germany itself. But, with the notable exception of Sir Charles Dilke, they seem to know nothing of, and learn nothing from, the Democratic communities of the South Seas, whose experience of Cabinet administration is extensive and peculiar ... Australia sadly needs studying, as Mr Bryce studied the American Commonwealth, and such a work would be of enormous value.[48]

Sidney admired Australia in direct proportion to the fact that it was so unlike America; in that sense Australia was for him an attractive Fabian alternative to the dominant Liberal tendency to look to the United States for refractions of Anglo-Saxon ideals. Australia was to be admired, in short, because it was not about abstractions or 'arbitrary psychology'. It was here, in its English-inspired disposition towards practicalities, that 'the extraordinary interest of Australian political experience to the English student' lay.[49] Even more remarkable was Beatrice Webb's take on New Zealand. Not known to wax enthusiastic about many subjects, Beatrice declared that if she had to raise a family outside Great Britain she would choose New Zealand. While not totally uncritical, as with Sidney on Australia she took America as her main point of comparison. In contrast to both Britain and the United States, she found in New Zealand 'no millionaires and hardly any slums ... a people characterised by homely refinement, and by a large measure of vigorous public spirit'.[50]

The Webbs' experience in Australasia may have been a wake-up call for them about the pedagogical value of colonial experiments, but, as I have suggested, they somewhat belatedly joined a growing group of metropolitan politicians and reformers for whom the view from the Antipodes was less a mirror than a kind of visionary political possibility. In any event, the story of the Webbs' Antipodean experience has several ramifications for the provocation about reverse flow that animates this volume. In the first instance, it's quite likely that the Webbs' determination to visit Australia and New Zealand was the result of their encounter with

[48] Quoted in A. G. Austin (ed.), *The Webbs' Australian Diary* (Melbourne, 1965), 113.
[49] *Ibid.*, 114–15.
[50] Quoted in Bassett, *The State in New Zealand*, 9 and 93.

two New Zealanders in London: William Pember Reeves and his wife
Maud Pember Reeves. Reeves had been a member of the Liberal
government in New Zealand that oversaw much of the progressive
legislation Britons admired in the early 1890s (especially, in his capacity
as minister for Labour, the Arbitration Act), and from 1896 he became
the New Zealand Agent-General in London. Maud had political creden-
tials in her own right, having participated in the agitation for women's
suffrage in New Zealand resulting in the franchise in 1893. William
Pember Reeves had been an admirer of Fabian Socialism since reading
Essays in Fabian Socialism, published in 1889; he had corresponded with
Sidney from New Zealand and when he came to London the two met and
he and Maud were quickly taken into the Fabians' circle.[51] Reeves' bio-
grapher intimates that the Webbs' visit to New Zealand in order to get
first-hand impressions of a socialist state in action was one consequence of
their friendship.[52]

In addition to whetting the Webbs' appetite for what he would later
call 'experiments in state socialism', Reeves was an active contributor to
the dissemination of information about New Zealand, its political
accomplishments and its imperial allegiances in metropolitan opinion
forums like the *National Review* and several Fabian tracts as well.[53] So
confident were the Webbs in Reeves' *bona fides*, they entrusted him with
the directorship of their most enduring Fabian product of all, the London
School of Economics.[54] In terms of direct influence on Fabian Socialism,
however, Maud's role was even more significant, though perhaps still
largely underappreciated. For not only did she become a member of the
Fabian executive committee, taking H. G. Wells' side in his failed bid to
take control of the Society in 1906–7, she was instrumental in getting and
keeping 'the woman question' on the Fabian agenda into the early years
of the twentieth century, as evidenced in her contributions to the eventual
formation of the Fabian Women's Group in 1908.[55] Nor was her role
limited to the suffrage question *per se*. Maud Pember Reeves was the
author of a celebrated Fabian pamphlet, later expanded into a book,
which documented the struggles of English working-class mothers and
became a best-seller and a classic in both liberal-left and feminist circles

---

[51] See Keith Sinclair, *William Pember Reeves, New Zealand Fabian* (Oxford, 1965).
[52] *Ibid.*, 270.   [53] *Ibid.*, 249.   [54] *Ibid.*, ch. 21.
[55] Sally Alexander (ed.), *Women's Fabian Tracts* (London, 1988), 5–7. See also Ruth Fry, *Maud and
     Amber: A New Zealand Mother and Daughter and the Women's Cause, 1865 to 1981* (Canterbury,
     1992); Patricia Pugh, *Educate, Agitate, Organize: 100 years of Fabian Socialism* (London, 1984),
     ch. 10; and Ruth Brandon, *The New Women and the Old Men: Love, Sex and the Woman Question*
     (London, 1990).

down until the end of the twentieth century: *Round About a Pound a Week*.[56] As late as the 1990s historian David Vincent was still citing it as an authority on the Victorian social welfare mind, its aspirations and its strategies for reform.[57]

Maud Pember Reeves was not, of course, alone in her efforts to propel women's issues to the centre of the Fabian platform. But her experiences in the New Zealand suffrage struggle undoubtedly helped her to strategise the necessary ways and means for fighting the confident but ultimately sexist sexual liberation programme at the heart of Wells' version of socialism, at any rate. Nor was she the only Fabian woman to draw on colonial experiences to make her case for the necessity of state support for working women and mothers. In 1907 B. L. Hutchins wrote Fabian Tract no. 130, *Home Work and Sweating: The Causes and Remedies*, in which she extensively referenced legislation in Australia and especially New Zealand, and in which the Arbitration Act figured prominently in her case for the regulation of sweating. As John Rickard has shown, this was part of a larger cross-relay between Australia, New Zealand and Britain over the question of labour policy and social reform in the first decade of the twentieth century.[58] Once again, although the heightened attention brought to these questions by, for example, the Exhibition of Sweated Labour at Queen's Hall in 1906, has given them prominence in twentieth-century narratives, this should not occlude the late Victorian roots of these imperial networks. In 1890 Lady Emilia Dilke, in her capacity as President of the Women's Trade Union, had used the example of striking women in Melbourne in 1882 to make her point to English women about the importance of tenacity in their labour struggles as well as the object lesson their colonial 'sisters' could teach them about the path to unionisation.[59]

What we see, then, is a pattern not just of reference but of example from colonial to metropole: a discursive universe of cross-relay with pedagogical effects on the political culture of Britain – persuasive evidence of what Lester calls 'diverse and dynamic but interconnected imperial terrain[s]' across considerable geographical space – and, most significantly perhaps, equally powerful evidence of the movement of ideas and policies not from home to empire but the reverse. For some the evocation of this discursive terrain may not be sufficient 'proof' that empire was constitutive of

---

56 Brandon, *The New Women*, 200–23; see also Sally Alexander, 'Introduction', in Maud Pember Reeves, *Round About a Pound a Week* (London, 1979), ix–xxi.

57 David Vincent, *Poor Citizens: The State and the Poor in the 20th Century* (London, 1991), 10.

58 Reprinted in Alexander (ed.), *Women's Fabian Tracts*, 33–52.

59 Lady Emilia Dilke, 'Trades Unionism for Women', in Burton (ed.), *Politics and Empire*, 265.

'domestic' politics. For sceptics, the accomplishments of Maud Pember Reeves may well seem marginal, despite the impact of a book like *Round About a Pound a Week* on shaping the culture of care at the heart of the emergent late-Victorian/Edwardian welfare state.[60] In this respect, the political work of William Pember Reeves in London is a useful counterpoint. Although he was best known then, and remains so now, chiefly for his promotion in Britain of information about the New Zealand Arbitration Act, he also played a role in the creation of a crucial piece of social welfare legislation: the Old Age Pensions Act. New Zealand's Pensions Bill – first proposed in 1896 and passed after several failed starts in 1898 – was lauded as the first such provision in the British Empire.[61] This was virtually simultaneous with the publication of the Report of the Committee on Old-Age Pensions in Britain, chaired by Lord Rothschild.[62] Though not mentioned in that Report, the New Zealand bill was much talked about in the metropolitan press in the years leading up to the 1908 British Act, with particular emphasis placed on the means tests that the government of New Zealand had applied.[63] Reeves contributed actively to this public discussion, providing valuable evidence about the workings of the New Zealand scheme and thereby contributing to the debate about what kind of pension model should be enacted in Britain.[64] Clearly Reeves was not directly or even indirectly responsible for the provision of Old Age Pensions, which grew out of a discussion that had been going on in Britain at least since the 1880s; it had deep roots in Victorian Poor Law and Elizabethan pauper relief systems as well.[65] At the same time, the Pension Act that eventuated in Britain in 1908 borrowed from the Antipodean model rather than the German one (by relying on a redistribution of income rather than taxes to pay for the outlays).[66] Nor is

---

[60] The Reeves are still probably best known for being the parents of Amber Reeves, who had a liaison and a daughter with H. G. Wells. See Brandon, *The New Women*, 181ff. and Andrea Lynn, *Shadow Lovers: The Last Affairs of H. G. Wells* (Boulder, CO, 2001).

[61] Bassett, *The State in New Zealand*, 99.

[62] See *Report of the Departmental Committee on Old-Age Pensions*, British Parliamentary papers (Aged Poor), 1898. I am most grateful to Danielle Kinsey for tracking down this reference for me.

[63] Vaughan Nash, 'The Old-Age Pension Movement', *Contemporary Review* (April 1899), 503.

[64] See Anne Freemantle, *This Little Band of Prophets: The British Fabians* (New York, 1959), 149 and William Pember Reeves, 'The New Zealand Old-Age Pension Act', *National Review*, 32 (February 1899), 818–25. This was part of the larger Fabian influence on the development of Old Age Pensions and of course the reform of the Poor Law. The former was heavily influenced by the New Zealand case. See A. M. McBriar, *Fabian Socialism and English Politics, 1884–1918* (Cambridge, 1962), 128–9.

[65] See Nash, 'Old-Age Pension Movement', 495–504 and Vincent, *Poor Citizens*, 27ff.

[66] See Peter J. Coleman, *Progressivism and the World of Reform: New Zealand and the Origins of the American Welfare State* (Lawrence, KS, 1987), 82.

this the full extent of colonial influence on the making of the social welfare state in Britain. Although the 'native' English roots and the European contexts of that debate have been scrutinised, the ways in which public discussion in Britain was imprinted with imperial reference points, as writings by Canon Samuel Barnett and others in the press at the time testify, have not been fully considered.[67] Reeves is not, in the end, the proverbial smoking gun, proof positive that imperial experience 'made' the proto-welfare state in Britain, as Peter Coleman has claimed for New Zealand's role in US Progressivism.[68] And his role in imperial social reform politics is in many ways 'fitful' if not tenuous with respect to the larger story of political imperial culture writ large, especially given the unrepresentativeness of the Fabians in the socialist and the larger political landscape.[69] But Pember Reeves' post-1896 career in London does offer persuasive evidence that politics and even some policy outcomes in modern Britain were influenced by colonial encounters 'at home', if not by the total experience of imperial power abroad as well.[70]

Such evidence does not mean that the 'domestic' and European contexts of incipient welfare statism are to be eclipsed by new imperialised narratives, though this seems often to be one fear-effect of the new imperial studies. And yet the imperial context of continental references and borrowings should not be discounted either. Recourse to German examples can easily be seen as a reflection of larger imperial competitive anxieties in the aftermath of the partition of Africa. In any case, Reeves himself was a political polyglot, gleaning what he knew and valued about progressive politics and reform from contemporary English, German, French, American and Australian writers and practices, so that it would be a mistake to see his contributions to metropolitan debates as purely 'colonial' – or to view the

---

[67] Samuel Barnett referred to the views of Sir Harry Johnson, the African colonial administrator and botanist, as grounds for the kind of remedies he thought Poor Law reform could accomplish. Johnston, 'who speaks with rare authority, has told us how negroes with a reputation for idleness respond to treatment which, showing them respect, calls out their hope and their manhood. Treat them, he implies, as children, drive them as cattle, and you are justified in your belief in their idleness. Treat them as men, give them wages and money, open to them the hope of better things, and they work as men.' *Contemporary Review*, 94 (1908), 565. See also Sidney Low, 'Old Age Pensions and Military Service: A Suggestion', *Fortnightly Review*, (n.s.) 73 (April 1903), 606–16.

[68] Coleman, *Progressivism and the World of Reform*.

[69] See Royden Harrison, *The Life and Times of Sidney and Beatrice Webb 1858–1905: The Formative Years* (London, 2000), esp. ch. 8, 'Squalid Opportunism: Fabianism and Empire 1893–1903'.

[70] As Rickard has shown, Reeves was not a one-off example: Charles Dilke credited Alfred Deakin, whose practical discussions with him about a wages board scheme resulted in the Trades Board Act of 1909 (which Rickard says was derivative of the earlier Victorian model in Australia as well). This was part of a larger cross-relay between Britain and the white settler colonies over wages and sweating more generally. See 'The Anti-Sweating Movement', 585.

vectors of imperial political culture as linear (rather than multidirectional or 'web-like', to invoke Ballantyne's metaphor).[71] It is also worth remarking that, as did his late-Victorian and Edwardian contemporaries, Reeves articulated colonial whiteness as a 'component of imperial governmentality' (at least in his metropolitan self-representations), in ways that underscore the racialist agendas of fin-de-siècle liberal and reformist thinking.[72] Indeed, much remains to be said about how the suppression of evidence about 'aliens' and treaty work with aboriginal peoples both erased evidence of racial practices in Australasia *and* encoded the social-experiment discourses in the metropole with a certain fictive, if powerful, claim to Anglo-Saxon purity and white supremacist triumphalism.

Given the fact that, together with democracy, the provision of services of the kind that the incipient welfare state sought to institutionalise is thought to be one of the legacies of the Victorian state to the present (and by implication, to the world), it is worth lingering on the significance of colonial contributions to social insurance schemes of the kind which Reeves championed during his residence in Britain. This is especially warranted in light of recent work on India and Egypt which points to traditions of both colonial/state-sponsored philanthropy *and* indigenous forms of provision that belie the highly naturalised and historically ungrounded assumption that Britain and/or the West is the original home of 'welfare' broadly conceived. Although he does not pursue this line of questioning, Sanjay Sharma's work on north India, for example, opens the door to future scholars interested in tracing the connections between famine relief on the subcontinent and in Ireland in the 1830s and 1840s.[73] He and the late Mine Ener both excavate examples of poor relief provision by local elites in north India and Cairo/Alexandria respectively, thereby implicitly challenging the chronology of first-the-West-then-the-rest when it comes to concerted efforts at managing the indigent in self-conscious and systematic ways.[74] Relocating the Pember Reeves and their contemporaries in the long story of imperial state formation – in the combined, uneven, geographically dispersed but ideologically and practically linked imperial developments that Sharma's and Ener's work points to – is admittedly an enormous project, but it is essential to the counter-narratives of political history that we must

---

[71] Bassett, *The State in New Zealand*, 97; Sinclair, *William Pember Reeves*, 209–10.
[72] The phrase is Ian Fletcher's. See his 'Double Meanings: Nation and Empire in the Edwardian Era', in Burton (ed.), *After the Imperial Turn*, 254.
[73] Sanjay Sharma, *Famine, Philanthropy and the Colonial State: North India in the Early Nineteenth Century* (Oxford, 2001).
[74] See Mine Ener, *Managing Egypt's Poor and the Politics of Benevolence, 1800–1952* (Princeton, 2003).

develop if we are to challenge the persistent insularity of Whig history *in toto*. It is equally crucial for combating the archaic but still powerful idea that Britain's empire was acquired and sustained in a 'fit of absence of mind'.[75] By understanding the workings of imperial political culture (which I intend as an analogue of Sinha's 'imperial social formation'), we can, I think, appreciate the ways in which imperial ideologies and practices were not orchestrated or coordinated in any necessarily deliberate way, even as we understand how a variety of local, unlooked-for and ultimately quixotic events and players helped to suture it together – with authority as well as with the kind of porousness and flexibility which allowed for contest and resistance – across space and place.

In the end, the concept of 'reverse flow' that the Antipodean example illustrates may not prove the most useful metaphor for understanding how imperial political culture was made, in so far as it proceeds from a home/empire imaginary rather than evoking a multiplicity of influences (English, colonial, continental) which could account for what modern Britain looked like at the turn of the century. Indeed, the very question of 'flow' has come in for some criticism for the way it allegedly reproduces 'durable liberal conceptions' of movement, though it need not, and I would say does not, perforce do so in the new scholarship.[76] Whatever model we adopt, the history of imperial political culture – its uneven development, and the convergences and divergences of people, ideas and power it produced – is surely in the details. Of course, there will always be connections that cannot be cemented, outcomes whose genealogies we can but imperfectly trace, and evidence that the archive, however nimbly we negotiate it, and even exceed it, cannot yield. To admit as much is to acknowledge that, in Jed Esty's evocative words, 'we must chart imperial presence not only as visible and narrative data but as unexpected formal encryptments and thematic outcroppings' in presumptively 'domestic' contexts.[77] It is these unanticipated codes and recurrent if fugitive instances that require our attention. And this is the terrain on which anti-imperial histories of the British Empire – political or otherwise – can, should and doubtless will be written.

---

[75] For the persistence of this view in contemporary analyses see Gore Vidal, 'Requiem for the American Empire' (11 January 1986), in *Perspectives on The Nation, 1865–2000* (New York, 2004), 115 and Martin Walker, 'America's Virtual Empire', *World Policy Journal*, 19 (2) (2002), 149.

[76] See Tim Pratt and James Vernon, '"Appeal From this Fiery Bed . . . ": The Colonial Politics of Gandhi's Fasts and their Metropolitan Reception', *Journal of British Studies*, 44 (1) (2005), 92. See also Michael Fisher, *Counterflows to Colonialism: Indian Travellers and Settlers in Britain, 1600–1857* (Delhi, 2004).

[77] Jed Esty, *A Shrinking Island: Modernism and National Culture in England* (Princeton, 2004), 6.

CHAPTER ELEVEN

Bringing the Empire home: women activists in imperial Britain, 1790s–1930s

Clare Midgley

This chapter focuses on women's metropolitan-based activism on imperial issues in the period between the 1790s and the outbreak of the Second World War. The women concerned are mainly British-born, white and middle or upper class as it was from this sector of the population that the leadership for most empire-focused campaigns came. However, there is also some consideration of white working-class women's relationship to these campaigns, and of both white colonial women and black and Asian women who were active within or without these movements, and often challenged hegemonic discourses. Discussion concentrates on women's activism within organisations with a specifically imperial focus, rather than imperial activism within the organised feminist movement or the relationship between feminism and imperialism, aspects of which are covered in chapters by Jane Rendall and Keith McClelland and Sonya Rose.[1]

The chapter covers a long time-span, which saw major developments both in the politics of empire and in women's relationship to public life and politics.[2] It explores the interconnecting dynamics of these two arenas of change through discussing women's involvement in movements aiming to reform the Empire and the colonised, in organisations promoting support for imperialism, and in anti-imperial and anti-racist activism. Chronologically, these campaigns overlapped with each other, but they peaked in succeeding periods: the nineteenth century, the Edwardian period and the interwar period respectively. The chapter explores the diverse ways in which a range of female activists, varied in their ideological stance towards imperialism, played a crucial role in bringing imperial concerns 'home' to the British public. In the process, it will be

---

[1] The most influential study of the relationship between British feminism and imperialism is Antoinette Burton, *Burdens of History: British Feminists, Indian Women and Imperial Culture, 1865–1915* (Chapel Hill, 1994). Barbara Caine, *English Feminism, 1780–1980* (Oxford, 1997) is a pioneering attempt to incorporate consideration of imperialism within a general history of British feminism.

[2] Susan Kingsley Kent, *Gender and Power in Britain, 1640–1990* (London, 1999) devotes considerable attention to the impact of empire in shaping the politics of gender in Britain.

shown, they opened up new roles for women in public and political spheres and contributed to shaping gendered class identities constituted through whiteness, Englishness and Protestantism in imperial Britain.

IMPERIAL PHILANTHROPY AND SOCIAL REFORM

Women activists were crucial to the successful operation of both the anti-slavery and the foreign missionary movements. The discursive dimensions of women's engagement with these two movements are discussed by Jane Rendall: here, the focus will be on women's organisations, campaigns and imperial agency. Interconnected enterprises, the movements were among the most widely supported networks of voluntary organisation of the first half of the nineteenth century, drawing a large portion of the public into engagement with imperial issues.[3] They also lay at the heart of the development of female philanthropy and women's involvement in social reform: there were close links between the domestic and imperial dimensions of middle-class women's public activism.[4] A study of women's empire-focused activism thus throws new light on the intersections between gendered ideologies of race and class in early nineteenth-century Britain.[5] It also complicates our understanding of the relationships between 'public' and 'private' spheres, between 'domestic' and 'political' life and between evangelicalism and feminism.[6]

Women's roles were vital to both anti-slavery and missionary movements despite the fact that they were excluded from the national committees of

[3] For the anti-slavery movement see: Adam Hochschild, *Bury the Chains: The British Struggle to Abolish Slavery* (London, 2005); J. R. Oldfield, *Popular Politics and British Anti-Slavery: The Mobilisation of Public Opinion Against the Slave Trade, 1787–1807* (Manchester, 1995); David Turley, *The Culture of English Anti-slavery, 1780–1860* (London, 1991); James Walvin (ed.), *Slavery and British Society, 1776–1846* (London, 1982). For differing interpretations of the missionary movement and its relationship to empire see: Andrew Porter, *Religion Versus Empire? British Protestant Missionaries and Overseas Expansion, 1700–1914* (Manchester, 2004) and Susan Thorne, *Congregational Missions and the Making of an Imperial Culture in Nineteenth-Century England* (Stanford, 1999).

[4] F. K. Prochaska, *Women and Philanthropy in 19th Century England* (Oxford, 1980); Alison Twells, '"Let Us Begin Well at Home": Class, Ethnicity and Christian Motherhood in the Writing of Hannah Kilham, 1774–1832', in Eileen Janes Yeo (ed.), *Radical Femininity: Women's Self-representation in the Public Sphere* (Manchester, 1998), 25–51; Alison Twells, '"Happy English Children": Class, Ethnicity and the Making of Missionary Women, 1800–50', *Women's Studies International Forum*, 21 (1998), 235–46.

[5] Catherine Hall, *Civilising Subjects: Metropole and Colony in the English Imagination* (Cambridge, 2002), a key exploration of these issues, focuses on the period when ideologies were shifting and concentrates on male activists.

[6] Leonore Davidoff and Catherine Hall, *Family Fortunes: Men and Women of the English Middle Class, 1780–1850*, rev. edn (London, 2002); Sue Morgan (ed.), *Women, Religion and Feminism in Britain, 1750–1900* (Basingstoke, 2002).

the main societies, which attempted to channel all women's activities into local support groups under the supervision of local men's auxiliaries. These local ladies' societies actually became crucial to the spread of propaganda and the raising of funds for both causes. In addition, women organised themselves into separate societies at both local and national levels. An independent women's society in Birmingham acted as the national organisational hub for female abolitionism, while the London-based interdenominational Female Education Society organised the sending out of single women as Christian educators to British India and elsewhere independently of the main missionary societies, and developed its own network of auxiliaries.[7]

Women's commitment to the two movements also pushed them into their earliest concerted attempts to directly impact on British parliamentary politics. Women's petitions against *sati* (widow-burning) in India and their much more extensive petitioning against slavery predated the earliest petitions calling for British women's legal and political rights by several decades. Such overtly political acts, which apparently posed a direct challenge to the ideology of 'separate spheres', were successfully justified as an exceptional response to exceptional circumstances, motivated by women's special empathy for female suffering, a matter of humanity and morality rather than politics. They were framed as appeals to men in power to extend their paternal protection to their suffering fellow subjects rather than as open challenges to male authority. Women activists thus placed their concerns before the imperial parliament while avoiding an explicit assertion of their own political rights.[8]

In the anti-slavery movement, middle-class white British women, in contrast to the radical women abolitionists in the USA, generally stopped short of asserting their own right to equal participation in the movement.[9] However, they did at times directly challenge gender and class hierarchies. Quaker campaigner Elizabeth Heyrick's controversial pamphlet *Immediate, not Gradual Abolition* was influenced by the rights-based agenda of 1790s'

---

[7] Clare Midgley, *Women Against Slavery: The British Campaigns, 1780–1870* (London, 1992), esp. 43–50; Margaret Donaldson, ' "The cultivation of the Heart and the Moulding of the Will ... ": The Missionary Contribution of the Society for Promoting Female Education in China, India and the East', in W. J. Sheils and Diana Wood (eds.), *Women in the Church* (Oxford, 1990), 429–42.

[8] Clare Midgley, 'Female Emancipation in an Imperial Frame: English Women and the Campaign Against *Sati* (Widow-burning) in India, 1813–30', *Women's History Review*, 9 (2000), 95–121; Midgley, *Women Against Slavery*, 62–71.

[9] Kathryn Kish Sklar, ' "Women Who Speak for an Entire Nation": American and British Women at the World Anti-Slavery Convention, London, 1840', in Jean Fagan Yellin and John C. Van Horne (eds.), *The Abolitionist Sisterhood: Women's Political Culture in Antebellum America* (Ithaca, 1994); Clare Midgley, 'Anti-slavery and Feminism in Britain', *Gender and History*, 5 (1993), 343–62.

radicalism, one of the main roots of opposition to slavery. It called for direct action by ordinary people to bring about the rapid downfall of the slave system. By abstaining en masse from slave-grown produce, Heyrick argued, ordinary people, particularly women in their role as purchasers of consumer produce, had the power to bring about the eradication of slavery, bypassing the cautious male leadership of the Anti-Slavery Society – the 'worldly politicians' who had 'converted the great business of emancipation into an object of political calculation'. Moral and financial pressure from ladies' anti-slavery associations who backed Heyrick was an important factor in pushing that leadership to shift from their policy of promoting amelioration and gradual abolition.[10]

While male campaigners sought support through public meetings and sermons and debated issues in parliament, middle-class women were largely responsible for systematic door-to-door visiting, reaching working-class women in the home and drawing them into penny-a-week support for foreign missionary societies, anti-slavery petitioning campaigns and the boycott of slave-grown produce. Such activities were crucial in broadening popular support for, and bringing in vital funds to, male-led national organisations. Women of all classes were shown that their private role as consumers was one which bore public responsibilities. Consumer power could be used to achieve imperial reform, tea parties transformed from trivial social events into political statements by the use of free-grown sugar and tea sets bearing images of female suffering under slavery. In addition, women's feminine skills were channelled into the production of anti-slavery work-bags and goods for missionary bazaars.[11]

Although the main foreign missionary societies did not directly employ women until the second half of the nineteenth century, women played a crucial role in the mission field overseas as missionaries' wives and as single women employed by women-run societies to undertake the Christian education of 'native females'. Women activists in the imperial metropole presented such women's work in ways which emphasised female imperial agency and encouraged middle-class women to broaden their vision of appropriate feminine roles beyond the domestic, the voluntary and the locally based. Jemima Thompson's 1841 *Memoirs of*

---

[10] Midgley, *Women Against Slavery*, 103–20. The quotes are from Elizabeth Heyrick, *Immediate, not Gradual Abolition* (London, 1824), 18.

[11] Clare Midgley, 'Slave Sugar Boycotts, Female Activism and the Domestic Base of Anti-slavery Culture', *Slavery and Abolition*, 17 (1996), 137–62; Charlotte Sussman, *Consuming Anxieties: Consumer Protest, Gender and British Slavery, 1713–1833* (Stanford, 2000), esp. ch. 4; Prochaska, *Women and Philanthropy*, 47–72.

British Female Missionaries, a manifesto promoting female missionary endeavour, began with a strong assertion that 'missionary biography ought not ... be limited to ... laborious and apostolic men'. Questioning evangelical prescriptions of appropriate roles for women, the text lamented that many girls 'spend several years of their most valuable part of their lives in a kind of restless indolence' and argued that 'had they before them some great and benevolent object, such as taking a share in the regeneration of the world, they would be much happier, and much more amiable'. Here a much wider sphere of activity is envisioned for middle-class British women than that laid out in Sarah Lewis' recently published *Women's Mission*. Women's different but complementary qualities to men, which Lewis argued were best cultivated and properly utilised from a domestic base, were presented in Thompson's tract as particularly suiting them to missionary work among the 'heathen'. In the mission field, where the boundary between preaching and teaching was blurred, women were presented with new opportunities at just the time when their roles within mainstream Protestantism at home were being constricted.[12] From the 1860s onwards, the major missionary societies, finally acknowledging the vital work of women, began to directly employ female missionaries and, when the continuing important work of missionary wives is also taken into account, by the late nineteenth century women formed the majority of those sent out as missionary workers overseas: what had initially been seen by British evangelicals as an exclusively male role had become feminised.[13]

In missionary writings directed at a British female audience a global comparative framework which contrasted the privileges of Christian women with the sufferings of 'heathen' women formed the basis of the assertion of British women's duty towards their less privileged sisters. British women's Christian duty was linked to a sense of female imperial responsibility and British women were presented as 'the natural guardians of these unhappy

---

[12] Clare Midgley, 'Can Women Be Missionaries? Envisioning Female Agency in the Early Nineteenth-century British Empire', *Journal of British Studies*, 45 (2) (April 2006). The quotes are from Jemima Thompson, *Memoirs of British Female Missionaries* (London, 1841), preface, ix, xxvi. For women and preaching see Jocelyn Murray, 'Gender Attitudes and the Contribution of Women to Evangelism and Ministry in the Nineteenth Century', in John Wolffe (ed.), *Evangelical Faith and Public Zeal: Evangelicals and Society in Britain 1780–1980* (London, 1995), 97–116; Beverly Mayne Kienzle and Pamela J. Walker (eds.), *Women Preachers and Prophets through Two Millennia of Christianity* (Berkeley, 1998).

[13] Rhonda Anne Semple, *Missionary Women: Gender, Professionalism and the Victorian Idea of Christian Mission* (Woodbridge, 2003); Steven S. Maughan, 'Civic Culture, Women's Foreign Missions, and the British Imperial Imagination, 1860–1914', in Frank Trentmann (ed.), *Paradoxes in Civil Society: New Perspectives on Modern German and British History* (New York, 2000), 199–219.

Widows and Orphans in British India'. Their missionary work was placed as part of providential imperialism – the belief that Britain's imperial expansion was a God-given opportunity to spread Christianity through the world. Paradoxically, then, evangelical discourse, generally seen as encouraging women's confinement within the domestic sphere, could, through the marriage of concepts of woman's mission, Christian female privilege and providential imperialism, be deployed to create an expansive vision of independent British female agency on the global stage, enacting a maternalist Christian imperial mission to 'heathen' women.[14]

In highlighting the sufferings of colonised women and presenting them as passive victims of colonial slavery or of 'heathen' patriarchy, British women activists played a key role in justifying a reformed imperialism, and presenting this to the British public as a civilising project in which women could play a vital part. Anti-slavery, it should be stressed, was not an anti-imperial movement, but rather about the reform of empire to accord to British middle-class definitions of freedom based around the promotion of male waged labour and female domesticity.[15] In this context, female abolitionists presented themselves as saviours of, and ideal models for, 'other' women. While encouraging empathetic identification with enslaved black women through adopting the slogan 'Am I not a woman and a sister', they simultaneously reinforced a sense of white women's maternalistic and superior position as saviours through the visual image of the keeling enchained black woman appealing to an invisible white female audience. This double-edged message is very apparent in 'The negro mother's appeal'. Addressing the 'white lady, happy, proud, and free' and urging her to 'Dispel the Negro Mother's fears', the poem was illustrated with the image of a white woman taking coffee in her home with her child on her lap; an enchained black woman has entered the room appealing for help and in the background this woman's child is shown being dragged away into slavery by a white man. Anti-slavery women thus brought the horrors of slavery home to British women while stressing their own superior domesticity.[16]

[14] Midgley, 'Can Women Be Missionaries?'; the quote is from the British and Foreign School Society's 'Appeal in Behalf of Native Females', *Missionary Register* (1820), 434. For the concept of providential imperialism see Brian Stanley, *The Bible and the Flag: Protestant Missions and British Imperialism in the Nineteenth and Twentieth Centuries* (Leicester, 1990).
[15] Hall, *Civilising Subjects*; Thomas C. Holt, *The Problem of Freedom: Race, Labor, and Politics in Jamaica and Britain, 1832–1938* (Baltimore, 1992).
[16] An example of a roundel with the illustrated slogan 'Am I not a woman and a sister' can be viewed in the Wilberforce House, Hull, England; 'The negro mother's appeal' in *Anti-Slavery Scrap Book* (London, 1829).

Women active in the foreign missionary movement aligned with anti-slavery women in asserting non-Western women's potential to be educated, civilised and Christianised. However, they also widely disseminated visual images of non-Western women which associated cultural inferiority with physical appearance: 'immodest' dress was associated with dark skin, in contrast to images of the angelic white female missionary teacher, armed with bonnet and Bible.[17] The dissemination of such imagery by middle-class women to working-class families may have helped bridge the class divide around which domestic philanthropy was structured through offering a vision of shared cross-class ethnic and racial identity based on a sense of superiority to, and a maternalistic 'helping' stance towards, black and brown women in Britain's empire. Working-class women, however, were confined to supportive roles in both movements. Chartist women, making analogies between their own position and that of slaves, challenged the hypocrisy of the privileged who focused on the ill-treatment of British subjects abroad while ignoring injustice at home.[18]

White middle-class activists' gendered ideologies of race and class were also called into question by black and Asian women activists in Britain. Such individuals, while small in number, brought the Empire home to British people in the most literal sense. As women of colour from the colonies they made spaces for themselves within the metropole and their varied backgrounds and self-presentations challenged racial and ethnic stereotypes of colonised women. Their very presence unsettled essentialised notions of ethnic and racial difference and easy equations between colonised peoples in the Empire and the labouring poor at home.

Mary Prince, an enslaved African-Caribbean woman brought to Britain by her owners, petitioned parliament for her legal freedom and dictated her life-story in order to promote the emancipation of all slaves, providing evidence not only of the victimisation of enslaved women but also of their resistance.[19] Her petition asserted a black woman's right to freedom over thirty years before white women began to petition for their own legal rights. However, Prince's movement from slave-servant to paid servant in a leading British abolitionist household, her treatment by white abolitionist women not as a fellow activist but as a victim of slavery,

---

[17] For a fascinating discussion of the significance of bonnet-wearing as a marker of civility and Christian conversion see Anna Johnston, *Missionary Writing and Empire, 1800–1860* (Cambridge, 2003), 147–54.

[18] Jutta Schwarzkopf, *Women in the Chartist Movement* (Basingstoke, 1991), esp. 95.

[19] For the lives of other enslaved men and women in England at this period see Gretchen Gerzina, *Black England: Life Before Emancipation* (London, 1995).

whose suffering had to be confirmed through examination of the whip marks on her body, and the suppression of elements of her story relating to extra-marital sexual relationships, are together suggestive of the limits of expression and opportunity for black women in early nineteenth-century Britain. Such boundaries were framed by hierarchies based on class as well as race, and by middle-class notions of respectability which hinged on the rigid control of female sexual behaviour.[20]

Rather similar obstacles confronted another African-Caribbean woman, Mary Seacole, in the post-emancipation period. Positioning herself as a loyal British imperial subject, she travelled to Britain in the 1850s to offer her help in the Crimean War effort. However, she was turned down for employment as a nurse by Florence Nightingale, who was endeavouring to transform nursing into a 'respectable' profession for middle-class English women. She ascribed this rejection to her race but, as a free woman with financial resources, she was far less dependent on white patronage than Mary Prince had been. Through her self-financed work running a hotel for soldiers near the front line, and later through her autobiographical *Wonderful Adventures*, Seacole was able to successfully challenge her marginalisation within Britain and its empire. An interesting shift in her image in Britain is discernible, from the motherly and down-to-earth brown-skinned 'doctress' of the 1857 *Punch* cartoon, presented in contrast to the angelic image of Florence Nightingale as the 'lady with the lamp', to the dignified Victorian lady of the marble bust produced by the royal sculptor Count Gleichen in 1871, a sculpture which monumentalised Seacole's public recognition at the heart of empire.[21]

In the late Victorian period a number of educated black and Asian women came to Britain as students, and some were active in opening up new opportunities for women in the Empire, interacting with British female reform and feminist circles. In the 1880s Pandita Ramabai, a widowed woman from a Hindu Brahmin family, travelled to Britain to gain a medical training with the aim of serving Indian women as a doctor.

---

[20] *The History of Mary Prince* was originally published in London in 1831. Two recent editions contain extensive new critical introductions: Moira Ferguson (ed.), *The History of Mary Prince, a West Indian Slave, Related by Herself*, rev. edn (Ann Arbor, 1997); Sarah Salih (ed.), *The History of Mary Prince*, updated edn (London, 2004). See also Jennifer DeVere Brody, *Impossible Purities: Blackness, Femininity, and Victorian Culture* (Durham, NC, 1998).

[21] Ziggi Alexander and Audrey Dewjee (eds.), *Wonderful Adventures of Mrs Seacole in Many Lands* (Bristol, 1984), which includes reproductions of the *Punch* cartoon of 30 May 1857 and the Gleichen sculpture. See also Lizabeth Paravisini-Gebert, 'Mrs Seacole's *Wonderful Adventures in Many Lands* and the Consciousness of Transit', in Gretchen Holbrook Gerzina (ed.), *Black Victorians, Black Victoriana* (New Brunswick, 2003), 71–87.

However, as Antoinette Burton observes, 'imperial England proved to be inhospitable ground for Ramabai's developing female reform conscious-ness'. Amid pressure from her white patrons not to undertake public speaking in order to safeguard her respectability, and attempts to remould her into a Christian missionary to Indian women, she sought her own path, questioning Anglican orthodoxy and asserting her own agenda of social reform. Two years after her departure Cornelie Sorabji, a single woman from a Parsi Christian family, also came to Britain to study, becoming the first women to qualify as a lawyer in this country, a pioneering figure in the feminist campaign to open up new educational and employment opportunities for women in the late Victorian period. As highly educated women Ramabai and Sorabji's very presence in the imperial metropole called into question both missionary and Western feminist representations of Indian women as passive, ignorant and superstitious.[22]

FEMALE IMPERIALISTS

From the late Victorian period, public activism in Britain increasingly focused less on the social reform of empire than on promoting support for it in the face of threats to British imperial supremacy from the growing power of other industrialising Western nations, and on strengthening imperial bonds through cementing links with the self-governing white settler colonies of 'Greater Britain'. Imperialist and patriotic organisations proliferated in the Edwardian period, fostered by the impact of the South African War of 1899–1902. Historians have remarked on the very mas-culinist and militaristic imperial ethos of this period.[23] However, this did not preclude an important role for female activists, and female imperialism gained increasing significance after the First World War. The discussion that follows, focusing on female imperial activism between the 1880s and the 1930s, complements Keith McClelland and Sonya Rose's discussion in this volume of the politics of gender, citizenship and empire over this period.[24]

[22] Antoinette Burton, At the Heart of Empire: Indians and the Colonial Encounter in Late-Victorian Britain (Berkeley, 1998), quote from 109. See also Rozina Visram, Ayahs, Lascars and Princes: Indians in Britain, 1700–1947 (London, 1986).
[23] John M. Mackenzie, Propaganda and Empire (Manchester, 1984); John M. Mackenzie (ed.), Imperialism and Popular Culture (Manchester, 1986); Dane Kennedy, Britain and Empire, 1880–1945 (London, 2002); John Tosh, 'Manliness, Masculinities and the New Imperialism, 1880–1900', in his Manliness and Masculinities in Nineteenth-Century Britain (Harlow, 2005), 192–214.
[24] For comparative material on German women imperialists at the period see Lora Wildenthal, German Women for Empire, 1884–1945 (Durham, NC, 2001).

As Paula Krebs has noted, in the new, more virulently racist environment of the late Victorian period, public criticisms of British imperialism, even in progressive circles, were more likely to take the form of advocacy of the Boer cause in South Africa than concern over racism towards Africans. Olive Schreiner, the South African feminist writer, wrote a series of articles for major British periodicals in the 1890s which put a sympathetic view of Afrikaners before the public and sought to justify their genocide against indigenous peoples. In a chilling passage she mocked 'the fair European woman' for criticising Boers from the safety of her drawing-room in the metropole:

But if, from behind some tapestry-covered armchair in the corner, a small, wizened, yellow face were to look out now, and a little naked arm guided an arrow, tipped with barked bone dipped in poison, at her heart, the cry of the human preserving itself would surely arise; Jeaves would be called up, the policeman with his baton would appear, and if there were a pistol in the house, it would be called into requisition! The little prehistoric record would lie dead upon the Persian carpet.[25]

Schreiner's social Darwinist language contrasted sharply with the sympathetic anti-slavery image of the black woman entering the English woman's home in the 'Negro mother's appeal', and instead evoked images which had circulated during the Indian Rebellion of 1857–8. This event, widely interpreted by historians as marking a shift to much more negative attitudes to colonised peoples, saw a threat to British imperial dominance presented to the public as a threat to helpless English women, under attack in their colonial homes by wild Indian men.[26]

A few years later, when the concentration camps controversy became the biggest scandal of the South African War, it was the sufferings of Boers, not the substantial number of Africans who were also confined to camps, which was the focus of debate. This controversy is a key moment in the history of British women's imperial activism: it was the first time that women were the leading public advocates on opposing sides of a major debate concerning British imperial policy. Emily Hobhouse, who visited the camps for the anti-war and pro-Boer South African Women and Children's Distress Fund, published a highly critical report in 1901 which gained widespread coverage in the press and stimulated anti-war

[25] Olive Schreiner, *Thoughts on South Africa* (London, 1923), 154, quoted in Paula Krebs, *Gender, Race and the Writing of Empire: Public Discourse and the Boer War* (Cambridge, 1999), 132.
[26] Christine Bolt, *Victorian Attitudes to Race* (London, 1971); Sara Suleri, *The Rhetoric of English India* (Chicago, 1992).

activism and heated parliamentary debate. The government responded by setting up its own Ladies Commission, led by leading women's suffrage campaigner and Liberal Unionist Millicent Fawcett, to investigate the camps and suggest reforms.[27] It was the first government commission made up entirely of women and is suggestive of the way in which well-connected white middle-class women, even before they gained the vote, were becoming a part of the political nation, accepted as experts on issues relating to the treatment of women in the Empire, as British feminists had hoped. As Paula Krebs points out, the question of racial difference was central to the debate between Hobhouse and Fawcett: were Boer women more like 'us', the English, or more like 'them', the Africans? Hobhouse sought to evoke empathy for dignified suffering mothers under threat from sexually predatory Africans; in contrast, Fawcett sought to blame deaths in the camps on ignorant inadequate mothers who were part of a backward enemy 'race'.[28]

The South African War was a major catalyst for the emergence in Edwardian Britain of an imperialist women's movement. One organisation directly stimulated by the war was the Girl Guides, which developed from 1909 as the female wing of the Boy Scouts, founded by the hero of the siege of Mafeking, Robert Baden-Powell; it was a patriotic movement aiming to encourage 'womanly' qualities at home and on the imperial frontier.[29] Another influential organisation set up in the aftermath of the war was the Victoria League, the only women-run empire propaganda society in Britain. At its foundation in 1901 its president Lady Jersey asserted that 'they were English women and the impulse of their race was not to sit with folded hands and tremble for the future', presenting women as active rather than passive in the face of a threat to empire.[30] Women's organisations founded in the late Victorian period, including the Girls' Friendly Society (f. 1874) and the British Women's Emigration

---

[27] For Fawcett's pro-imperial politics, including her opposition to Irish Home Rule, see David Rubinstein, *A Different World for Women: The Life of Millicent Garrett Fawcett* (Columbus, OH, 1991), ch. 10. For the perspective of another leading 'imperial feminist' on the war see Antoinette Burton, '"States of Injury": Josephine Butler on Slavery, Citizenship, and the Boer War', in Ian Christopher Fletcher, Laura E. Nym Mayhall and Philippa Levine (eds.), *Women's Suffrage in the British Empire: Citizenship, Nation and Race* (London, 2000), 18–32.

[28] Krebs, *Gender, Race and the Writing of Empire*, esp. 64–6, 69–79.

[29] Allen Warren, '"Mothers for the Empire"? The Girl Guides Association in Britain, 1909–1939', in J. A. Mangan (ed.), *Making Imperial Mentalities: Socialisation and British Imperialism* (Manchester, 1990), 96–109.

[30] Lady Jersey, 'The Victoria League', *National Review*, 52 (1909), 317–18, quoted in Eliza Reidi, 'Imperialist Women in Edwardian Britain: The Victoria League 1899–1914' (PhD, University of St Andrews, 1998), 29.

Association (f. 1884), also adopted an increasingly imperialist agenda in the Edwardian period. As Julia Bush points out, this imperialist women's movement was led by upper middle-class and aristocratic ladies, often politically Conservative and High Church, with close links to leading male imperialists. They were adept at using their social position to exert informal influence on powerful men and asserting a 'womanly' imperialism to complement the approach of the masculine imperial elite.[31]

Female emigration societies combined woman-oriented and empire-oriented agendas.[32] White settler colonies were promoted as alternative homes for British women who lacked opportunities in the metropole, and female migration was presented as a solution to the shortage of white women, and a way of strengthening the British settler community at the expense of Afrikaners in South Africa. Female emigrators took it for granted that Britons had a right to settle in lands over which they had seized control from indigenous peoples, and in their propaganda the violence of male conquest and land appropriation was rendered invisible. The activists presented women as consolidating empire through the creation of settled communities, tempering the masculine frontier mentality with feminine domesticity. Influenced by social Darwinism and eugenics, they developed the concept of 'imperious maternity', expressing concern for emigrating 'the right sort of women' who would become 'nursing mothers of the English race to be' and spread the English way of life.[33] Tensions, however, arose between women-run voluntary societies, who were keen to place middle-class women as teachers and governesses, and the British imperial government and colonial authorities, who wanted working-class women to be sent as domestic servants and potential farmers' wives.

If female emigration societies focused on exporting the English way of life, the women of the Primrose League concentrated on fostering public support for empire at home as part of the agenda of popular Conservatism. Concerned to gain support from the expanding working-class male electorate, the League set out to promote Conservative values,

[31] Julia Bush, *Edwardian Ladies and Imperial Power* (Leicester, 2000). For earlier influence by aristocratic women on politics see K. D. Reynolds, *Aristocratic Women and Political Society in Victorian Britain* (Oxford, 1998); Amanda Vickery (ed.), *Women, Privilege and Power: British Politics, 1750 to the Present* (Stanford, 2001), esp. chs. 1, 2, 4.

[32] The standard history of female emigration societies, A. James Hammerton, *Emigrant Gentlewomen: Genteel Poverty and Female Emigration, 1830–1914* (London, 1979), does not directly address the issue of the societies' support for empire.

[33] J. Bush, ' "The Right Sort of Woman": Female Emigrators and Emigration to the British Empire, 1890–1910', *Women's History Review*, 3 (1994), 385–409. Bush is quoting Mrs Chapin in *Imperial Colonist*, 2 (August 1903), Dora Browne's poem 'To England's Daughters', *Imperial Colonist*, 3 (December 1904) and Susan Countess of Malmesbury in *Imperial Colonist*, 1 (January 1903).

defined as 'the maintenance of Religion, the Estates of the Realm, and of the unity of the British Empire under our Sovereign'. While the League was not a female-led organisation, women comprised nearly half its membership, which reached two million by 1910.[34] Its Ladies' Grand Council undertook its own propaganda initiatives, and established local 'habitations' in which women were frequently more active than men, forming an army of unpaid canvassers and organisers. These women were vital to the League's agenda, which Matthew Hendley describes as an attempt to 'domesticize politics', acting as a bridge between the remote world of Westminster politics and everyday life in family and local community and creating 'an arena in which politics were never completely absent but were conducted subtly in a non-confrontational atmosphere and absorbed almost unconsciously'.[35] The provision of free social entertainments was central to this: lantern slide shows, *tableaux vivants* and speakers promoted the cult of the hero, patriotism and militarism, and the report of one such event, in which a platform speaker was sandwiched 'between a nigger song and a conjuror',[36] is suggestive of the casual racism which imbued popular imperialism at this period.

Leading Dames were highly politically engaged women and at times their activities had major repercussions for the Conservative Party's male leadership. This happened in the 1900s over Tariff Reform, when leading Dames defected from the League to form a Women's Committee of the Tariff Reform League in 1904, contributing to a crisis in the Party over the policy by stoking fears that the popular support base of Conservatism would be undermined. Less controversially, Dames played an important role in promoting the maintenance of Union with Ireland, seen by the Conservative Party as crucial to the survival of the Empire. Liberal introduction of a new Home Rule Bill in 1912 led Dames to launch a 'Help the Ulster Women' committee to aid those expected to flee Ulster in the event of civil war. The League's 'most notable pre-war political philanthropic endeavour',[37] it provided a way for unenfranchised women to show their strong views on a key political issue.

In contrast to the Primrose League, the Victoria League prided itself on its 'non-political' stance, numbering Liberal Unionists and Liberals as

---

[34] Martin Pugh, *The Tories and the People, 1880–1935* (Oxford, 1985), 13, 27. See also G. E. Maguire, *Conservative Women: A History of Women and the Conservative Party, 1874–1997* (London, 1998).

[35] Matthew Hendley, 'Patriotic Leagues and the Evolution of Popular Patriotism and Imperialism in Great Britain, 1914–1932' (PhD, University of Toronto, 1998), 105.

[36] *Primrose League Gazette*, 24 May 1890, quoted in Pugh, *The Tories and the People*, 35.

[37] Hendley, 'Patriotic Leagues', 107.

well as Conservatives among its leadership. Developing innovative propaganda methods, it sought to maintain imperial unity not through
'male' political, administrative or military means but through the promotion of 'imperial sentiment' among the general public in both Britain
and its empire. A key aspect of its work was the imperial education of
children and the cultural spread of pro-imperial ideas in both Britain and
the Dominions. Its branches organised lectures, lantern slide talks,
reading circles, essay competitions and Empire Day celebrations. It also
fostered personal ties between British and white colonial children through
extensive school linking and pen-friend schemes. However, it never
became a mass organisation in the way that the Primrose League was,
gaining support mainly from the upper and middle classes.[38]

One way in which the Victoria League attempted to appeal to the
working class and draw in a wider social and political spectrum of female
activists was through the promotion of social imperialism. Linking social
reform at home with the strengthening of the Empire overseas in varying
ways this, as Keith McClelland and Sonya Rose discuss, became a
dominant element of British political culture in the late nineteenth
century. Female social imperialism, which combined women's imperial
interest with their established role in philanthropy, social reform and
local government, remains an under-researched area. Violet Markham
was a pivotal figure in this regard. A leading figure in the Victoria League,
she combined a radical Liberalism with Milnerite imperialism, public
prominence with opposition to women's suffrage. In 1905 she was
involved in forming the League's Industrial Committee, on which she
worked in cooperation with leading female social reformers, feminists and
Fabian socialists including May Tennant and Maud Pember Reeves. The
Committee collected together material for a 1908 handbook comparing
factory laws in Britain and the self-governing colonies. Markham's
interest in the issue was tied to her social Darwinist and eugenicist
concerns: protective legislation, she believed, would safeguard the welfare
of mothers of the 'imperial race'. She followed up the Committee's
initiative by organising the Victoria League Imperial Health Conference
and Exhibition, which focused on town planning and housing, and on
infant health and 'mothercraft'.[39] Markham, together with Flora Shaw
(Lady Lugard), the colonial editor of *The Times* from 1893 to 1900,

[38] Eliza Reidi, 'Women, Gender, and the Promotion of Empire: The Victoria League, 1901–1914',
Historical Journal, 45 (2002), 569–99.
[39] Eliza Reidi, 'Options for an Imperialist Woman: The Case of Violet Markham, 1899–1914', *Albion*,
32 (2000), 59–84.

emerged as leading public 'crusaders for empire' in late Victorian and Edwardian Britain, breaking into hitherto male preserves with their journalism and their authoritative studies of South Africa and Nigeria.[40]

In keeping with its concern for sustaining the 'imperial race' and maintaining imperial unity, the upper-class ladies of the Victoria League also drew on their traditional role as society hostesses to organise extensive hospitality for white female colonial visitors, to help them feel at home at the heart of empire.[41] However, relations between metropolitan and colonial women were not always smooth. While colonial women increasingly demanded a relationship of equal sisterhood to women in Britain, British women were accustomed to seeing themselves in a superior maternal role in relation to Britain's overseas empire and were not always sympathetic to white settler women's role in the nation-building process which accompanied the shift to Dominion status.[42] By 1914, Angela Woollacott argues, Antipodean feminists in the metropole were positioning themselves as 'an imperial feminist vanguard', having already won the vote in advance of women in Britain itself.[43] This challenged British women's view of themselves as the leaders of the women of the Empire. Despite these tensions, however, white women in Britain and the settler colonies articulated a strong familial bond based explicitly on assertions of a common cultural heritage and less openly on white racial solidarity and anti-black racism.[44]

During the First World War, while feminist activists divided between a pro- and anti-war stance, female imperialist and patriotic organisations united in organising practical contributions to the 'home front' and promoting the war effort in patriotic and imperial terms.[45] The Primrose League urged women to use their power as household consumers to support the Empire by purchasing imperial produce. The Victoria League set up clubs in London for imperial soldiers and nurses, organised public

---

[40] Helen Callaway and Dorothy O. Helly, 'Crusader for Empire: Flora Shaw / Lady Lugard', in Nupur Chaudhuri and Margaret Strobel (eds.), *Western Women and Imperialism: Complicity and Resistance* (Bloomington, 1992), 79–97.

[41] Reidi, 'Women, Gender and the Promotion of Empire', 585. For women and 'Society' in Victorian and Edwardian Britain see Leonore Davidoff, *The Best Circles*, new edn (London, 1986).

[42] Bush, *Edwardian Ladies and Imperial Power*, ch. 6.

[43] Angela Woollacott, *To Try Her Fortune in London: Australian Women, Colonialism, and Modernity* (Oxford, 2001), 119. See also Angela Woollacott, 'Australian Women's Metropolitan Activism: From Suffrage, to Imperial Vanguard, to Commonwealth Feminism', in Fletcher, Mayhall and Levine (eds.), *Women's Suffrage in the British Empire*, 207–23; Bush, *Edwardian Ladies and Imperial Power*, ch. 6.

[44] Bush, *Edwardian Ladies and Imperial Power*, ch. 7; Reidi, 'Women, Gender and the Promotion of Empire', 197–200.

[45] For feminists and the war see Johanna Alberti, *Beyond Suffrage: Feminists in War and Peace, 1914–1928* (Basingstoke, 1989).

lecture series on 'the Empire and the War', and mass-produced pamphlets which stressed the vital contributions of colonial troops to the war effort. Both organisations saw the war as a crucial time for determining the future of the British Empire.[46]

The organisations continued to be very active after the war, a period when, as Matthew Hendley points out, the militaristic and acquisitive imperialism promoted by many male-dominated organisations had lost its appeal to the public. It was also one when there was a renewed emphasis on domesticity within British society as a whole, and in this context, women activists, with their 'domesticated imperial message' were well placed to take a central role in ensuring the continued success of organised patriotism and imperialism.[47] This message was directed at the new mass electorate, particularly women, reflecting the importance of securing female support for empire at a time when communism, socialism and anti-colonial nationalism were on the rise. The new social imperialist agenda developed at government level recognised 'the importance of women to any comprehensive strengthening of empire' and was concerned to address the new 'surplus woman' problem, as the large numbers of single women facing unemployment at the end of the war led to fears of a revival of militant feminism.[48] Single women were targeted for assisted emigration to the colonies through the Society for the Oversea Settlement of British Women, a hybrid voluntary–state organisation representative of the way in which women, now full citizens, promoted welfare agendas in coop-eration with an increasingly interventionist state.[49]

The Primrose League helped promote the Conservative government's Empire Settlement scheme while also targeting the new female electorate, urging them to vote for a candidate who 'stands as representative of the British Empire and as imperialist'.[50] Its promotion of Empire Shopping targeted women as imperial consumers who 'as the shoppers of the empire, could insure that trade followed red routes'.[51] The Victoria

[46] Hendley, 'Patriotic Leagues', chs. 2 and 4.

[47] *Ibid.*, II, 415, 8. For interwar gender relations and domesticity see Susan Kingsley Kent, *Making Peace: The Reconstruction of Gender in Interwar Britain* (Princeton, 1993).

[48] Brian Blakely, 'The Society for the Oversea Settlement of British Women and the Problems of Empire Settlement, 1917–1936', *Albion*, 20 (1988), 421–44, quote from 421.

[49] Dane Kennedy, 'Empire Settlement in Postwar Reconstruction: The Role of the Oversea Settlement Committee, 1919–1922', *Albion*, 20 (1988), 403–19.

[50] 'The Vote: What I Want Before I Get It', *Primrose League Gazette*, 26 August 1918, 4, quoted in Hendley, 'Patriotic Leagues', 161. For female support for the Conservative Party in the interwar period see David Jarvis, '"Behind Every Great Party": Women and Conservatism in Twentieth-century Britain', in Vickery (ed.), *Women, Privilege and Power*, 289–316.

[51] Blakely, 'The Society for the Oversea Settlement of British Women', 432.

League organised thousands of lectures on imperial topics, many of them to Women's Institutes, intended to bolster interest in empire among newly enfranchised rural women.[52] The League also offered support to Malayan students studying in London. This decision to move beyond its earlier exclusive focus on white settler visitors was promoted by concern at the rise of anti-colonial activism in London. The League hoped to create a new generation of imperial subjects who were loyal to empire while avoiding over-close social contact with those of 'other' races: it set up a student hostel rather than offering home hospitality.[53]

ANTI-IMPERIAL AND ANTI-RACIST ACTIVISTS

Women's pro-empire activism thus took place against a background of, and was in part a defensive response to, the rise of anti-colonial nationalisms, the growth of Pan-Africanism, and critiques of Western imperialism from communists and those on the labour left. London began to become the hub of nascent anti-colonial nationalist activism at the turn of the century and by the interwar period it was the home of a number of transnational organisations and a crossroads for international contacts.[54]

While such organisations tended to be male-dominated, partly reflecting the disproportionate number of men to women in the black British population at the period, a number of individual women rose to prominence. White British women, newly empowered through winning the vote and the right to stand as Members of Parliament, responded to such development in diverse ways. Some, like the activists discussed above, opposed them outright; others, notably Margery Perham, one of the first British women to become recognised as an academic expert on colonial issues, promoted official attempts to preserve empire through remoulding colonial administration in more 'progressive' but still fundamentally paternalistic directions. Another set, on the political left, aligned themselves with the new radical movements.[55]

---

[52] For the history of the WI see M. Andrews, *The Acceptable Face of Feminism: The Women's Institute Movement* (London, 1997).

[53] Hendley, 'Patriotic Leagues', 463–4, 446.

[54] Peter Fryer, *Staying Power: The History of Black People in Britain* (London, 1984), 262–97; Hakim Adi, *West Africans in Britain, 1900–1960: Nationalism, Pan-Africanism and Communism* (London, 1998); Jonathan Schneer, *London 1900: The Imperial Metropolis* (Newhaven, CT, 1999), chs. 8–9; Ron Ramdin, *The Making of the Black Working-Class in Britain* (London, 1987).

[55] Barbara Bush, '"Britain's Conscience on Africa": White Women, Race and Imperial Politics in interwar Britain', in Clare Midgley (ed.), *Gender and Imperialism* (Manchester, 1998), 200–23; A. Smith and M. Ball (eds.), *Margery Perham and British Rule in Africa* (London, 1991).

Anti-racist and anti-imperialist activism began to develop in Britain in the late Victorian period, partly connected with the earlier anti-slavery movement, but mainly associated with the increasingly organised demands for racial equality and self-government by black people themselves. In response, more radical white women began to move from a philanthropic approach to cooperation with black activists. One of the pioneers in this regard was English Quaker Catherine Impey. Her magazine *Anti-Caste*, launched in 1888, campaigned against racism throughout the world, with a dual focus on the USA and the British Empire, and Impey also organised British lecture tours by African-American anti-lynching campaigner Ida B. Wells.[56] In the 1910s another white woman activist, the feminist and theosophist Annie Besant, played a pivotal role in cementing organisa- tional links between Indian- and British-based supporters of nationalism. Her *India: A Nation, a Plea for Self Government* was published in London in 1915.[57] Radical women's interest in Indian nationalism persisted into the interwar period. Socialist feminist MP Ellen Wilkinson was one of a group of 100 MPs who pledged their support for the India League, which campaigned for complete self-rule within the Commonwealth. In 1932 Wilkinson, Leonard Matters (another Labour MP) and Monica Whately, a spokeswoman of the 'equal rights' feminist Six Point Group and an Independent Labour Party activist, went on a long fact-finding mission to India for the League. Their subsequent report, *Condition of India* (1934), is described by Rozina Visram as 'a searing indictment of the Raj in India'.[58]

Pan-Africanism was also a major political current in interwar Britain, with many transnational organisations having their bases in London. Such groups combined opposition to racism within Britain with pro- motion of anti-colonial nationalisms, pan-African cooperation, and opposition to racial discrimination within the USA. Organisations, many of which were formed by student activists, ranged in focus from the welfare-orientated to the overtly political, and in political orientation from reformist to communist.[59] Among the most prominent of women

---

[56] Vron Ware, *Beyond the Pale: White Women, Racism and History* (London, 1992), ch. 4, quote from 215; entry on Catherine Impey by David M. Fahey in the *Oxford Dictionary of National Biography* (Oxford, 2004).

[57] Nancy Paxton, 'Complicity and Resistance in the Writings of Flora Annie Steel and Annie Besant', in Chaudhuri and Strobel (eds.), *Western Women and Imperialism*, 158–76.

[58] Visram, *Ayahs, Lascars and Princes*, quote from 163. Visram (178–9) points out that by 1934 there were 100 Indian female students studying in Britain, but it is unclear how many were involved in any form of political activity.

[59] Hakim Adi and Marika Sherwood, *Pan-African History: Political Figures from Africa and the Diaspora since 1787* (London, 2003); Adi, *West Africans in Britain;* Imanuel Geiss, *The Pan-African Movement*, trans. Ann Keep (London, 1974).

active in the radical wing of the Pan-Africanist movement was Amy Ashwood Garvey, who played a crucial role in linking West African activists to West Indians and African-Americans. Garvey, drawing on her experience in Jamaica and the USA in founding and running the Universal Negro Improvement Association with her ex-husband Marcus Garvey, assisted in forming the Nigerian Progress Union in London in 1924. Through this organisation she sought to forward her agendas of promoting education as a necessary precursor to black political emancipation, encouraging self-help and improving the lives of black women. In the 1930s she was vice-president and spokesperson of the International African Service Bureau, an organisation combining Marxism, anti-imperialism and Pan-Africanism. The Florence Mills Social Parlour in Carnaby Street, which she set up as a social centre for black people in London, formed part of a web of social support sustained by black women which was vital both to cementing black political networks and in creating homes-from-home within an alien and racist environment.[60]

Another leading black woman activist in 1930s' Britain was Una Marson, described by Delia Jarrett-Macauley as 'the first black British feminist to speak out against racism and sexism in Britain'. The Jamaican playwright, poet and journalist became editor of *The Keys*, the journal of Harold Moody's League of Coloured Peoples, and a leading spokesperson for the League. In contrast to Garvey, she was a reformist and opponent of communism, who participated in many British women's organisations, particularly those with an internationalist and pacifist focus. These included the British Commonwealth League, formed in 1925 to encourage the development of women's groups within the Commonwealth. She brought feminist ideas into black-led organisations and simultaneously pressed the white-dominated British and international women's movement to treat black women on terms of equality and take their concerns seriously.[61]

The Ethiopian cause was one which united black and white women activists of varying political hues from 1935, when Italy under Mussolini's fascist regime invaded the only African country hitherto free from European imperial conquest. Amy Ashwood Garvey organised fund-raising in defence of the people of Ethiopia, while Una Marson became the secretary to the Ethiopian minister in London, and after Emperor Haile Selassie's exile to London she accompanied him as a personal secretary to

---

[60] Adi and Sherwood, *Pan-African History*, 69–75. For racism in interwar Britain see Fryer, *Staying Power*, 298–366; Laura Tabili, *'We Ask for British Justice': Workers and Racial Difference in Late Imperial Britain* (Ithaca, 1994).

[61] Delia Jarrett-Macauley, *The Life of Una Marson, 1905–65* (Manchester, 1998).

Geneva to plead for help from the League of Nations. Ethiopia also became the central focus of activism for white British feminist Sylvia Pankhurst (1882–1960). She had already turned her focus to anti-racism and anti-imperialism in her paper the *Workers' Dreadnought*. Jamaican poet and activist Claude McKay, who wrote for the paper, later recalled that 'whenever imperialism got drunk and went wild among native peoples, the Pankhurst paper would be on the job'.[62] To promote the Ethiopian cause she launched a new paper, the *New Times and Ethiopian News*, which at its height sold 40,000 copies weekly in Britain, West Africa and the West Indies. While better known in Britain today as a feminist and socialist, on her death in Ethiopia in 1960 the leading African-American activist W. E. B. DuBois asserted that 'the great work of Sylvia Pankhurst was to introduce black Ethiopia to white England'.[63]

Other white women active in socialist and feminist politics also supported the Ethiopian cause and combined anti-racist, anti-imperialist and anti-fascist agendas in the 1930s, among them Ellen Wilkinson, Monica Whately, the former militant suffragist Charlotte Despard, the writers and close friends Vera Brittain and Winifred Holtby, and Nancy Cunard. Cunard came out of a very different social milieu from Pankhurst, and was representative of a new generation of 'modern' women, influenced by the modernist movement in the arts and espousing alternative bohemian lifestyles, for whom personal liberation and political commitment were closely intertwined. From a privileged upper-class background, the rebellious Nancy took advantage of her financial independence to escape England in 1920 for a bohemian life on the Parisian left bank, an avant-garde milieu within which African art and jazz music were espoused as rejections of bourgeois European values. Cunard's relationship with African-American jazz musician Henry Crowder caused a scandal in Britain, tapping into eugenic concerns which placed white women as the insurers of racial purity and condemned interracial relationships.[64]

Cunard's major achievement was the compilation of *Negro: An Anthology*, an 850-page tome published in 1934, a record of 'the struggles and achievements, the persecutions and the revolts against them, of the Negro peoples'. Its Pan-Africanist perspective was combined with explicit endorsement of the Communist Party line on the question of race,

---

[62] Claude McKay, *A Long Way from Home* (New York, 1970), 27, quoted in Mary Davis, *Sylvia Pankhurst: A Life in Radical Politics* (London, 1999), 105.

[63] *Ethiopia Observer*, 5 January 1961, quoted in Davis, *Sylvia Pankhurst*, 116.

[64] Lucy Bland, 'White Women and Men of Colour: Miscegenation Fears in Britain After the Great War', *Gender and History*, 17 (1) (2005), 29–61.

reflecting the strength of black Marxism in this period. As Maureen Moynagh discusses, the volume included written and visual material by key African-American, West Indian and West African intellectual and cultural workers and members of international modernist circles in Paris and London, exposing the extent to which modernism was dependent on black labour and cultural production.[65]

CONCLUSION

Research on women's empire-based activism in Britain between the 1790s and the 1930s remains patchy and incomplete, despite the burgeoning of scholarly interest in the topic since the early 1990s. In particular, more work needs to be done on the 'rank and file' female membership of the diverse range of organisations discussed, on local activism outside the imperial capital, on the impact of women's activism on the broader public, and on white working-class women's relationship to imperial campaigns.

What is clear is that empire-focused activism was a central component of middle- and upper-class white women's public work and political engagements throughout the period of study, and that for women imperial and domestic concerns were intermeshed. Women of colour also made crucial contributions to debates on race and empire throughout the period. The form that women's imperial activism took varied in response to shifts in imperial politics and changes in the position of women within British society. However, anti-slavery and missionary women, female imperialists and female anti-imperialists all contributed in vital ways to shaping public debate on empire, to bringing empire home to the British public and highlighting its relevance to their everyday lives, and to forging links between women based in the imperial metropole and the colonies. Seeking to bring the specific concerns of women to the fore in imperial politics, women claimed a place in the imperial nation. In the process, they were involved in shaping gendered class identities through articulating feminine visions of racial and ethnic belonging within imperial Britain.

---

[65] Maureen Moynagh, *Essays on Race and Empire: Nancy Cunard* (Peterbrough, ON, 2002), introduction, 11.

CHAPTER TWELVE

Taking class notes on empire

James Epstein

The impact of empire on British class formation and identities was uneven, varying across different social groups and at different historical moments. Unfortunately, the scholarship on the relationship between class and empire is itself fragmented and sometimes inadequate for answering some of the most pressing questions. In part, this has to do with the disciplinary division between domestic history, including 'history from below', and imperial history in its more traditional guise; a separation which a new generation of scholars has challenged, although class has not been high on the agenda of the new imperial history. Moreover, as a category of historical understanding, class has been under fire for some time. And yet like an earlier generation of Marxist historians against whom they have set their sights, scholars most intent on undermining class's status as a master category of British history have themselves left the division between domestic and imperial history largely undisturbed, reconfirming (at least implicitly) the assumption that empire had little impact on metropolitan society and political culture.[1] Nonetheless, in revisiting class from the perspective of empire, we should acknowledge the artificiality of pulling class out of a matrix of hierarchically ordered identities – gender, ethnicity, nation, race, etc. – that impinged on people's lives. We must also take care not to treat empire as a unitary object or static formation; different sties of empire were subject to different forms of rule and thus differing connotations for class identities.

A further difficulty arises from the range of approaches available for discussing both how and to what extent imperialism affected British class relations. So, one of the classic questions of imperial history concerns the benefits of empire: in whose interests did the maintenance and expansion of empire operate? The question has obvious implications for wealth and

[1] See Catherine Hall, 'Remembering Edward Said', *History Workshop Journal*, 57 (2004), 240–1. My own published work on nineteenth-century popular politics reflects the same implicit assumptions.

class formation. The issue of imperial benefits may in turn be linked
cautiously to party politics, government policy, popular movements,
manifestos and the like; to how imperial issues were translated into
political action and ideology, and to how such political manifestations
may or may not express class feeling or interest. The most difficult
questions, however, relate to broader cultural understandings of empire,
to how empire was perceived more generally and what bearing such an
imperial *mentalité* may have had on class identities. While it may well be
that members of Britain's ruling elite viewed empire in what David
Cannadine has termed 'ornamentalist' terms, as elaborate figurations of
sameness based on status hierarchy, we cannot assume that such was the
view of the British public at large.[2] Indeed, this vision of hierarchically
ordered society, one that British colonial administrators found mirrored
in subject colonial settings, can itself be regarded as a class ideology, part
of the common sense of a ruling elite identified in the first instance with
landed wealth.

By way of introduction, something should be said about my chosen
period, the 'long' nineteenth century. The 1780s corresponds to the
quickened pace of domestic industrialisation and the emergence of class
discourses; it also corresponds to the beginnings of what C. A. Bayly
identifies as an imperial regime characterised by a form of 'aristocratic
military government supporting a viceregal autocracy, by a well-developed
imperial style which emphasised hierarchy and racial subordination, and
by the patronage of indigenous landed elites'.[3] The nineteenth century
takes in important changes, including the 'new imperialism' of the final
third of the century, and the formation of cultural and social patterns
which to some extent remained in place to the Great War, and beyond.[4]
The chapter is divided into four parts, designed to illustrate different
instances of class, or ways in which class was manifest in the mutual
constitution of imperial and domestic social formations. The first part of
this essay offers a schematic view of empire's role in the foundation and
sustaining of elite rule, in both material and cultural terms. The second
section considers the anti-slavery movement as an example of the complex
ways in which interchanges between imperial and domestic sites could
shape class meanings. In the third section, I consider how the experience of

---

[2] David Cannadine, *Ornamentalism: How the British Saw Their Empire* (London, 2001). The broad
   claim that distinctions based on class prevailed over race, even if restricted to the ruling elite,
   remains questionable.
[3] C. A. Bayly, *Imperial Meridian: The British Empire and the World 1780–1830* (London, 1989), 7–15.
[4] See P. J. Cain and A. G. Hopkins, *British Imperialism, 1688–2000* (London, 2001), 30–1, 48–9.

empire itself, in the case of military service, might affect class identities of ordinary people. The essay concludes with a brief consideration of the late nineteenth century, as an intensified moment when the culture of empire produced not only feelings of national and imperial belonging but also generated terms of social exclusion.

GENTLEMAN CAPITALISTS AND EMPIRE

If the most striking characteristic of the Empire's contribution to British constructions of class was its unevenness, it was among sections of Britain's ruling elite that empire's influence was most strongly manifest, producing an imperial ethos that was in turn related to the creation and maintenance of economic power linked to class rule. However, rather than following Joseph Schumpeter in viewing imperialism as incompatible with a 'purely capitalist world', and thus necessarily 'atavistic' in character, it makes better sense to follow Mrinalini Sinha in stressing the uneven and contradictory impulses and intersections within what she terms a modern 'imperial social formation'.[5]

P. J. Cain and A. G. Hopkins provide the most sophisticated and wide-ranging interpretation of the class character of such an 'imperial social formation'. To summarise a highly nuanced and learned argument, they trace the origins of 'gentlemanly capitalism' and the impetus behind imperial expansion and policy to its origins in the eighteenth century and to a commercially oriented oligarchy of landowners who became increasingly allied to metropolitan financiers and merchant capital. Not only did this impart an aristocratic tone and style to imperialism as it turned from North America to India and beyond, it served to broaden and consolidate the ranks of a gentlemanly elite who came to dominate British economic life and policy. Cain and Hopkins thus shift economic emphasis away from industrialisation and industrial wealth to non-industrial forms of capitalism, particularly in the commercial and service sectors, to the City of London rather than the industrial north and midlands.[6] While during the second half of the nineteenth century landed wealth yielded its predominance to wealth generated from the service or finance sector, 'a

[5] Joseph Schumpeter, *Imperialism and Social Classes: Two Essays*, trans. Heinz Norden (New York, 1955), 64–9; Mrinalini Sinha, *Colonial Masculinity: The 'Manly Englishman' and the 'Effeminate Bengali' in the Late Nineteenth Century* (Manchester, 1995), 2, 182–4.

[6] Also see W. D. Rubinstein, *Men of Property: The Very Rich in Britain since the Industrial Revolution* (New Brunswick, NJ, 1981). For a critique of their thesis, see Andrew Porter, '"Gentlemanly Capitalism" and Empire: The British Experience since 1750?', *Journal of Imperial and Commonwealth History*, 18 (1990), 265–95.

tight bond' had been forged between elements within this sector, resulting in a gentlemanly elite possessed of 'a common view of the world and how it should be ordered'. 'The imperial mission', they continue, 'was the export version of the gentlemanly order. In some respects, indeed, the gentlemanly code appeared in bolder format abroad in order to counter the lure of an alien environment.'[7]

Such an interpretation owes an obvious debt to J. A. Hobson's *Imperialism: A Study* (1902), and Hobson's recognition of the role of finance capitalists – capitalists rooted in a pre-industrial mercantilist class – in modern imperialism, although Cain and Hopkins not only extend Hobson's chronological reach, but strip his thesis of its conspiratorial theories and his identification of imperial expansion with economic and social backwardness. Cain and Hopkins demonstrate that by the second half of the nineteenth century the City and the south of England were established as the epicentre of British economic activity, with steady increases in earnings from trade in services and overseas investments. Still, the importance of exports of manufactured goods to the Empire, particularly to the settlement colonies and India, is also clear. As Hopkins points out, many sectors of private wealth were directly linked to empire, including the tobacco lords of Glasgow, the jute manufacturers of Dundee, the steel manufacturers of Sheffield, the mill owners of Lancashire, along with the financiers and merchant princes of London. Despite vicissitudes over the long nineteenth century, imperial earnings made a significant contribution to the wealth of Britain's industrial and non-industrial elites.[8]

Of course, the empire had to be ruled and recruitment into colonial service provided a significant source of employment for aristocrats, military officers and gentlemen. The most lucrative colonial offices were usually filled from the highest reaches of the British aristocracy. Imperial service also provided avenues of advancement for well-connected or talented members of the Scottish and Anglo-Irish gentry, helping to integrate these groups into the ranks of the British upper class through their strong connections to empire.[9] By the early nineteenth century an

---

[7] Cain and Hopkins, *British Imperialism*, 43, 47.

[8] *Ibid.*, ch. 5, particularly tables 5.2, 5.3, 5.8; A. G. Hopkins, 'Back to the Future: From National History to Imperial History', *Past and Present*, 164 (1999), 210; P. J. Cain, 'Economics and Empire: The Metropolitan Context', in Wm. Roger Louis (ed.), *The Oxford History of the British Empire*, 5 vols. (Oxford, 1998–9), vol. III: *The Nineteenth Century*, ed. Andrew Porter (1999), 31–52.

[9] Linda Colley, *Britons: Forging the Nation, 1707–1837* (New Haven and London, 1992), 127–32; John M. MacKenzie, 'Essay and Reflection: On Scotland and the Empire', *International History Review*, 15 (1993), 714–39.

ever-closer alliance was forged among traditional landed interests, the Church, a reinvigorated monarchy, and increasingly powerful financial and commercial interests.[10] At the same time, attitudes to Indian service softened. Thus P. J. Marshall observes that 'some of the esteem which service in India gained was no doubt a rationalization of class interest. For the British upper class to continue to revile service in India into the nineteenth century would have been a quixotic luxury.'[11] Correspondingly, there was a shift in official morality within the service that discouraged interracial mixing and was underpinned by the force of evangelical Christianity.

Along with the consolidation of elite power, an 'aristocratic reaction' developed in response to a crisis in ruling-class legitimacy and to revolutionary upheavals spread not only throughout Europe but on a global scale, including Ireland, the West Indies and India. During the French Wars (1793–1815), Britain's aristocratic and gentlemanly elite became more militarised, recreating, according to Bayly, a *noblesse d'épée*.[12] Colonial regimes magnified reactionary and military trends, as they did earning power.[13] The repressive authority of the aristocratic state, which found expression at 'home' in treason trials, the suspension of habeas corpus, the infamous 'Two Acts' and anti-trade-union legislation, was more fully manifest at the 'peripheries' of the imperial state, visited most violently on the Irish peasantry following the insurrection of 1798 and the enslaved rebels of the Caribbean.[14] So, for example, in the newly seized island of Trinidad, the colony's first British governor, General Thomas Picton (himself a member of the Welsh lesser gentry), imposed order through a regime of tyranny and punishments so brutal that it led to his removal and proceedings brought against him in Privy Council.[15]

---

[10] See David Cannadine, *Aspects of Aristocracy* (New Haven and London, 1994), ch. 1, for what he terms, 'the making of the British upper class'.

[11] P. J. Marshall, 'The Moral Swing to the East: British Humanitarianism, India and the West Indies', in Kenneth Ballhatchet and John Harrison (eds.), *East India Company Studies* (Hong Kong, 1986), 84–5.

[12] See Bayly, *Imperial Meridian*, 133–4, 164–6, and *Indian Society and the Making of the British Empire* (Cambridge, 1988), ch. 3, for the 'crisis of the Indian state'; Colley, *Britons*, 184–5.

[13] See Douglas M. Peers, *Between Mars and Mammon: Colonial Armies and the Garrison State in Early Nineteenth-Century India* (London, 1995), ch. 1.

[14] See Marianne Elliot, *Partners in Revolution: The United Irishmen and France* (New Haven and London, 1982); Michael Craton, *Testing the Chains: Resistance to Slavery in the British West Indies* (Ithaca, 1982), particularly parts 3–5; Michael Duffy, 'War, Revolution and the Crisis of the British Empire', in Mark Philp (ed.), *The French Revolution and British Popular Politics* (Cambridge, 1991), 118–45.

[15] William Fullarton, *Substance of the Evidence Delivered before the Lords of His Majesty's Most Honourable Privy Council, in the Case of Governor Picton* (London, 1807).

The imperial ideal was sustained by more than the prerequisites of office and an expanding system of colonial honours conferred by the imperial state. Over the long nineteenth century, as imperial authoritarianism was tempered by pragmatic reform, the codes and bonds of imperial service were reproduced within an evolving culture and distinctly class-based milieu. This milieu was inextricably linked to a gender regime based on ideals of 'adventure, male comradeship, and licensed aggression'.[16] Central to this masculine culture was the reformed and enlarged system of public schools of mid-Victorian Britain. The values of muscular Christianity, patriotism, fellowship, and chivalric visions of honour and loyalty were forged on the playing fields, in the sixth forms and houses of the ancient and newly founded public schools. Fostering an elite code of service based on classical models and 'the habit of authority', public schools staffed the Empire. While Eton produced cabinet ministers, viceroys and field marshals, newer schools like Clifton more typically trained the larger cadre of gentlemen who moved into lesser positions in the military and imperial service. The public schools played a critical role in blending the broadened ranks of Britain's gentlemanly elite. As preferment shifted from patronage to merit, the public schools helped to rig the reformed system of examination and recruitment.[17] Below this level, a group of minor public schools emulating the public-school ethos catered to a wider range of middle-class boys, helping to sustain multi-generational patterns of recruitment.[18] The lodges of public-school freemasonry spread throughout the Empire and became part of its power structure.[19]

The public schools formed part of a network of associations sustaining a gentlemanly ethos of privilege manifest in the practice of elite domestic and imperial rule. For example, like the public schools, 'clubland' expanded during the nineteenth century, including clubs such as the East India United Services Club and Oriental Club which owed their existence solely to empire. As Mrinalini Sinha argues, the model of elite masculinity associated with the concept of clubbability 'leads beyond the network of power relations produced by the internal politics of Britain to include

---

[16] John Tosh, 'Masculinities in an Industrializing Society: Britain, 1800–1914', *Journal of British Studies*, 44 (2005), 342.

[17] A. P. Thornton, *The Habit of Authority: Paternalism in British History* (Toronto, 1966); Anthony Kirk-Greene, *Britain's Imperial Administrators, 1858–1966* (Basingstoke, 2000), 9–22, 97–8; Mark Girouard, *The Return to Camelot: Chivalry and the English Gentleman* (New Haven and London, 1981), ch. 11, also ch. 14; Cain and Hopkins, *British Imperialism*, 45–7, 119–21.

[18] Elizabeth Buettner, *Empire Families: Britons and Late Imperial India* (Oxford, 2004), 163–80.

[19] Paul J. Rich, 'Public-school Freemasonry in the Empire: "Mafia of the Mediocre"?', in J. A. Mangan (ed.), *'Benefits Bestowed'?: Education and British Imperialism* (Manchester, 1988), 174–92.

the wide set of class, gender, and race relations that was produced and enabled by British imperialism'.[20] Looking beyond the domestic context for understanding how social and cultural relations were enabled by imperialism, we must also recognise that various cultural manifestations of rule – found in modes of education, sociability, architecture, etc. – were marked not merely by a desire for affinity but by differential or asymmetrical modes of authority and subjugation, by difference between 'home' and 'away'.

ANTI-SLAVERY AND CLASS POLITICS

Turning from those who ruled, most benefited from and most clearly identified with empire to consider imperialism's broader reach and impact on the experiences and representations of class, we move on to more difficult and more contested ground.[21] What follows is a provisional, three-part sketch of broader, popular notations and intersections between class and empire, stressing the conjunctional, uneven and often fragmented character of such moments of intersection.

The anti-slavery campaign fused dual concerns of domestic and imperial reform. The movement was sustained organisationally by the provincial middle class; it embodied middle-class aspirations for social and political recognition; and the ultimate triumph allowed middle-class men and women to identify with the nation in its virtue. In conjunction with a wider complex of middle-class reform, it did much to foster a sense of class identity among its supporters.[22] At its height, however, anti-slavery mobilised national support across a broad social spectrum, from sections of the ruling elite, including Pitt as Prime Minister, to artisans, shopkeepers, labourers and domestic servants; women were especially active in the movement, particularly in its later stages. Judging from subscription lists, from the wide support for consumer boycotts of West Indian sugar and rum and from anti-slavery petitions, anti-slavery mobilised extraordinarily large numbers.[23] The abolition of British slavery

---

[20] Mrinalini Sinha, 'Britishness, Clubbability, and the Colonial Public Sphere: The Genealogy of an Imperial Institution in Colonial India', *Journal of British Studies*, 40 (2001), 489–521, 496–7 (quotation).

[21] See John M. Mackenzie, 'Empire and Metropolitan Cultures', in *Oxford History of the British Empire*, ed. Porter, III, 270–93. Cf. Bernard Porter, *The Absent-Minded Imperialists* (Oxford, 2004).

[22] David Turley, *The Culture of English Anti-slavery, 1780–1860* (London, 1991), ch. 5; J. R. Oldfield, *Popular Politics and British Anti-Slavery: The Mobilisation of Public Opinion Against the Slave Trade, 1787–1807* (Manchester, 1995), ch. 5.

[23] Seymour Drescher, *Capitalism and Anti-slavery: British Mobilization in Comparative Perspective* (New York and Oxford, 1987), 93–4 and chs. 4–5; David Turley, 'British Anti-slavery Reassessed', in

in 1833 became a hallmark of British national identity: as a nation, Britain was redeemed by an act of disinterested, Christian benevolence.[24]

However, if the abolition of slavery was seen as a distinguishing act of British humanitarianism, this hardly exhausts the complex meanings associated with anti-slavery, a movement whose character was multi-faceted, often contradictory and shifted over time. Although opponents continued to associate the anti-slavery campaign with subversion, the taint of 'Jacobinism' was relatively short-lived; anti-slavery in its official guise purged itself of radicalism; its national leaders emphasised support for traditional authority and hierarchical order.[25] Operating outside the bounds of such authority, planters' power was condemned in abolitionist writings as unauthorised and arbitrary; planters became the incarnation of imperial avarice, licence and excess. The image of the fabulously wealthy, degenerate planter inverted the presumed norms of 'English' civility and moral restraint.[26] Such images cannot in themselves account for the abolition of British slavery, but they suggest an aspect of the ideological work of anti-slavery, allowing Britain's ruling elite to legitimate its own authority by disavowing connections to the social world of Caribbean slavery. It was no accident that when successful abolition of the slave trade finally came in 1807, the bill originated in the House of Lords. Given a fundamentally conservative and oligarchic political system, abolition of the slave trade became, as Robin Blackburn argues, 'not so much the most urgent, as the least controversial, reform that could be undertaken'.[27]

The intersection between domestic industrialisation, the British slave system and the abolition of slavery has preoccupied historians ever since the publication of Eric Williams' seminal work, *Capitalism and Slavery* (1944). Developing a thesis first articulated by C. L. R. James, Williams linked the investment of profits from slavery to the requirements of early industrialism and attributed slave abolition to the declining economic prospects of the British West Indies after the loss of the thirteen North American colonies and the eventual demise of mercantilism.[28] In contrast to Cain and

---

Arthur Burns and Joanna Innes (eds.), *Rethinking the Age of Reform: Britain, 1780–1850* (Cambridge, 2003), 182–99; James Walvin, 'The Rise of British Sentiment for Abolition, 1787–1832', in Christine Bolt and Seymour Drescher (eds.), *Anti-Slavery, Religion, and Reform* (Folkestone, 1980), 149–62; Clare Midgley, *Women Against Slavery: The British Campaigns, 1780–1870* (London, 1992).

[24] Colley, *Britons*, 354–60.

[25] David Brion Davis, *The Problem of Slavery in the Age of Revolution, 1770–1823* (Ithaca, 1975), ch. 8.

[26] Kathleen Wilson, *The Island Race: Englishness, Empire and Gender in the Eighteenth Century* (London, 2003), 130.

[27] Robin Blackburn, *The Overthrow of Colonial Slavery, 1776–1848* (London, 1988), 295; chs. 8, 11.

[28] Eric Williams, *Capitalism and Slavery* (Chapel Hill, NC, 1944/1994), particularly chs. 7–9.

Hopkins' gentlemanly capitalists, the debate over what made abolition politically possible has turned on conflicting assessments of the shift towards capitalist industrialisation and the ideological character of humanitarianism.

The most compelling case for linking anti-slavery to class rule and capitalist hegemony has been offered by David Brion Davis. In his *The Problem of Slavery in the Age of Revolution*, and subsequent writings, he argues that while serving 'conflicting ideological functions', abolition reinforced the normative requirements of industrial capitalism. Without discounting the religious sources of anti-slavery thought and 'the profound sense of religious transformation', Davis stresses the centrality of class and social context to understanding anti-slavery's full ideological implications.[29] He writes: 'The new hostility to human bondage cannot be reduced simply to the needs of particular classes. Yet the needs and interests of particular classes had much to do with a given society's receptivity to new ideas and thus to the ideas' historical impact.'[30] How, for example, are we to interpret the fact that the 'humanitarian triumph' of 1807 coincided roughly with the parliamentary attack on the last vestiges of legislative protection for various trades and to their full exposure to capitalist market forces? According to Davis, the connection between the two forms of 'abolition' was not direct or causal, but was rather to be found in an emerging mindset and a transitional (and highly unstable) class alliance, including sections of the landed elite, commercial and merchant interests and provincial manufacturers. At this point Davis' argument links to E. P. Thompson's detailing of the steady erosion of working people's independence, the introduction of new forms of labour discipline and manufacturers' desire for greater control over the work process and its rewards.[31] Davis' analysis helps to explain the coincidence between the 'benevolence' extended by the reformed British parliament to distant Afro-American slaves and the same assembly's utilitarian indifference to human suffering encoded in the provisions of the new Poor Law (1834).[32] The same parliament that abolished Caribbean slavery

---

[29] David Brion Davis, 'Reflections on Abolitionism and Ideological Hegemony', in Thomas Bender (ed.), *The Anti-slavery Debate* (Berkeley and Los Angeles, 1992), 161–2, 171. Also see David Brion Davis, *Slavery and Human Progress* (New York and Oxford, 1984), chs. 5 and 6; Thomas C. Holt, *The Problem of Freedom: Race, Labor, and Politics in Jamaica and Britain, 1832–1938* (Baltimore, 1992), ch. 1.; cf. Christopher Leslie Brown, *Moral Capital: Foundations of British Abolitionism* (Chapel Hill, NC, 2006).

[30] Davis, *Problem of Slavery*, 49.

[31] *Ibid.*, 453, 455–68; E. P. Thompson, *The Making of the English Working Class* (London, 1963), ch. 6, and *Customs in Common* (London, 1991), ch. 6. Also see Peter Linebaugh, *The London Hanged: Crime and Society in the Eighteenth Century* (London, 1992), ch. 11; David Eltis, *Economic Growth and the Ending of the Transatlantic Slave Trade* (New York and Oxford, 1987), ch. 2.

[32] Davis, *Slavery and Human Progress*, 122.

was also concerned with reform legislation and institutions (workhouses, penitentiaries, schools, reformatories) aimed at disciplining recalcitrant members of Britain's own labouring class.[33]

Significantly, Davis does not propose a conscious or coordinated attempt merely to deflect public attention away from harsh domestic policies aimed at disciplining Britain's labouring poor. The relationship between anti-slavery and the search for domestic social order was more finely tuned, more conflicted and perhaps more akin to an instance of ideological 'misrecognition'. Although the rise of anti-slavery sentiment coincided with new regimes of labour discipline and support for the campaign to reform working-class habits, Davis notes that abolitionists were themselves often ambivalent towards social changes associated with industrialisation. He goes on to argue that because the slave system was 'both distinctive and remote, it could become a subject of experimental fantasies that assimilated traditional [i.e. paternalist] values to new economic needs ... By picturing the slave plantation as totally dependent upon physical torture, abolitionist writers gave sanction to less barbarous modes of social discipline.'[34] What is important here is the double move of separation and projection: on the one hand, the abolitionists' sharp distinction between the plantation system of slave labour and domestic practices linked to free-wage labour; and on the other hand, their fantasies of a new, post-emancipation order projected on to an idealised regime of free labour at once distanced and returned 'home'.[35]

From the 1790s, plebeian radicals contested abolitionists' insistence on slavery as a singular and remote manifestation of inhumanity, drawing parallels between the cause of liberty in Europe and the West Indies. Thus John Thelwall, the most talented 'Jacobin' orator and theorist, admonished William Wilberforce: 'seek not so wide for the objects of thy benevolence ... If we would dispense justice to our distant colonies, we must begin by rooting out from the centre the corruption by which that cruelty and injustice is countenanced and defended.'[36] The frontispiece to William Hodgson's *Commonwealth of Reason* (1795), his utopian vision of an egalitarian society, pictures a classically robed black man and a white

---

[33] Holt, *Problem of Freedom*, 37.
[34] Davis, *Problem of Slavery*, 466.
[35] Also see David Eltis, 'Abolitionist Perceptions of Society after Slavery', in James Walvin (ed.), *British Slavery and Society, 1776–1846* (Baton Rouge, LA, 1982), 195–213.
[36] Quoted in James Walvin, 'The Impact of Slavery on British Radical Politics: 1787–1838', in Vera Rubin and Arthur Tuden (eds.), *Comparative Perspectives on Slavery in New World Plantation Societies, Annals of the New York Academy of Sciences*, 292 (1977), 347–8. Also see Marcus Wood, *Slavery, Empathy and Pornography* (Oxford, 2002), 172–7.

man hand in hand. The standing figures hold aloft a cap of liberty along with a banner reading 'Liberty Fraternity Equality', and proclaiming 'Liberty is the Right and Happiness of all, for all by Nature are equal and free, and no one can without the utmost injustice become the Slave of his like.' The iconography and French Revolutionary symbolism contrast to Wedgwood's famous abolitionist seal of the supplicant slave kneeling in chains with the motto 'Am I not a man and a brother?' Hodgson was a leading member of the London Corresponding Society. Radicals were alive to the forms of unfree or coerced labour on which Britain's Atlantic empire relied. Thus Peter Linebaugh and Marcus Rediker draw attention to circuits linking plebeian radicalism to the transatlantic world of sailors, displaced workers and slaves.[37] The involvement of black writers and activists in metropolitan radicalism is well documented. Olaudah Equiano, the most famous member of London's black community, joined the London Corresponding Society in 1792; on his book tours he recruited supporters and linked London's artisans to radical abolitionists outside London.[38] The next generation of radicals included the cabinetmaker Thomas 'Black' Davidson and the mulatto tailor Robert Wedderburn; both men were Jamaicans and ex-sailors active in London's revolutionary circles. Davidson died on the gallows in 1820 for his part in the Cato Street conspiracy. Wedderburn gave a distinctly West Indian tone to radicalism; he frequently compared the fate of British workers to that of West Indian slaves and used the Haitian revolution to inspire audiences. He also adapted Thomas Spence's communitarian theory to a model of free black smallholders as an alternative to both slave and wage labour.[39]

As Catherine Hall has shown, in both 1832 and 1867 the construction of the white British citizen and black colonial subject were mutually constituted, and they were constituted partially in class terms.[40] Matters of class, gender, race and ethnicity, as well as domestic and colonial security,

---

[37] Peter Linebaugh and Marcus Rediker, *The Many-Headed Hydra: Sailors, Slaves, Commoners, and the Hidden History of the Revolutionary Atlantic* (Boston, 2000).

[38] *Ibid.*, 334–41; Vincent Carretta, *Equiano the African* (Athens, GA, 2005), 297, 349–50, 353, 361–2.

[39] Iain McCalman, 'Anti-Slavery and Ultra-Radicalism in Early Nineteenth England: The Case of Robert Wedderburn', *Slavery and Abolition*, 7 (1986), 99–117, and McCalman (ed. and intro.), *The Horrors of Slavery and Other Writings by Robert Wedderburn* (Edinburgh, 1993); Linebaugh and Rediker, *Many-Headed Hydra*, ch. 9.

[40] Catherine Hall, 'The Rule of Difference: Gender, Class and Empire in the Making of the 1832 Reform Act', in Ida Blom, Karen Hagemann and Catherine Hall (eds.), *Gendered Nations: Nationalisms and Gender Order in the Long Nineteenth Century* (Oxford, 2000), 107–35; Catherine Hall, Keith McClelland and Jane Rendall, *Defining the Victorian Nation: Class, Race, Gender and the British Reform Act of 1867* (Cambridge, 2000); also Miles Taylor, 'Empire and the 1832 Parliamentary Reform Act Revisited', in Burns and Innes (eds.), *Rethinking the Age of Reform*, 295–311.

converged during the first reform crisis. In 1829, confronted by a mass mobilisation of the Irish population under the leadership of Daniel O'Connell and the Catholic Association, the Tory government of Wellington and Peel conceded Catholic Emancipation. Yet violence directed against landlords and the established church remained endemic to rural Ireland; in 1833 the Whig government introduced the Irish Coercion Bill aimed at pacifying the countryside of this 'internal' colony.[41] At 'home', the Whig ministry sent Special Commissions to agricultural districts throughout England to punish agricultural labourers who had destroyed threshing-machines and burnt corn ricks in the 'Swing' riots of 1830.[42] At the end of 1831, slave rebellion in Jamaica left a landscape of burnt sugar factories and devastated cane fields. Just as the implications of the Haitian revolution for Britain's Caribbean empire helped frame debates over the abolition of the slave trade, the Christmas slave revolt (or 'Baptist war' as it became known) forced the issue of abolition.[43] 'Our brethren of Jamaica', announced the *Poor Man's Guardian*, 'have revolted, and taken into their hands the abolition of that slavery which a *Christian* people has imposed, and a *Christian* government of Whig *liberals* has countenanced.' The journal went on to compare the treatment of slave rebels to domestic reform rioters, 'being savages, their lives were not their own but the *property* of their masters, and that, therefore, it was wrong to let the bloodhounds destroy them in the same manner as if they were so many *civilised* fellow-country-men of Bristol or Nottingham'.[44] Working-class radicals were quick to see correspondences among these multifaceted challenges to elite authority and in repressive government measures to quell popular resistance in urban and rural Britain, Ireland and the West Indies.

Undoubtedly, large numbers of working people opposed slavery. Plebeian radicals and abolitionists shared a language of natural or God-given rights, equality and liberty, although accented differently. Historians differ as to whether abolitionism served to sharpen or ameliorate class antagonisms. In part, differing interpretations are sustained by genuine ambivalence on the part of working-class radicals and the overtures of a

---

[41] Galen Broeker, *Rural Disorder and Police Reform in Ireland, 1812–1836* (London, 1970), ch. 11; Stanley Palmer, *Police and Protest in England and Ireland, 1780–1850* (Cambridge, 1988), 316–31.

[42] E. J. Hobsbawm and George Rudé, *Captain Swing* (London, 1969), ch. 13; George Rudé, 'English Rural and Urban Disturbances on the Eve of the First Reform Bill', *Past and Present*, 37 (1967), 87–102.

[43] Holt, *Problem of Freedom*, 13–21; Craton, *Testing the Chains*, ch. 22; Drescher, *Capitalism and Antislavery*, 100–10.

[44] *Poor Man's Guardian*, 25 February 1832, 289–90.

small group of middle-class abolitionists sympathetic to popular radic-alism's programme.[45] Nonetheless, by the early nineteenth century, the emergent working-class movement turned increasingly hostile to official abolitionism due in large part to anti-slavery's close identification with political economy and evangelicalism, as well as its role in helping to define a 'permissible limit' to reform demands and a 'respectable' style to reform agitation.[46] In the event, the emancipation of West Indian slaves sharpened working-class resentment. Parliament's grant of twenty million pounds compensation to the planters, along with the introduction of the apprenticeship system, undercut any moral claims. James Bronterre O'Brien, the most sophisticated ultra-radical writer of the day, main-tained: 'The people of England would doubtless give liberty to the negro, but they never proposed doing so at the expense of mortgaging their industry to the planter.' He opined that West Indian proprietors would continue to live off the fruits of others' labour. As for the blacks, pre-viously 'free from the deadly effects of competing with each other as labourers', they soon would become like British workers subject to the 'tyranny of capital'. But a just legislature 'would begin by abolishing domestic slavery' and passing the ten-hours bill to protect children working in factories. O'Brien expressed his disgust for 'that bastard philanthropy which, while it affects to weep over well-fed negroes abroad, has the baseness to connive at child-murder at home'.[47] Middle-class advocates of political economy, such as Henry Brougham and Daniel O'Connell – who opposed protective legislation for factory workers, supported the new Poor Law and championed slave abolition – became targets of working-class scorn. Thus the final triumph of abolition was linked to a system of domestic oppression separating working-class democrats from middle-class, 'sham' reformers.

For most working-class radicals, 'freedom' meant freedom from wage labour, expressed as a desire for lost independence associated with self-employment on the land or in the workshop. Certainly critiques of plantation slavery and the factory system drew on a common stock of

---

[45] My own view is close to that of Patricia Hollis, 'Anti-Slavery and British Working-Class Radicalism in the Years of Reform', in Bolt and Drescher (eds.), *Anti-Slavery*, 294–315; also Turley, *Culture of Anti-slavery*, 181–95. Cf. Betty Fladeland, ' "Our Cause Being One and the Same": Abolitionists and Chartism', in Walvin (ed.), *British Slavery and Society*, 69–99; Drescher, *Capitalism and Anti-slavery*, ch. 7.

[46] Davis, *Problem of Slavery*, 350; James Walvin, 'The Public Campaign in England against Slavery, 1787–1834', in David Eltis and James Walvin (eds.), *The Abolition of the Atlantic Slave Trade* (Madison, WI, 1981), 65.

[47] *Poor Man's Guardian*, 15 June 1833, 189–90.

assumptions and discourses.[48] And no one did more to popularise the interchangeable terms 'wage slavery' and 'white slavery' than Richard Oastler, himself an evangelical and abolitionist. The champion of York-shire's factory children, he admonished, 'in this boasted land of liberty' tender children 'are Hired – not sold – as Slaves, and daily forced to *hear* that they are free'.[49] As they opposed liberalism's association of free-wage labour with 'progress', popular radicals walked an uneasy line in their construction of hierarchies of oppression; as they appropriated the humanitarian rhetoric of suffering pioneered by abolitionists, working-class radicals often downplayed the horrors of slavery in comparison to their own plight.[50] At their most extreme, claims made about the miseries of Britain's labouring poor in contrast to the comfort of colonial subjects exposed populism's 'dark side'. This was most evident in the rabid racism of William Cobbett, the period's most popular radical writer.[51] Moreover, as Marcus Wood argues, Cobbett's ideas on race, miscegenation and colonialism should not be written off as merely eccentric; on the contrary, they provided a framework for Thomas Carlyle's insistence on the unique suffering of British industrial workers and his view of Afro-Americans as unfit for non-coerced labour.[52]

IMPERIAL ENCOUNTERS: TWO SOLDIERS' STORIES

Anti-slavery was the most sustained and visible movement in which class and imperial relations converged. Certainly we can discern imperial themes in other nineteenth-century social movements. Thus Chartists supported the Canadian rebels of 1837; the Chartist press developed a class-based critique of the British government's pursuit of the First Opium War against China; the second National Petition (1842) demanded the repeal of the Act of Union with Ireland along with the Charter's six points; and Chartist activists faced transportation to the convict settlements of Australia and the Cape.[53] Moreover, Miles Taylor has recently traced the

---

[48] Robert Gray, *The Factory Question and Industrial England, 1830–1860* (Cambridge, 1996), 37–47.

[49] *Leeds Times*, 16 October 1830, 4; also see Marcus Cunliffe, *Chattel Slavery and Wage Slavery: The Anglo-American Context, 1830–1860* (Athens, GA, 1979), ch. 1.

[50] See, for example, the speech of the sawyer and trade union leader, John Jackson, *Poor Man's Guardian*, 22 June 1833, 199.

[51] W. D. Rubinstein, 'British Radicalism and the "Dark Side" of Populism', in his *The Elite and the Wealthy in Modern British History* (Brighton, 1987), 339–73. For Cobbett at his worst, see *Cobbett's Weekly Political Register*, 16 June 1804, cols. 933–7.

[52] Wood, *Slavery, Empathy and Pornography*, 152–69, and ch. 7.

[53] Dorothy Thompson, *The Chartists: Popular Politics in the Industrial Revolution* (London, 1984), 46, 264; Shijie Guan, 'Chartism and the First Opium War', *History Workshop*, 24 (1987), 17–31; George

complex ways in which imperial policy helped to stabilise British society in 1848: middle-class loyalty was partly secured by displacing the domestic tax burden on to the colonies themselves; colonial emigration may have provided a safety valve, reducing social tensions by absorbing surplus population; the transportation of political protestors, most notably Irish nationalist leaders, as well as many of the more 'dangerous' criminal class, removed troublemakers. However, the cumulative effect of government policy radicalised colonial politics, with the result that by the 1850s the elective franchise was far more popular in most settlement and Crown colonies than at 'home'. It proved difficult to separate modes of metro-politan and colonial authority, and in 1866–7 democratisation at the periphery shaped debate over metropolitan parliamentary reform.[54]

But the impact of empire varied enormously; if the lives of many were touched more indirectly, the lives of others were indelibly marked by empire. The more than six million who left Britain between 1815 and 1914 for the colonies, men and women mostly drawn from the labouring poor and bound predominantly for Australia and Canada, often transformed their lives for the better.[55] Letters home commonly drew attention to the differences in social relations. 'Dear Brother, we have no overseers to tred us under foot', wrote one such emigrant.[56] Thousands of Christian missionaries, many of them women, were intimately involved in the imperial project; their encounters with colonised peoples were not only intense and often subject to conflicting sympathies, but served to mediate imperial and domestic identities, including those of class.[57] As the Empire expanded over the course of the century, the number of colonial administrators grew, with district officers increasingly recruited from the ranks of the professional middle class.[58] Moreover, despite the Raj's image

Rudé, *Protest and Punishment: The Story of the Social and Political Protesters Transported to Australia, 1788–1868* (Oxford, 1978). Also see Andrew Charles Messner, 'Chartist Political Culture in Britain and Colonial Australia, c. 1835–1860', unpublished PhD thesis, University of New England, Australia (2000).

[54] Miles Taylor, 'The 1848 Revolutions and the British Empire', *Past and Present*, 166 (2000), 146–80.

[55] A. N. Porter (ed.), *Atlas of British Overseas Expansion* (London, 1991), 85–6; Robin F. Haines, *Emigration and the Labouring Poor: Australian Recruitment in Britain and Ireland, 1831–60* (Basingstoke, 1999); A. James Hammerton, 'Gender and Migration', in Philippa Levine (ed.), *Gender and Empire* (Oxford, 2004), 156–80.

[56] Quoted in K. D. M. Snell, *Annals of the Labouring Poor: Social Change and Agrarian England, 1660–1900* (Cambridge, 1985), 13.

[57] See, in particular, Susan Thorne, *Congregational Missions and the Making of an Imperial Culture in Nineteenth-Century England* (Stanford, 1999); Catherine Hall, *Civilising Subjects: Metropole and Colony in the English Imagination, 1830–1867* (Chicago, 2002); also Jeffrey Cox, 'Were Victorian Nonconformists the Worst Imperialists of All?', *Victorian Studies*, 46 (2004), 243–55.

[58] Kirk-Greene, *Imperial Administrators*, 15–16, 99–101.

of itself 'as a relatively homogenous elite', it also included a substantial European population of 'poor whites'.[59] To these groups we might add travellers, journalists and businessmen. Yet by far the largest number of British people directly participating in empire, besides settlers, consisted of ordinary soldiers. In a sense, the making of the English working class was, as Linda Colley points out, 'a phenomenon acted out on a global scale'.[60] The army's rank and file represented a sampling of the lesser skilled working class, including large but relatively declining numbers from rural districts and Ireland.[61] While living conditions and terms of service slowly improved, soldiers remained poorly paid, drilled to mono-tonous routine and subject to privations, high mortality rates and until 1881 the lash. The continuous warfare of the last third of the century, the 'small wars' against the Maoris, Ashanti, Afghans, Zulus, Boers and Dervishes, together with the introduction of short-term enlistment, necessitated an increased number of recruits.[62]

A brief comparison of two soldiers' memoirs of Indian service offers some insight into the implications of military service for class and imperial understandings. John Pearman served in the King's Own Light Dragoons between 1843 and 1856, fighting as a cavalryman in the Sikh Wars (1845–6 and 1848–9) that preceded the annexation of the Punjab.[63] Portrayed as an exotic country where adventurous young men might make their way, India possessed an appeal that should not be under-estimated.[64] A sawyer by trade, Pearman was working as a railway guard when a dispute with his supervisor, together with a desire 'to travel and see other Countries', impelled him to enlist in the army. Pearman probably wrote his 'memoirs' in 1881–2, on retiring from a long career in the Buckinghamshire Constabulary. There is no evidence that he inten-ded to publish his story; indeed, until 1988 the full text remained unpublished. As Carolyn Steedman shows, the imperial events of the late 1870s and of 1880–1 'gave contemporary shape' to his memories of serving

---

[59] David Arnold, 'European Orphans and Vagrants in India in the Nineteenth Century', *Journal of Imperial and Commonwealth History*, 7 (1979), 104, and 'White Colonization and Labour in Nineteenth-Century India', *ibid.*, 11 (1983), 133–58; Buettner, *Empire Families*, 7–8.

[60] Linda Colley, *Captives: Britain, Empire and the World, 1600–1850* (London, 2002), 334–5, and ch. 10.

[61] Edward M. Spiers, *The Army and Society, 1815–1914* (London, 1980), 46–7, 50–1, and ch. 2 generally, and *The Late Victorian Army, 1868–1902* (Manchester, 1992), 129–31, and ch. 5.

[62] Spiers, *Army and Society*, 35–9.

[63] Bryon Farwell, *Queen Victoria's Little Wars* (New York, 1972), chs. 4–5, for the two Sikh Wars.

[64] Peter Stanley, *White Mutiny: British Military Culture in India, 1825–1875* (London, 1998), 13.

in 'John Company' in India.[65] Pearman was an anti-imperialist, yet he recorded that soldiering was the part of his life 'the most worth living'. Against the army's hierarchical authority, Pearman juxtaposed death's ultimate reversal of class relations. 'We oftentimes had to face Death in the worse form,' he explained. 'But there is a pleasure in that for it places the great man and the poor on a footen. I have oftimes put my foot on a Dead officer as we put his body under ground and said to myself where is your Rank now.' Rather than regretting his loss of personal freedom, Pearman recorded that 'India was to the White man a free Country we Could go where we liked no Trespass out there and John Company behaved well to us shared some of the Plunder.' He reflected that 'with all the faults of a Military life there is more to live for then the poor man who in England is a free paid Slave'.[66]

By the late nineteenth century, as Steedman writes, there was 'an increased and general expectation that the private soldier would *personally* embrace the principles of imperial expansion', and the small but growing 'literature of working-class military autobiography came increasingly to frame its narrative by this assumption'. But by the time he came to write his account, Pearman understood 'that the wars against the Sikhs were not his wars: that they were wars of capital, of the landed interest, of the rich and powerful, of official Christianity'.[67] In his memoirs, the romance narrative of a soldier's life gave way under the pressure of his anti-imperialism; unable to resolve the contradictions in his own experience, he failed to produce a coherent narrative. As his memoirs shift to a more reflective engagement with his past in terms of his freethinking and republican beliefs, India offers the site for transforming his earlier experience through the filter of new ideas. Thus Pearman remembered conversations that he had had in the Punjab. 'Were I an Englishman', he was told, probably by a Zoroastrian (perhaps a servant or camp follower from Gujerat), 'I would worship the gun and Bayonet only. See what it had brought your country. All her possessions, all her liberties all her money, all her commerce all her advantages.'[68] Pearman's reading of secularist publications such as the *Republican*, the *Freethinker* and Charles Bradlaugh's *National Reformer* clearly helped to shape his ideas about empire, land redistribution, religion and class – about what constituted

---

[65] Carolyn Steedman, *The Radical Soldier's Tale, John Pearman, 1819–1908* (London, 1988), 15. The following paragraphs are heavily indebted to Steedman's superb introduction to Pearman's memoirs.

[66] *Ibid.*, 208–9. Quotations from Pearman's text are in their original form.   [67] *Ibid.*, 20, 42.

[68] *Ibid.*, 49–50, 212 (quotation).

social and moral justice in an unfair world. Bradlaugh's own military service, as a private stationed in Ireland during the early 1840s, had deepened his sympathy for the Irish peasantry, and perhaps drew Pearman to Bradlaugh's publications.[69] Pearman came to see common humanity among the dispossessed, including the peoples of India, Africa and Ireland. His imperial service fostered a social critique based on class and imperial subjugation, focusing particularly on questions of land-ownership.

Pearman's reflections may not be 'typical', but they serve to unsettle easy assumptions about how ordinary soldiers felt, restoring imaginative complexity to their worldview.[70] Frank Richards' *Old Soldier Sahib*, published in 1936, conforms more closely to the dominant narrative of imperial soldiering. At the turn of the century, the era of high British imperial culture, Richards served a seven-year stint as a private in India. Born in 1884 and orphaned at a young age, he was raised by his uncle and aunt in the South Wales' mining and iron region of Blaina. Having worked in the coal mines and followed his uncle into the local tin works as a lad, he became captivated by India and the stories told by an old soldier about life there. Unlike most working people in a district that became a Labour stronghold (previously a major Chartist centre), Richards embraced his family's Conservative politics, commenting: 'in spite of all the Socialist propaganda that goes on about me I remain a rank Imperialist a heart'.[71] However, for most working people, 'to go for a soldier' was not seen as a desirable option or higher calling – on this point Richards' family conformed to social type. Thus he recorded his aunt's dismay in 1898 when his cousin, out of work due to the South Wales miners' strike, joined the army. Although there was a strong correlation between military recruitment and unemployment, the memoirs of work-ing-class volunteers often stress motives other than those of sheer des-peration or economic need. Like Pearman, Richards was a restless young man, discontented with his working life and in search for adventure. In 1900, during the Boer War, Richards joined the Welch Fusiliers.[72]

Richards was a diehard, Tory imperialist. Nonetheless, he had no doubt as to the class hierarchy of the British army in India: 'It was class

---

[69] *Ibid.*, 86–103. For Bradlaugh's experience in Ireland, see Hypatia Bradlaugh Bonner and J. M. Robertson, *Charles Bradlaugh: A Record of His Life and Work*, 2 vols. (London, 1895), I, 33–4, 40.
[70] Cf., however, Corporal John Ryder's indictment of the brutalities of imperial soldiering in his *Four Years' Service in India* (Leicester, 1853), particularly 128–30.
[71] Frank Richards, *Old Soldier Sahib* (London, 1936), 30. Thanks to Philippa Levine for drawing my attention to this work.
[72] *Ibid.*, 26, 30–1. Cf., for example, Robert Blatchford, *My Life in the Army* (London, 1904), 13–14.

distinction with a vengeance.'[73] His disdain for native people, whom he insisted must always be kept down, was unqualified, as was his reiteration of the military adage 'that what is won by the sword must be kept by the sword'.[74] In fact, Richards and Pearman agreed that imperial rule was fundamentally based on military conquest and subjugation; it was just that Richards saw imperial dominion as part of the world's natural order. He also cherished the freedom this 'land of milk and honey' accorded the working-class soldier with their own 'cleaning-boys' paid a few rupees per month to care for their uniforms and equipment and a medley of native barracks servants: the 'punkah-wallahs', 'tatty-wallahs' and 'bhisti-wallahs' to help cool rooms, 'dhobis' to do the washing, the sweepers and cooks. Richards gave a graphic account of the brothels and native prostitutes reserved for British soldiers' cheap pleasure.[75] It was a life that he liked. On returning to South Wales in 1907, Richards writes, it was not long before 'My delight with home wore off', as he drifted back into the mines, working as a timberman and longing for India. After work, he spun yarns about India; he told his workmates, 'what I was thinking of when I left it to come back home here and work again deep in the bowels of the earth, I'm damned if I know'. At the local pub, he socialised with fellow veterans, who concurred that they had been 'utter fools' to have ever left the service.[76] Looking back from the depths of the Depression, his military youth in India took on an understandably warm glow.

What then are we to make of these two soldiers' life stories? First, their memories of Indian service were marked by more than nostalgia for lost youth and exotic lands. While their 'freedom' in India was a product of empire's racial and gender hierarchies, the masculine freedom they enjoyed was set against domestic life as 'a free paid Slave', against working the night shift underground as a timberman. What became explicit critique for Pearman remained oblique in Richards' memoirs; in both cases, however, domestic class relations and working-class subordination were refracted through their experience of empire. Both men experienced the dislocation of returning home and remained on the margins of local working-class culture and community. Yet they told stories to their families, to their workmates, at the pub or working-men's club, to anyone willing to listen to a soldier's tale of India; they wrote memoirs, and in

[73] Richards, *Soldier Sahib*, 150.   [74] *Ibid.*, 79–80, 136, 310.
[75] *Ibid.*, 179–89. For prostitution in the colonial-military context, see Philippa Levine, *Prostitution, Race, and Politics: Policing Venereal Disease in the British Empire* (New York, 2003), part 2.
[76] Richards, *Soldier Sahib*, 306–10. Cf. Robert Bickers, *Empire Made Me: An Englishman Adrift in Shanghai* (London, 2003).

this they were unusual. Like many soldiers, Pearman and Richards conveyed impressions of empire to a broader audience, although it is extremely difficult to assess how they were received.[77] But we must allow that sharpened class awareness, feelings of resentment and injustice at 'home' were not necessarily incompatible with allegiance to nation and empire.

WAYS OF BELONGING

The last thirty years of the century witnessed major territorial expansion of Britain's overseas empire; the era of 'new imperialism' shifted the tone of metropolitan imperial culture, as empire's appeal became more deeply embedded within British society. The late nineteenth century was also a period of renewed class antagonism, gender crisis and rising concerns about the urban underclass, the residuum, and the advent of modern 'mass' society. The 1880s and 1890s were decades in which many middle-class intellectuals, social reformers and urban missionaries discovered that they had lost touch with a large and increasingly estranged population of outcasts, slum dwellers subject to chronic unemployment and moral and physical degeneration.[78] The extent to which the labour movement, socialists or working people more generally identified with late nineteenth-century empire or to which 'social imperialism' undercut the politics of class remains an open question.[79] Nonetheless, during these decades languages and ways of belonging – to society, nation and empire – were reworked. Like all codes of inclusion, the rhetoric of imperial belonging, articulated in part as an alternative to class, was predicated on terms of exclusion, although the controlling boundaries remained insecure. By way of conclusion, I want to suggest how some of those terms of belonging were reconstituted.

[77] For the broader cultural resonances, see John M. MacKenzie (ed.), *Popular Imperialism and the Military, 1850–1950* (Manchester, 1992).

[78] Gareth Stedman Jones, *Outcast London: A Study in the Relationship between Classes in Victorian Society* (Oxford, 1971), part 3; Judith R. Walkowitz, *City of Dreadful Delight: Narratives of Sexual Danger in Late Victorian London* (Chicago, 1992), ch. 1; Jose Harris, *Private Lives, Public Spirit: A Social History of Britain, 1870–1914* (Oxford, 1993), ch. 1.

[79] See Richard Price, *An Imperial War and the British Working Class: Working-Class Attitudes and Reactions to the Boer War* (London, 1972); Henry Pelling, 'British Labour and British Imperialism', in his *Popular Politics and Society in Late Victorian Britain* (London, 1968), 82–100; Gareth Stedman Jones, 'Working-Class Culture and Working-Class Politics in London, 1870–1900: Notes on the Remaking of a Working Class', in his *Languages of Class: Studies in English Working Class History* (Cambridge, 1983), 179–238; Neville Kirk, *Comrades and Cousins: Globalization, Workers and Labour Movements in Britain, the USA and Australia from the 1880s to 1914* (London, 2003), ch. 3.

During the later Victorian period, the Empire was often imagined metaphorically as a family, with Queen Victoria (empress of India) as its mother. However, the language of kith and kin was itself constructed against an enlarged exclusionary field, as imperial Britain expanded into vast new territories in Africa and Asia. This aggressive expansion confounded notions of empire as one of settlement as opposed to conquest. The 'greater Britain' of Charles Dilke and later J. R. Seeley was based on the English-speaking world and those of Anglo-Saxon descent, including the United States but excluding India, as well as the Aborigines of Australia, the Maoris of New Zealand, or the indigenous peoples of the Dominions.[80] The appeal to the unity of the Anglo-Saxon race blended distinctions based on history, culture and biology.

On his return from travelling throughout the English-speaking countries in 1867, Dilke declared that the Anglo-Saxon was 'the only extirpating race on earth'. While predating the 'new' imperial expansion, his influential *Greater Britain* anticipated the intensified Anglo-Saxonism and social Darwinism of the late nineteenth century.[81] Moreover, despite the triumphal tones of cultural and racial superiority, Dilke's work was suffused with inconsistency (not least regarding his notion of 'race') and doubt. 'Are we English in turn to degenerate abroad', asked Dilke, in accord with 'a great natural law?' To ask the question was to confront the possibility that 'Englishness' would succumb in its very triumph, that the conquerors would be absorbed, amalgamated, transformed – would cease to be English. In his concluding chapter, Dilke predicted that racial distinctions would in fact continue – miscegenation would not produce racial blending – with the 'dearer races . . . likely to destroy the cheaper peoples, and that Saxondom will rise triumphant from the doubtful struggle'. But the struggle was always 'doubtful'. The Empire offered some reassurance: 'The countries ruled by a race whose very scum and outcasts have founded empires in every portion of the globe' that were four and a half times larger than Rome's empire.[82] And yet the reminder that the Empire's own white settlers were themselves outcasts might have troubled middle-class readers, particularly in light of the sudden

---

[80] See Andrew Thompson, 'The Language of Imperialism and the Meanings of Empire: Imperial Discourse in British Politics, 1895–1914', *Journal of British Studies*, 36 (1997), 147–77, and *Imperial Britain: The Empire in British Politics c. 1880–1932* (Harlow, 2000), ch. 1.

[81] See Bernard Semmel, *Imperialism and Social Reform: English Social-Imperial Thought, 1895–1914* (London, 1960); also Paul Kramer, 'Empires, Exceptions, and Anglo-Saxons: Race and Rule Between the British and United States Empires, 1880–1910', *Journal of American History*, 88 (2002), 1315–53.

[82] Charles W. Dilke, *Greater Britain: A Record of Travel in English Speaking Countries during 1866 and 1867*, 2 vols. (London, 1868), I, 310; II, 405.

expansion of the electorate at 'home'. Indeed, at twenty-four, Dilke was returned at the 1868 General Election, as a radical Liberal, for the huge new constituency of Chelsea, which included the working-class districts of Fulham, Hammersmith and Kensal Green.

Arguably, in *Greater Britain* Dilke displaced concerns about the purity and well-being of Britain's own working class. Fears of internal contamination – from Irish immigration into British cities or later from eastern-European Jewish immigration into London's East End – and the physical deterioration of the working class were rife.[83] Moreover, from the mid-century, as racist attitudes became more pronounced, and the differences between race and class became more sharply articulated, not only were 'blacks' deemed biologically inferior, but sections of Britain's labouring poor might be judged as biologically unfit subjects, a 'race' apart.[84] Colonial resistance to imperial authority – the Indian 'Mutiny' of 1857, the Waikato War of 1863 against New Zealand's Maori, the Morant Bay 'riots' of 1865 in Jamaica – marked turning points in the attitudes of government, settlers and 'home' opinion. A reconfiguration took place whereby a decline in 'humanitarian liberalism' fostered increasingly punitive attitudes towards indigenous colonial peoples, while bringing the metropolitan middle class and colonial settlers together on the basis of shared racial superiority. This reformulation paralleled, as well as helped to set the terms for, hardened attitudes towards the 'undeserving' domestic poor.[85] By the 1880s, the imperial metropolis, the world's largest city and the Empire's financial and cultural capital, was represented as socially and graphically divided, suffering from an urban pathology and subject to political disorder spilling out from working-class districts into London's fashionable West End. Gareth Stedman Jones argues that in response to the social crisis of the 1880s a new style of middle-class liberalism drew a sharper distinction between the respectable, 'true' working class who were to be trusted and wooed, and the residuum.

[83] See, for example, Mary Poovey, *Making a Social Body: British Cultural Formation, 1830–1864* (Chicago, 1995), ch. 2; David Feldman, 'The Importance of Being English: Jewish Immigration and the Decay of Liberal England', in Feldman and Gareth Stedman Jones (eds.), *Metropolis: London: Histories and Representations since 1800* (London, 1989), 56–84.

[84] Douglas Lorimer, *Colour, Class and the Victorians: English Attitudes to the Negro in the Mid-Nineteenth Century* (Leicester, 1978), 12–13, 204–5.

[85] Martin Daunton and Rick Halpern, 'Introduction: British Identities, Indigenous Peoples and the Empire', in their co-edited *Empire and Others: British Encounters with Indigenous Peoples, 1600–1850* (London, 1999), 12–13, and Andrew Bank, 'Losing Faith in the Civilizing Mission: The Premature Decline of Humanitarian Liberalism at the Cape, 1840–60', 364–83; Alan Lester, 'British Settler Discourse and Circuits of Empire', *History Workshop Journal*, 54 (2002), 25–48.

In a related development, missionary efforts shifted from foreign to home work, as the Empire now returned in the guise of 'social imperialist' healing.[86] Missionaries, journalists, novelists and sociologists frequently mapped the urban jungle in terms of its African counterpart, drawing on metaphors of race to characterise the marginalised segment of the working class, which in turn became central to the era's social imagination.[87] Thus in 1890, the Salvation Army's 'General' William Booth published *In Darkest England and the Way Out* in which he compared the 'wooded wilderness' of Stanley's 'Darkest Africa' to London's slums and their inhabitants. 'As there is a darkest Africa', he asked, 'is there not also a darkest England? Civilization, which can breed its own barbarians, does it not also breed its own pygmies?' Was the plight of 'a negress in the Equatorial Forest', for example, really worse than that of an orphan girl in London who must choose between starvation and sin, and once consenting to sell herself will be 'treated as a slave and an outcast by the very men who have ruined her'?[88] The book's sustained sensationalism, due probably to W. T. Stead, who drafted much of the text from Booth's notes, deflected attention from its actual plan to rehabilitate London's 'submerged tenth'; it also helped to make *In Darkest England* a best-seller. Gertrude Himmelfarb perceptively notes the connection of the Salvation Army's image of poverty to the earlier language of Henry Mayhew who divided all societies into 'nomadic and civilised tribes' or 'races', comparing London's street folk to the Bushmen and Sonquas among the Hottentots, the Fingoes among the Kafirs and the Bedouins among the Arabs, alike in their savage lusts and immorality.[89]

But Booth's work reflected the new social and imperial context, popularising strands of social-imperialist thought and schemes of social regeneration, including settling the residuum in labour colonies.[90] Booth proposed the formation of self-sustaining communities, 'a kind of co-operative society, or patriarchal family', based on the Salvation Army's 'principles of discipline'. The scheme called for society's 'ship-wrecked' to be rescued by first joining the City Colony. From here, those who did not return regenerated to city life would move to the Farm community,

[86] Thorne, *Congregational Missions*, ch. 4.
[87] Elaine Showalter, *Sexual Anarchy: Gender and Culture at the Fin de Siècle* (London, 1990), 5–6; Seth Koven, *Slumming: Sexual and Social Politics in Victorian London* (Princeton, 2004), 237, 254.
[88] General (William) Booth, *In Darkest Africa and the Way Out* (London, 1890), 9–13.
[89] Gertrude Himmelfarb, *Poverty and Compassion: The Moral Imagination of the Late Victorians* (New York, 1991), 221–6, and *The Idea of Poverty: England in the Early Industrial Age* (New York, 1984), 323–46, for Mayhew.
[90] Stedman Jones, *Outcast London*, 303–12.

where they would be resuscitated by the same methods of religious, moral and industrial discipline. Some might find employment in the country-side, while the 'great bulk' would move on to the Overseas Colony. Impressed with successful British settlement in South Africa, Canada and Australia, he proposed to secure land and establish a colony ready to receive the city's most 'depraved and destitute' for reformation. Thus the willing poor would move from the city to the country, 'and then pouring them on to the virgin soils that await their coming', free men and women under 'strong government' who were prepared to lay 'the foundations, perchance, of another Empire to swell to vast proportions in later times'.[91]

Booth's plan was not put into practice as conceived; the point, how-ever, is to recognise its imaginative range and how the social space of outcast London was refigured within that of empire. Booth's aim was to regenerate and thus incorporate the residuum within the family of greater Britain. Yet a contradiction remained between the Empire's capacity for inclusion and opportunity for its white settlers and its association with the outcast poor and racial 'others'. The settlement colonies could not entirely escape their image as a space for society's recalcitrant poor. In the emblematic works of Booth and Dilke, class is not an operative category as such; Dilke's Anglo-Saxonism subsumed or transcended class, while Booth separated the 'submerged tenth' from the trustworthy majority of British working people. Yet the terms of inclusion, within the nation, the imperial family or Anglo-Saxon 'race', remained troubled. If the Empire's white settlers and the domestic working class had become fit for measured inclusion, set off against indigenous peoples and the metropolitan resi-duum, belonging and trust could never simply be taken for granted. Over the long nineteenth century, configurations of belonging varied greatly. The constitutive impact of empire on class was at best uneven; going beyond such generalisations requires analysing specific contexts. It also depends on one's methodological approach to 'class', as well as decisions about what constitutes historical evidence. However, I hope at least to have done enough to indicate the benefits of viewing class and empire within the same historical frame.

[91] Booth, *In Darkest England*, 90–3.

CHAPTER THIRTEEN

Citizenship and empire, 1867–1928

Keith McClelland and Sonya Rose

This chapter explores how Britain's status as an imperial nation shaped debates about and changes in the nature of citizenship between roughly 1867 when some working-class men were granted the parliamentary franchise and 1928 when adult suffrage was made universal. It was during this period that empire and nation became linked in new ways, marked by Britain taking a 'more consciously imperialist course', especially prior to World War I,[1] and its empire becoming an increasingly visible symbol of national worth. The chapter will explore how Britain's status as an imperial nation informed debates about political citizenship, influenced responses to the broadening of the franchise and, in turn, produced new understandings of and concerns with the nature of citizenship. While both the meanings of citizenship and considerations of Britain's imperial project were contested throughout the period, the chapter focuses primarily on those hegemonic understandings and their various articulations that dominated public culture, both shaping political debate and infusing everyday life.

Between 1866 and 1928 the size of the electorate in Britain multiplied by about twenty times, from about 1.4 million in 1866 to 28.5 million by 1929. Thus it was during this period that British liberal democratic citizenship was consolidated.[2] But this process of consolidation or development was a highly contested one; throughout, those who had a political stake in the nation guarded their prerogative jealously and it was as a consequence of debate and struggle over the terms of political fitness that new classes of individuals were enfranchised.

These changes in the franchise were part of a major transformation in the role, practice and ideologies of the state.[3] There developed a new

[1] Dane Kennedy, *Britain and Empire, 1880–1945* (London, 2002), 5.
[2] Laura E. Nym Mayhall, *The Militant Suffrage Movement: Citizenship and Resistance in Britain, 1860–1930* (Oxford, 2003), 12.
[3] *Ibid.*; for a lucid account of the changing state, Stuart Hall and Bill Schwarz, 'State and Society, 1880–1930', in Mary Langan and Bill Schwarz (eds), *Crises in the British State 1880–1930* (London, 1985), 7–32.

understanding of its role – as the 'special institution that acts for the *general* interest, and according to the principles of *public* service'.[4] As Charles Dilke put it in 1892: 'The state represents the common good of its citizens. It is the basis of their higher life. It secures to its subjects the only possibility for the exercise – for the full development – of their faculties. It supplies them with the ideal aim of a common good.'[5]

One variant of this revived notion of the 'common good' was understood at the time as 'collectivism'.[6] There was no single version of this; it was, rather, a discourse into which several strands fed, including varieties of imperialist, conservative, liberal, labourist and socialist thought. Taken together these variants of collectivism comprised the 'principal political-ideological programme through which a variety of social forces attempted to transform the state' as Stuart Hall has put it.[7] For Hall and his colleagues, '[c]ollectivism assumes that society consists, not of "bare individuals" but of corporate classes, groups and interests. The state should therefore plan and act on behalf of society conceived as an organic whole – a "collectivity".'[8] There were two associated developments in the meaning of citizenship: first, a general concern with what was termed 'good citizenship' – the idea that citizenship was a practice concerned with obligations; and second, a new understanding of the state's responsibilities for its citizenry that foreshadowed what was later to be articulated as 'social rights' or 'social citizenship'. This essay focuses primarily on the former.

The development of collectivism has a complex history: this is not the place to detail it. But within the spectrum of collectivist thought and practice one figure in particular was at the centre of much of the post-1870 reconfiguration of politics and the state, Joseph Chamberlain.[9] Rising to prominence in Birmingham in the 1870s, he was within the orbit of radical liberalism, from which he took a concern with the social conditions of the people, a realisation of the potential force of demos, an emphasis upon the virtues of civic duty as well as the civic gospel, and a

---

[4] Colin Gordon, 'Governmental Rationality: An Introduction', in Graham Burchell, Colin Gordon and Peter Miller (eds.), *The Foucault Effect: Studies in Governmentality* (Chicago, 1991), 32.
[5] Charles Dilke and Spenser Wilkinson, *Imperial Defence* (London, 1892), 8–9.
[6] See Hall and Schwarz, 'State and Society', 16–24; cf. the earlier and more comprehensive assessment: Stuart Hall, 'The Rise of the Representative/Interventionist State 1880s–1920s', in Gregor McLennan, David Held and Stuart Hall (eds), *State and Society in Contemporary Britain: A Critical Introduction* (Cambridge, 1984), 7–49.
[7] Hall, 'The Rise', 27.   [8] *Ibid.*
[9] There is a great deal of work on Chamberlain. But essential for an understanding of the context is E. H. H. Green, *The Crisis of Conservatism: The Politics, Economics, and Ideology of the Conservative Party, 1880–1914* (London, 1995).

stress upon the political and social purchase of the pursuit of 'Greater Britain' (partly derived from Charles Dilke). Forming Unionism in the 1880s following the crisis of the Liberal Party over Home Rule for Ireland, the key imperial issue of its time, he pursued an aggressive imperialism which focused on the white settler Empire and attempted to wed this to the popularisation of imperialism. Concretely, this meant social imperialism: a programme of social reform which sought to incorporate the popular enfranchised constituency and those identified as the socially excluded with a political economy centred on tariff reform. If Chamberlain himself was wrecked in the vain pursuit of tariff reform, part of what he helped to make possible was a whole shift of the centre of gravity of British political culture to one in which social imperialism became a dominant element.[10] Some of these elements are ones to which we shall return; but for the moment it is necessary to outline in a little more detail what we mean by citizenship in legal and political terms.

WHAT IS CITIZENSHIP?

The concept of citizenship is one with a number of different meanings and usages. In the modern era it signifies belonging or membership in a nation state, and in this sense it is a synonym for nationality. At the same time citizenship refers to the rights and duties of full membership in that society. It is a legal concept and it also refers to 'the moral and performative dimensions of membership which define the meanings and practices of belonging in society'.[11]

Needless to say every one of these elements has been contested; and while we may suppose that citizenship is a set of more or less formal rights and duties inscribed in law, claims by individuals for rights and demands upon them for duties have always drawn upon a shifting discursive terrain. It is useful, then, to think of citizenship not only in terms of nationality and as a formal rights and obligations-bearing relationship between individuals and the nation state, but also as a language by means of which people can make claims on the political community concerning rights and duties, political and moral or ethical practices, and criteria of membership.[12] These claims have concerned not only political rights but

---

[10] The major work on social imperialism remains Bernard Semmel, *Imperialism and Social Reform: English Social-Imperial Thought, 1895–1914* (London, 1960).

[11] James Holston and Arjun Appadurai, 'Cities and Citizenship', *Public Culture*, 8 (1996), 200.

[12] For a similar conceptualisation see Frederick Cooper, *Colonialism in Question: Theory, Knowledge, History* (Berkeley, 2005), 24.

during the twentieth century have broadened to incorporate social and economic entitlements and obligations. And it is on the grounds of the discursive, as well as the legal, framework of citizenship that the nation state can expect or demand various forms of reciprocity from its members.

SUBJECTS, NATIONALS AND ALIENS

At the most basic level, the government, informed by culturally significant civic ideals, defines who can and who cannot belong to the nation state. In Britain, until 1981 however, the official term for British national was British subject, and British subjecthood was based on the principle of *jus soli* (born in a territory under the British Crown). British subjecthood, then, was an imperial form of belonging as well as a form of 'nationality'.

Subjecthood denoted primarily a status of obedience and loyalty to the Crown. In the late nineteenth and early twentieth centuries, empire was to influence in complex ways the variable meanings and prerogatives of British subjecthood for those born outside the United Kingdom and the ability of non-British subjects or aliens to reside in the metropole and possibly become naturalised as well.

Economic depression from the 1870s, coupled with increasing public attention to poverty and urban crowding, produced an undercurrent of dissatisfaction with Britain's 'open door' policy to asylum seekers, one that had been in place since the end of the Napoleonic Wars. With the mass immigration of Jews from eastern Europe in the wake of the pogroms of 1881–2, popular opinion about alien immigration became increasingly hostile. It took more than another twenty years, significant public protests, several parliamentary commissions and a particular conjunctural context for parliament to pass the Aliens Act of 1905, designed to reduce the number of destitute Jewish immigrants. As David Feldman has suggested, immigration became the focus of increasing political militancy as the 'emphasis of debate ... shifted from the domestic to the imperial consequences of poverty' and led to the passage of the 1905 Aliens Act.[13]

The problems exposed by the military failures of the Boer War, increasing competition from other imperial powers, public debate about a loss of 'national efficiency' and the circulation of social Darwinist ideas, fuelled anxieties that Britain would lose its imperial pre-eminence. Immigrants were believed to be threatening to the nation's physical health

---

[13] David Feldman, 'The Importance of Being English: Jewish Immigration and the Decay of Liberal England', in Feldman and Gareth Stedman Jones (eds), *Metropolis: London: Histories and Representations since 1800* (London, 1989), 57.

and moral fibre. Anti-alien discourse highlighted the idea that alien immigrant men were incapable of masculine respectability because they sent their wives to work, and their 'unmanliness was further marked out by their aversion to manual labour, and their incapacity for trade union organization'.[14] More important than the actual effectiveness of the 1905 Act in stemming immigration, was that it opened the way to future, more restrictive Acts.[15]

Anti-alienism continued through to World War I amidst fears of invasion, anarchism and subversion that heightened British concerns about national and imperial decline. The Aliens Restriction Act of 1914 gave the Home Secretary discretionary powers to refuse entry and deport people whom 'he deemed not to be conducive to the public good',[16] and it mandated that all aliens must register with the police. Subsequently the Act was reinforced by an Amendment in 1919.

The imperial context was fundamental both to official rhetoric and to various purportedly 'race-neutral' practices regarding non-white, colonial British subjects. Through the late Victorian period, Great Britain's official posture was that while the rights of British subjects might vary, a British subject anywhere was a British subject without distinction based on race or ethnicity. While this was the official stance, the actual import of being a British subject and the meaning of British subjecthood depended on race.[17]

Deploying particular race-neutral regulations was a time-tested way for Great Britain, as well as the Dominions, to differentiate among British subjects (as well as among aliens) without officially sanctioning racial discrimination. The white settler colonies adopted various ways to do this. But it was South Africa through the Natal Act of 1867 that pioneered a language test as a way of discriminating among British subjects and aliens to control immigration.[18]

The Merchant Shipping Act of 1906 required such a language test for seamen signing on to British ships (purportedly to assure safety at sea).

---

[14] *Ibid.*, 72–3.
[15] David Cesarani, ' "An Alien Concept?" The Continuity of Anti-alienism in British Society before 1940', in David Cesarani and Tony Kushner (eds.), *The Internment of Aliens in Twentieth Century Britain* (London, 1993), 31.
[16] Ann Dummett and Andrew Nicol, *Subjects, Citizens, Aliens and Others: Nationality and Immigration Law* (London, 1990), 107.
[17] *Ibid.*, 113–27.
[18] *Ibid.*, 118–21. Importantly, Marilyn Lake has argued that Natal emulated the US in using literacy 'to patrol racial borders'. See Marilyn Lake, 'From Mississippi to Melbourne via Natal: The Invention of the Literacy Test as a Technology of Racial Exclusion', in Ann Curthoys and Marilyn Lake (eds.), *Connected Worlds: History in Transnational Perspective* (Canberra, 2005), 213.

The Board of Trade's instructions were that '[n]o Asiatic seaman or other person of apparently foreign origin should be regarded as exempt unless he produces a certificate of nationality, a birth certificate or other official certificate'.[19] Such certificates were not issued in most of the countries from which non-white British seamen came and so non-European seamen were generally required to take the test.

After 1918 the British government's policies with regard to racial discrimination were to become more explicit with the Special Restriction (Coloured Alien Seamen) Order of 1925. The order allowed the Home Office to exclude non-white or 'coloured' seamen from Britain.[20]

These attempts to exclude non-white British subjects and aliens who were believed to be unassimilable would become critical to post-World War II debates about immigration. However, in our period, the concept of citizenship generally was used not as a synonym for nationality, but rather referred to claims for and acquisition of political rights, and in discussions concerning obligations to the imperial nation, to which we now turn.

POLITICAL CITIZENSHIP AND THE EXPANSION OF THE SUFFRAGE BEFORE WORLD WAR I

Debates about franchise extension between 1867 and 1884 focused primarily upon the respectable and independent working men, the core of whom were married householders or single men with sufficient income to pay substantial rent as lodgers. Cumulatively the Second and Third Reform Acts enfranchised only about 60 per cent of adult men. After 1884–5 debates about suffrage within and without parliament largely focused on the vital issue of enfranchising women. Further reform of the parliamentary franchise for men living in the metropole became a much less visible issue from the 1880s: those men excluded were generally the unorganised and politically unrepresented – sons living at home, lodgers in humble dwellings, those men who were residentially mobile including soldiers living in barracks.

Changes in the franchise in the metropole had an imperial dimension, notably in the germination of nationalist politics in India. The year 1885 was not only the year that the male franchise was extended to householders in the counties of Britain, but also saw the founding of the Indian

---

[19] *Ibid.*, 164.
[20] Laura Tabili, *'We Ask for British Justice': Workers and Racial Difference in Late Imperial Britain* (Ithaca, 1994), 114.

National Congress. While in its early years the rhetoric of its leaders was painfully conciliatory towards British rule in the subcontinent, Congress politicians in the period prior to World War I emphasised the desirability of some limited form of representative government. As W. C. Bonnerjee put it in his presidential address to the first Congress meeting held in Bombay in 1885: 'All that they desired was that the basis of the government should be widened and that the people should have their proper and legitimate share in it.'[21]

More pointedly George Yule, the first non-Indian president and revered Calcutta businessman, addressed the Fourth Congress in Allahabad in 1888. He considered what the so-called 'qualifications' might be that Indians were supposed to attain in order to have the 'political institutions of the country ... placed on a wider basis'. He wondered if the British who talked of 'qualifications' were 'thinking of the qualifications of ordinary English constituencies at a somewhat more rudimentary stage of their development than they are to-day?' He suggested that India's rulers consult the Blue Book publications produced by the government to show the 'material, the moral, and the educational state of the country'. The books, he argued, indicate that 'there are large bodies of men in this country fitted in every way for the proper discharge of duties connected with a constitutional form of Government'.[22]

Yule went further, saying:

There are many thousands of Hindu, Mohammedan, Eurasian, Parsee and other gentlemen in the country who, if they were to transfer their persons to England for twelve months or more and pay certain rates, would be qualified to enjoy all the rights and privileges of British subjects. If you and I go to England we are qualified. If we return to India our character changes, and we are not qualified. In England we should be trusted citizens. In India well, the charitably-minded among our opponents say that we are incipient traitors! (Loud and prolonged cheers and laughter.)[23]

Yule used a potent symbol of racial solidarity to say that some form of

limited enfranchisement ... would draw into closer connection the two extreme branches of the Aryan race, the common subjects of the Queen-Empress; a measure which would unite England and India, not by the hard and brittle bonds of arbitrary rule which may snap in a moment, but by the flexible and more enduring ligaments of common interests promoted, common duties discharged, by means of a common service, chosen with some regard to the principle of representative government.[24]

---

[21] W. C. Bonnerjee (intro.), *Indian Politics* (Madras, 1898), part II, 5.
[22] Presidential address of Mr George Yule, Fourth Congress, Allahabad, 1888, in *ibid.*, 25–6.
[23] *Ibid.*, 7. [24] *Ibid.*, 31–2.

Four years after Yule had made his powerful speech for extending political rights within India, Dadabhai Naoroji, a Parsee, was elected as a Liberal MP for Finsbury Central in London, becoming the first Indian to serve in parliament.[25]

Further enfranchisement for British men was no longer a matter of anxious debate after 1885. The issue of women's suffrage, however, had emerged in the 1860s and persisted with increasing vehemence thereafter. Although from 1870 women in Britain were granted the rights of local political participation, their attempts to gain the parliamentary suffrage were continually rebuffed.

Prior to the turn of the twentieth century and the South African War some suffragists adapted not only classic liberalism's arguments about rights and equality, but also stressed duty, civic virtue and the value of political participation for individual development that was being articulated in 'popular liberalism' and elaborated later in New Liberalism. Significantly, Victorian feminists prioritised the nation and its needs in arguing for the emancipation of British women. They forged a discursive link between women's emancipation and Britain's moral progress as a nation, building upon imperialist ideas viewing empire 'as a means of moral self-elevation'.[26]

A key argument against suffrage for women was the so-called 'physical force argument'. Thus F. E. Smith maintained in the suffrage debate in July 1910: 'Votes are to swords exactly what bank notes are to gold – the one is effective only because the other is believed to be behind.'[27] Empire was critical to the 'antis' physical force argument in very direct ways. Although the overlap between imperialists and anti-suffragists was only partial, leading imperialists were major figures in anti-suffrage leagues.[28] One of the most prominent, Lord Curzon, maintained that granting votes to women would 'weaken Great Britain in the estimation of foreign powers' and would be 'a source of weakness in India'.[29] A. V. Dicey expressed a common fear about women becoming a majority of a greatly expanded electorate: 'Is this the body to whom any patriot is willing

---

[25] Naoroji was not the first Indian to stand for election in the metropole. See Rozina Visram, *Asians in Britain: 400 Years of History* (London, 2002), 130–5.

[26] Antoinette Burton, *Burdens of History: British Feminists, Indian Women and Imperial Culture, 1865–1915* (Chapel Hill and London, 1994), 41.

[27] Quoted in Brian Harrison, *Separate Spheres: The Opposition to Women's Suffrage in Britain* (London, 1978), 73.

[28] *Ibid.*, 75–6.

[29] NLOS Fawcett Archives Box 298 cited in Lisa Tickner, *The Spectacle of Women: Imagery of the Suffrage Campaign 1907–1914* (Chicago, 1988), 155.

deliberately to confide the government of England and the destinies of the British Empire?'[30]

Advocates for women's suffrage also appealed to imperialist and nationalist sentiments in their arguments for the vote.[31] Suffragists claimed that their campaign was international, with the Dominions leading the mother country.[32] Indeed Australian feminist Vida Goldstein came to London to lend support to the movement in Britain. As Angela Woollacott described her London visit in 1911, her stance was not that 'of a white colonial "coming to learn from the metropolitan power", but rather that of an experienced woman voter from a progressive country who could extend the benefits of her knowledge to her beleaguered English sisters'.[33] The antis, however, were quick to point out that using the Dominions' lead to argue for the suffrage in Britain was pointless. As a *Times* editorial put it in 1910: 'what value have the precedents of . . . our Dominions between the Pacific and the Indian Oceans when applied to an Empire such as ours'?[34]

Even more critically, Victorian feminists maintained that women's moral influence was significant for Britain's imperial duties.[35] In the late nineteenth century, the rhetoric of imperial feminists emphasised indigenous women's suffering and the need for reform and uplift, but did 'little to critique British colonialism or to distance The Cause from it'.[36] Millicent Fawcett wrote to *The Times* in January 1889, recalling 'the work of Englishwomen in India . . . who have given up their lives in order to lift up even by a little the lot of women in India. The touching affection and reverence felt by native women in India to the English women who have been thus their friends, so far from being likely to . . . "set Hindostan on fire" ' would be of great 'political value if periods of storm and stress should arise for our Indian Empire'.[37] This was a sharp rebuke to Goldwin Smith who had cautioned the public that enfranchised women might 'commence a political crusade against the Hindoo zenanas which would set Hindostan on fire'.[38]

---

[30] A. V. Dicey, letter to the editor of *The Times*, 23 March 1909, 6.

[31] Harrison, *Separate Spheres*, 76; Burton, *Burdens of History*, ch. 6.

[32] Christine Bolt, *The Ideas of British Suffragism* (London, 2000), 46.

[33] Angela Woollacott, *To Try Her Fortune in London: Australian Women, Colonialism, and Modernity* (Oxford, 2001), 116.

[34] *The Times*, 'The Women's Franchise Debate', 12 July 1910, 13.   [35] Burton, *Burdens*, 48.

[36] Antoinette Burton, '"States of Injury": Josephine Butler on Slavery, Citizenship, and the Boer War', in Ian Christopher Fletcher, Laura E. Nym Mayhall and Philippa Levine (eds), *Women's Suffrage in the British Empire: Citizenship, Nation and Race* (London and New York, 2000), 19.

[37] *Ibid.*

[38] Quoted by Millicent Garrett Fawcett in her letter to *The Times*, 4 January 1889, 5.

The Boer War was a crucial period for the suffrage movement. When the conflict started, pro-Boer War suffragists Millicent Fawcett and Josephine Butler argued that the suffrage should be expanded to those women who met property qualifications on the grounds of their service to the nation and empire.[39] The Boer War highlighted other arguments for the suffrage, most importantly for the militant suffrage movement, the relationship between consent of the governed and governmental legitimacy.[40] The issues of consent and the principle of resistance were central to suffrage militancy up until World War I, earning the respect of Indian nationalists including Gandhi until the militants engaged in violence.[41] Some Indian women resident in the metropole were members of the Women's Social and Political Union and were active as tax resisters in the Women's Tax Resistance League founded in 1909, an offshoot of the Women's Freedom League.[42] The theme of 'no taxation without representation' was also one central to leaders of the early Indian National Congress as it was to Henry Sylvester Williams, a founder of the Pan-African Conference.[43] Although the principle of resistance continued to be a feature of some militants' understanding of citizenship during World War I, service to the nation and empire became critical to debates about franchise reform in the metropole and self-governance in India, to which we shall return.

GOOD CITIZENSHIP

From the 1880s the term 'citizenship' was increasingly used in public debate and discussion to speak of duties that individuals owed to their communities, the nation and the Empire. In the context of the expansion of the suffrage, 'New Imperialism' and the spread of militarism, patriotic leagues, religious associations, educationalists and youth groups became preoccupied with 'good citizenship', a concern which ran across the political spectrum.[44]

The values of good citizenship were most prominent in discussions about educating the country's youth in the years between the mid-1880s and 1914. As Mangan argues, 'the concept of imperial service was honed

[39] Mayhall, *Militant Suffrage Movement*, 26. [40] *Ibid.* [41] Visram, *Asians in Britain*, 162.
[42] *Ibid.*, 163–8.
[43] See, for example, Romesh C. Dutt, 'Indian Aspirations Under British Rule', in Bonnerjee, *Indian Politics*, 49–58. On Williams and the Pan-African Conference, see Jonathan Schneer, *London 1900: The Imperial Metropolis* (New Haven and London, 1999), 218. See also Schneer's discussion of the British Committee for the Indian National Congress, 188–202.
[44] Bernard Shaw (ed.), *Fabianism and the Empire: A Manifesto by the Fabian Society* (London, 1900), 88–90.

and rehoned by public school masters' and 'the beau ideal was the warrior and the ultimate glory, sacrificial'.[45] In an address, 'Eton and the Empire', at the school in November 1890, Geoffrey Drage, an 'old boy', ended his speech with a clarion call:

Strive to be ready when the call shall come, to whatever duty, to whatever sacrifice, in whatever part of Her Majesty's dominions. For you shall leave father and mother and wife, and children for your Queen, your country or your faith. You shall conquer and rule others as you have learnt to conquer and rule yourselves.[46]

Such addresses were symptomatic of a culture which was increasingly militaristic (although not without substantial opposition), and in which the association between militarism, empire and citizenship lent a decidedly masculinist tone to the language of citizenship.[47] This was evident in magazines for middle-class boys that equated citizenship with patriotism,[48] while similar themes coloured children's books and magazines.[49]

It was not just public schools that were concerned with empire and citizenship. From the 1880s empire was also stressed in state schools. The new voter, as Joseph Bristow has argued, 'had to be trained not only to read the right things ... but he had also to meet the demands of becoming a responsible citizen. Imperialism made the boy into an aggrandized subject – British born and bred with the future of the world lying upon his shoulders.'[50] In 1886, Freeman Wills expressed the importance of education about empire and citizenship for those boys, who might now as adults be able to vote: 'These are the future electors who ... ought to be educated with a view to the power they will wield ... He cannot, with safety to the empire, be allowed to be so ignorant as to be unfit for his political trust, like a loose ballast in a vessel, liable, in any agitation that may arise, to roll from side to side and so destroy national stability.'[51]

---

[45] J. A. Mangan, 'Images of Empire in the Late Victorian Public School', *Journal of Educational Administration and History*, 12 (1) (1980), 37.

[46] Geoffrey Drage, *Eton and the Empire: An Address* (Eton, 1890), 39–40.

[47] Among others, see Kennedy, *Britain and Empire*, 26.

[48] Robert H. MacDonald, 'Reproducing the Middle-Class Boy: From Purity to Patriotism in the Boys' Magazines, 1892–1914', *Journal of Contemporary History*, 24 (3) (1989), 519–39; Kelly Boyd, *Manliness and the Boys' Story Paper in Britian: A Cultural History, 1855–1940* (Basingstoke, 2003).

[49] Kathryn Castle, *Britannia's Children: Reading Colonialism Through Children's Books and Magazines* (Manchester, 1996); Jeffrey Richards (ed.), *Imperialism and Juvenile Literature* (Manchester, 1989).

[50] Joseph Bristow, *Empire Boys: Adventures in a Man's World* (London, 1991), 19.

[51] Quoted in *ibid.*, 19. See Freeman Wills, 'Recreative Evening Schools', *The Nineteenth Century*, 20 (1886), 133. See also, for example, R. S. S. Baden-Powell, *Scouting for Boys: A Handbook for Instruction in Good Citizenship*, rev. edn (London, 1908), 262–3.

Imperial nationalism infused elementary education in England from the 1880s.[52] Books written on teaching methods advocated the importance of teaching history so as to inculcate 'patriotism and good citizenship . . . as well as . . . moral training'.[53] An array of voluntary associations, such as the Victoria League, the Navy League and the League of Empire, actively promoted and sponsored the publication of texts for elementary and secondary schools that would give students knowledge of the Empire and foster a sense of citizenly duty to the imperial nation.[54] Even if school boards cautioned teachers not to adopt overtly political and/or ideological texts – and some teachers were opposed to blatantly imperialist ideas – textbooks and readers generally were deeply engaged with imperialist ideas.[55]

Youth groups, with the Boy Scout movement being the most important and popular, also stressed these virtues. The first edition of *Scouting for Boys* (1908) was subtitled, 'A Handbook for Instruction in Good Citizenship'. Martial virility exemplified by the movement's founder, Baden-Powell, the hero of Mafeking, was central to the image of Scouting, although Baden-Powell himself attempted to distance his movement from the contemporaneous debates about the military training of youth.[56] The movement grew rapidly in the years before World War I, offering in its initial years an ideology that was 'conservative and defensive, seeking to find in patriotism and imperialism the cure for an apparently disintegrating society . . . Its orientation was aggressively masculine, its mission to save boys from the sapping habits of domestic and urban life.'[57] Baden-Powell also founded the Girl Guides Association in 1909 to respond to the need to train girls to be responsible mothers in England and in the Empire, but until World War I its popularity paled when contrasted with the Boy Scouts.[58]

While the main thrust of education and training for citizenship was aimed at young children, especially boys, voluntary associations concerned

---

[52] Stephen Heathorn, *For Home, Country, and Race: Constructing Gender, Class, and Englishness in the Elementary School, 1880–1914* (Toronto, 2000).

[53] John Mackenzie, *Propaganda and Empire* (Manchester, 1986), 177. For an insightful discussion of English elementary education, see Pamela Horn, 'English Elementary Education and the Growth of the Imperial Ideal: 1880–1914', in J. A. Mangan (ed.), *'Benefits Bestowed'? Education and British Imperialism* (Manchester, 1988), 39–55.

[54] Mackenzie, *Propaganda and Empire*, ch. 6.   [55] Heathorn, *For Home*, esp. 205–18.

[56] Bristow, *Empire Boys*, 177.

[57] Robert H. MacDonald, *Sons of the Empire: The Frontier and the Boy Scout Movement, 1890–1918* (Toronto, 2003), 8.

[58] Allen Warren, '"Mothers for the Empire"? The Girl Guides Association in Britain, 1909–1939', in J. A. Mangan (ed.), *Making Imperial Mentalities: Socialisation and British Imperialism* (Manchester, 1990), 101.

with education attempted to reach adults through, for instance, Frederick Swann's text, *English Citizenship* (1913), used in education classes held for soldiers and written with 'older pupils' in mind or through Violet Markham's work for the Victoria League, lecturing about empire to 'working men in the North of England'.[59]

These preoccupations with the inculcation of good citizenship among boys and men were connected to wider concerns within the context of the Boer War and after. There was a melding together of a concern with empire, a din about national efficiency and a challenge to gender relations embodied in the suffrage movement.

There developed a new focus on the bodies of the working class and the poor amid fears of physical and 'racial' degeneration and of the fitness of potential recruits to the military. Further, there was an elaboration of social policies and ideas of welfare that began to generate ideas about social rights.[60] The Liberal reforms of 1906–14 carried the idea of benefits commensurate with the 'contributions' of individuals and groups to the society. They were bounded by a concern with distinctions within the male working class, the male breadwinner, and an effective demarcation between 'native citizens' who might be entitled to support and 'aliens' who were to be excluded.[61]

But if, at this period, men were to be physically trained and morally educated to stave off fears of 'degeneration', it was particularly maternity that became central. Fears of degeneration were tied to expectations of reforming mothers who would fulfil their duties to the imperial nation. After the Boer War women were to be imperial mothers, just as men were to be imperial soldiers,[62] which was reflected in a 'domestic' bias in the curriculum for elementary schoolgirls, evident as early as 1905 in the Board of Education's assertion that 'girls must ... be taught to set a high value on the housewife's position'.[63]

---

[59] Violet Markham to Hilda Cashmore, 1 October 1911, repr. in Violet Markham, *Duty and Citizenship: The Correspondence and Political Papers of Violet Markham, 1896–1953*, ed. Helen Jones (London, 1994), 40.

[60] These ideas and practices clearly prefigure the more elaborate articulations of 'social citizenship' and the elaboration of the 'social democratic state' from the First World War onwards. Cf. for instance the discussion in Susan Pedersen, 'Gender, Welfare, and Citizenship in Britain During the Great War', *American Historical Review*, 95 (1990), 983–1006. But this is a theme which we cannot pursue here.

[61] We are thinking here of the recommendations of the Report of the Inter-Departmental Committee on Physical Deterioration (1904) and the subsequent policies introduced under the Liberals (1906–14), including national insurance (1911), free school meals (1906) and grants for maternal and child welfare. In the Old Age Pensions Act (1908), for example, pensions were to be denied to 'aliens or the wives of aliens'.

[62] Anna Davin, 'Imperialism and Motherhood', *History Workshop Journal*, 5 (1978), 9–65.

[63] Horn, 'English Elementary Education', 52.

While there certainly were differences in the way that 'good citizenship' was articulated, the omnipresence of the term reflects a major shift in how the concept of citizenship was understood. It was part and parcel of a transformation in ideas about the state, homed in on from radically different perspectives as the source of the imperial nation's 'common good'.

CITIZENSHIP AND EMPIRE, 1914—1928

During the First World War the concept of 'good citizenship' meant service to the nation. In the context of the horrific loss of life the consequences of this emphasis were profound. In 1918, manhood suffrage became universal and the vote was extended to women over thirty who, on their own, were entitled to vote in local government elections, or were married to men who were so entitled. Whereas militant suffragists had emphasised the notion of 'consent' in arguing for the suffrage after the Boer War, many of them as well as others in the larger movement refashioned the idea of service. They publicly demonstrated their patriotism emphasising their own sacrifices for the war effort. Christabel and Emmeline Pankhurst along with Millicent Fawcett and other suffragists, using 'the spectacle of female patriotism that featured a condemnation of pacifist male cowardice, disrupted a notion of citizenship based on manhood alone'.[64] The prominence in wartime culture of the notions of service and sacrifice, including mothers sacrificing sons and the war service of those soldier-sons who before 1918 would have been excluded from the vote because of residency requirements, led to a widespread transformation of political sensibility and a massive expansion of the electorate. As Gullace has argued, 'Instead of vindicating the "physical force" argument, war ironically revealed its two fundamental flaws: first, that not all men able to bear arms were willing to do so and, second, that women's contribution to making war was far from negligible.'[65]

Although the vote for women's suffrage in both Houses of Parliament was overwhelmingly positive, diehard antis continued to press the idea that women were unfit to participate in the imperial parliament.[66] In the House of Lords debate on 9 June 1918, which approved the clause for women's suffrage by a large majority, the dedicated anti, Earl Loreburn, argued that he wouldn't object to women's suffrage if parliament only

---

[64] Nicoletta F. Gullace, 'The Blood of Our Sons': Men, Women, and the Renegotiation of British Citizenship During the Great War (New York, 2002), 6.
[65] Ibid., 9.
[66] Harold L. Smith, The British Women's Suffrage Campaign, 1866–1928 (London, 1998), 68.

dealt with domestic issues, but the House of Commons decided issues relating to Crown colonies and India. The Earl asked rhetorically, 'was it desirable in the interest of the Empire that feminine influence should be very powerful at once, and most probably predominant in the very near future of questions of peace and war?'[67] Lord Crewe, in his response to such arguments and in supporting the clause for women's suffrage, 'recalled that women had taken a far greater share in the service of the nation and the Empire during the war than anybody had previously thought possible'.[68] While suffragists like Millicent Fawcett had always touted women's positive role in the Empire as a reason for their being deserving of the suffrage, people such as Lord Crewe became convinced by the dramatic enactments of patriotism, love of country and loyalty to the Empire that suffragists had displayed during the war.[69]

Indian nationalists in Britain and in India were keenly interested in the debates on the Women's Suffrage clause of the Representation of the People Bill. The British Committee for the Indian National Congress, in its weekly newspaper published in London, *India*, commented on Tory MP Sir Frederick Banbury's rejection of the clause in a 1917 debate because of the 'effect which would be produced upon the Oriental mind by the admission of women to the franchise'. While the MP argued that 'Orientals would distrust government by women', *India* retorted, 'We do not know what authority [he] has for his statement ... But we can assure him that Indians will most certainly want to know why men in India are to be denied a "right" which is conceded to women in England.'[70]

Importantly, in the special session of the Indian National Congress held in Bombay in 1918 to formulate demands for Home Rule, Mrs Sarojini Naidu introduced Resolution VIII, Women's Franchise. The speech by Shrimati Ansuya Sarabar seconding the resolution is especially relevant to this essay:

If women's rights as citizens of this land ... are not granted now, the time will surely come when they will secure them by their own efforts. You cannot but be acquainted with the struggle of the English women for justice. Such a struggle is not wanted in this country ... You are all assembled here to preserve your self-respect, to free yourselves from the fetters of dependency. You have fully realized what it is to submit to injustice and tyranny ... I, therefore ask you – my countrymen, whether you will deny to your sisters the rights you demand for yourselves? India's heart is not England's.[71]

---

[67] As reported in *The Times*, 10 January 1918, 10.   [68] *Ibid.*, 7.
[69] This point is made forcefully by Gullace, '*Blood of Our Sons*', 188–91.
[70] *India*, 22 June 1917, 236.
[71] Report of the Special Session of the Indian National Congress, Bombay 29 August–1 September 1918, reprinted in K. C. Sankarakrishna (ed.), *India's Demands for Home Rule* (Madras, 1918).

A majority carried the resolution.

Wartime propaganda in Britain had especially highlighted imperial contributions and the cooperation of the dependencies and the Dominions in the war effort. Books, pamphlets and speeches praised the contributions of the various members of the Empire, doing so in ways that underscored Great Britain's benevolence and predicting that as a consequence of the war, the Empire would be made stronger. Basil Mathews, writing in 1917, for example, spoke of 'the flaming response of a world-wide Empire to the need of the Mother-country. The secret of the rally ... lies hidden in that word "Mother-country". Our men from the dominions, the Crown Colonies, and the Dependency of India are sons, not subjects of the Home-land.'[72] Sir Harry H. Johnston, former First Commissioner and Consul General in British Central Africa, wrote in the same year of 'the principle that the dark-skinned races of every degree of civilization have come to the assistance of the (British and Belgian and French) White peoples *because* our recent treatment of them has, in the main, won their gratitude'.[73] He also interestingly insisted that Great Britain would have an obligation, after the war, 'to recognize and affirm his [the black man's] rights as a citizen of the Empire'.[74]

While the war may have been a high point of imperial unity, it also was a turning point in British imperial relations.[75] As a consequence of their wartime contributions, the Dominions and colonies began 'to claim with greater vigour new rights and privileges'.[76] Thus at the thirty-first meeting of the Indian National Congress, Pandit Jagat Narain, Chairman of the Reception Committee, argued that India should have the same status as the Dominions and that Britain should announce that 'Self-Governing India is the goal of her policy and grant us a substantial instalment of reform after the war, as a step towards that goal'.[77] He argued:

[T]he assistance rendered by India during the War has fired her imagination ... She has acquired a new spirit of self-reliance and dignity, and

---

[72] Basil Mathews, *Three Years' War for Peace* (London, 1917), 37.

[73] Sir Harry H. Johnston, GCMG, *The Black Man's Part in the War* (London, 1917), 9–10.

[74] *Ibid.*, 9.

[75] On wartime tensions within the Empire see Stephen Constantine, Maurice W. Kirby and Mary B. Rose (eds.), *The First World War in British History* (London, 1995), 264–70.

[76] Quote from George Robb, *British Culture and the First World War* (Basingstoke, 2002), 6. See also Robert Holland, 'The British Empire and the Great War, 1914–1918', in Wm. Roger Louis (ed.), *The Oxford History of the British Empire*, 5 vols. (Oxford, 1998–9), vol. IV: *The Twentieth Century*, ed. Judith M. Brown and Wm. Roger Louis (1999), 114–37; Judith M. Brown, 'India', in *ibid.*, 421–46, esp. 429–30. Especially relevant and helpful on this is Richard Smith, *Jamaican Volunteers in the First World War: Race, Masculinity and the Development of National Consciousness* (Manchester, 2004).

[77] Quoted in Sankarakrishna, *India's Demands*, 6.

realised her own worth by coming to Britain's help at a critical juncture. The battlefields of Europe, Africa and Asia bear witness to the fighting qualities of her sons, and their deeds of heroism, written in characters of blood, have thrilled every Indian heart.[78]

Although the demands for representative institutions in India had grown louder in the years just prior to the war, the war accelerated their pace and the principle of Home Rule was first articulated by Congress in 1914.[79] Following the very limited reforms of the Government of India Act of 1919 and the Rowlatt Bill curtailing civil liberties, there was widespread disaffection and protest, including the Amritsar massacre and the beginnings of Gandhi's satyagraha movement in Bombay.[80]

Predictably, one response to the expansion of the electorate in the metropole was once again to insist that voters needed to be educated for citizenship, and that with rights came duties: 'democracy meant active participation in citizenship and that in consequence adult education was not a luxury, but a permanent national necessity inseparable from citizenship, and should be both permanent and life long'.[81]

The message sounds similar to the pre-war one. Indeed, many of the same history texts that had been taught in schools as part of the effort to teach citizenship and imperial responsibility continued to be used. But there was a shift in the larger political culture of the time that affected how empire was represented and how the meanings of citizenship were articulated. Dominating public and political culture in the postwar years was the Russian Revolution and rising fears of Bolshevism in the metropole and in the Empire which shifted the framework in which empire was understood.

Social divisiveness and rising nationalism in India were widely feared to be inspired by communists.[82] This fear was critical to reshaping the meanings of citizenship. The Primrose League couched its mission to keep women 'on ... the side of Imperial thought and Imperial Action' within the horror it called 'the Bolshevik Bacillus'.[83] The British Empire

---

[78] *Ibid.*, 4–5.

[79] Harish P. Kaushik, *Indian National Congress in England* (Delhi, 1991), 98.

[80] Derek Sayer, 'British Reaction to the Amritsar Massacre 1919–1920', *Past and Present*, 131 (1991), 135.

[81] Ministry of Reconstruction: *Adult Education Committee: Final Report*, PP1919 (321) XXVIII, 453.

[82] The Indian Political Intelligence files held in the Oriental and India Office Collections, British Library, contain extensive material bearing on this. For a guide see A. J. Farrington (ed.), *Indian Political Intelligence (IPI) Files, 1912–1950* (London, 2000), available at http://www.idc.nl/pdf/335_guide.pdf.

[83] 'The Bolshevik Bacillus', *Primrose League Gazette*, 26 No. 106 (August 1918), 4, cited in Matthew Hendley, 'Constructing the Citizen: The Primrose League and the Definition of Citizenship in the Age of Mass Democracy in Britain, 1918–1928', *Journal of the Canadian Historical Association*, 7 (1996), 136.

Union, founded in 1915 originally named the Anti-German Union, shifted its focus to the Labour Party and the threat of socialism, issuing a series of pamphlets from 1918 denouncing the party as an 'internal peril' and lambasting Russia.[84] As they put it in 1928, they opposed 'all those who by word or deed do anything against the interests of the British Empire – Our Motherland – by ... undermining the loyalty of our people, by fomenting and encouraging strikes or sedition, by attempting to overthrow the Constitution of the country'.[85]

In the tumultuous years of the immediate postwar period contemporary perception focused on fears 'that the barbarism of war had left an indelible mark on British society'.[86] As a consequence, Jon Lawrence suggests, by 1921 militarism 'had been banished to the margins of political life'.[87]

Some historians have argued that along with the fading of militarism, the late Victorian and Edwardian imperialist creed fell out of favour as it became 'identified with war and came under attack from the growing pacifist element in British society'.[88] Additionally, a refurbished construction of masculinity came into prominence – one with echoes of the mid-nineteenth-century middle-class manly ideal that emphasised domesticity. This new home-loving, family-oriented quintessentially middle-class and conservative vision of masculinity promised to heal the dislocations of war and return the nation to normalcy.[89]

A new or modified discourse of masculine citizenship centred on a reimagined ideal of respectable manliness and focused on the necessity of behaving in a 'constitutional' manner and exercising 'responsible' citizenship. This revised version of masculine citizenship was constructed in opposition to those 'unconstitutional' working-class militants protesting against unemployment or engaged in events such as the General Strike of 1926. This conception of masculine citizenship was promulgated with extraordinary effectiveness by Stanley Baldwin, Conservative Prime Minister for much of the period, who continually reminded his audiences of the disaster of war and the need to avert conflict and 'elided in his

---

[84] For the World War I period, see Panikos Panayi, 'The British Empire Union in the First World War', in Tony Kushner and Kenneth Lunn (eds.), *The Politics of Marginality: Race, the Radical Right and Minorities in Twentieth Century Britain* (London, 1990), 113–30.

[85] British Empire Union, *Annual Report, 1928*, 51.

[86] Jon Lawrence, 'Forging a Peaceable Kingdom: War, Violence and the Fear of Brutalization in Post First World War Britain', *Journal of Modern History*, 75 (2004), 557–89, quotation at 558.

[87] *Ibid.*, 557.

[88] James G. Greenlee, *Education and Imperial Unity, 1901–1926* (New York and London, 1987), 178.

[89] Alison Light, *Forever England: Femininity, Literature and Conservatism Between the Wars* (London, 1991).

speeches the violence of the trenches with the violence of domestic social conflict'.[90]

Along with his focus on 'constitutionalism', Baldwin underscored the equation between citizenship and service that had been reinvigorated during the war, especially when he spoke of the Empire. Men's responsibility lay in helping to spread 'the peoples of our Empire, the ideals of our Empire, the trade of our Empire from one side of the world to the other'.[91] He tied this to a theme that peppered his speeches and radio broadcasts – the Englishman's 'love of home . . . that makes our race seek its new home in the Dominions overseas . . . They go overseas, and they take with them what they learned at home: Love of justice, love of truth, and the broad humanity that are so characteristic of English people.'[92]

Baldwin's emphasis on service and respectful behaviour was echoed in publications such as *Scouting for Boys*. In the twelfth edition of the book, published in 1926, Baden-Powell emphasised that the aim of Scout training was to 'replace Self with Service, to make the lads . . . efficient, morally and physically, with the object of using that efficiency for the service of the community . . . I don't mean by this the mere soldiering and sailoring services; we have no military aim or practice in our movement; but I mean the ideals of service for their fellow-men.'[93]

According to Williamson, Baldwin's pronouncements on empire had three goals: to reinforce the aim of domestic stabilisation and consolidate support for the Conservative Party; to persuade voters to support the continuance of empire, being concerned that postwar popular prejudice might mount against imperial defence; and to help convince the Dominions and India that their future lay with the Empire.[94] With the formal bonds of empire loosening, Baldwin found it necessary to distance himself and his party from an 'imperialist assertiveness'. Empire was no longer to be associated with militarism and aggression.[95]

When Baldwin spoke of empire he generally referred to the white, self-governing Dominions, and during the 1920s he repeatedly expressed his

---

[90] Bill Schwarz, 'The Language of Constitutionalism: Baldwinite Conservatism', in *Formations of Nation and People* (London, 1984), 7.

[91] Stanley Baldwin, 'Democracy and the Spirit of Service' (speech given at Albert Hall, 4 December 1924), in *On England* (London, 1926), 84.

[92] Stanley Baldwin, 'On England and the West' (speech at the annual dinner of the Royal Society of St George, 6 May 1924), in *On England*, 8.

[93] R. Baden-Powell, *Scouting for Boys*, 12th edn (London, 1926), 5–6.

[94] Philip Williamson, *Stanley Baldwin: Conservative Leadership and National Values* (Cambridge, 1999), 262–3.

[95] *Ibid.*, 264.

desire for a 'unified Empire – with one home and one people' with 'one citizenship'.[96] In his Empire Day broadcast of 1927 he said, speaking of the Dominions, 'we must devote our best energies in the years to come ... to make our unity such a reality that men and women regard the Empire as one, and that it may become possible for them to move within its bounds to New Zealand, to Australia, to South Africa, to Canada, as freely as from Glasgow to London or Bristol to Newcastle'.[97] Then he spoke of the 'direct responsibilities' that the British had for the 'Colonies, Protectorates, and Mandated Territories', and with regard to India talked about Britain's policy of 'progressive realization of responsible Government'.[98] In closing he talked of the ethic of service: 'In a world still suffering from the shock of war, the British Empire stands firm as a great force for good ... It invites and requires some service of us all.'[99]

Although certainly trade within the Empire had been central to debates in the late Victorian and Edwardian era with Chamberlain's Free Trade Association, 'buying empire' without a change in tariff laws became a major focus of imperial advocates both in and out of government in the 1920s leading to the establishment of the Empire Marketing Board in 1926.

The Primrose League, while supporting Britain's imperial role, increasingly focused its efforts on encouraging women to purchase empire products. The British citizen was someone who supported the Empire as a citizen-consumer,[100] a theme echoed by the British Women's Patriotic League that established in 1922 an annual Empire Shopping Week to encourage trade with the Dominions.

Perhaps the most important event bringing the Empire home in these years was the 1924 Wembley British Empire Exhibition. Over twenty-seven million people visited it – equivalent to over half the British population – with some going several times. It was staged again in 1925. According to Denis Judd, the exhibition was partly 'a celebration of the imperial achievement, partly a gigantic advertisement for the Empire ... and partly an exercise in reassurance'.[101] As he put it, it was staged to 'promote and reinterpret the imperial ideal amid the fresh challenges of the postwar world'.[102] The organisers promoted the 'Fellowship of the British Empire Exhibition' which, like a museum

---

[96] *Ibid.*, 261, 272.

[97] Stanley Baldwin, 'The Privilege of Empire' (Empire Day Broadcast, 1927), in *Our Inheritance: Speeches and Addresses* (London, 1928), 68–9.

[98] *Ibid.*, 70–1.   [99] *Ibid.*, 71.   [100] Kennedy, *Britain and Empire*, 5.

[101] Denis Judd, *Empire: The British Imperial Experience, from 1765 to the Present* (London, 1996), 275.

[102] *Ibid.*, 276.

membership, allowed members unlimited access to the exhibition for its duration. With the proceeds from the Fellowships being used for imperial education, membership was advertised as 'a certificate of active citizenship, neither more nor less. It [the Fellowship] proclaims the men and women who realise that the British heritage was not won and cannot be sustained without effort, and this effort must not be limited to the few who in every generation sacrifice their lives for the Empire.'[103]

Importantly, the displays of imperial products, like those in department stores, were addressed to women, especially to middle-class women, as consumers.[104] Men at the exhibition were specifically addressed in the Palace of Engineering and His Majesty's Government Building as builders and developers of the Empire. The exhibition also advertised the raw materials produced in the Empire for British manufacturing firms and, like a gigantic and spectacular Empire Shopping Week, it promoted food and consumer products from Great Britain and the Empire to British women.[105]

The themes of women citizens as consumers of empire and men as producers and builders of empire were also to shape the promotional material produced by the Empire Marketing Board established in 1926. Chaired by Colonial Secretary Leo Amery, it aimed 'to project an image of the British Empire to the general public in order to stimulate empire trade'.[106] The Board was disbanded in 1933 after Britain and the Dominions adopted a tariff-driven 'imperial preference' scheme. Until then its primary efforts had been educational, producing material for schools along with posters, films and radio broadcasts for the general public, and it organised Empire Shopping Weeks in over two hundred towns.[107] The posters put out by the EMB depicted men as 'Empire Builders' and showed women buying empire products, especially food.[108] The idea of women as citizen-consumers was spread further by the BBC's

---

[103] 1924 *Official Guide*, 105 cited in Emily Klancher, 'Consuming the British Empire at the Wembley Exhibition, 1924–1925' (unpublished paper, 2004).

[104] Interestingly, Judith Walkowitz has suggested that the first department stores in London emulated colonial exhibitions. Judith Walkowitz, *City of Dreadful Delight: Narratives of Sexual Danger in Late Victorian London* (Chicago, 1992), 48.

[105] We are indebted to Emily Klancher for permitting us to draw from her as yet unpublished work.

[106] David Meredith, 'Imperial Images: The Empire Marketing Board, 1926–32', *History Today*, 37 (1987), 3.

[107] For a brief discussion of the EMB, see Thomas G. August, *The Selling of the Empire: British and French Imperialist Propaganda, 1890–1940* (Westport, CT and London, 1985), esp. 74–9.

[108] Stephen Constantine, '"Bringing the Empire Alive": The Empire Marketing Board and Imperial Propaganda, 1926–33', in J. M. MacKenzie (ed.), *Imperialism and Popular Culture* (Manchester, 1986), ch. 9; Stephen Constantine, *Buy and Build: The Advertising Posters of the Empire Marketing Board* (London, 1986).

Household Talks in 1928 in collaboration with the EMB to encourage and instruct women in the use of empire materials and goods. These Talks were published with notes by the EMB, proclaiming 'Empire buying offers to us all an opportunity of national service. To us and to our fellow-citizens overseas the task is entrusted of securing the happiness and prosperity of a quarter of the world.'[109]

While women were being drawn into the project of imperial consumption, the mid-1920s witnessed a revival of pre-war agitation for universal suffrage on an equal basis for women and men although a variety of feminist groups had been active since 1918. Lady Rhondda's Equal Political Rights Demonstration Committee organised a mass march from the Embankment and rally in Hyde Park on 2 July 1926 with 3,500 women participating while Mrs Eliott Lynn flew over the marchers in an aeroplane.[110] The press portrayed it as a revival of the spirit of pre-war militancy.[111]

A primary concern of those who were chary of extending the suffrage to women over twenty-one was that women would be a significant majority of the electorate. While there was no large-scale opposition to equalising the franchise in the bill's second reading of 1928, Conservatives had earlier expressed considerable hostility to adding younger women to the registers. Anxiety that women, as a majority of voters, would 'swamp' the elections became entangled in some sectors of public opinion with the threat of socialism.[112] But it was the idea that women would be a majority of electors that was at the basis of the opposition to the 1928 franchise bill, especially as women rather than men would determine the fate of the Empire. As the Tory MP, Colonel Applin, said:

We are governing a great Empire ... and that Empire comprises not only our ... Dominions, but the largest Mohammedan population in the world. We are the greatest Mohammedan power in the world ... What will be the effect on the great Mohammedan population of the world of granting the franchise in this country – the governing country – to a majority of 2,200,000 women over men? [*Laughter*] ... We are trying to give India Home Rule, but we are asking the people not to be in a hurry ... If this Bill becomes law, what a weapon we will put into the hands of the agitators if we tell the Hindus of India that they are to be ruled by a majority of women![113]

[109] *BBC Household Talks, 1928: Extracts ... with Notes by the Empire Marketing Board* (London, 1929), 172.
[110] Johanna Alberti, ' "A Symbol and a Key": The Suffrage Movement in Britain, 1918–1928', in June Purvis and Sandra Stanley Holton (eds), *Votes for Women* (London, 2000), 283.
[111] Smith, *British Women's Suffrage*, 77.   [112] Alberti, 'A Symbol', 274.
[113] *Parliamentary Debates*, 5th ser., vol. CCXV, Representation of the People (Equal Franchise) Bill (2nd reading), col. 1391, 29 March 1928.

The Labour MP Ellen Wilkinson responded:

really, are British women to be kept down to the level of any backward races that happen to be under the British Crown? Mohammedans may not be backward culturally, but they are certainly backward, or were backward – they have come along astonishingly in the last year or two – in their treatment of women, and we hope that the example set in this country will bring them along still more ... India was governed with apparently great success by a woman ruler, namely the late Queen Victoria, and, as a matter of fact, in every Province of India to-day, women already have the vote.[114]

At the end of the debate Stanley Baldwin encouraged parliament 'to fall in line with Australia, Canada, New Zealand and the United States of America, to mention only the English-speaking countries' because women's part in the war made it seem 'to be something almost ridiculous in refusing her [woman's] claim to equal citizenship'.[115] There were but ten votes opposing the bill. Universal suffrage was now a fact.

The domestic debates about citizenship did not, of course, end with the granting of universal suffrage. The rights and duties of citizens were of primary concern to political parties and others in the 1930s and beyond.[116] At the same time, Ellen Wilkinson's tortured response evokes themes which both reach back into the domestic debates about citizenship and look forward to later discourses. Here is an advocate of women's rights, the defender of the right to work for working-class men – she was associated above all with the Jarrow marches of the 1930s – and a leading figure in the claims of Labour to create a wider, more participatory citizenship within the nation. Yet her placing of 'Mohammedans' within a hierarchy of race in the context of a discussion of citizenship rights could only be possible because of the shifting terrain of discourses of race and nation, class and gender. Far from the expansion of citizenship being a more or less unproblematic widening of rights within Britain, the shaping of the meanings of citizenship was always, as we have shown in this paper, entwined with questions of empire.

---

[114] *Ibid.*, col. 1403.   [115] *Ibid.*, cols. 1472, 1474.

[116] See, e.g., The Labour Party, *The Citizen*, issued by the Party between March 1928 and August 1934 and, for Conservatism, Clarisse Berthezène, 'Creating Conservative Fabians: The Conservative Party, Political Education and the Founding of Ashridge College', *Past and Present*, 182 (2004), 211–40.

Select bibliography

Abrahams, Yvette, 'Images of Sara Bartman: Sexuality, Race and Gender in Early Nineteenth-Century Britain', in Ruth Roach Pierson and Nupur Chaudhuri, eds., *Nation, Empire, Colony: Historicizing Gender and Race* (Bloomington, 1998).

Achebe, Chinua, 'An Image of Africa: Racism in Conrad's *Heart of Darkness*', *Massachusetts Review*, 18 (1977).

Adi, Hakim, *West Africans in Britain, 1900–1960: Nationalism, Pan-Africanism and Communism* (London, 1998).

Adi, Hakim and Marika Sherwood, *Pan-African History: Political Figures from Africa and the Diaspora since 1787* (London, 2003).

Alberti, Johanna, *Beyond Suffrage: Feminists in War and Peace, 1914–1928* (Basingstoke, 1989).

Alexander, M. Jacqui and Chandra Talpede Mohanty, eds., *Feminist Genealogies, Colonial Legacies, Democratic Futures* (New York, 1997).

Alexander, Sally, ed., *Women's Fabian Tracts* (London, 1988).

Alexander, Ziggi and Audrey Dewjee, eds., *Wonderful Adventures of Mrs Seacole in Many Lands* (Bristol, 1984).

Ali, Yasmin, 'Muslim Women and the Politics of Ethnicity and Culture in Northern England', in Gita Sanghaza and Nira Yuval-Davis, eds., *Refusing Holy Orders: Women and Fundamentalism in Britain* (London, 1992).

Alloula, M., *The Colonial Harem* (Manchester, 1986).

Altick, Richard D., *The Shows of London* (Cambridge, 1978).

Anderson, David, *Histories of the Hanged: The Dirty War in Kenya and the End of Empire* (New York, 2005).

Anderson, Olive, 'Women Preachers in Mid-Victorian Britain: Some Reflexions on Feminism, Popular Religion and Social Change', *Historical Journal*, 12 (3) (1969).

Andrew, Donna, *Philanthropy and Police: London Charity in the Eighteenth Century* (Princeton, 1989).

Andrews, M. *The Acceptable Face of Feminism: The Women's Institute Movement* (London, 1997).

Appadurai, A., ed., *The Social Life of Things* (Cambridge, 1986).

Armitage, David, 'Greater Britain: A Useful Category of Historical Analysis?', *American Historical Review*, 104 (2) (1999).

The Ideological Origins of the British Empire (Cambridge, 2000).

Arnold, David, 'European Orphans and Vagrants in India in the Nineteenth Century', *Journal of Imperial and Commonwealth History*, 7 (1979).

'White Colonization and Labour in Nineteenth-Century India', *Journal of Imperial and Commonwealth History*, 11 (1983).

Auerbach, Jeffery, The Great Exhibition of 1851: A Nation on Display (New Haven, 1999).

August, Thomas G., The Selling of the Empire: British and French Imperialist Propaganda, 1890–1940 (London, 1985).

Austen, R. and W. Smith, 'Private Tooth Decay as Public Economic Virtue: The Slave-Sugar Triangle, Consumerism, and European Industrialisation', *Social Science History*, 14 (1990).

Ayandele, Emmanuel Ayankanmi, The Missionary Impact on Modern Nigeria, 1842–1914: A Political and Social Analysis (London, 1966).

Backhouse, Constance, Colour-coded: A Legal History of Racism in Canada, 1900–1950 (Toronto, 1999).

Ballantyne, Tony, Orientalism and Race: Aryanism in the British Empire (Basingstoke, 2002).

'The Sinews of Empire: Ireland, India and the Construction of British Colonial Knowledge', in McDonough, ed., *Was Ireland a Colony?*

Ballantyne, Tony and Antoinette Burton, eds., Bodies, Empires and World History (Durham, NC, 2005).

Ballhatchet, Kenneth, Race, Sex and Class Under the British Raj: Imperial Attitudes and Policies and their Critics, 1793–1905 (London, 1980).

Bank, A. 'Losing Faith in the Civilizing Mission: The Premature Decline of Humanitarian Liberalism at the Cape, 1840–60', in Daunton and Halpern, eds., *Empire and Others*.

Banton, Michael, The Coloured Quarter: Negro Immigrants in an English City (London, 1955).

'The Race Relations Problematic', *British Journal of Sociology*, 42 (1) (1991).

Barber, Ross, 'The Criminal Law Amendment Act of 1891 and the "Age of Consent" Issue in Queensland', *Australia and New Zealand Journal of Criminology*, 10 (1977).

Barratt Brown, Michael, After Imperialism (London, 1963).

Bartlett, Robert, The Making of Europe: Conquest, Colonization and Cultural Change, 950–1350 (Princeton, 1993).

Bassett, Michael, The State in New Zealand 1840–1984: Socialism without Doctrines? (Auckland, 1998).

Bayly, C. A., Indian Society and the Making of the British Empire (Cambridge, 1988).

Imperial Meridian: The British Empire and the World 1780–1830 (London, 1989).

The Birth of the Modern World, 1780–1914 (Oxford, 2004).

'The British and Indigenous Peoples, 1760–1860: Power, Perception and Identity', in Daunton and Halpern, eds., *Empire and Others*.

Bays, Daniel H. and Grant Wacker, eds., *The Foreign Missionary Enterprise at Home: Explorations in North American Cultural History* (Tuscaloosa and London, 2003).

Bean, Philip and Joy Melville, *Lost Children of the Empire* (London, 1989).

Bebbington, D. W., *The Nonconformist Conscience: Chapel and Politics, 1870–1914* (London, 1982).

Evangelicalism in Modern Britain: A History from the 1730s to the 1980s (London, 1989).

Belchem, John, 'English Working Class Radicals and the Irish 1815–50', in Swift and Gilley, eds., *The Irish in the Victorian City*.

'Nationalism, Republicanism and Exile: Irish Emigrants and the Revolution of 1848', *Past and Present*, 146 (1995).

Benson, J., *The Rise of Consumer Society in Britain 1880–1980* (London, 1994).

Berg, M. and H. Clifford, eds., *Consumers and Luxury: Consumer Cultures in Europe 1650–1850* (Manchester, 1999).

Berg, M. and E. Eger, eds., *Luxury in the Eighteenth Century* (London, 2002).

Berthezène, Clarisse, 'Creating Conservative Fabians: The Conservative Party, Political Education and the Founding of Ashridge College', *Past and Present*, 182 (2004).

Bhabha, Homi K., 'Dissemination: Time, Narrative and the Margins of the Modern State', in Bhabha, ed., *Nation and Narration* (London, 1990).

Bickers, Robert, *Empire Made Me: An Englishman Adrift in Shanghai* (London, 2003).

Billig, Michael, *Banal Nationalism* (London, 1995).

Birkett, Dea, *Mary Kingsley: Imperial Adventuress* (London, 1992).

Bivona, D., *Desire and Contradiction: Imperial Visions and Domestic Debates in Victorian Literature* (Manchester, 1990).

British Imperial Literature 1870–1940: Writing and the Administration of Empire (Cambridge, 1998).

Blackburn, Robin, *The Overthrow of Colonial Slavery, 1776–1848* (London, 1988).

Blakely, Brian, 'The Society for the Oversea Settlement of British Women and the Problems of Empire Settlement, 1917–1936', *Albion*, 20 (1988).

Bland, Lucy, 'White Women and Men of Colour: Miscegenation Fears in Britain After the Great War', *Gender and History*, 17 (1) (2005).

Blunt, Alison and Robyn Dowling, *Home* (London, 2005).

Bocock, R., *Consumption* (London, 1993).

Bolt, Christine, *The Ideas of British Suffragism* (London, 2000).

Victorian Attitudes to Race (London, 1971).

Boyce, George, 'British Conservative Opinion, the Ulster Question and the Partition of Ireland 1919–21', *Irish Historical Studies*, 17 (65) (1970).

Boyd, Kelly, *Manliness and the Boys' Story Paper in Britain: A Cultural History, 1855–1940* (Basingstoke, 2003).

Bradshaw, B., 'Nationalism and Historical Scholarship in Modern Ireland', in C. Brady, ed., *Interpreting Irish History: The Debate on Historical Revisionism 1938–1994* (Dublin, 1994).

Brandon, Ruth, *The New Women and the Old Men: Love, Sex and the Woman Question* (London, 1990).

Brantlinger, Patrick, *Rule of Darkness: British Literature and Imperialism* (Ithaca, 1988).

Dark Vanishings: Discourse on the Extinction of Primitive Races, 1800–1930 (Ithaca, 2003).

Brasted, H., 'Indian Nationalist Development and the Influence of Irish Home Rule, 1870–1886', *Modern Asian Journal of the Asiatic Society of Bangladesh*, 22 (1977).

Bressey, Caroline, 'Forgotten Histories: Three Stories of Black Girls from Barnardo's Victorian Archive', *Women's History Review*, 11 (3) (2002).

Brewer, John and Roy Porter, eds., *Consumption and the World of Goods* (London, 1993).

Bridge, Carl and Kent Fedorowich, eds., *The British World: Diaspora, Culture and Identity* (London, 2003).

Bristow, Joseph, *Empire Boys: Adventures in a Man's World* (London, 1991).

Brody, Jennifer DeVere, *Impossible Purities: Blackness, Femininity, and Victorian Culture* (Durham, NC, 1998).

Broeker, Galen, *Rural Disorder and Police Reform in Ireland, 1812–1836* (London, 1970).

Brown, Callum G., *Religion and Society in Scotland Since 1707* (Edinburgh, 1997).

Brown, Judith M., 'India', in Brown and Louis, eds., *The Oxford History of the British Empire*, vol. IV.

Brown, Judith M. and William Roger Louis, eds., *The Oxford History of the British Empire*, vol. IV: *The Twentieth Century* (Oxford, 1999).

Brubaker, Rogers, *Citizenship and Nationhood in France and Germany* (Cambridge, MA, 1992).

Buckman, Joseph, *Immigrants and the Class Struggle: The Jewish Immigrant in Leeds 1880–1914* (Manchester, 1983).

Buckner, Philip and Doug Francis, eds., *Rediscovering the British World* (Calgary, 2005).

Buettner, Elizabeth, *Empire Families: Britons and Late Imperial India* (Oxford, 2004).

Burnett, J., *Plenty and Want: A Social History of Food in England from 1815 to the Present* (London, 1989).

Liquid Pleasures: A Social History of Drink in Modern Britain (London, 1999).

Burrow, J. W., *A Liberal Descent: Victorian Historians and the English Past* (Cambridge, 1981).

Burton, Antoinette, *Burdens of History: British Feminists, Indian Women and Imperial Culture, 1865–1915* (Chapel Hill and London, 1994).

At the Heart of the Empire: Indians and the Colonial Encounter in Late-Victorian Britain (Berkeley, 1998).

'Tongues Untied: Lord Salisbury's "Black Man" and the Boundaries of Imperial Democracy', *Comparative Studies in Society and History*, 43 (2) (2000).

'Women and "Domestic" Imperial Culture: The Case of Victorian Britain', in Marilyn J. Boxer and Jean H. Quataert, eds., *Connecting Spheres: Women in a Globalizing World, 1500 to the Present*, 2nd edn (Oxford, 2000).

'"States of Injury": Josephine Butler on Slavery, Citizenship, and the Boer War', in Fletcher, Mayhall and Levine, eds., *Women's Suffrage in the British Empire*.

ed., *Politics and Empire in Victorian Britain* (Palgrave, 2001).

After the Imperial Turn: Thinking With and Through the Nation (Durham, NC, 2003).

'The Visible Empire at Home, 1832–1905', *Empire On-Line*: www.adam-matthew-publications.co.uk.

Bush, Barbara, '"Britain's Conscience on Africa": White Women, Race and Imperial Politics in Inter-war Britain', in Clare Midgley, ed., *Gender and Imperialism* (Manchester, 1998).

Bush, Julia, '"The Right Sort of Woman": Female Emigrators and Emigration to the British Empire, 1890–1910', *Women's History Review*, 3 (1994).

Edwardian Ladies and Imperial Power (Leicester, 2000).

Byrne, David, 'The 1930 "Arab Riot" in South Shields: A Race Riot That Never Was', *Race and Class*, 18 (3) (1977).

Cain, P. J. 'Economics and Empire: The Metropolitan Context', in Porter, ed., *Oxford History of the British Empire*, vol. III.

Cain, P. J. and A. G. Hopkins, *British Imperialism, 1688–2000* (London, 2001).

Caine, Barbara, *English Feminism, 1780–1980* (Oxford, 1997).

'Feminism, Journalism and Public Debate', in Joanne Shattock, ed., *Women and Literature in Britain 1800–1900* (Cambridge, 2001).

Callaway, Helen and Dorothy O. Helly, 'Crusader for Empire: Flora Shaw / Lady Lugard', in Nupur Chaudhuri and Margaret Strobel, eds., *Western Women and Imperialism: Complicity and Resistance* (Bloomington, 1992).

Cannadine, David, 'The British Monarchy, c. 1820–1977', in Eric Hobsbawm and Terence Ranger, eds., *The Invention of Tradition* (Cambridge, 1983).

Aspects of Aristocracy (New Haven and London, 1994).

Ornamentalism: How the British Saw Their Empire (London and New York, 2001).

Carretta, Vincent, *Equiano the African: Biography of a Self-made Man* (Athens, GA, 2005).

Castle, Kathryn, *Britannia's Children: Reading Colonialism Through Children's Books and Magazines* (Manchester, 1996).

Cayford, Joanne M., 'In Search of "John Chinaman": Press Representations of the Chinese in Cardiff, 1906–1911', *Llafur: Journal of Welsh Labour History*, 5 (4) (1991).

Centre for Contemporary Cultural Studies (CCCS), *The Empire Strikes Back: Race and Racism in 70s Britain* (London, 1982).

Cesarani, David, '"An Alien Concept?"' The Continuity of Anti-alienism in British Society before 1940', in David Cesarani and Tony Kushner, eds., *The Internment of Aliens in Twentieth Century Britain* (London, 1993).

Chakrabarty, Dipesh, *Provincializing Europe: Postcolonial Thought and Historical Difference* (Princeton, 2000).

'Foreword', in *The Bernard Cohn Omnibus* (Oxford, 2004; New York, 2006).

Chakravarti, Uma, 'Whatever Happened to the Vedic *Dasi?* Orientalism, Nationalism, and a Script for the Past', in Kumkum Sangari and Sudesh Vaid, eds., *Recasting Women: Essays in Indian Colonial History* (New Brunswick, NJ, 1990).

Chancellor, Valerie E., *History for their Masters: Opinion in the English History Textbook, 1900–1914* (Bath, 1970).

Chandavarkar, Rajnarayan, *The Origins of Industrial Capital in India: Business Strategies and the Working Classes in Bombay, 1900–1940* (Cambridge, 1994).

Chapman, S. and S. Chassagne, *European Textile Printers in the Eighteenth Century* (London, 1981).

Chatterjee, Partha, *The Nation and its Fragments: Colonial and Post-Colonial Histories* (Princeton, 1993).

Chaudhuri, Nupur, 'Race, Gender and Nation in *Englishwoman's Domestic Magazine* and *Queen*, 1850–1900', in Finkelstein and Peers, eds., *Negotiating India*.

Cherry, Deborah, *Beyond the Frame: Feminism and Visual Culture, Britain 1850–1900* (London, 2000).

Chinn, C., *They Worked All Their Lives: Women of the Urban Poor in England 1880–1939* (Manchester, 1988).

Clive, John, *Thomas Babington Macaulay: The Shaping of the Historian* (London, 1973).

Cohen, Robin, 'Diasporas, the Nation-State, and Globalisation', in Wang, *Global History and Migrations*.

Cohn, Bernard S., *An Anthropologist Among the Historians and Other Essays* (Oxford, 1990).

Colonialism and its Forms of Knowledge: The British in India (Princeton, 1996).

Colley, Linda, 'Britishness and Otherness: An Argument', *Journal of British Studies*, 31 (4) (1992).

Britons: Forging the Nation, 1707–1837 (London and New Haven, 1992).

Captives: Britain, Empire and the World, 1600–1850 (London, 2002).

Colls, Robert and Philip Dodd, eds., *Englishness: Politics and Culture, 1880–1920* (London, 1986).

Colpi, Terry, *The Italian Factor: The Italian Community in Great Britain* (Edinburgh, 1991).

'The Impact of the Second World War on the British Italian Community', *Immigrants and Minorities*, 11 (3) (1992).

Comaroff, Jean and John L. Comaroff, *Of Revelation and Revolution*, 2 vols. (Chicago, 1991–7).

Comaroff, John, 'Images of Empire, Contests of Conscience: Models of Colonial Domination in South Africa', in Cooper and Stoler, eds., *Tensions of Empire*.

Connolly, S. J., ed., *The Oxford Companion to Irish History* (Oxford, 1998).

Constantine, Stephen, *The Making of British Colonial Policy 1914–1940* (London, 1984).

Buy & Build: The Advertising Posters of the Empire Marketing Board (London, 1986).

' "Bringing the Empire Alive": The Empire Marketing Board and Imperial Propaganda, 1926–33', in MacKenzie, ed., *Imperialism and Popular Culture*.

ed., *Migrants and Empire: British Settlement in the Dominions between the Wars* (Manchester, 1990).

Constantine, Stephen, Maurice W. Kirby and Mary B. Rose, eds., *The First World War in British History* (London, 1995).

Coombes, Annie E., *Reinventing Africa: Museums, Material Culture and Popular Imagination in Late Victorian and Edwardian England* (London and New Haven, 1994).

Cooper, Frederick, *Colonialism in Question: Theory, Knowledge, History* (Berkeley, 2005).

Cooper, Frederick and Ann L. Stoler, eds., *Tensions of Empire: Colonial Cultures in a Bourgeois World* (Berkeley, 1997).

Costa, Emlia Viotti da, *Crowns of Glory, Tears of Blood: The Demerara Slave Rebellion of 1823* (New York, 1994).

Coulter, Mark, 'Field-Marshal Sir Henry Wilson: Imperial Soldier, Political Failure', *History Ireland*, 13 (1) (2005).

Cox, Jeffrey, *Imperial Fault Lines: Christianity and Colonial Power in Punjab, 1830–1930* (Stanford, 2001).

'Were Victorian Nonconformists the Worst Imperialists of All?', *Victorian Studies*, 46 (2004).

Craik, Dinah Mulock, *Olive*, ed. and intro. Cora Kaplan (Oxford, 1999).

Craton, Michael, *Testing the Chains: Resistance to Slavery in the British West Indies* (Ithaca, 1982).

Crowder, M., *West Africa under Colonial Rule* (London, 1968).

Cumpston, Mary, 'Some Early Indian Nationalists and their Allies in the British Parliament, 1851–1906', *English Historical Review*, 76 (1961).

Cunliffe, Marcus, *Chattel Slavery and Wage Slavery: The Anglo-American Context, 1830–1860* (Athens, GA, 1979).

Curtis, L. P., *Apes and Angels: The Irishmen in Victorian Caricature* (London, 1971).

Curtis, Liz, *Nothing But The Same Old Story: Roots of Anti-Irish Racism* (London, 1984).

The Cause of Ireland (Belfast, 1994).

Darian-Smith, Kate, Patricia Grimshaw and Stuart Macintyre, eds., *Britishness Abroad: Transnational Movements and Imperial Cultures* (Melbourne, forthcoming).

Daunton, Martin and Rick Halpern, eds., *Empire and Others: British Encounters with Indigenous Peoples, 1600–1850* (London, 1999).

David, Deirdre, *Rule Britannia: Women, Empire and Victorian Writing* (Ithaca, 1995).

David, Rob, *The Arctic in the British Imagination, 1818–1914* (Manchester, 2000).

Davidoff, Leonore, 'Class and Gender in Victorian England: The Case of Hannah Cullwick and A. J. Munby', in Judith L. Newton, Mary P. Ryan and Judith R. Walkowitz, eds., *Sex and Class in Women's History* (London, 1983).

The Best Circles, new edn (London, 1986).

Davidoff, Leonore and Catherine Hall, *Family Fortunes: Men and Women of the English Middle Class, 1780–1850* (London, 1987; rev. edn, 2002).

Davin, Anna, 'Imperialism and Motherhood', *History Workshop Journal*, 5 (1978); repr. in Cooper and Stoler, *Tensions of Empire*.

Davis, David Brion, *The Problem of Slavery in the Age of Revolution, 1770–1823* (Ithaca, 1975).

Davis, David Brion, *Slavery and Human Progress* (New York and Oxford, 1984).
'Reflections on Abolitionism and Ideological Hegemony', in Thomas Bender, ed., *The Antislavery Debate* (Berkeley and Los Angeles, 1992).

Davis, Mary, *Sylvia Pankhurst: A Life in Radical Politics* (London, 1999).

Davis, R., *The Industrial Revolution and English Overseas Trade* (Leicester, 1979).

Davis, Richard, *Revolutionary Imperialist: William Smith O'Brien 1803–1864* (Dublin, 1998).

Dawson, Graham, *Soldier Heroes: British Adventure, Empire and the Imagining of Masculinities* (London, 1994).

Denean Sharpley-Whiting, T., *Black Venus: Sexualized Savages, Primal Fears, and Primitive Narratives in French* (Durham, 1999).

Devine, T. M., *Scotland's Empire, 1600–1815* (London, 2003).

deVries, Jacqueline, 'Rediscovering Christianity after the Postmodern Turn', *Feminist Studies*, 31 (1) (2005).

Dirks, Nicholas, 'History as a Sign of the Modern', *Public Culture*, 2 (1990).
The Scandal of Empire (Cambridge, MA, 2006).

Dixon, Joy, *Divine Feminine: Theosophy and Feminism in England* (Baltimore, 2001).

Donald, James and Ali Rattansi, eds., *'Race', Culture and Difference* (London, 1992).

Donaldson, Margaret. ' "The Cultivation of the Heart and the Moulding of the Will ... ": The Missionary Contribution of the Society for Promoting Female Education in China, India and the East', in W. J. Sheils and Diana Wood, eds., *Women in the Church* (Oxford, 1990).

Douglas, M. and B. Isherwood, eds., *The World of Goods: Towards an Anthropology of Consumption*, rev. edn (London, 1996).

Drescher, Seymour, *Capitalism and Antislavery: British Mobilization in Comparative Perspective* (New York and Oxford, 1987).

Duffield, Ian, 'Skilled Workers or Marginalised Poor? The African Population of the United Kingdom, 1812–52', *Immigrants and Minorities*, 12 (3) (1993).

Duffy, Michael, 'War, Revolution and the Crisis of the British Empire', in Mark Philp, ed., *The French Revolution and British Popular Politics* (Cambridge, 1991).

Dummett, Ann and Andrew Nicol, *Subjects, Citizens, Aliens and Others: Nationality and Immigration Law* (London, 1990).

Dunnae, Patrick A., 'Boys' Literature and the Idea of Empire, 1870–1914', *Victorian Studies*, 24 (1) (1980).

Dwight Culler, A., *The Victorian Mirror of History* (New Haven, 1985).

Eagleton, Terry, 'Afterword: Ireland and Colonialism', in McDonough, ed., *Was Ireland a Colony?*

Easley, Alexis, *First-Person Anonymous: Women Writers and the Victorian Print Media, 1830–70* (Aldershot, 2004).

Eberle, Roxanne, 'Amelia Opie's *Adeline Mowbray*: Diverting the Libertine Gaze; or, The Vindication of a Fallen Woman', *Studies in the Novel*, 26 (1994).

Edwards, Paul and James Walvin, *Black Personalities in the Era of the Slave Trade* (Baton Rouge, 1983).

Elbourne, Elizabeth, *Blood Ground: Colonialism, Missions, and the Contest for Christianity in the Cape Colony and Britain, 1799–1853* (Montreal, 2002).

Elkins, Caroline, *Britain's Gulag: The Brutal End of Empire in Kenya* (London, 2005). Published in the USA as *Imperial Reckoning: The Untold Story of Britain's Gulag in Kenya* (New York, 2005).

Elliott, Marianne, *Partners in Revolution: The United Irishmen and France* (New Haven and London, 1982).

Ellis, S., 'Representations of the Past in Ireland: Whose Past and Whose Present?', *Irish Historical Studies*, 27 (1991).

Eltis, David, 'Abolitionist Perceptions of Society after Slavery', in James Walvin, ed., *British Slavery and Society, 1776–1846* (Baton Rouge, LA, 1982).

Economic Growth and the Ending of the Transatlantic Slave Trade (New York and Oxford, 1987).

Ener, Mine, *Managing Egypt's Poor and the Politics of Benevolence, 1800–1952* (Princeton, 2003).

Esty, Jed, *A Shrinking Island: Modernism and National Culture in England* (Princeton, 2004).

Evans, Neil, 'The South Wales Race Riots of 1919', *Llafur*, 3 (1) (1980).

Fahrmeir, Andreas, *Foreigners and Law in Britain and German States 1789–1870* (Oxford, 2000).

Fanon, Franz, *The Wretched of the Earth* (London, 1967).

Farwell, Bryon, *Queen Victoria's Little Wars* (New York, 1972).

Fausto-Sterling, Anne, 'Gender, Race, and Nation: The Comparative Anatomy of "Hottentot" Women in Europe, 1815–17', in Kimberley Wallace, ed., *Skin Deep, Spirit Strong: The Black Female Body in American Culture* (Ann Arbor, 2002).

Feldman, David, 'The Importance of Being English: Jewish Immigration and the Decay of Liberal England', in Feldman and Gareth Stedman Jones, eds., *Metropolis: London: Histories and Representations since 1800* (London, 1989).

Englishmen and Jews: Social Relations and Political Culture 1840–1914 (New Haven, 1994).

Ferguson, Moira, *Subject to Others: British Women Writers and Colonial Slavery, 1670–1834* (London and New York, 1992).

Ferguson, Niall, *Empire: The Rise and Demise of the British World Order and the Lessons for Global Power* (New York, 2002).

Fields, Barbara Jeanne, 'Ideology and Race in American History', in J. Morgan and James M. McPherson Kousser, eds., *Region, Race, and Reconstruction* (London, 1982).
'Slavery, Race and Ideology in the United States of America', *New Left Review*, 181 (1990).
'Of Rogues and Geldings', *American Historical Review*, 108 (2003).
Finkelstein, David and Douglas M. Peers, eds., *Negotiating India in the Nineteenth-Century Media* (Basingstoke, 2000).
Fisher, Michael, *Counterflows to Colonialism: Indian Travellers and Settlers in Britain, 1600–1857* (Delhi, 2004).
Fishman, W. J., *Jewish Radicals: From Tsarist Stetl to London Ghetto* (New York, 1974).
Fitzpatrick, David, 'Ireland and the Empire', in Porter, ed., *Oxford History of the British Empire*, vol. III.
Fladeland, Betty, ' "Our Cause Being One and the Same": Abolitionists and Chartism', in Walvin, ed., *British Slavery and Society*.
Fletcher, Ian, 'Double Meanings: Nation and Empire in the Edwardian Era', in Burton, ed., *After the Imperial Turn*.
Fletcher, Ian Christopher, Laura E. Nym Mayhall and Philippa Levine, eds., *Women's Suffrage in the British Empire: Citizenship, Nation and Race* (London, 2000).
Flint, Kate, *The Woman Reader 1837–1914* (Oxford, 1993).
Foot, Paul, *Immigration and Race in British Politics* (London, 1968).
Foster, Roy, 'We Are All Revisionists Now', *Irish Review*, 1 (1986).
Modern Ireland (London, 1988).
'History and the Irish Question', in his *Paddy and Mr Punch: Connections in English and Irish History* (London, 1993).
Franey, L., *Victorian Travel Writing and Imperial Violence* (London, 2003).
Fraser, T. G., 'Ireland and India', in Jeffery, ed., *'An Irish Empire'*.
Fraser, W. H., *The Coming of the Mass Market 1850–1914* (London, 1981).
Fry, Michael, *The Scottish Empire* (Edinburgh, 2001).
Fryer, Peter, *Staying Power: The History of Black People in Britain* (London, 1984).
Fulford, Tim and Peter J. Kitson, 'Romanticism and Colonialism: Texts, Contexts, Issues', in Fulford and Kitson, eds., *Romanticism and Colonialism: Writing and Empire 1780–1830* (Cambridge, 1998).
Fussell, Paul, *The Great War and Modern Memory* (Oxford, 1975).
Gainer, Bernard, *The Alien Invasion: The Origins of the Aliens Act, 1905* (London, 1972).
Gallagher, Tom, 'A Tale of Two Cities: Communal Strife in Glasgow and Liverpool Before 1914', in Swift and Gilley, eds., *The Irish in the Victorian City*.
Gates, Henry Louis, ed., *'Race', Writing and Difference* (Chicago, 1985).
Geoghegan, Patrick M., *The Irish Act of Union: A Study in High Politics, 1798–1801* (Dublin, 1999).

George, Rosemary Marangoly, *The Politics of Home: Postcolonial Relocations and Twentieth-century Fiction* (Cambridge, MA, 2002).

Gerzina, Gretchen, *Black England: Life Before Emancipation* (London, 1995).

Ghose, Indira, *Women Travellers in Colonial India* (Delhi, 1998).

Ghosh, Durba, 'Decoding the Nameless: Gender, Subjectivity and Historical Methodologies in Reading the Archives of Colonial India', in Wilson, ed., *New Imperial History*.

Ghosh, P. R., 'Macaulay and the Heritage of the Enlightenment', *English Historical Review*, 112 (446) (April 1997).

Gikandi, Simon, *Maps of Englishness: Writing Identity in the Culture of Colonialism* (London and New York, 1996).

Giles, J., *The Parlour and the Suburb: Domestic Identities, Class, Femininity and Modernity* (London, 2004).

Gilman, Sander L., 'Black Bodies, White Bodies: Toward an Iconography of Female Sexuality in Late Nineteenth-Century Art, Medicine, and Literature', in Gates, ed., *'Race', Writing and Difference*.

Difference and Pathology: Stereotypes of Sexuality, Race, and Madness (Ithaca, 1985).

Gilroy, Paul, *'There Ain't No Black in the Union Jack': The Cultural Politics of Race and Nation* (Chicago, 1987).

The Black Atlantic: Modernity and Double Consciousness (Cambridge, MA, 1993).

'One Nation Under a Groove: The Cultural Politics of Race and Racism in Britain', in Geoff Eley and Ronald Grigor Suny, eds., *Becoming National: A Reader* (Oxford, 1996).

Girouard, Mark, *The Return to Camelot: Chivalry and the English Gentleman* (New Haven and London, 1981).

Goodman, J., *Tobacco in History: The Cultures of Dependence* (London, 1993).

Gould, Eliga, *The Persistence of Empire: British Political Culture in the Age of the American Revolution* (Chapel Hill, 2000).

Grayzel, Susan R., *Women's Identities At War: Gender, Motherhood and Politics in Britain and France during the First World War* (Chapel Hill, 1999).

Green, E. H. H., *The Crisis of Conservatism: The Politics, Economics, and Ideology of the Conservative Party, 1880–1914* (London, 1995).

Green, Jeffrey, *Black Edwardians: Black People in Britain 1901–1914* (London, 1998).

Greenhut, Jeffrey, 'Race, Sex, and War: The Impact of Race and Sex on Morale and Health Services for the Indian Corps on the Western Front, 1914', *Military Affairs*, 45 (2) (1981).

Greenlee, James G., *Education and Imperial Unity, 1901–1926* (New York and London, 1987).

Gregory, Derek, *The Colonial Present* (Oxford, 2004).

Grimshaw, Patricia, Marilyn Lake, Ann McGrath and Marian Quartly, *Women's Suffrage in Zealand* (Auckland, 1972).

Creating a Nation (Ringwood, Victoria, 1994).

Groot, Joanna de, ' "Sex" and "Race": The Construction of Language and Image in the Nineteenth Century', in Hall, ed., *Cultures of Empire*.

Guan, Shijie, 'Chartism and the First Opium War', *History Workshop*, 24 (1987).

Guha, Ranajit, *Elementary Aspects of Peasant Insurgency in Colonial India* (Delhi, 1983).

'Not at Home in Empire', *Critical Inquiry*, 23 (3) (1997).

Gullace, Nicoletta F., *'The Blood of Our Sons': Men, Women, and the Renegotiation of British Citizenship During the Great War* (New York, 2002).

Haines, Robin F., *Emigration and the Labouring Poor: Australian Recruitment in Britain and Ireland, 1831–60* (Basingstoke, 1999).

Hall, Catherine, *White, Male and Middle Class: Explorations in Feminism and History* (Cambridge, 1992).

'Missionary Stories: Gender and Ethnicity in England in the 1830s and 1840s', in her *White, Male, and Middle Class*.

' "From Greenland's Icy Mountains … to Afric's Golden Sand": Ethnicity, Race and Nation in Mid-Nineteenth-Century England', *Gender and History*, 5 (1993).

'Gender Politics and Imperial Politics: Rethinking the Histories of Empire', in Verene Shepherd, Bridget Brereton and Barbara Bailey, eds., *Engendering History: Caribbean Women in Historical Perspective* (New York, 1995).

ed., *Cultures of Empire: Colonizers in Britain and the Empire in the Nineteenth and Twentieth Centuries: A Reader* (Manchester, 2000).

'The Rule of Difference: Gender, Class and Empire in the Making of the 1832 Reform Act', in Ida Blom, Karen Hagemann and Catherine Hall, eds., *Gendered Nations: Nationalisms and Gender Order in the Long Nineteenth Century* (Oxford, 2000).

Civilising Subjects: Metropole and Colony in the English Imagination, 1830–1867 (Cambridge and Chicago, 2002).

'Remembering Edward Said', *History Workshop Journal*, 57 (2004).

'Imperial Careering at Home: Harriet Martineau on Empire', in Alan Lester and David Lambert, eds., *Colonial Lives across the British Empire: Imperial Careering in the Long Nineteenth Century* (Cambridge, 2006).

Hall, Catherine, Keith McClelland and Jane Rendall, *Defining the Victorian Nation: Class, Race, Gender and the British Reform Act of 1867* (Cambridge, 2000).

Hall, Stuart, 'The Rise of the Representative/Interventionist State 1880s–1920s', in Gregor McLennan, David Held and Stuart Hall, eds., *State and Society in Contemporary Britain: A Critical Introduction* (Cambridge, 1984).

'Conclusion: The Multi-Cultural Question', in Barnor Hesse, *ed., Un/Settled Multiculturalisms: Diaspora, Entanglements, 'Transruptions'* (London, 2000).

Hall, Stuart, Chas Critcher, Tony Jefferson, John Clarke and Brian Roberts, *Policing the Crisis: Mugging, the State, and Law and Order* (London, 1978).

Hall, Stuart and Bill Schwarz, 'State and Society, 1880–1930', in Mary Langan and Bill Schwarz, eds., *Crises in the British State 1880–1930* (London, 1985).

Hamburger, Joseph, *Macaulay and the Whig Tradition* (Chicago, 1976).

Hammerton, A. James, *Emigrant Gentlewomen: Genteel Poverty and Female Emigration, 1830–1914* (London, 1979).

'Gender and Migration', in Philippa Levine, ed., *Gender and Empire* (Oxford, 2004).

Hampshire, James, *Citizenship and Belonging: Immigration and the Politics of Demographic Government in Postwar Britain* (Basingstoke, 2005).

Harcourt, Freda, 'Disraeli's Imperialism, 1866–1868: A Question of Timing', *Historical Journal*, 23 (1) (1980).

Harlow, Barbara and Mia Carter, eds., *Imperialism and Orientalism: A Documentary Sourcebook* (Oxford, 1999).

Harnetty, P., *Imperialism and Free Trade: Lancashire and India in the 19th Century* (Manchester, 1972).

Harris, Clive and Gail Lewis, 'Black Women's Employment and the British Economy', in Winston James and Clive Harris, eds., *Inside Babylon: The Caribbean Diaspora in Britain* (London, 1993).

'Post-war Migration and the Industrial Reserve Army', in Winston James and Clive Harris, eds., *Inside Babylon: The Caribbean Diaspora in Britain* (London, 1993).

Harris, Jose, *Private Lives, Public Spirit: A Social History of Britain, 1870–1914* (Oxford, 1993).

Harrison, Brian, *Drink and the Victorians: The Temperance Question in England, 1815–1872* (London, 1971; rev. edn, Keele, 1994).

Separate Spheres: The Opposition to Women's Suffrage in Britain (London, 1978).

Harrison, Royden, *The Life and Times of Sidney and Beatrice Webb 1858–1905: The Formative Years* (London, 2000).

Havinden, M., *Colonialism and Development: Britain and its Tropical Colonies 1850–1960* (London, 1993).

Heathorn, Stephen, *For Home, Country, and Race: Constructing Gender, Class, and Englishness in the Elementary School, 1880–1914* (Toronto, 2000).

Hechter, Michael, *Internal Colonialism: The Celtic Fringe in British National Development, 1536–1966* (London and Berkeley, 1975).

Hendley, Matthew, 'Constructing the Citizen: The Primrose League and the Definition of Citizenship in the Age of Mass Democracy in Britain, 1918–1928', *Journal of the Canadian Historical Association*, 7 (1996).

Himmelfarb, Gertrude, *The Idea of Poverty: England in the Early Industrial Age* (New York, 1984).

Poverty and Compassion: The Moral Imagination of the Late Victorians (New York, 1991).

Hindley, D. and G. Hindley, *Advertising in Victorian England 1837–1901* (London, 1972).

Hobsbawm, Eric and Terence Ranger, eds., *The Invention of Tradition* (Cambridge, 1983).

Hobsbawm, E. J. and George Rudé, *Captain Swing* (London, 1969).

Hochschild, Adam, *Bury the Chains: The British Struggle to Abolish Slavery* (London, 2005).

Hoffenberg, Peter, *An Empire on Display: English, Indian and Australian Exhibitions from the Crystal Palace to the Great War* (California, 2001).

Holland, Robert, 'The British Empire and the Great War, 1914–1918', in Brown and Louis, ed., *The Oxford History of the British Empire*, vol. IV.

Hollis, Patricia, ed., *Pressure From Without in Early Victorian England* (London, 1974).

'Anti-Slavery and British Working-Class Radicalism in the Years of Reform', in Christine Bolt and Seymour Drescher, eds., *Anti-Slavery, Religion and Reform* (Folkestone, Kent, 1980).

Holmes, Colin, *John Bull's Island: Immigration and British Society, 1871–1971* (Basingstoke, 1988).

'Historians and Immigration', in Michael Drake, ed., *Time, Family and Community: Perspectives on Family and Community in History* (Oxford, 1994).

Holston, James and Arjun Appadurai, 'Cities and Citizenship', *Public Culture*, 8 (1996).

Holt, Thomas C., ' "An Empire Over the Mind": Emancipation, Race, and Ideology in the British West Indies and the American South', in J. Morgan Kousser and James M. McPherson, eds., *Region, Race and Reconstruction: Essays in Honor of C. Vann Woodward* (New York, 1982).

The Problem of Freedom: Race, Labor, and Politics in Jamaica and Britain, 1832–1938 (Baltimore, 1992).

'Race, Race-making and the Writing of History', *American Historical Review*, 100 (1) (1995).

Hopkins, A. G., 'Back to the Future: From National History to Imperial History', *Past and Present*, 164 (1999).

ed., *Globalization in World History* (London, 2002).

Horn, Pamela, 'English Elementary Education and the Growth of the Imperial Ideal: 1880–1914', in Mangan, ed., *Benefits Bestowed?*

Howard, Carol, ' " The Story of the Pineapple": Sentimental Abolitionism and Moral Motherhood in Amelia Opie's *Adeline Mowbray*', *Studies in the Novel*, 30 (1998).

Howe, Stephen, *Anticolonialism in British Politics: The Left and the End of Empire, 1918–1964* (Oxford, 1993).

Ireland and Empire: Colonial Legacies in Irish History and Culture (Oxford, 2000).

Empire: A Very Short Introduction (Oxford, 2002).

'Internal Decolonisation? British Politics since Thatcher as Postcolonial Trauma', *Twentieth Century British History*, 14 (2003).

Hughes, Robert, *The Fatal Shore* (New York, 1987).

Hyam, R., *Britain's Imperial Century* (London, 1974).

Hyam, Ronald, 'Concubinage and the Colonial Service: The Crewe Circular (1909)', *Journal of Imperial and Commonwealth History*, 14 (3) (1986).

Jackson, Alvin, 'The Irish Act of Union', *History Today*, 51 (1) (2001).

James, C. L. R., *The Black Jacobins* (New York, 1989).

Jarrett-Macauley, Delia, *The Life of Una Marson, 1905–65* (Manchester, 1998).

Jarvis, David, '"Behind Every Great Party": Women and Conservatism in Twentieth-century Britain', in Vickery, ed., *Women, Privilege and Power.*

Jeffery, Keith, ed., *'An Irish Empire? Aspects of Ireland and the British Empire* (Manchester, 1996).

Jenkinson, Jacqueline, 'The Glasgow Race Disturbances of 1919', *Immigrants and Minorities*, 4 (2) (1985).

'The Black Community of Salford and Hull, 1919–21', *Immigrants and Minorities*, 7 (2) (1988).

Johnson, Dale, *The Changing Shape of English Nonconformity 1825–1925* (New York, 1999).

Johnston, Anna, *Missionary Writing and Empire, 1800–1860* (Cambridge, 2003).

Jones, Aled and Bill Jones, 'The Welsh World and the British Empire, c. 1851–1939', in Bridge and Fedorowich, eds., *The British World.*

Jones, Gareth Stedman, *Outcast London: A Study in the Relationship between Classes in Victorian Society* (Oxford, 1971).

'Working-Class Culture and Working-Class Politics in London, 1870–1900: Notes on the Remaking of a Working Class', in his *Languages of Class: Studies in English Working Class History* (Cambridge, 1983).

Jones, Vivien, 'Reading for England: Austen, Taste and Female Patriotism', *European Romantic Review*, 16 (April 2005).

Joshua, Harris, Tina Wallace and Heather Booth, *To Ride the Storm: The 1980 Bristol 'Riot' and the State* (London, 1983).

Journal of Colonialism and Colonial History, 3 (1) (2002), Special Issue: 'From Orientalism to Ornamentalism: Empire and Difference in History'.

Judd, Denis, *Empire: The British Imperial Experience, from 1765 to the Present* (London, 1996).

Kaplan, Amy, *The Anarchy of Empire in the Making of U.S. Culture* (Cambridge, MA, 2002).

Kaplan, Cora, '"A Heterogeneous Thing": Female Childhood and the Rise of Racial Thinking in Victorian Britain', in Diana Fuss, ed., *Human, All Too Human* (London and New York, 1996).

'Black Heroes/White Writers: Toussaint L'Ouverture and the Literary Imagination', *History Workshop Journal*, 46 (1998).

Kaushik, Harish P., *Indian National Congress in England* (Delhi, 1991).

Kearney, Hugh, *The British Isles: A History of Four Nations* (Cambridge, 1989).

Kennedy, Dane, 'Empire Settlement in Post-war Reconstruction: The Role of the Oversea Settlement Committee, 1919–1922', *Albion*, 20 (1988).

Britain and Empire, 1880–1945 (London, 2002).

Kenny, Kevin, ed., *Ireland and the British Empire* (Oxford, 2004).

Kent, Susan Kingsley, *Making Peace: The Reconstruction of Gender in Interwar Britain* (Princeton, 1993).

Gender and Power in Britain, 1640–1990 (London, 1999).

Kidd, A. and D. Nicholls, eds., *Gender, Civic Culture and Consumerism: Middle Class Identity in Britain 1800–1940* (Manchester, 1999).

Kienzle, Beverly Mayne and Pamela J. Walker, eds., *Women Preachers and Prophets through Two Millennia of Christianity* (Berkeley, 1998).

Kiernan, V. G., *The Lords of Human Kind: European Attitudes to the Outside World in the Imperial Age* (London, 1969).

Killingray, David, 'Africans in the United Kingdom: An Introduction', *Immigrants and Minorities*, 12 (3) (1993).

Kinealy, Christine, *This Great Calamity: The Irish Famine 1845–52* (Dublin, 1994; 2nd edn, 2006).

'Beyond Revisionism: Reassessing the Irish Famine', *History Ireland*, 4 (4) (1995).

A Disunited Kingdom? England, Ireland, Scotland and Wales 1800–1949 (Cambridge, 1999).

'The Orange Order and Representations of Britishness', in Stephen Caunce, Ewa Mazierska, Susan Sydney-Smith and John K. Walton, eds., *Relocating Britishness* (Manchester, 2004).

'Was Ireland a Colony? The Evidence of the Great Famine', in McDonough, ed., *Was Ireland a Colony?*

King, Anthony, *Urbanism, Colonialism and the World-Economy: Cultural and Spatial Foundations of the World Urban System* (London, 1990).

Kirk, Neville, *Comrades and Cousins: Globalization, Workers and Labour Movements in Britain, the USA and Australia from the 1880s to 1914* (London, 2003).

Kirk-Greene, Anthony, *Britain's Imperial Administrators, 1858–1966* (Basingstoke, 2000).

Klug, Francesca, ' "Oh, To Be in England": The British Case Study', in Nira Yuval-Davis and Floya Anthius, eds., *Woman-Nation-State* (London, 1989).

Koditschek, Theodore, *Class Formation and Urban Industrial Society* (Cambridge, 1990).

Kolchin, Peter, 'Whiteness Studies: The New History of Race in America', *Journal of American History*, 89 (1) (2003).

Koven, Seth, *Slumming: Sexual and Social Politics in Victorian London* (Princeton, 2004).

Koven, Seth and Sonya Michel, eds., *Mothers of a New World: Maternalist Politics and the Origins of Welfare States* (London, 1993).

Kowaleski-Wallace, E., *Consuming Subjects: Women, Shopping, and Business in the Eighteenth Century* (New York, 1997).

Kramer, Paul, 'Empires, Exceptions, and Anglo-Saxons: Race and Rule Between the British and United States Empires, 1880–1910', *Journal of American History*, 88 (4) (2002).

Krebs, Paula, *Gender, Race and the Writing of Empire: Public Discourse and the Boer War* (Cambridge, 1999).

Kriegel, Lara, 'The Pudding and the Palace: Labor, Print Cultures and Imperial Britain in 1851', in Burton, *After the Imperial Turn*.

Lahiri, Shompa, *Indians in Britain: Anglo-Indian Encounters, Race and Identity 1880–1930* (London, 2000).

Lake, Marilyn, 'From Mississippi to Melbourne via Natal: The Invention of the Literacy Test as a Technology of Racial Exclusion', in Ann Curthoys and

Marilyn Lake, eds., *Connected Worlds: History in Transnational Perspective* (Canberra, 2005).

Landau, Paul Stuart, *The Realm of the Word: Language, Gender, and Christianity in a Southern African Kingdom* (Portsmouth, 1995).

Laqueur, Thomas, *Religion and Respectability: Sunday Schools and Working-Class Culture 1780–1850* (New Haven, 1976).

Lawless, Richard, *From Ta'izz to Tyneside: An Arab Community in the North-East of England During the Early Twentieth Century* (Exeter, 1995).

Lawrence, Jon, 'Forging a Peaceable Kingdom: War, Violence and the Fear of Brutalization in Post First World War Britain', *Journal of Modern History*, 75 (2004).

Lawson, Philip, *The East India Company: A History* (London, 1993).

A Taste for Empire and Glory: Studies in British Overseas Expansion, 1660–1800 (Aldershot, 1997).

Leask, Nigel, *Curiosity and the Aesthetics of Travel Writing, 1770–1840* (Oxford, 2002).

Ledbetter, Kathryn, 'Bonnets and Rebellions: Imperialism in the *Lady's Newspaper*', *Victorian Periodicals Review*, 37 (2004).

Lee, Debbie, *Slavery and the Romantic Imagination* (Philadelphia, 2002).

Lees, P. J., B. Piatek and I. Curyllo-Klag, eds., *The British Migrant Experience, 1700–2000: An Anthology* (London, 2002).

Lemire, Beverly, *Fashion's Favourite: The Cotton Trade and the Consumer in Britain, 1660–1800* (Oxford, 1991).

'Fashioning Cottons: Asian Trade, Domestic Industry and Consumer Demand 1660–1780', in D. Jenkins, *Cambridge History of Western Textiles* (Cambridge, 2003).

Lester, Alan, *Imperial Networks: Creating Identities in Nineteenth-century South Africa and Britain* (London, 2001).

'British Settler Discourse and Circuits of Empire', *History Workshop Journal*, 54 (2002).

'Constructing Colonial Discourse', in Alison Blunt and Cheryl McEwan, eds., *Postcolonial Geographies* (London, 2002).

Levine, George, *The Boundaries of Fiction: Carlyle, Macaulay, Newman* (Princeton, 1968).

Levine, Philippa, 'The Humanising Influences of Five O'clock Tea', *Victorian Studies*, 33 (1990).

'Battle Colors: Race, Sex, and Colonial Soldiery in World War I', *Journal of Women's History*, 9 (4) (1998).

'The White Slave Trade and the British Empire', *Criminal Justice History*, 17 (2002).

Prostitution, Race, and Politics: Policing Venereal Disease in the British Empire (London and New York, 2003).

Levy, Andrea, *Small Island* (London, 2004).

Lew, Joseph, ' "That Abominable Traffic": *Mansfield Park* and the Dynamics of Slavery', in Beth Fowkes Tobin, ed., *History, Gender and Eighteenth Century Literature* (Athens, GA, 1994).

Lewis, Gail, 'From Deepest Kilburn', in Liz Heron, ed., *Truth, Dare, or Promise: Girls Growing Up in the Fifties* (London, 1985).

'Racialising Culture is Ordinary', in Elizabeth B. Silva and Tony Bennett, eds., *Contemporary Culture and Everyday Life* (Durham, 2004).

Lewis, Gail and Sarah Neal, 'Introduction: Contemporary Political Contexts, Changing Terrains and Revisited Discourses', *Ethnic and Racial Studies*, 28 (3) (2005).

Lewis, Martin W. and Kären E. Wigen, *The Myth of Continents: A Critique of Metageography* (Berkeley, 1997).

Light, Alison, *Forever England: Femininity, Literature and Conservatism Between the Wars* (London, 1991).

Lindfors, Bernth, ' "The Hottentot Venus" and Other African Attractions in Nineteenth-Century England', *Australasian Drama Studies*, 1 (2) (1983).

Linebaugh, Peter, *The London Hanged: Crime and Society in the Eighteenth Century* (London, 1992).

Linebaugh, Peter and Marcus Rediker, *The Many-Headed Hydra: Sailors, Slaves, Commoners, and the Hidden History of the Revolutionary Atlantic* (Boston, 2000).

Little, Kenneth Lindsay, *Negroes in Britain: A Study of Race Relations in an English City* (1948, rev. edn, London, 1972).

Logan, M., *Narrating Africa: George Henty and the Fiction of Empire* (New York, 1999).

Loomba, Ania, *Colonialism/Postcolonialism*, 2nd edn (London, 2005).

Shakespeare, Race and Colonialism (Oxford, 2002).

Lorimer, Douglas, *Colour, Class and the Victorians: English Attitudes to the Negro in the Mid-Nineteenth Century* (Leicester, 1978).

'Reconstructing Victorian Racial Discourse: Images of Race, the Language of Race Relations, and the Context of Black Resistance', in Gretchen Holbrook Gerzina, ed., *Black Victorians/Black Victoriana* (New Brunswick, NJ, 2003).

Louis, Wm. Roger, 'Introduction', in Robin W. Winks, ed., *The Oxford History of the British Empire*, vol. V: *Historiography* (Oxford, 1999).

Lovegrove, Deryck W., *Established Church, Sectarian People: Itinerancy and the Transformation of English Dissent, 1780–1830* (Cambridge, 1988).

McBriar, A. M., *Fabian Socialism and English Politics, 1884–1918* (Cambridge, 1962).

McCalman, Iain, 'Anti-Slavery and Ultra-Radicalism in Early Nineteenth England: The Case of Robert Wedderburn', *Slavery and Abolition*, 7 (1986).

McClintock, Anne, 'The Angel of Progress: Pitfalls of the Term "Post-colonialism" ', in P. Williams and L. Chrisman, eds., *Colonial Discourse and Postcolonial Theory* (New York, 1994).

Imperial Leather: Race, Gender and Sexuality in the Colonial Context (London and New York, 1995).

McCracken, Donal P., 'MacBride's Brigade in the Anglo-Boer War', *History Ireland*, 8 (1) (2000).

MacDonald, Robert H., 'Reproducing the Middle-Class Boy: From Purity to Patriotism in the Boys' Magazines, 1892–1914', *Journal of Contemporary History*, 24 (3) (1989).

Sons of the Empire: The Frontier and the Boy Scout Movement, 1890–1918 (Toronto, 2003).

McDonough, Terrence, ed., *Was Ireland a Colony? Economics, Politics and Culture in Nineteenth-Century Ireland* (Dublin, 2005).

McDowell, R. B., *The Irish Administration 1801–1914* (London, 1964).

McGovern, Mark, 'The Siege of Derry', in D. George Boyce and Roger Swift, eds., *Problems and Perspectives in Irish History since 1800* (Dublin, 2003).

Machin, G. I. T., *Politics and the Churches in Great Britain, 1832–1868* (Oxford, 1977). *Politics and the Churches in Great Britain, 1869 to 1921* (Oxford, 1987).

McKay, Claude, *A Long Way from Home* (New York, 1970).

MacKenzie, John M., *Propaganda and Empire: The Manipulation of British Public Opinion, 1880–1960* (Manchester, 1984).

ed., *Imperialism and Popular Culture* (Manchester, 1986).

ed., *Popular Imperialism and the Military, 1850–1950* (Manchester, 1992).

'Essay and Reflection: On Scotland and the Empire', *International History Review*, 15 (1993).

'Empire and Metropolitan Cultures', in Porter, ed., *Oxford History of the British Empire*, vol. III.

McLeod, Hugh, *Class and Religion in the Late Victorian City* (London, 1974).

MacRaild, Donald, ed., *The Great Famine and Beyond: Irish Migration in Britain in the Nineteenth and Twentieth Centuries* (Dublin, 2000).

Maguire, G. E., *Conservative Women: A History of Women and the Conservative Party, 1874–1997* (London, 1998).

Malchow, Howard L., *Population Pressures: Emigration and Government in Late Nineteenth-Century Britain* (Palo Alto, 1979).

Maly, Willy, 'Nationalism and Revisionism: Ambivalences and Dissensus', in Scott Brewster, Virginia Crossman, Fiona Beckett and David Alderson, eds., *Ireland in Proximity: History, Gender, Space* (London, 1999).

Mandler, Peter, *History and National Life* (London, 2002).

Mangan, J. A., 'Images of Empire in the Late Victorian Public School', *Journal of Educational Administration and History*, 12 (1) (1980).

Athleticism in the Victorian and Edwardian Public School (Cambridge, 1981).

The Games Ethic and Imperialism: Aspects of the Diffusion of an Ideal (Harmondsworth, 1986).

ed., *'Benefits Bestowed'? Education and British Imperialism* (Manchester, 1988).

ed., *Making Imperial Mentalities: Socialisation and British Imperialism* (Manchester, 1990).

Marriott, John, 'In Darkest England: The Poor, the Crowd and Race in the Nineteenth-Century Metropolis', in Phil Cohen, ed., *New Ethnicities, Old Racisms?* (London, 1999).

Marsh, Jan, ed., *Black Victorians: Black People in British Art 1800–1900* (Manchester and Birmingham, 2005).

Marshall, P. J., 'The Moral Swing to the East: British Humanitarianism, India and the West Indies', in Kenneth Ballhatchet and John Harrison, eds., *East India Company Studies* (Hong Kong, 1986).

Bengal: The British Bridgehead, Eastern India, 1740–1828. The New Cambridge History of India, vol. II, part 2 (Cambridge, 1987).

'Empire and Authority in the Later Eighteenth Century', *Journal of Imperial and Commonwealth History*, 15 (2) (1987).

Trade and Conquest: Studies in the Rise of British Dominance in India (Aldershot, 1993).

'No Fatal Impact? The Elusive History of Imperial Britain', *Times Literary Supplement*, 12 March 1993.

Massey, Doreen, *Space, Place and Gender* (Cambridge, 1994).

Maughan, Steven S., 'Civic Culture, Women's Foreign Missions, and the British Imperial Imagination, 1860–1914', in Frank Trentmann, ed., *Paradoxes of Civil Society: New Perspectives on Modern German and British History* (New York and Oxford, 2000).

Mavor, Carol, *Pleasures Taken: Performances of Sexuality and Loss in Victorian Photographs* (Durham, 1995).

May, Roy and Robin Cohen, 'The Interaction Between Race and Colonialism: A Case Study of the Liverpool Race Riots of 1919', *Race and Class*, 14 (2) (1974).

Mayhall, Laura E. Nym, *The Militant Suffrage Movement: Citizenship and Resistance in Britain, 1860–1930* (Oxford, 2003).

Meredith, David, 'Imperial Images: The Empire Marketing Board, 1926–32', *History Today*, 37 (1) (1987).

Merians, Linda E., *Envisioning the Worst: Representations of 'Hottentots' in Early-modern England* (Newark, London and Cranbury, 2001).

Metcalf, Thomas R., *Ideologies of the Raj* (Cambridge, 1994).

Meyer, Susan, *Imperialism at Home: Race and Victorian Women's Fiction* (Ithaca, 1996).

Midgley, Clare, *Women Against Slavery: The British Campaigns, 1780–1870* (London, 1992).

'Anti-slavery and Feminism in Britain', *Gender and History*, 5 (1993).

'Slave Sugar Boycotts, Female Activism and the Domestic Base of Anti-slavery Culture', *Slavery and Abolition*, 17 (1996).

'Anti-slavery and the Roots of Imperial Feminism', in Midgley, ed., *Gender and Imperialism* (Manchester, 1998).

'Female Emancipation in an Imperial Frame: English Women and the Campaign Against *Sati* (Widow-burning) in India, 1813–30', *Women's History Review*, 9 (2000).

'Can Women Be Missionaries? Envisioning Female Agency in the Early Nineteenth-century British Empire', *Journal of British Studies*, 45 (2) (April 2006).

Millgate, Jane, *Macaulay* (London, 1973).

Mintz, Sidney, *Sweetness and Power: The Place of Sugar in Modern History* (Harmondsworth and New York, 1985).

Mitchell, Sally, *The Fallen Angel: Chastity, Class, and Women's Reading, 1835–1880* (Bowling Green, KY, 1981).

Moch, Leslie Page, *Moving Europeans: Migration in Western Europe since 1650* (Bloomington, 1992).

Moore, Jonathan, *Ulster Unionism and the British Conservative Party: A Study of a Failed Marriage* (London, 1997).

Morawska, Ewa and Willfried Spohn, 'Moving Europeans in the Globalizing World: Contemporary Migrations in a Historical-Comparative Perspective (1855–1994 v. 1870–1914)', in Wang, ed., *Global History and Migrations.*

Morgan, Cecilia, ' "A Wigwam to Westminster": Performing Mohawk Identities in Imperial Britain, 1890s–1900s', *Gender and History*, 15 (2) (2003).

Morgan, Jennifer L., ' "Some Could Suckle over Their Shoulder": Male Travelers, Female Bodies, and the Gendering of Racial Ideology, 1500–1770', *William and Mary Quarterly*, 3rd ser., 54 (1) (1997).

Morgan, Sue, ed., *Women, Religion and Feminism in Britain, 1750–1900* (Basingstoke, 2002).

Morrison, Toni, *Playing in the Dark: Whiteness and the Literary Imagination* (Cambridge, MA and London, 1993).

Mosse, Werner E., ed., *Second Chance: Two Centuries of German Speaking Jews in the United Kingdom* (Tubingen, 1991).

Moynagh, Maureen, *Essays on Race and Empire: Nancy Cunard* (Peterbrough, ON, 2002).

Munck, R., *The Irish Economy: Results and Prospects* (London, 1993).

Murdoch, Alexander, *British Emigration 1603–1914* (London, 2004).

Murray, Jocelyn, 'Gender Attitudes and the Contribution of Women to Evangelism and Ministry in the Nineteenth Century', in John Wolffe, ed., *Evangelical Faith and Public Zeal: Evangelicals and Society in Britain 1780–1980* (London, 1995).

Nair, Janaki, 'Uncovering the Zenana: Visions of Indian Womanhood in Englishwomen's Writings, 1813–1940', *Journal of Women's History*, 2 (1) (1990).

Neal, Frank, *Sectarian Violence: The Liverpool Experience 1819–1914: An Aspect of Anglo-Irish History* (Manchester, 1988).

Neill, Stephen, *Colonialism and Christian Missions* (New York, 1966).

Newsinger, John, *Fenianism in Mid-Victorian Britain* (London, 1994).

Newton, Judith, 'Sex and Political Economy in the *Edinburgh Review*', in her *Starting Over: Feminism and the Politics of Cultural Critique* (Ann Arbor, 1994).

Nightingale, P., *Trade and Empire in Western India 1784–1806* (Cambridge, 1970).

Nirenberg, David, *Communities of Violence: Persecution of Minorities in the Middle Ages* (Princeton, 1996).

Noiriel, Gerard, *The French Melting Pot: Immigration, Citizenship, and National Identity* (Minneapolis, 1996).

Nussbaum, Felicity, *Torrid Zones: Maternity, Sexuality and Empire in Eighteenth Century English Narratives* (Baltimore, 1995).

O'Brien, Patrick and Stanley Engerman, 'Exports and the Growth of the British Economy', in B. Solow, ed., *Slavery and the Rise of the Atlantic System* (Cambridge, 1991).

O'Tuathaigh, M. A. G., 'The Irish in Nineteenth-Century Britain: Problems of Integration', in Swift and Gilley, eds., *The Irish in the Victorian City*.

Oddy, D. and D. Miller, *The Making of the Modern British Diet* (London, 1976).

Ofonagoro, W., *Trade and Imperialism in Southern Nigeria* (New York, 1979).

Ogborn, Miles, 'Gotcha!', *History Workshop Journal*, 56 (2003).

Ohlmeyer, Jane H., 'A Laboratory for Empire?: Early Modern Ireland and English Imperialism', in Kenny, ed., *Ireland and the British Empire*.

Oldfield, J. R., *Popular Politics and British Anti-Slavery: The Mobilisation of Public Opinion Against the Slave Trade, 1787–1807* (Manchester, 1995).

Olorunfemi, A., 'The Liquor Traffic Dilemma in British West Africa', *International Journal of African Historical Studies*, 17 (1984).

Opie, Amelia, *Adeline Mowbray*, ed. Shelly King and John B. Pierce ((1805) Oxford, 1999).

Orazem, Claudia, *Political Economy and Fiction in the Early Works of Harriet Martineau* (Frankfort, 1999).

Page, Judith W., *Wordsworth and the Cultivation of Women* (Berkeley, 1994).

Paisley, Fiona, 'Performing "New Zealand": Maori and Pakeha Delegates at the Pan-Pacific Women's Conference, Hawai'i, 1934', *New Zealand Journal of History*, 38 (1) (2004).

Palmer, Stanley, *Police and Protest in England and Ireland, 1780–1850* (Cambridge, 1988).

Panayi, Panikos, 'The British Empire Union in the First World War', in Tony Kushner and Kenneth Lunn, eds., *The Politics of Marginality: Race, the Radical Right and Minorities in Twentieth Century Britain* (London, 1990).

The Enemy in Our Midst: Germans in Britain During the First World War (New York, 1991).

Immigration, Ethnicity and Racism in Britain, 1815–1945 (Manchester, 1994).

'Anti-German Riots in Britain During the First World War', in Panayi, ed., *Racial Violence in Britain in the Nineteenth and Twentieth Centuries* (London, 1996).

'The Historiography of Immigrants and Ethnic Minorities: Britain Compared with the USA', *Ethnic and Racial Studies*, 19 (4) (1996).

Paravisini-Gebert, Lizabeth, 'Mrs Seacole's *Wonderful Adventures in Many Lands* and the Consciousness of Transit', in Gretchen Holbrook Gerzina, ed., *Black Victorians, Black Victoriana* (New Brunswick, 2003).

Parker, Andrew, Nancy Russo, Doris Sommer and Patricia Yeager, eds., *Nationalisms and Sexualities* (New York, 1992).

Paul, Kathleen, *Whitewashing Britain: Race and Citizenship in the Postwar Era* (Ithaca, 1997).

Paxton, Nancy, 'Complicity and Resistance in the Writings of Flora Annie Steel and Annie Besant', in Nupur Chaudhuri and Margaret Strobel, eds., *Western Women and Imperialism: Complicity and Resistance* (Bloomington, 1992).

Writing Under the Raj: Gender, Race and Rape in the British Imagination, 1830–1857 (New Brunswick, 1999).

Peach, Ceri, *West Indian Migration to Britain: A Social Geography* (Baltimore, 1965).

Pearson, Jacqueline, *Women's Reading in Britain 1750–1835: A Dangerous Recreation* (Cambridge, 1999).

Pedersen, Susan, 'Gender, Welfare, and Citizenship in Britain During the Great War', *American Historical Review*, 95 (1990).

   Family, Dependence and the Origins of the Welfare State: Britain and France, 1914–1945 (Cambridge, 1993).

Peers, Douglas M., *Between Mars and Mammon: Colonial Armies and the Garrison State in Early Nineteenth-Century India* (London, 1995).

   'Privates off Parade: Regimenting Sexuality in the Nineteenth-Century Indian Empire', *International History Review*, 20 (4) (1998).

Pelling, Henry, 'British Labour and British Imperialism', in his *Popular Politics and Society in Late Victorian Britain* (London, 1968).

Penn, Alan, *Targeting Schools: Drill, Militarism and Imperialism* (London, 1999).

Perry, Adele, *On the Edge of Empire: Gender, Race, and the Making of British Columbia, 1849–1871* (Toronto, 2000).

Peterson, Linda, 'Women Writers and Self-writing', in Joanne Shattock, ed., *Women and Literature in Britain 1800–1900* (Cambridge, 2001).

Phillips, Caryl, *The Final Passage* (London, 1985).

Pieterse, Jan Niederven, *White on Black: Images of Africa and Blacks in Western Popular Culture* (New Haven, 1992).

Piggin, Frederic Stuart, 'Halévy Revisited: The Origins of the Wesleyan Methodist Missionary Society: An Examination of Semmel's Thesis', *Journal of Imperial and Commonwealth History*, 9 (1) (1980).

   Making Evangelical Missionaries, 1789–1858: The Social Background, Motives, and Training of British Protestant Missionaries to India (Abingdon, 1984).

Pivar, David J., 'The Military, Prostitution, and Colonial Peoples: India and the Philippines, 1885–1917', *Journal of Sex Research*, 17 (3) (1981).

Pocock, J. G. A., 'British History: A Plea for a New Subject', *New Zealand Historical Journal*, 8 (1974).

   'The Limits and Divisions of British History: In Search of the Unknown Subject', *American Historical Review*, 87 (2) (1982).

Pollock, Griselda, 'The Dangers of Proximity: The Spaces of Sexuality and Surveillance in Word and Image', *Discourse*, 16 (2) (1993–4).

Pooley, Colin G., 'The Residential Segregation of Migrant Communities in Mid-Victorian Liverpool', *Transactions of the Institute of British Geographers*, 2nd ser., 2 (1977).

Poovey, Mary, *Making a Social Body: British Cultural Formation, 1830–1864* (Chicago, 1995).

Porter, Andrew, 'Cambridge, Keswick, and Late-Nineteenth-Century Attitudes to Africa', *Journal of Imperial and Commonwealth History*, 5 (1) (1976).

   The Origins of the South African War: Joseph Chamberlain and the Diplomacy of Imperialism 1895–99 (Manchester, 1980).

   ' "Gentlemanly Capitalism" and Empire: The British Experience since 1750?', *Journal of Imperial and Commonwealth History*, 18 (1990).

ed., *Atlas of British Overseas Expansion* (London, 1991).

'Religion and Empire: British Expansion in the Long Nineteenth Century, 1780–1914', *Journal of Imperial and Commonwealth History*, 20 (3) (1992).

ed., *The Oxford History of the British Empire*, vol. III: *The Nineteenth Century* (Oxford, 1999).

'Religion, Missionary Enthusiasm, and Empire', in Porter, ed., *Oxford History of the British Empire*, vol. III.

Religion Versus Empire? British Protestant Missionaries and Overseas Expansion, 1700–1914 (Manchester, 2004).

Porter, Bernard, *The Absent-Minded Imperialists: Empire, Society, and Culture in Britain* (Oxford, 2004).

Pratt, Mary Louise, *Imperial Eyes: Travel Writing and Transculturation* (London, 1992).

Pratt, Tim, and James Vernon, ' "Appeal From this Fiery Bed ... ": The Colonial Politics of Gandhi's Fasts and their Metropolitan Reception', *Journal of British Studies*, 44 (1) (2005).

Price, Richard, *An Imperial War and the British Working Class: Working-Class Attitudes and Reactions to the Boer War 1899–1902* (London, 1972).

Prochaska, F. K., 'Little Vessels: Children in the Nineteenth-Century English Missionary Movement', *Journal of Imperial and Commonwealth History*, 6 (2) (1978).

Women and Philanthropy in 19th Century England (Oxford, 1980).

Pugh, Martin, *The Tories and the People, 1880–1935* (Oxford, 1985).

Purbrick, Louise, ed., *The Great Exhibition of 1851: New Interdisciplinary Essays* (Manchester, 2002).

Rajan, Balachandra, *Under Western Eyes: India from Milton to Macaulay* (Durham, NC, 1999).

Ramamurthy, A., *Imperial Persuaders: Images of Africa and Asia in British Advertising* (Manchester, 2003).

Ramdin, Ron, *The Making of the Black Working-Class in Britain* (London, 1987).

Reimaging Britain: Five Hundred Years of Black and Asian History (London, 1999).

Rappoport, E., *Shopping for Pleasure* (Princeton, 2000).

Raza, Rosemary, *In Their Own Words: British Women Writers on India 1740–1857* (Delhi, 2006).

Reidi, Eliza, 'Options for an Imperialist Woman: The Case of Violet Markham, 1899–1914', *Albion*, 32 (2000).

'Women, Gender, and the Promotion of Empire: The Victoria League, 1901–1914', *Historical Journal*, 45 (2002).

Rendall, Jane, 'Citizenship, Culture and Civilisation: The Languages of British Suffragists 1866–74', in Melanie Nolan and Caroline Daley, eds., *Suffrage and Beyond: International Feminist Perspectives* (Auckland, 1994).

Reynolds, David, 'The Churchill Government and the Black Troops in Britain During World War II', *Transactions of the Royal Historical Society*, 5th ser., 35 (1985).

Reynolds, K. D., *Aristocratic Women and Political Society in Victorian Britain* (Oxford, 1998).

Rich, Paul J., 'Public-school Freemasonry in the Empire: "Mafia of the Mediocre"?', in J. A. Mangan, ed., *'Benefits Bestowed'?: Education and British Imperialism* (Manchester, 1988).

Richards, Eric, *Britannia's Children: Emigration from England, Scotland, Wales, and Ireland since 1600* (London, 2004).

Richards, Jeffrey, ed., *Imperialism and Juvenile Literature* (Manchester, 1989).

Imperialism and Music: Britain 1876–1953 (Manchester, 2001).

Richards, T., *The Commodity Culture of Victorian England: Advertising and Spectacle 1851–1914* (London, 1991).

Richardson, D., 'The Slave Trade, Sugar, and Economic Growth', in B. Solow and S. Engerman, eds., *British Capitalism and Caribbean Slavery* (Cambridge, 1987).

Rickard, John, 'The Anti-Sweating Movement in Britain and Victoria: The Politics of Empire and Social Reform', *Historical Studies: Australia and New Zealand*, 18 (1979).

Robb, George, *British Culture and the First World War* (Basingstoke, 2002).

Robinson, Ronald and John Gallagher, 'The Imperialism of Free Trade', *Economic History Review*, 2nd ser., 6 (1) (1953).

Rogers, Helen, *Women and the People: Authority, Authorship and the Radical Tradition in Nineteenth-Century England* (Aldershot, 2000).

Rose, Sonya O., 'Girls and GIs: Race, Sex, and Diplomacy in Second World War Britain', *International History Review*, 19 (1) (1997).

Which People's War? National Identity and Citizenship in Wartime Britain, 1939–1945 (Oxford, 2003).

Ross, Ellen, 'Fierce Questions and Taunts: Married Life in Working-Class London, 1870–1914', *Feminist Studies*, 8 (1982).

Rowe, Michael, 'Sex, "Race" and Riot in Liverpool, 1919', *Immigrants and Minorities*, 19 (2) (2000).

Ruane, J., 'Colonialism and Interpretation of Irish Historical Development', in M. Silverman and P. H. Gulliver, eds., *Approaching the Past: Historical Anthropology through Irish Case Studies* (New York, 1992).

Rubinstein, David, *A Different World for Women: The Life of Millicent Garrett Fawcett* (Columbus, OH, 1991).

Rubinstein, W. D., *Men of Property: The Very Rich in Britain since the Industrial Revolution* (London and New Brunswick, NJ, 1981).

'British Radicalism and the "Dark Side" of Populism', in his *The Elite and the Wealthy in Modern British History* (Brighton, 1987).

Rudé, George, *Protest and Punishment: The Story of the Social and Political Protesters Transported to Australia, 1788–1868* (Oxford, 1978).

Rushdie, Salman, 'The New Empire within Britain', in his *Imaginary Homelands: Essays and Criticism 1981–1991* (London, 1991).

Said, Edward, *Orientalism* (New York and London, 1978).

Culture and Imperialism (New York and London, 1993).

Samuel, Raphael, *Theatres of Memory*, vol. II: *Island Stories: Unravelling Britain* (London, 1998).

Saville, John, *1848: The British State and the Chartist Movement* (Cambridge, 1990).

Sayer, Derek, 'British Reaction to the Amritsar Massacre 1919–1920', *Past and Present*, 131 (1991).

Scally, Robert James, *The Origins of the Lloyd George Coalition: The Politics of Social-Imperialism, 1900–1918* (Princeton, 1975).

Schaffer, Talia, 'Taming the Tropics: Charlotte Yonge takes on Melanesia', *Victorian Studies*, 47 (2005).

Schama, Simon, *A History of Britain: The Fate of Empire 1776–2000* (New York, 2003).

Schneer, Jonathan, *London 1900: The Imperial Metropolis* (New Haven and London, 1999).

Schumpeter, Joseph, *Imperialism and Social Classes: Two Essays*, trans. Heinz Norden (New York, 1955).

Schwarz, Bill, 'The Language of Constitutionalism: Baldwinite Conservatism', in *Formations of Nation and People* (London, 1984).

    'Black Metropolis, White England', in Mica Nava and Alan O'Shea, eds., *Modern Times: Reflections on a Century of English Modernity* (London, 1996).

    ed., *West Indian Intellectuals in Britain* (Manchester, 2003).

    Memories of Empire (Oxford, forthcoming).

Scola, Roger, *Feeding the Victorian City: The Food Supply of Manchester 1780 to 1870* (Manchester, 1992).

Scott, David, 'Modernity that Predated the Modern: Sidney Mintz's Caribbean', *History Workshop Journal*, 58 (2004).

Scully, Pamela, *Liberating the Family? Gender and British Slave Emancipation in the Rural Western Cape, S. Africa, 1823–1854* (Portsmouth, NH, 1997).

Searle, G. R., *A New England? Peace and War, 1886–1918* (Oxford, 2004).

Sebastiani, Silvia, ' "Race", Women and Progress in the Scottish Enlightenment', in Sarah Knott and Barbara Taylor, eds., *Women, Gender and Enlightenment* (London, 2005).

Semmel, Bernard, *Imperialism and Social Reform: English Social-Imperial Thought, 1895–1914* (London, 1960; repr. New York, 1969).

    The Governor Eyre Controversy (London, 1962).

    The Methodist Revolution (New York, 1973).

Semple, Rhonda Anne, *Missionary Women: Gender, Professionalism and the Victorian Idea of Christian Mission* (Woodbridge and Rochester, NY, 2003).

Sen, Amartya, *Poverty and Famine: An Essay on Entitlement and Deprivation* (Oxford, 1981).

Sharma, Sanjay, *Famine, Philanthropy and the Colonial State: North India in the Early Nineteenth Century* (Oxford, 2001).

Sharpe, Jenny, *Allegories of Empire: The Figure of Woman in the Colonial Text* (Minneapolis, 1993).

Showalter, Elaine, *Sexual Anarchy: Gender and Culture at the Fin de Siècle* (London, 1990).

Silva, Elizabeth B. and Tony Bennett, eds., *Contemporary Culture and Everyday Life* (Durham, 2004).

Silver, A., *Manchester Men and Indian Cotton* (Manchester, 1966).

Simoes da Silva, A. J., *The Luxury of Nationalist Despair: George Lamming's Fiction as Decolonizing Project* (Amsterdam, 2000).

Sinha, Mrinalini, *Colonial Masculinity: The 'Manly Englishman' and the 'Effeminate Bengali' in the Late Nineteenth Century* (Manchester, 1995).

'Mapping the Imperial Social Formation: A Modest Proposal for Feminist History', *Signs*, 25 (4) (2000).

'Britishness, Clubbability, and the Colonial Public Sphere: The Genealogy of an Imperial Institution in Colonial India', *Journal of British Studies*, 40 (2001).

Sivanandan, A., *A Different Hunger: Writings on Black Resistance* (London, 1982).

Sklar, Kathryn Kish, '"Women Who Speak for an Entire Nation": American and British Women at the World Anti-Slavery Convention, London, 1840', in Jean Fagan Yellin and John C. Van Horne, eds., *The Abolitionist Sisterhood: Women's Political Culture in Antebellum America* (Ithaca, 1994).

Smith, A. and M. Ball, eds., *Margery Perham and British Rule in Africa* (London, 1991).

Smith, Graham A., 'Jim Crow on the Homefront (1942–1945)', *New Community*, 8 (3) (1980).

Smith, Harold L., *The British Women's Suffrage Campaign, 1866–1928* (London, 1998).

Smith, Richard, *Jamaican Volunteers in the First World War: Race, Masculinity and the Development of National Consciousness* (Manchester, 2004).

Smith, Zadie, *White Teeth* (London, 2000).

Spencer, Ian R. G., *British Immigration Policy since 1939: The Making of Multi-Racial Britain* (London, 1997).

Spiers, Edward M., *The Army and Society, 1815–1914* (London, 1980).

The Late Victorian Army, 1868–1902 (Manchester, 1992).

Spivak, Gayatri Chakravorty, 'Three Women's Texts and a Critique of Imperialism', in Gates, ed., *Race, Writing, and Difference*.

Sponza, Lucio, *Italian Immigrants in Nineteenth Century Britain: Realities and Images* (Leicester, 1988).

Springhall, John, *Youth, Empire and Society, 1883–1940* (London, 1977).

Decolonization since 1945: The Collapse of European Overseas Empires (London, 2001).

Spurr, D., *The Rhetoric of Empire: Colonial Discourse in Journalism, Travel Writing, and Imperial Administration* (Durham, NC, 1993).

Stanley, Brian, *The Bible and the Flag: Protestant Missions and British Imperialism in the Nineteenth and Twentieth Centuries* (Leicester, 1990).

Stanley, Peter, *White Mutiny: British Military Culture in India, 1825–1875* (London, 1998).

Steedman, Carolyn, *The Radical Soldier's Tale, John Pearman, 1819–1908* (London, 1988).

Stepan, Nancy, *The Idea of Race in Science: Great Britain, 1800–1960* (London, 1982).

'Race, Gender, Science and Citizenship', in Hall, ed., *Cultures of Empire*.

Stocking, George, *Victorian Anthropology* (New York, 1987).

Stoler, Ann L., *Race and the Education of Desire: Foucault's History of Sexuality and the Colonial Order of Things* (Durham, NC, 1995).

Carnal Knowledge and Imperial Power: Race and the Intimate in Colonial Rule (Berkeley, 2002).

'Haunted by Empire: Domains of the Intimate and the Practices of Comparison', in Stoler, ed., *Haunted by Empire* (Durham, NC, forthcoming).

Streets, Heather, *Martial Races and Masculinity in the British Army, 1857–1914* (Manchester, 2004).

Strother, Z. S., 'Display of the Body Hottentot', in Bernth Lindfors, ed., *Africans on Stage: Studies in Ethnological Show Business* (Bloomington, 1999).

Suleri, Sara, *The Rhetoric of English India* (Chicago, 1992).

Sussman, C., *Consuming Anxieties: Consumer Protest, Gender, and British Society, 1713–1833* (Stanford, 2000).

Swift, Roger, 'The Outcast Irish in the British Victorian City: Problems and Perspectives', *Irish Historical Studies*, 25 (1987).

Irish Migrants in Britain 1815–1914: A Documentary History (Cork, 2002).

Swift, Roger and Sheridan Gilley, eds., *The Irish in the Victorian City* (London, 1985).

Tabili, Laura, *'We Ask for British Justice': Workers and Racial Difference in Late Imperial Britain* (Ithaca, 1994).

'Empire is the Enemy of Love: Edith Noor's Progress and Other Stories', *Gender and History*, 17 (1) (2005).

' "Having Lived Close Beside Them All the Time": Negotiating National Identities Through Personal Networks', *Journal of Social History*, 39 (2) (2005).

'Outsiders in the Land of Their Birth: Exogamy, Citizenship, and Identity in War and Peace', *Journal of British Studies*, 44 (2005).

Taylor, Miles, 'Imperium et Libertas? Rethinking the Radical Critique of Imperialism during the Nineteenth Century', *Journal of Imperial and Commonwealth History*, 19 (1) (1991).

'John Bull and the Iconography of Public Opinion in England c1712–1929', *Past and Present*, 134 (1992).

'The 1848 Revolutions and the British Empire', *Past and Present*, 166 (2000).

'Empire and the 1832 Parliamentary Reform Act Revisited', in Arthur Burns and Joanna Innes, eds., *Rethinking the Age of Reform: Britain, 1780–1850* (Cambridge, 2003).

Thomas, William, *The Quarrel of Macaulay and Croker: Politics and History in the Age of Reform* (Oxford, 2000).

Thompson, Andrew, 'The Language of Imperialism and the Meanings of Empire: Imperial Discourse in British Politics, 1895–1914', *Journal of British Studies*, 36 (1997).
  Imperial Britain: The Empire in British Politics c. 1880–1932 (Harlow, 2000).
  The Empire Strikes Back? The Impact of Imperialism on Britain from the Mid-Nineteenth Century (Harlow, 2005).
Thompson, Dorothy, *The Chartists: Popular Politics in the Industrial Revolution* (London, 1984).
Thompson, E. P., *The Making of the English Working Class* (London, 1963).
  Customs in Common (London, 1991).
Thorne, Christopher, 'Britain and the Black GIs: Racial Issues and Anglo-American Relations in 1942', *New Community*, 3 (3) (1974).
Thorne, Susan, ' "The Conversion of Englishmen and the Conversion of the World Inseparable": Missionary Imperialism and the Language of Class in Early Industrial Britain', in Cooper and Stoler, eds., *Tensions of Empire*.
  Congregational Missions and the Making of an Imperial Culture in Nineteenth-Century England (Stanford, 1999).
Thornton, A. P., *The Habit of Authority: Paternalism in British History* (Toronto, 1966).
Tickner, Lisa, *The Spectacle of Women: Imagery of the Suffrage Campaign 1907–1914* (Chicago, 1988).
Tosh, John, *A Man's Place: Masculinity and the Middle-Class Home in Victorian England* (New Haven, 1999).
  'Manliness, *Masculinities* and the New Imperialism, 1880–1900', in his *Manliness and Masculinities in Nineteenth-Century Britain* (Harlow, 2005).
  'Masculinities in an Industrializing Society: Britain, 1800–1914', *Journal of British Studies*, 44 (2005).
Turley, David, *The Culture of English Antislavery, 1780–1860* (London, 1991).
  'British Antislavery Reassessed', in Arthur Burns and Joanna Innes, eds., *Rethinking the Age of Reform: Britain, 1780–1850* (Cambridge, 2003).
Turner, Mary, *Slaves and Missionaries: The Disintegration of Jamaican Slave Society, 1787–1834* (Urbana, 1982).
Twells, Alison, ' "Happy English Children": Class, Ethnicity and the Making of Missionary Women, 1800–50', *Women's Studies International Forum*, 21 (1998).
  ' "Let Us Begin Well at Home": Class, Ethnicity and Christian Motherhood in the Writing of Hannah Kilham, 1774–1832', in Eileen Janes Yeo, ed., *Radical Femininity: Women's Self-representation in the Public Sphere* (Manchester, 1998).
  ' "A Christian and Civilised Land": The British Middle Class and the Civilising Mission, 1820–42', in Alan Kidd and David Nicholls, eds., *Gender, Civic Culture and Consumerism: Middle-class Identity in Britain, 1800–1940* (Manchester, 1999).
Tyrell, Ian, *Woman's World, Woman's Empire: The Woman's Christian Temperance Union in International Perspective, 1880–1930* (Chapel Hill, 1991).

Valenze, Deborah M., *Prophetic Sons and Daughters: Female Preaching and Popular Religion in Industrial England* (Princeton, 1985).

van der Veer, Peter, *Imperial Encounters: Religion and Modernity in India and Britain* (Princeton, 2001).

Vernon, James, 'Narrating the Constitution: The Discourse of "the Real" and the Fantasies of Nineteenth Century Constitutional History', in Vernon, ed., *Re-reading the Constitution: New Narratives in the Political History of England's Long Nineteenth Century* (Cambridge, 1996).

Vicinus, Martha, *Independent Women: Work and Community for Single Women, 1850–1920* (Chicago, 1985).

Vickery, Amanda, ed., *Women, Privilege and Power: British Politics, 1750 to the Present* (Stanford, 2001).

Vidal, Gore, 'Requiem for the American Empire' (11 January 1986), in his *Perspectives on The Nation, 1865–2000* (New York, 2004).

Vincent, David, *Poor Citizens: The State and the Poor in the 20th Century* (London, 1991).

Vincent, J. R., *The Formation of the Liberal Party, 1857–1868* (London, 1966).

Visram, Rozina, *Ayahs, Lascars and Princes: Indians in Britain, 1700–1947* (London, 1986).

Asians in Britain: 400 Years of History (London, 2002).

Walker, B. M., *Ulster Politics: The Formative Years 1868–86* (Belfast, 1989).

Walker, Martin, 'America's Virtual Empire', *World Policy Journal*, 19 (2) (2002).

Walker, Pamela J., *Pulling the Devil's Kingdom Down: The Salvation Army in Victorian Britain* (Berkeley, 2001).

Walkowitz, Judith R., *City of Dreadful Delight: Narratives of Sexual Danger in Late Victorian London* (Chicago, 1992).

Walvin, James, 'The Impact of Slavery on British Radical Politics: 1787–1838', in Vera Rubin and Arthur Tuden, eds., *Comparative Perspectives on Slavery in New World Plantation Societies, Annals of the New York Academy of Sciences*, 292 (1977).

'The Rise of British Sentiment for Abolition, 1787–1832', in Christine Bolt and Seymour Drescher, eds., *Anti-Slavery, Religion, and Reform* (Folkestone, 1980).

'The Public Campaign in England against Slavery, 1787–1834', in David Eltis and James Walvin, eds., *The Abolition of the Atlantic Slave Trade* (Madison, WI, 1981).

ed., *Slavery and British Society, 1776–1846* (London, 1982).

Wang, G., ed., *Global History and Migrations* (Boulder, CO, 1997).

Ward, Margaret, 'Gendering the Union: Imperial Feminism and the Ladies' Land League', *Women's History Review*, 10 (2001).

Ward, Paul, *Red Flag and Union Jack: Englishness, Patriotism and the British Left, 1881–1924* (Woodbridge, 1998).

Ward, Stuart, ed., *British Culture and the End of Empire* (Manchester, 2001).

Ware, Vron, *Beyond the Pale: White Women, Racism and History* (London, 1992).

Warren, Allen, ' "Mothers for the Empire"? The Girl Guides Association in Britain, 1909–1939', in J. A. Mangan, ed., *Making Imperial Mentalities: Socialisation and British Imperialism* (Manchester, 1990).

Waters, Chris, ' "Dark Strangers" in Our Midst: Discourses of Race and Nation in Britain, 1947–1963', *Journal of British Studies*, 36 (April 1997).

Weatherill, Lorna, *Consumer Behaviour and Material Culture in Britain 1660–1760* (London, 1988).

Webb, R. K., *Harriet Martineau: A Radical Victorian* (London, 1960).

Webster, Wendy, *Imagining Home: Gender, 'Race' and National Identity, 1945–64* (London, 1998).

  Englishness and Empire, 1939–1965 (Oxford, 2005).

Wheeler, Roxanne, *The Complexion of Race: Categories of Difference in Eighteenth-Century British Culture* (Philadelphia, 2000).

Whelan, K., 'Come All You Staunch Revisionists: Towards a Post-revisionist Agenda for Irish History', *Irish Reporter*, 2 (1991).

Whelan, Y., 'The Construction and Destruction of a Colonial Landscape: Monuments to British Monarchs in Dublin Before and After Independence', *Journal of Historical Geography*, 28 (4) (2002).

Whitlock, Gillian, *The Intimate Empire: Reading Women's Autobiography* (London, 2000).

Wildenthal, Lora, *German Women for Empire, 1884–1945* (Durham, NC, 2001).

Williams, Bill, *The Making of Manchester Jewry, 1740–1875* (Manchester, 1976).

Williams, Eric, *Capitalism and Slavery* ((1944) Chapel Hill, NC, 1994).

Williams, Leslie A., *Daniel O'Connell, the British Press and the Irish Famine: Killing Remarks*, ed. W. H. A. Williams (Aldershot, 2003).

Williamson, Philip, *Stanley Baldwin: Conservative Leadership and National Values* (Cambridge, 1999).

Wilson, Kathleen, 'Citizenship, Empire and Modernity in the English Provinces, c. 1720–90', *Eighteenth Century Studies*, 29 (1) (1995).

  The Island Race: Englishness, Empire and Gender in the Eighteenth Century (London, 2003).

  ed., *A New Imperial History: Culture, Identity and Modernity in Britain and the Empire 1660–1840* (Cambridge, 2004).

Winder, Robert, *Bloody Foreigners: The Story of Immigration to Britain* (London, 2004).

Wolf, Eric R., *Europe and the People Without History* (London and Berkeley, 1982).

Wong, Maria Lin, *Chinese Liverpudlians: A History of the Chinese Community in Liverpool* (Liverpool, 1989).

Wood, Marcus, *Slavery, Empathy and Pornography* (Oxford, 2002).

Woollacott, Angela, ' "Khaki Fever" and Its Control: Gender, Class, Age and Sexual Morality on the British Homefront in the First World War', *Journal of Contemporary History*, 29 (1994).

  To Try Her Fortune in London: Australian Women, Colonialism, and Modernity (Oxford, 2001).

'Australian Women's Metropolitan Activism: From Suffrage, to Imperial Vanguard, to Commonwealth Feminism', in Fletcher, Mayhall and Levine, eds., *Women's Suffrage in the British Empire*.

Wright, Patrick, *On Living in an Old Country* (London, 1985).

Young, L., *Middle Class Culture in the Nineteenth Century* (London, 2003).

Young, Robert J. C., *Colonial Desire: Hybridity in Theory, Culture and Race* (London, 1995).

Zolberg, Aristide, 'Global Movements, Global Walls: Responses to Migration, 1855–1925', in Wang, ed., *Global History and Migrations*.

'International Migration Policies in a Changing World System', in William H. McNeill and Ruth S. Adams, eds., *Human Migration: Patterns and Policies* (Bloomington, 1978).

Zonona, Joyce, 'The Sultan and the Slave: Feminist Orientalism and the Structure of *Jane Eyre*', *Signs*, 18 (1993).

Index